Endorseme

"Dr. Ronald Ramsey has written a very practical forty-day guide to help people on a journey of forgiveness. Each day has a meditation and an exercise that guides your experience toward the destination of forgiving. The approach is thoroughly biblical and yet draws on the most up-to-date science of forgiveness. If you've been struggling to forgive, this is well worth your investment of time."

Everett L. Worthington Jr., PhD
Commonwealth Professor Emeritus
Department of Psychology
www.EvWorthington-forgiveness.com

"There are many books on forgiveness available, and Dr. Ramsey has provided a uniquely accessible addition to the genre. His conversational style makes this an easy read for almost anyone. That is good because the depth of the experiential material he offers throughout will make Forty Days to Forgiveness, by design, slow going. This is not a page-turner. To get full benefit, the reader will need to thoughtfully consider the material and apply the ideas to the exercises provided. As a pastoral psychotherapist for nearly fifty years, I know that forgiveness is a major issue for many people. I would have liked to have had a book like this one that I could put in the hands of my clients to help them work through the process of forgiveness. It is a difficult journey through that wilderness, but Dr. Ramsey's book provides a helpful guide."

Rev. Wayne Perry, DMin, PhD, LMFT

"A practical, insightful guide to such a vital topic—forgiveness. Both biblical and relevant, Forty Days to Forgiveness was written from Dr. Ramsey's thorough personal and professional experience as an expert on the topic. This is a much-needed book in today's day and age for some much-needed forgiveness fuel—stronger than your morning coffee to start your day."

Charlie Lapastora, Fox TV reporter and producer

"There are thousands of illnesses that plague humankind, which in medicine we seek not to only treat but also to identify the root cause. The countless deaths and lives detoured from their purpose because of the internal turmoil of unforgiveness are why you must read this book. Dr. Ramsey details the methodology to forgiveness and freedom. Adhere and be healed."

Earlexia M. Norwood, MD
Service Chief, Family Medicine
West Bloomfield Hospital

Director, Practice Development and Community Education
Henry Ford Health System

Assistant Clinical Professor
Wayne State University School of Medicine

President
Jackson State University National Alumni Association, Inc.

"Forty Days to Forgiveness offers a clear, practical, intelligent, and highly spiritual approach to the vexing topic of forgiveness. Readers from many perspectives will be glad to take Dr. Ramsey's journey along with him."

J. Morris
Writer and editor
www.jmorrisbooks.com

"Forty Days to Forgiveness is a voyage inward, to the deepest recesses of the heart, where unforgiveness is exchanged for freedom. Dr. Ramsey does a marvelous job of combining the truth of God's Word with experiences filtered through God's love. His practical approach to forgiveness compels the reader to honesty, healing, and reconciliation. This is a voyage that I will return to often."

Kenny Holland, Pastor
Peacemakers International

"Forty Days to Forgiveness is an inordinately well-organized collection of descriptions, explanations, exercises, supporting scriptures, and encouraging prompts to aid a reader in moving through unforgiveness to forgiveness, relying on the example of Christ and reaching for the promise of a closer relationship with self, others, and God as a result of opening his or her heart to a transgressor and coming to develop compassion, mercy, and other such Christian traits. That Dr. Ron Ramsey has undertaken this journey himself and has struggled with forgiveness is clear, and this serves to establish his ethos, making him a credible narrator in whom the reader may have confidence. Guiding readers through the journey with actionable steps and ways to gain insight into their own thoughts, feelings, and behaviors to effect positive change, Dr. Ramsey performs a very valuable service, namely, instructing people on how to obey the biblical commandment that they forgive even when the Bible is largely silent on how to go about doing so. Forty Days to Forgiveness therefore fills a gap and meets a real need."

WestBow Press editor

Forty Days
to
Forgiveness

A Christian's Field Guide
to the Forgiveness Journey

Ronald D. Ramsey, MEd, DMin, LMFT

WESTBOW
PRESS®
A DIVISION OF THOMAS NELSON
& ZONDERVAN

WestBow Press books may be ordered through booksellers or by contacting:

WestBow Press
A Division of Thomas Nelson & Zondervan
1663 Liberty Drive
Bloomington, IN 47403
www.westbowpress.com
844-714-3454

Because of the dynamic nature of the Internet, any web addresses or links contained in this book may have changed since publication and may no longer be valid. The views expressed in this work are solely those of the author and do not necessarily reflect the views of the publisher, and the publisher hereby disclaims any responsibility for them.

Any people depicted in stock imagery provided by Getty Images are models, and such images are being used for illustrative purposes only.
Certain stock imagery © Getty Images.

Unless marked otherwise, all Scripture quotations are taken from The Holy Bible, English Standard Version® (ESV®), Copyright © 2001 by Crossway, a publishing ministry of Good News Publishers. All rights reserved.

Scripture quotations marked NIV are taken from The Holy Bible, New International Version®, NIV® Copyright © 1973, 1978, 1984, 2011 by Biblica, Inc.® Used by permission. All rights reserved worldwide.

Scripture quotations marked KJV are taken from the King James Version.

ISBN: 978-1-6642-1763-8 (sc)
ISBN: 978-1-6642-1764-5 (hc)
ISBN: 978-1-6642-1762-1 (e)

Library of Congress Control Number: 2020925482

Printed in United States of America.

WestBow Press rev. date: 6/8/2021

Contents

Dedication xiii

Foreword xv

Preface xvii

CHAPTER 1: WHY FORGIVE? 1

Day 1: Forty Days to Forgiveness—Introduction 3

    Journal Exercise 1a: Getting Started 12

    Journal Exercise 1b: Selecting the Transgressor 13

        INTERPRETING YOUR RESULTS 15

Day 2: The Bible and Forgiveness 16

    Journal Exercise 2: Prayer for Guidance 22

        A PERSONAL PRAYER FOR STRENGTH AND GUIDANCE 22

Day 3: Reasons to Forgive 23

    Journal Exercise 3a: Letter to Self 29

    Journal Exercise 3b: Forgiveness Readiness Survey 30

Day 4: The Core of the Matter 32

    Journal Exercise 4a: What Do You Need? 40

    Journal Exercise 4b: Getting a New Perspective 41

    Chapter 1 Summary 43

        DRAWING STRENGTH FROM SCRIPTURE 44

        DEVOTIONAL PRAYER 44

        RESOURCES FOR FURTHER STUDY 45

        CHAPTER 1 ENDNOTES 46

CHAPTER 2: ACKNOWLEDGING THE HURT 51

Day 5: Acknowledging the Unforgiveness Life Cycle—Introduction 53

    Journal Exercise 5: Your Forgiveness GPS 61

        INTERPRETING YOUR RESULTS 63

Day 6: Acknowledging the Type of Transgression 64

    Journal Exercise 6a: Acknowledging How You Are Affected 69

    Journal Exercise 6b: Acknowledging Degrees of Transgression 71

Day 7: Acknowledging Your Emotions and Feelings 72
Journal Exercise 7: Acknowledging Emotions and Feelings..78

Day 8: Acknowledging Unenforceable Rules 79
Journal Exercise 8: Unenforceable Rules 83

Day 9: Acknowledging How You Are Coping with the Transgression.........................84
Journal Exercise 9: Coping with Offenders 89
INTERPRETING YOUR RESULTS 90

Day 10: Acknowledging the Vicious Cycle 93
Journal Exercise 10a: Acknowledging Your Negative Intentions 97
Journal Exercise 10b: Acknowledging Your Rumination...98
Journal Exercise 10c: Reducing Unforgiveness 99
Journal Exercise 10d: My State of Unforgiveness 100
Chapter 2 Summary 101
DEVOTIONAL PRAYER 102
CHAPTER 2 ENDNOTES..102

CHAPTER 3: COMMITMENT TO FORGIVE **105**

Day 11: Why Commitment Is Critical—Introduction 107
FORGIVENESS IS CRITICAL FOR EMOTIONAL PEACE 110
Journal Exercise 11: Readiness to Forgive 116

Day 12: Alternatives to Trying to Forgive 117
Journal Exercise 12: Motivations for Unforgiveness 121

Day 13: Justice, Fairness, and Safety 123
Journal Exercise 13a: Justice, Fairness, Safety...127
Journal Exercise 13b: Knowing When You Have Forgiven 128
INTERPRETING YOUR RESULTS 129

Day 14: What Forgiveness Looks Like 130
Journal Exercise 14: What Forgiveness Looks Like 134

Day 15: Committing to Trying to Forgive 135
Journal Exercise 15a: Deciding to Commit to Trying to Forgive..............................140
Journal Exercise 15b: Committing to Trying to Forgive 141
Chapter 3 Summary 142
SCRIPTURE FOR STRENGTH...142
DEVOTIONAL PRAYER 143
CHAPTER 3 ENDNOTES..143

CHAPTER 4: TRANSITIONING TO A GODLY PERSPECTIVE **147**

Day 16: A Christian View of Forgiveness—Introduction 149
    Journal Exercise 16: Finding Your Forgiveness Strengths 160
        INTERPRETING YOUR RESULTS 161

Day 17: Coping with the Stress of Unenforceable Rules 163
    Journal Exercise 17a: Coping Style 168
        INTERPRETING YOUR SCORES 169
    Journal Exercise 17b: Coping Action Planner 171

Day 18: Short-Circuiting the Vicious Cycle 174
    Journal Exercise 18: Your Anger Style 177
        INTERPRETING YOUR SCORES 178

Day 19: Positive Intentions 179
    Journal Exercise 19a: Negative to Positive Intentions 181
    Journal Exercise 19b: Visualization Activity 182

Day 20: Forgiveness Outcomes 183
    Journal Exercise 20: Activity to Assess Well-Being[85] 185
        INTERPRETING YOUR RESULTS 187

Day 21: Empathy 189
    Journal Exercise 21a: Activity to Build Empathy 192
    Journal Exercise 21b: Mindful Empathy 194
    Chapter 4 Summary 196
        SCRIPTURE FOR STRENGTH 196
        DEVOTIONAL PRAYER 197
        RESOURCES TO HELP WITH COPING 197
        CHAPTER 4 ENDNOTES 198

CHAPTER 5: INTERNALIZING FORGIVENESS THROUGH SPIRITUAL MATURITY **201**

Day 22: The Condition of the Heart—Introduction 203
    Journal Exercise Part 22a: Setting Your Mind on Things Above 217
    Journal Exercise 22b: Inhibitors to Spiritual Maturity 218

Day 23: Internalizing Forgiveness through Spiritual Formation 220
    Journal Exercise 23a: Current State of Your Spiritual Disciplines 226
        INTERPRETATION 228
    Journal Exercise 23b: Committing to Improve 229

Day 24: Internalizing Forgiveness through Scripture Study 230
Journal Exercise 24a: Inductive Bible Study of Forgiveness 237
Journal Exercise 24b: Assessing Your Bible Study 240
MAKING MEANING OUT OF YOUR RESULTS 240

Day 25: Internalizing Forgiveness through Meditation 243
Journal Exercise 25: Assessing Your Meditation Practices 246
MAKING MEANING OUT OF YOUR RESULTS 246

Day 26: Internalizing Forgiveness through Prayer..249
Journal Exercise 26: Assessing Your Prayer Practices 260
MAKING MEANING OUT OF YOUR RESULTS 260

Day 27: Internalizing Forgiveness through Fellowship 262
Journal Exercise 27: Assessing Your Fellowship Practices 267
MAKING MEANING OUT OF YOUR RESULTS 267
Summary of Chapter 5........................270
SCRIPTURE FOR STRENGTH........................271
DEVOTIONAL PRAYER........................271
CHAPTER 5 ENDNOTES........................272

CHAPTER 6: OPENING YOUR HEART TO FORGIVENESS **279**

Day 28: Opening Your Heart to Forgiveness—Introduction........................281
Journal Exercise 28a: The Stronghold of Unforgiveness 290
Journal Exercise 28b: Prayer for Release from Strongholds........................291

Day 29: Opening Strongholds with Gratitude........................292
Journal Exercise 29: Overcoming Strongholds with Gratitude 294

Day 30: Opening Up to Meet Your Needs........................296
Journal Exercise 30a: Meeting Your Needs 301
Journal Exercise 30b: A Letter to the Transgressor........................302

Day 31: Openness to Empathy—the Gift of Forgiveness........................303
Journal Exercise 31a: Openness to Build Empathy 312
Journal Exercise 31b: Prayer for Empathic Release 314

Day 32: Opening Up to a New Story........................316
Journal Exercise 32: Rewriting Your Story........................318

Day 33: Opening the Door to Reconciliation 330
  Journal Exercise 33a: Opening Your Heart to Reconciliation 334
  Journal Exercise 33b: Checklist for Considering Reconciliation 335
    INTERPRETING YOUR RESPONSES 336
  Chapter 6 Summary 337
    DEVOTIONAL 338
    CHAPTER 6 ENDNOTES 339

CHAPTER 7: NEXT STEPS TO SUSTAIN EMOTIONAL FREEDOM......................**343**

Day 34: Next Steps for Emotional Healing—Introduction....................345
  Journal Exercise 34: Forgiveness Readiness Survey Revisited 354
    INTERPRETING YOUR RESULTS 355

Day 35: Love, Grace, and Gratitude..356
  Journal Exercise 35a: Love and Grace Meditation 359
  Journal Exercise 35b: Gratitude Journal 360

Day 36: Character Strengths...361
  Journal Exercise 36: Assessing Character Strengths 365

Day 37: A Dynamic Narrative...367
  Journal Exercise 37a: Creating a Dynamic Narrative 369
  Journal Exercise 37b: A Dynamic Narrative 373
  Journal Exercise 37c: A Letter to the Transgressor 374
    A LETTER TO THE TRANSGRESSOR 375

Day 38: Nurturing Positive Intentions 376
  Journal Exercise 38: Reflecting on Growth 377

Day 39: Reconciliation..378
  Journal Exercise 39: To Reconcile or Not to Reconcile.....................382
    INTERPRETING YOUR RESULTS 387

Day 40: Reflecting on Your Progress...388
  Journal Exercise 40a: Reflecting on Your Forgiveness Journey 389
  Journal Exercise 40b: Forgiveness Tune-Up 390
  Chapter 7 Summary 403
    DEVOTIONAL 404
    CHAPTER 7 ENDNOTES 405

Index..407

Dedication

I could not have written this book without the support and encouragement of many people, especially some key people whom God brought across my path on my own personal journey.

First, I dedicate *Forty Days to Forgiveness* to my mother, Nell Ramsey, whose tireless efforts as a chaplain inspired so many people to find that sacred place in their hearts where Jesus blossoms and brings peace and healing. She demonstrated to me an unconditional love for all people and the conviction that all people are children of God who deserve His abiding presence during the storms of their lives.

Second, I dedicate this book to my wife, Nina, whose counsel, love, and support has motivated me to stick with this project to its completion. More importantly, she has demonstrated in her own life a deep, abiding love for all people, including me. Her unconditional love and forgiveness for my shortcomings without judgment or rejection has helped shape who I am today.

Third, I dedicate *Forty Days to Forgiveness* to my colleague and chaplain associate Steve Axe, whose tremendous knowledge of God's Word helped to ensure that my application of the scriptures is clear and illustrates the intended messages in an uncompromising way.

Fourthly, I dedicate *Forty Days to Forgiveness* to my editor, Beth VanRheenen. Her knowledge and skill in English composition, coupled with her love of the Lord and her knowledge of His Word, provided the means for me to explain difficult ideas in a clear and more accessible way.

I would be remiss if I did not also acknowledge my daughter, Christina, whose patience with my inaccessibility while writing this book has been an encouragement for me. And finally there is Theo, my service dog, whose place by my side and whose unconditional love has helped me to withstand the storms and emotional difficulties in my own life throughout the latter stages of this journey.

Foreword

The forty exercises are razor-sharp, brilliantly worded, and spiritually solid. They are filled with the sunlight of the Spirit. These exercises will break the cycle of anger and blame, which will lead to forgiveness, if my own experience is any guide. The exercises act to expand our awareness of how forgiveness can offer emotional relief and peace of mind.

In addition to the guidance for walking through the forgiveness process, Dr. Ramsey offers hope, reassurance, and inspiration that peace of mind, compassion, and contentment can be achieved. Some examples of his golden nuggets are as follows:

- "Gratitude works its magic by serving as an antidote to negative emotions" (p. 448).
- "Forgiveness requires the offended person to reject the role of victim and decide to return to a state of peace" (p. 184).
- "With God's help, we can take back control of our thoughts, break down the walls that trap our hearts, and respond to transgressors with compassion and empathy" (p. 265).
- "I've found that prayer is not something that we 'do.' Instead, it is a way of living, a lifestyle; it is who we are at every point of every day" (p. 267).
- "Negative stories become … ruts in the neural pathways. These ruts become 'schemas.' When we change the schema, that is, our negative stories, we pull down the strongholds of our negative thoughts and behaviors" (p. 321).

Since I began my own recovery journey over thirty-nine years ago, I have sponsored many men in recovery. I've also worked as a lead high school counselor in a large suburban area. From teenagers to old-timers, I've found, the inability to forgive is a major stumbling block to emotional maturity.

The principles and practical exercises in *Forty Days to Forgiveness* align beautifully with the twelve steps of recovery outlined in Alcoholics Anonymous, as I will note. Turning our will over to the "care of a higher power as we [understand] Him," step 3, is a must. "We made a searching and fearless moral inventory of ourselves" (step 4) is stressed throughout *Forty Days to Forgiveness*. We continue with the all-important need to forgive (step 9), which says of recovering alcoholics, "We made direct amends to such people [whom we have offended] wherever possible, except when to do so would injure them or others."

If we continue, we will improve "our conscious contact with God as we [understand] Him, praying only for knowledge of His will for us and the power to carry that out" (step 11). "Having had a spiritual awakening as the result of these steps, we [try] to carry this message to alcoholics, and to practice these principles in all our affairs" (step 12).

For all those who are truly seeking to stop fighting with anyone or anything, *Forty Days to Forgiveness* will become a valuable resource in the lifelong journey of living and loving one day at a time.

William Ramsey
Lead High School Counselor (ret.)
Rockville High School, Rockville, Maryland

Preface

Thank you for choosing Forty Days to Forgiveness. With it, you are about to embark on a journey of a lifetime: the forgiveness journey. This journey will not be quick or easy; it will require time, commitment, and effort. However, it will be worthwhile since it will likely transform your understanding of forgiveness and transform your heart in ways that will enrich your life. In fact, you may not be the same person you are now once you finish.

Forty Days to Forgiveness was designed to take forty days to complete. It is broken into seven chapters with a total of forty sections, each with a reading portion and one or more journal exercises. However, finishing in forty consecutive days is not necessary. In fact, it is ill-advised. According to behavioral science studies, forgiveness interventions that take place over a longer period of time have a longer lasting effect. It's just common sense to know that changing one's habits and one's mindset takes time. If we look at the Bible for guidance, we see that forty is a number that recurs in situations where change was required: sometimes forty days and sometimes forty years. For example, at the time of the Flood, rain fell for forty days and forty nights; after fleeing from Egypt to save his life, Moses spent forty years in the desert of Midian; the Israelites wandered for forty years in the wilderness; the Philistines cruelly reigned over Israel for forty years; and Jesus was led into the wilderness to overcome Satan's temptations for forty days. None of these passages explains the significance of "forty," yet the Bible clearly associates forty with times of trouble, hardship, and change.

I encourage you to think of *Forty Days to Forgiveness* as going on a journey. While it's good to have a destination in mind, in the end it's the journey that matters. What's important is that you are consistent, persistent, and you stay the course. Randomly picking up where you left off "when you have time" is not likely to help bring the long-lasting emotional change you are seeking. I would suggest that you pick a time every week and use that time to avoid distractions and to focus. Doing everything on the same day and at the same time is not important but being intentional is.

Very probably, you picked up *Forty Days to Forgiveness* because you, too, are in a time of hardship with the enduring emotional upheaval caused by an offense or offenses committed against you. Like Noah, you are experiencing a flood of troubles and looking for a way to escape the storm. Like Jonah in the belly of a great fish, you are in the dark place of the soul, sometimes unable to see a way out. Like Jesus in the wilderness, you are experience temptations to your faith and feel like you are in a desert place. *Forty Days to Forgiveness* is designed to lead you through the deep waters of recovery to the emotional freedom that forgiveness brings.

Unfortunately, most of us have only a cursory understanding of forgiveness. We mistake it for saying the phrase *I forgive you*. We mistake it for the expectation of people who have been harmed to hear "Please forgive me" or "I'm sorry." We mistakenly believe that these phrases made by us or by those who harmed us will release us from the emotions that are stuck in our hearts. Nothing could be further from the truth. The reality is that the transgression you have experienced has contributed to emotions that disrupt your sense of peace and balance. Those emotions cannot be removed by words or phrases. You cannot undo the harm that has been done to you. You cannot "un-experience" a transgression.

Fortunately, however, those emotions can be reprogrammed with time and by submitting to an intentional process. God will help you make the time; *Forty Days to Forgiveness* provides the process. I pray that God will bless you on this journey, regardless of whether it is a literal or a figurative forty days to forgiveness and recovery.

With numerous books already on the market, why is another book on forgiveness needed? My experience in three divergent fields—organizational leadership development, marriage and family counseling, and palliative care chaplaincy — I have repeatedly seen unforgiveness at the center of interpersonal conflicts and a pervasive dissatisfaction with life. Unforgiveness is often the cause of illness, broken relationships, mental health challenges, shattered lives, relational conflict, and depression and anxiety. Whether at work or in family settings, tremendous negative energy is generated by grudges, vendettas, and bitterness.

From my professional experiences, from my own struggles to overcome mistreatment in the workplace, and from the pain and anger of being sexually abused as a child, I developed an intense interest in learning what forgiveness truly is and how it can help us achieve a life of fulfillment and peace. In all the professional roles I have had and still have, I have helped people establish goals for themselves and then navigate their way toward those goals with new ways of thinking and new behaviors. With God's help and blessings, that's what *Forty Days to Forgiveness* will do for you.

When I was working on my doctoral degree, I had to set a goal for what research I would do that would contribute to the growth of our knowledge in family therapy. I asked myself what contribution I wanted to make to God's kingdom on earth in my remaining years. In all my studies and all my research, I learned one important truth: At the heart of most conflict and the heart of broken marriages is the same issue—self-centeredness.

As disciples of Christ, we seek to emulate His behavior and thinking while He walked the earth. When you add up all His work, messages, and behavior, you find that the core message is love—the antithesis of self-centeredness. Love is a state of mind and a heart that seeks to put the interests of others before our own. The most difficult time to love others is when they have transgressed against us in some way, that is, when we have reason to hold unforgiveness toward others. In the end, I decided I would channel my energy toward helping people learn a Christ-centered approach to forgiving others.

In my research for *Forty Days to Forgiveness*, I discovered three different types of forgiveness: divine forgiveness, which is how God forgives us and how we release our belief that God has wronged us; self-forgiveness, which is how we overcome the regrets and failures of our own lives; and relational forgiveness, which is how we manage to forgive others. *Forty Days to Forgiveness* addresses only the last of these, relational forgiveness. Also, in reviewing the multitude of books and articles on forgiveness, I found four different approaches to the topic: (1) descriptions of what forgiveness is and how it functions from the behavioral sciences; (2) how to forgive another person from a secular, nonbiblical perspective; (3) the spiritual and/or Christian components of forgiveness; and (4) forgiveness from a philosophical perspective. As far as I could discover at the time I wrote *Forty Days to Forgiveness*, no other resource presents what *Forty Days to Forgiveness* does: a step-by-step, Christ-centered approach to forgiving another in order to achieve a life of peace and spiritual balance for oneself and, in some cases, for others.

Forty Days to Forgiveness draws from three different sources: The Bible, behavioral science research, and my personal and professional experience. Why was the Bible not my sole resource if it is, indeed, the "owner-operator manual for life" as some have called it? I agree that God made us and knows what is best for us, but each of us is unique with a wide range of experiences. While I believe the word of God is infallible and absolute truth for what God expects of His children, the Bible cannot possibly address the application of His Word to our unique situations. He leaves it up to us, in the context of Christian fellowship, to do that.

The Bible tells us to forgive, but it is unclear on "*how*" to forgive others in any direct and concise way. In my view, the Bible is more like a map than an owner's manual. A map does not lay out a single route for any journey; rather, it provides valuable information for the traveler to make informed decisions. Still, a map does not include *all* the information needed to get from point A to point B, especially when orange construction barrels appear, and the chosen route must be abandoned. Living life is like traveling on an unfamiliar route: each of us encounters challenges that the Bible cannot directly address. *Forty Days to Forgiveness* is like a map and a travel guide combined, laying out a Christ-inspired route to arrive at forgiveness while also highlighting the challenges you will encounter along the way.

Forty Days to Forgiveness is also based on the behavioral sciences, which is *not* to say that it is based on psychology; a discipline that some view as anti-Christian. Although psychology is a branch of the behavioral sciences, much of *Forty Days to Forgiveness* is based on a tremendous amount of research into human behavior to answer the question that motivated me to write it: Can people learn to forgive, and if so, what helps or hinders their success?

Forty Days to Forgiveness is also based on my twenty-five years of experience in designing and delivering training programs for all levels of leaders in the business world. I strongly believe that the Lord gave me those experiences so that I would have the skill and perspective to write a book like this.

All the training I have designed in my career was built around the belief that people learn best from their experiences. In similar form, you will learn best about the forgiveness journey by "experiencing" the journal exercises at the end of each section (or day). As you complete the journal exercises, you will experience forgiveness in bite-sized doses and will learn why and how to forgive as well as experience forgiveness in small measures throughout the book. This experiential learning process should not be hurried. As you complete each activity, let the ideas germinate in your thoughts and in your heart so that the concepts will take firm root in your soul.

Finally, it's important to say that *Forty Days to Forgiveness* doesn't have all the answers for forgiving others. *Forty Days to Forgiveness* is by no means perfect and does not offer absolutely every nuance of the forgiveness journey. No one resource can address all the needs represented in the diverse cases of unforgiveness. For that reason, I consider *Forty Days to Forgiveness* as a starting point for an ongoing dialogue about forgiveness. I am a student of forgiveness, and I'm inviting you to join me. My website (forgivenessinaction.com) includes a forum where readers can share their experiences, thoughts, and insights about their forgiveness journeys. Dissenting and divergent points of view are also welcome since conversation will refine and grow our understanding of a Christ-centered approach to forgiveness. Please go there and join in the learning community as you share lessons learned on your own journey.

As you begin this journey, I want to bestow a traditional blessing on you: I pray that "the Lord bless you and keep you; the Lord make his face shine upon you and be gracious to you; the Lord turn his face toward you and give you peace" (Numbers 6:24–26 NIV). I pray that God will bless you on your journey toward emotional freedom—during your engagement with *Forty Days to Forgiveness* and beyond.

Ronald D. Ramsey, MEd, DMin, LMFT, Clinical Chaplain
April 2020

CHAPTER 1

Why Forgive?

Bearing with one another and, if one has a complaint against another, forgiving each other; as the Lord has forgiven you, so you also must forgive.

—COLOSSIANS 3:13

Judge not, and you shall not be judged. Condemn not, and you shall not be condemned. Forgive, and you will be forgiven.

—LUKE 6:37

DAY 1

Forty Days to Forgiveness–Introduction

Forty Days to Forgiveness has three goals. The first is to help you forgive a specific person who has committed a trespass that hurt you. The second is to help you learn the skills required to become a more forgiving person. The third is to help you as a disciple of Christ to develop a biblical paradigm for forgiving in order to strengthen your relationship with God and His Church. This introductory chapter is divided into four sections, each intended to be completed at your own pace.

Day 1: Forty Days to Forgiveness—Introduction
Day 2: The Bible and Forgiveness
Day 3: Reasons to Forgive
Day 4: The Core of the Matter

Although anyone can learn about forgiveness through *Forty Days to Forgiveness*, the intended audience is followers of Christ. Jesus outlined expectations for His people to be forgiving, but forgiveness is not universally practiced. A single scripture will illustrate the high standard of behavior set by Jesus Christ. In the Gospel of Matthew, the writer quotes Jesus saying to his followers, "You have heard the law which says, 'Love your neighbor' and hate your enemy. But I say, love your enemies! Pray for those who persecute you! In that way, you will be acting as true children of your Father in heaven. For he gives his sunlight to both the evil and the good, and he sends rain on the just and unjust alike."[1]

Simply stated, Jesus has given Christians a pattern to live by that encourages living in a state of love toward both friends and foes, just as God does. This way of life, however, is contrary to most human emotion, instinct, wisdom, and practice.

In addition to being countercultural, forgiveness is also a broad topic. Therefore, we will look at forgiveness only from the interpersonal perspective, that is, when one person commits a transgression against another. We will not examine forgiveness in other situations, such as forgiving oneself, forgiving God for our belief He has wronged us, and forgiveness between groups. Though the principles in *Forty Days to Forgiveness* may be helpful in these other circumstances, focusing on these other types of forgiveness would dilute our thorough attention to interpersonal forgiveness. In some cases, I have suggested other resources throughout.

Forgiveness is a much-misunderstood concept that has been at the center of theological, philosophical, and scientific study for centuries. From the time of the Greek philosophers, such as Aristotle, to the days of the Old Testament Hebrews,[2] and even to contemporary times, the nature of and need for forgiveness has been debated. For example: What is it? How is it done? When is it appropriate or not appropriate? Are there some acts that are unforgiveable? *Forty Days to Forgiveness* is unique in its design to integrate what these various disciplines teach about forgiveness.

In books written from a behavioral science viewpoint, scripture is largely absent and replaced with a scientific view of forgiveness. Conversely, books about forgiveness written from a theological or philosophical perspective have little reference to what behavioral scientists have discovered about forgiveness. Often, rather than being validated by research, books written from a theological or philosophical perspective are the writers' opinions. Although forgiveness is at the core of the Christian faith, much can also be learned from the behavioral sciences.

The Bible talks about three types of forgiveness: divine, which is the forgiveness relationships between God and humankind; interpersonal forgiveness, which is one person forgiving another who has transgressed against him or her; and self-forgiveness, which entails individually letting go of our past mistakes and failings in order to live in the present under the atoning sacrifice of Jesus our Lord.

The Bible presents a clear, comprehensive story of the divine forgiveness God grants to His people through the atoning sacrifice of Jesus on the cross. We also see examples of people crying out to God, looking for a way to trust God and forgive Him for their misguided indictments against Him. The Bible also addresses self-forgiveness and the role it plays in our images of God and ourselves and in our usefulness as vessels through which God works in the world. Finally, the Bible talks about interpersonal forgiveness and emphasizes the importance of learning to forgive. Although scripture is less clear on how to forgive others, it clearly teaches that following God's direction to forgive will bring personal peace and a balanced life. By relying on God's wisdom, we can tackle the difficult task that forgiveness poses. A key verse from the book of Proverbs illustrates this point:

> *My son, do not forget my teaching, but let your heart keep my commandments, for length of days and years of life and peace they will add to you. Let not steadfast love and faithfulness forsake you; bind them around your neck; write them on the tablet of your heart. So you will find favor and good success in the sight of God and man. Trust in the Lord with all your heart, and do not lean on your own understanding. In all your ways acknowledge Him, and he will make straight your paths.[3]*

This next statement may come as a shock. It is interesting that the Bible provides no examples of interpersonal forgiveness. It gives us no role models for how to forgive our neighbors.[4] Some examples seem to indirectly apply, but many of those examples actually refer to reconciliation, which is not a synonym for forgiveness. Jesus talks about interpersonal forgiveness in some parables, which serve as the closest examples of interpersonal forgiveness that we have. Yet even these parables fall short of behavioral examples of interpersonal forgiveness that teach "how" to forgive. I believe they are important examples of the depth of intensity that forgiveness may require.

While the Bible stresses the importance of forgiveness, it also does not explicitly lay out a clear road map for *how* to forgive interpersonal transgressions. I believe that this is because specific examples of forgiveness might distract our learning from the ultimate forgiver: God Himself. I also believe that forgiveness is a means to an end. The end result our Lord expects is for us to love like He has loved us. When we forgive another person for some interpersonal transgression, we are expressing love. (We will talk about these points extensively throughout *Forty Days to Forgiveness*, so do not get too hung up on them here.)

The Bible also gives us information about many behaviors that, taken together, add up to an ability to forgive. Instead of specific explicit examples of interpersonal forgiveness, we are guided by Christ's demonstration of love and forgiveness for us. With God's demonstration of forgiveness, along with the best research from the disciplines of theology and the behavioral sciences, we can learn the forgiveness process in a way that is rarely experienced outside our Christian tradition and faith.

Forgiveness is behavior, not merely a feeling or an emotion. It is a skill that can be learned. As with learning any skill, work is involved. As you devote your time to work through the exercises in the following chapters, you will begin to flex your forgiveness muscles, building the skills and strength needed to be a truly forgiving person.

You will be asked later in this chapter to select a single person whom you are struggling to forgive. By focusing on a single hurt or offense that you have not been able to forgive, you will learn to stretch yourself to experience a new understanding of forgiveness. On the other hand, you may feel that you have already granted forgiveness for this offense, yet you have not experienced the peace and the emotional freedom that Christ-centered forgiveness offers. Again, working through the exercises and learning new skills will help you achieve the peace and emotional freedom you crave.

Forty Days to Forgiveness is designed for you if one or more of the following statements describe you:

- You are a disciple of Christ looking for biblical answers about how to forgive another person.
- You have experienced unjust, unfair, dismissive, inconsiderate, or harmful behavior from another person.

- You have struggled to forgive another person but are not finding emotional peace from your efforts.
- You cannot stop thinking about a transgression, the offender, and the situation that has caused you pain and suffering.
- You wish to reconcile with a person who has hurt or offended you, and you feel the need to forgive him or her first.
- You are the kind of person who finds something wrong with just about everything that crosses your path.

The mission of *Forty Days to Forgiveness* is to walk you through a proven process that will teach you the behaviors that combine to make you a more forgiving person. You will engage in forty daily readings and exercises that will lead you on a journey to build the skills and the strength needed to forgive someone and become a truly forgiving person.

Forty Days to Forgiveness is designed to be read and practiced over a period of time because the behavioral sciences have established a precedent for taking twenty days, plus or minus, to institute new sustainable habits. But learning the forgiveness process is more than simply changing a habit; it involves changing how we view the world around us and the world within us.

I have also chosen forty days because a number of significant life-altering events took place over a forty-day period of time in the scriptures. The Bible includes examples of people making a significant change, when God saw the need, from a world-focused view to a heaven-focused view. We can note that there seems to be a biblical precedent in the number "forty," which appears repeatedly: forty days of rain after Noah built the ark, forty days of Moses on Mount Sinai receiving the law, forty days for Nineveh to repent and turn from their evil, ungodly ways, forty days of Jesus in the wilderness after His baptism and before the start of His ministry. In some ways, the next forty days of your journey are like a time in the wilderness. It is a time for you to challenge your natural desire to seek justice and revenge for a transgression, and a time for you to look inward to learn what you can do to show up differently in the world.

By breaking *Forty Days to Forgiveness* into forty bite-sized chunks, or days, you can nurture the forgiveness process as you grow toward having more peace, enjoying better well-being, and—more importantly—moving nearer to the center of God's will. *Forty Days to Forgiveness* nestles the process into a period of time that will help you navigate the journey of decisional and emotional forgiveness.

What Forgiveness Is

Before we discuss *why* or *when* we forgive, we will first need to examine what forgiveness actually is. A broad biblical perspective on forgiveness will be presented in chapter 4; for now, we will be guided by Christ's expectation for us to forgive others as the Father has forgiven us, as described by the apostle Paul: "Since God chose you to be the holy people he loves, you must clothe yourselves with tenderhearted mercy, kindness, humility, gentleness, and patience. Make allowance for each other's faults and forgive anyone who offends you."[5]

Let me digress for a moment. Christ presents forgiveness as a natural occurrence, one that becomes a way of life for responding to transgressions. For example, Jesus told His disciples that if someone were to strike them on a cheek, they should turn the other cheek for the person to strike as well. I do not want to go into the theology behind this statement here. I simply want to make the point that Jesus does not view forgiveness as part of our response. Jesus simply says to turn the other cheek. No pause to forgive is stated or implied. As you will see, other verses like this one have suggestions on how to forgive embedded within them. I will point out many of these verses throughout *Forty Days to Forgiveness*.

Interestingly, behavioral science describes interpersonal forgiveness in ways that are consistent with biblical teachings. We learn from research done by behavioral scientists that forgiveness is a response entailing the replacing of negative thoughts toward someone who is threatening our well-being with more positive ones. Instead of responding with feelings and behaviors associated with unforgiveness (grudge holding, retaliation, avoidance, and so forth), a forgiving person endeavors to respond to a wrongdoer based on the moral principles of empathy, grace, and beneficence which may include compassion and unconditional positive regard for the offender's worth, generosity, and moral love.[6] At this point, these principles may seem absurd when thought of in the context of your feelings of unforgiveness. *Forty Days to Forgiveness* will help you to take the small steps necessary that add up to these behaviors and bring the emotional freedom that you are seeking.

My research has shown that theologians spend most of their time analyzing and unpacking divine forgiveness, that is, forgiveness between God and human beings. From a theological perspective, we may also see forgiveness as a human strength because it is an act that emulates God's grace: He forgave us before we deserved it and reconciled us to Himself; therefore, when I forgive, I am modeling my behavior after God's behavior toward me. In his book *Embodying Forgiveness: A Theological Analysis*,[7] Gregory Jones suggests that through forgiveness, we demonstrate key characteristics of God:

- truthful judgment about what has happened or is happening to us
- a willingness to acknowledge the propriety of anger, resentment, or bitterness, as well as a desire to overcome and be freed from these feelings
- a concern for the well-being of the other person, the transgressor, as a child of God
- recognition that we have all transgressed against others and have all needed to be forgiven, suggesting close links between forgiveness and other virtues such as humility, generosity, empathy, and compassion

- acknowledgment that truthful judgment requires accountability to God in order to honor our relationship with Him
- hope for eventual reconciliation with those who have transgressed against us, as well as hope that the transgressors will be reconciled to the blessings of living in God's will.

Theological explanations suggest that forgiveness contributes to individual fulfillment, satisfaction, physical well-being, and happiness. These insights are consistent with the scriptures paraphrased below. Theological explanations also suggest that withholding forgiveness contributes to stress, temptation to sin, conflict, and suffering. It is important to note that the scriptures do not teach that we will have a life without suffering caused by mistreatment. In fact, we are told that by suffering with Christ, we are heirs to His kingdom, and we will be glorified with Him.[8] Let's digress here briefly to debunk the myth that the Christian life brings only joy and that God will keep us from suffering. The following points about suffering paint a different picture.

- God allows suffering to increase our endurance, our character, and our hope in receiving God's love.[9]
- Suffering is temporary, but it leads to eternal presence in the glory of God.[10]
- When we share in Christ's sufferings, we share abundantly in His comfort.[11]
- It has been granted to us that for the sake of Christ we should not only believe in Him but also suffer for His sake.[12]
- Responding to suffering from transgressions with love, empathy, and good demonstrates our holy purpose: we are called to serve God.[13]
- The response to suffering from a transgression is to pray and sing songs of praise.[14]
- We have been called to endure when we suffer from the transgressions we have experienced.[15]
- For it is better to suffer for doing good, if that should be God's will, than for doing evil.[16]
- Those who do good while suffering entrust their souls to a faithful Creator.[17]
- After we have suffered for a little while, God will Himself restore, confirm, strengthen, and establish us.[18]
- We suffer with Him in order that we may also be glorified with Him. [19]

When we suffer because of a transgression we have experienced, we suffer because we judge the wrong from a worldly perspective. We associate the wrong done with the wrong-doer. Viewing the transgression as an act of injustice would not deter from God's perspective. God understands injustice and is opposed to it. Our suffering finds release when we view the transgressor, not the transgression, from God's perspective. Viewing a transgressor through God's lens of forgiveness and reconciliation empowers us to cope with the difficulty visited upon us.

When we are not able to cope with the transgression, we begin to develop negative thoughts about how we would like for the person who harmed us to be treated: taught a lesson, punished, humiliated, incarcerated, etc. However, when we view our transgressor (not the transgression) through God's eyes, He builds us up to experience peace in the face of our pain, a peace that comes only from our walk with Him. We have God's hand to strengthen us when we are *tempted* to withhold forgiveness. Paul told the Corinthian church, "No temptation has overtaken you that is not common to man. God is faithful, and he will not let you be tempted beyond your ability, but with the temptation he will also provide the way of escape, that you may be able to endure it."[20]

Forgiveness helps us to live at peace with others and at peace with ourselves. Even though forgiveness does not require reconciliation, the actions associated with forgiveness set the stage for reconciling broken relationships. As with any skill, however, some people are better at forgiveness than others. Improving our skill to forgive is done through the help of the Holy Spirit and through developing practices and behaviors that lead to spiritual maturity.

Unfortunately, forgiving a person for an interpersonal transgression does not guarantee that we will have a forgiving nature when we experience future hurts. We say that a person who can overcome unforgiveness for a onetime transgression has "state forgiveness," meaning that he or she is in a temporary *state* of forgiveness for a single episode of a broken relationship. While a person may have the emotional strength to forgive a single offense, he or she may not become a forgiving person by nature.

In contrast, when a person has a forgiving temperament, we say that he or she has "trait forgiveness" or "dispositional forgiveness." Trait forgiveness means one has developed the disposition of a forgiving person who has learned how to see the world through eyes of empathy and compassion for others. Harboring unforgiveness eclipses the disposition that fuels a forgiving heart. Disciples of Christ who have a forgiving nature understand that ultimately it is God who provides even when we do not immediately see the transgression from God's perspective.

Forty Days to Forgiveness is designed primarily to show how forgiveness is a *process* that can be learned and applied to a single transgression; however, as the process is learned, and the actions that lead to forgiveness are practiced, it can influence nurturance of a forgiving disposition and become a way of life. To put it succinctly: state forgiveness is what you "*do*" and trait forgiveness is who you "*are.*"

When you follow the multistep process outlined in this book, it will help you progress on your immediate forgiveness journey (state forgiveness) and help you begin the longer journey of shaping yourself into a more forgiving person (trait forgiveness).

In the approach I created for *Forty Days to Forgiveness*, I use the word *action* as a way to remember the steps in the forgiveness process. Each letter in the word ACTION is the first letter of each of the six steps of the forgiveness process as explained in *Forty Days to Forgiveness*. My goal for you is that once you complete the reading and journal exercises in *Forty Days to Forgiveness*, you will be able to take ACTION to forgive a person who has committed an offense against you. Here's what ACTION means:

- **Acknowledging how a hurt has affected you (chapter 2)**
  Acknowledging that a wrong has been done may seem obvious, but it is essential to reflect on the transgression to gain greater insight into the specific effects it has had on you.

- **Committing to trying to forgive (chapter 3)**
  Forgiveness begins with making a commitment to *try* to forgive. The commitment you will be asked to make is to try to replace unforgiving thoughts with positive ones.

- **Transitioning to a godly perspective (chapter 4)**
  Unforgiveness fuels a vicious cycle of negative thoughts about the transgressor and what you believe should happen to him or her as a result of the offense. This third step in the forgiveness process focuses on making the transition from this vicious thought cycle to one that is oriented toward forgiving thoughts.[21] Transitioning includes seeing the transgressor as a child of God rather than as a villain.

- **Internalizing spiritual maturity (chapter 5)**
  Internalizing your experience and viewing it through a godly lens will promote the development of Christlike behaviors, thoughts, and feelings.[22] The key goal for internalizing your forgiveness is[23] to begin to practice the disciplines that lead to ongoing spiritual maturity.

- **Opening your heart (chapter 6)**
  While you can take ACTION to forgive a transgression, forgiveness comes from the heart.[24] When there is an openness in your heart to forgive, you will begin to feel compassion toward the transgressor and to have a desire for his or her salvation.

- **Next steps for emotional healing (chapter 7)**
  Forgiveness is not an event that happens and then everything goes back to the way it was before the transgression. No, things will never be the same. You will continue the forgiveness journey and may have to refer again to some of the exercises in *Forty Days to Forgiveness*. You can build strength to resist a relapse to negative thoughts or behaviors by increasing your knowledge of God's Word and engaging in nurturing fellowship with like-minded disciples.[25]

As with any journey, knowing your starting point is important to navigate to where you want to be. Google can't provide a route to your destination unless it has data on where you're starting from. As you begin each chapter, you will be formulating where you are at that point in time regarding that step in the ACTION process. Journal exercises at the end of each chapter will help you understand your destination and your readiness to tackle the forgiveness step of that chapter. These exercises will help you find your current state of forgiveness in small, bite sized doses and help you to invite God along on your journey with you.

Each chapter is comprised of a series of sections, each designed in sequence to be completed in one day. In this case, I don't mean one day literally. One day represents whatever period of time you feel necessary to complete that component of the ACTION process before moving on to the next. In fact, it is preferable that you not rush through and do all the reading and activities in forty consecutive days. Give the lessons from each section (day) time to percolate in your mind and heart. Research shows that a longer-lasting effect on one's state of forgiveness is created by having a specific process to follow and by extending the steps in that process over time. People who experience short learning interventions are more likely to fall back into unforgiveness soon after the intervention is complete. Dr. Worthington, a renowned expert on forgiveness research (and a disciple of Christ) gave me a word of wisdom as I began writing this book: stretch out the forgiveness process over time – and that's what I have done.

At the end of each section is a summary and devotional. Do not skip the summary; it reinforces what you have learned. Read it and jot some notes on what you remember about each point in the summary in a personal journal. Do the devotional on a different day from when you do the journal exercises; perhaps do the devotion more than once. I would suggest starting a journal in a separate notebook. Write about the lessons learned, insights you've gained, direction you want to proceed in, and about parts of the devotional that resonate with you. It might be helpful to invite a friend to listen to your summary of the section and share in the devotional with you. As you'll see in later chapters, fellowship with other believers is a core component of building spiritual maturity.

Please know this: I will be praying to God on your behalf daily to bless you as you work your way through unforgiveness; as you learn and apply a forgiveness process. I am on your journey to emotional freedom with you, learning daily with you how to tame my own lingering unforgiveness. Thank you for the courage to buy this book and to engage in the steps outlined here; thank you for inviting me to take your journey with you through our mutual interaction in *Forty Days to Forgiveness*.

Journal Exercise 1a: Getting Started

PRAYER FOR GOD'S GUIDANCE

Gracious Lord, You are a God of mercy, and since the beginning of time You have granted forgiveness to all Your children. You granted me forgiveness when I [describe a time when you transgressed against someone and needed either that person's or God's forgiveness].

I am not sure where this forgiveness journey is going to lead me. I am having a hard time seeing my transgressor as anything but someone who has wrongfully hurt me and should be "dealt with." I know that from Your perspective, all have sinned, and You have forgiven us through the sacrifice made by Your Son. But You are God and I am me.

I pray that You walk beside me in this journey and give me a softened heart and open eyes, and please build my courage to try to forgive. Deliver me from the bondage of dark thoughts, stress, and unrest and into emotional peace and comfort.

I pray these things in the name of Jesus, my brother and Savior, who was tortured and shed His blood so that I may live in eternal glory with You in heaven when this life is over.

Amen.

Journal Exercise 1b: Selecting the Transgressor

This is a short exercise to help you walk before you run. This exercise will help you to prepare for the remainder of the exercises in *Forty Days to Forgiveness*. It is important to go slow and do this exercise thoughtfully. *Forty Days to Forgiveness* will use a variety of teaching methods to help you reach lasting *emotional* forgiveness. These methods include (1) reading insights into each step in the ACTION (forgiveness) process; (2) completing activities that illustrate key points about forgiveness; (3) keeping a journal to help you chart your progress; (4) participating in exercises that challenge you to think, feel, and grow; and (5) talking with a partner.

As you complete the exercises in *Forty Days to Forgiveness*, it will be important for you to think about a single transgression that you have experienced. To do this, think about the primary offense against you for which you feel you would like to find forgiveness. Choose a transgression or offense that focuses on one person and that is not too complex. When you near the end of your journey, you may want to return to the exercises you completed to strengthen what you have learned. You may think of more than one offense, but please narrow your focus to just one for the purposes of the exercises in *Forty Days to Forgiveness*.

It is also important to choose an interpersonal offense, that is, a transgression committed by someone against you personally, since *Forty Days to Forgiveness* does not address forgiving God or oneself. The following exercise will lead you through a set of questions to help you identify who the focus of your forgiveness goals will be.

Instructions

In the following worksheet, write the name of a single person whom you are struggling to forgive. Take your time and answer the questions thoughtfully and honestly. You will not be asked to share this worksheet with anyone else.

Journal Exercise 1c: Forgiveness Journey Worksheet

1. Name of transgressor		
2. Relationship to you		
3. Will your relationship continue?	[Yes] [No]	
4. Describe how often the transgression occurred.		
5. Briefly describe the offense.		

RATINGS	HIGH	MED.	LOW	DESCRIBE WHY YOU CHOSE THIS RATING.
6. How likely is future contact?	3	2	1	
7. What level of severity would you assign to the transgression?	3	2	1	
8. How distressing is this transgression to you?	3	2	1	
9. Why do you feel you need to forgive this person?				

Interpreting Your Results

Think of your choice of transgression as a social experiment—a learning laboratory. While this choice may begin the journey toward emotional peace, the key benefit is to provide a crucible in which you can begin to build the skills needed to forgive and to become more forgiving. Here are some important points to bear in mind as you review the worksheet you just completed:

- ✓ Your answers to **questions 2 and 3** are important to understand before you embark on this journey. For our initial purposes, the goal of this exercise is not necessarily to set the stage to reconcile your relationship with a wrongdoer who is still in your life. Forgiveness can be a stepping-stone to reconciliation; however, if the offender could hurt you again in the future, you may not want to pursue reconciliation.

- ✓ **Question 4** helps you to be clear about whether the transgressor is someone you interact with regularly. If so, it will be important to set boundaries for how often you interface with this person for the course of this journey. *Note:* At no point in *Forty Days to Forgiveness* will you be asked to approach the offender or interact with him or her.

- ✓ **Question 5** is asked so you will think about the type and magnitude of the transgression. A transgressor who has committed a very small offense may not present the details necessary for you to learn all the steps in the ACTION process. On the other hand, a transgression that is extremely egregious may have too many dynamics to sort out the first time through this ACTION process. Ultimately, the choice is yours. Once you select a transgression, you will need to stick with it throughout the course of this journey.

- ✓ **Questions 6–9** help to confirm that the selection you made in the successive previous step is the best one. In these questions, you have rated how much effect this offense is having on you now. An offense that carries a medium [M] severity is preferable; one that is too severe or too trivial may not be as helpful for your learning. You might want to reconsider the forgiveness issue you select to work on and choose a transgressor with whom you have a more moderate issue. However, this is a personal choice. Just be aware that your choice will affect the intensity with which you'll need to approach the activities in *Forty Days to Forgiveness*. Regardless of the forgiveness issue you want to work on, the goal is to help you see immediate results that will lead you to a greater sense of well-being.

DAY 2

The Bible and Forgiveness

In comparison to its descriptions of divine forgiveness, the Bible makes fewer explicit statements about interpersonal forgiveness. While forgiveness is a central theme in Judeo-Christian theology, most of the references to forgiveness in the Bible (particularly the Old Testament) relate to God's divine forgiveness of sin, rebellion against His commands, and worship of other gods, not to interpersonal forgiveness (that is, forgiveness between humans). We will first look at forgiveness in the Old Testament, especially in ancient Jewish culture, since it is the basis for New Testament forgiveness.

Several poignant stories about reconciliation in the Old Testament imply forgiveness, such as the stories of Jacob and Esau,[26] Joseph and his brothers,[27] David and Saul,[28] and David and Shimei.[29] On the surface, these stories seem to illustrate forgiveness, but they are actually about reconciliation. Reconciliation and forgiveness are two distinctly different but related processes. In our society today, we tend to think in linear logic: transgression leads to anger, which leads to forgiveness, which leads to reconciliation. However, in the Old Testament, the term *forgiveness* is used only once in the context of an interpersonal relationship: when, on his deathbed, Jacob told his older sons to seek Joseph's forgiveness. The timing here is illustrative because Jacob's request was made long after Joseph had fully demonstrated reconciliation with his family.[30]

In this context, *reconciliation* is the restoration of a relationship that has been broken because one person has treated another in a hurtful, unfair, or unjust way. In contrast, *forgiveness* is the replacing of feelings of retaliation and dislike with empathy and grace toward the transgressor. In some cases, reconciliation my lubricate our ability to experience state forgiveness. Forgiveness, however, may or may not include restoring a relationship, and it certainly does not absolve the transgressor of the consequences of his or her actions. Unfortunately, the terms reconciliation and forgiveness are often used interchangeably, but one is not necessarily required for the other. One can forgive without reconciling, and one can reconcile without forgiving, which was the case in the

Old Testament story of Joseph and his brothers. In order to understand forgiveness from a biblical perspective, we will turn first to forgiveness in the context of Judaism.

Judaism and Forgiveness[31]

In the Old Testament, God spoke extensively about seeking forgiveness for sins against Him. Despite God's love for and faithfulness to His chosen people, the Israelites, they maintained an on-again, off-again relationship with Him. One device God used to remedy the sinful nature of humankind was the introduction of the Ten Commandments through Moses. Before that, God issued his guidance through prophets and patriarchs. In conjunction with these commandments, God also supplied an extensive set of requirements for forgiveness of sins, including various types of gift offerings and animal sacrifices to be made through a priest (a Levite) at the temple. While God expected his people to treat one another justly and fairly, these offerings were primarily made to atone for sins against God as opposed to sins between people.

In addition to the Ten Commandments, God gave the Israelites a series of regulations that governed all life. These regulations are called the law of Moses and are known as the Torah, which is often identified as the first five books of the Old Testament. In addition to these biblical books, most sects of Judaism also followed a vast collection of rabbinic writings known as the Talmud, which is comprised of two sections: the Mishnah and the Gemara. The Mishnah is the part that contains many rules regarding interpersonal forgiveness.

The Mishnah instructs that a person who commits a transgression against another is required to apologize sincerely and publicly to the wronged individual in order to rectify the wrong. The transgressor is responsible for making things right with the victim; doing so, in some cases, requires monetary remuneration or acts of service. The Mishnah strongly encourages, but does not require, the wronged person to grant forgiveness. A transgressor can make up to three attempts to seek forgiveness; if unsuccessful, he or she is to return with three friends to solicit pardon. Even though the victim is still not required to grant forgiveness, he or she is forbidden to hold a grudge or take vengeance. Leviticus 19 commands, "You shall not hate your brother in your heart, but you shall reason frankly with your neighbor, lest you incur sin because of him. You shall not take vengeance or bear a grudge against the sons of your own people, but you shall love your neighbor as yourself: I am the Lord."[32]

The following is a summary of the Mishnah's teaching about forgiveness, which entails the following:

1. Acknowledgment by the transgressor that he or she has wronged another individual.
2. Public confession of one's wrongdoings to both God and the community.

3. Public expression of remorse.[33]
4. Public announcement of the offender's resolve not to sin in this way again.
5. Compensation of the victim for the injury inflicted, accompanied by acts of charity to others.
6. The transgressor's sincere request for forgiveness up to three times, and then with the help of friends if necessary.
7. Avoidance of the conditions that caused the offense, even to the point of changing one's name and/or moving to a new locale.
8. Acting differently when confronted with the same situation wherein the offender sinned the first time.

The offender's role in performing these steps determined whether he or she would be restored to the community or ostracized. Likewise, the victim had his or her own set of challenging responsibilities in the forgiveness process. As outlined in Leviticus, the victim not only was strongly encouraged to forgive in order to meet the expectations of God and community but also had to overcome feelings of hostility and vengefulness toward the transgressor. The community regarded forgiveness as going beyond duty: forgiveness was a series of actions rooted in charity and benevolence performed by both victim and transgressor.

An important concept regarding forgiveness in the Jewish faith is that a person cannot obtain forgiveness from God for wrongs done to others; forgiveness can only be obtained from the victim of the transgression.[34] Thus, when a transgressor desired forgiveness for committing a sin against someone, his or her primary source of relief was from the wronged person and, ultimately, the community. Although the transgressor could seek divine help in obtaining forgiveness from the wronged person, the ultimate goal was not to receive forgiveness from God but to be forgiven by the victim.

Another Jewish practice regarding forgiveness is the annual observance of the Day of Atonement, known as Yom Kippur. Just prior to Yom Kippur, transgressors ask for the forgiveness of those they have wronged during the prior year. Additionally, to repent from non-interpersonal wrongs committed, transgressors fast and pray for God's forgiveness for sins against Him. Sincere outward signs of repentance are required for both kinds of sin. But again, one sought God's forgiveness for sins committed against God; Jews were commanded to actively seek the forgiveness of the people they wronged.

Christian Forgiveness

As we look at the New Testament for guidance regarding forgiveness, we see that Christ's and the apostles' teachings were clearly influenced by Jewish culture, yet with a major distinction: Christ taught that the victim has the responsibility to forgive the offender. As Christians, we must "forgive as the Lord forgave [us]."[35] Under Jewish law, as explained earlier, the transgressor was to acknowledge wrongdoing and ask for forgiveness, but the wounded party was not obligated to forgive. The New Testament, in contrast, makes clear that the victim has as much obligation to forgive as the offender has obligation to seek forgiveness.

Jewish practice may have influenced Christ's teachings about forgiveness, but key differences exist. For example, in Matthew, Jesus instructs his followers to go to a brother who has sinned against them and tell him his fault privately, while the Jewish tradition instructs the transgressor to go to the victim publicly. Jesus said that if, after the private visit from the victim, the transgressor does not repent, the *victim is then to take one or two others* who can establish evidence of the sin.[36] In Jewish tradition, in contrast, when the *victim does not grant forgiveness* on the first request, the transgressor may take others with him to request forgiveness. In a clear reversal of Jewish practice, Jesus taught that His disciples are to take the initiative to forgive when they are sinned against, first privately and alone and then with witnesses. If the transgressor fails to respond appropriately, the next step is for the Christian community to withdraw from an unrepentant brother or sister, a concept that has some similarities with Jewish teaching.[37] As in Judaism, Christ's teaching requires outward evidence that the transgressor has repented and turned to God. We will talk more later about how this guidance applies to disciples with whom we are in fellowship, not to nonbelievers.[38]

Another distinction of Christian forgiveness is that we can call upon God to help us with interpersonal forgiveness, which we will discuss later in this chapter. Victims are to operate out of a sense of love and compassion for the offender, whereas in Judaism, a victim may or may not grant forgiveness despite the charity and benevolence extended by the transgressor. Essentially, in Jewish law, God is not involved in this human exchange. While New Testament descriptions of forgiveness and repentance bear some resemblance to the Jewish Mishnah (although often in reverse of the Jewish approach), the concept of interpersonal forgiveness is expanded in the New Testament and placed in a context of love, tolerance, and reconciliation. We will talk more later about the dearth of examples to illustrate this behavior (except for two of Jesus's parables) despite the clear directive to forgive others for wrongs committed against us.

The New Testament describes three different contexts for interpersonal forgiveness: (1) forgiveness of a fellow disciple of Christ (a brother/sister in the Lord), (2) forgiveness of others in general (neighbors and enemies), and (3) the impact of forgiving others on our relationship with God, a concept not explored in the Torah or the Mishnah.

Concerning the first context, Christian teaching emphasizes that God desires for us to live at peace with all people, but specifically with other members of the body of Christ.[39] We are also told, as much as it is up to us, to try to live peacefully with all people: "Do not repay anyone evil for evil. Carefully consider what is right in the eyes of everybody. If it is possible on your part, live at peace with everyone."[40] Christians are told to be tolerant and patient and to forgive one another,[41] forgiving as many times as someone requests forgiveness.[42] When a Christian sins against a brother or against God, he or she is to be admonished (warned), but in a spirit of love, patience, kindness, and restoration.[43] If the offense (sin) persists without true repentance, then the offended party is to take other Christians (which may include a church leader) with him or her, and if the offender still refuses to listen and respond, the offended party should bring the matter to the attention of the Church.[44] However, we are to be aware that no one is guiltless.[45] In the Sermon on the Mount, Jesus warned against pointing out the flaws of others when we have flaws of our own and, I might add, flaws that may be worse.[46]

The second context for interpersonal forgiveness, the forgiveness of others in general, is outside of our Christian fellowship and relationships and includes our neighbors, our persecutors, and our enemies. Thus, the requirement to forgive means forgiving everyone who crosses our path, whether we encounter them casually, regularly, or only once.[47] When forgiving those outside the church, the process is not as extensive, lacking the steps of reconciliation and restoration to the community. All are to be treated with love and shown the same mercy and forgiveness that God has shown to us.[48] Beyond that, we are to do good to those who mistreat us, not harming them or vengefully paying them back. Instead, we are to love them as we love ourselves.[49]

At the same time, it is virtually impossible to be at peace with everyone. Some people thrive on conflict and bitterness, and no matter what we do, we cannot make peace. We are only responsible for ourselves, however, and we make peace only to the extent that we can control.[50] Yet, when presented with the opportunity, we are to treat others with kindness regardless of the conflict they create.[51] This truth, though, does not mean that we are to seek out people who abuse us in order to "do good" to them. Instead, we are to release them to God for judgment of their sin.[52] However, we remain available as instruments that God may use to reach them for their salvation.[53]

As explained above, Jewish tradition requires that repentant individuals openly show that they have changed their ways. This stipulation regarding visible change particularly applies to serial transgressors or abusers who seemingly repent but remain the same in their hearts. Unless they demonstrate a change in their pattern of transgressions, such people need to be avoided. God does not wish for His people to be in harm's way. When possible, He provides a way of escape.[54] (More will be said about this later.) Yet, even in our avoidance, we can still forgive offenders, treat them with kindness and love when the opportunity presents, and pray for their redemption.

The third context regarding forgiveness in the New Testament concerns how it affects our relationship with God. In Matthew 6, Jesus said, "If you do not forgive others their trespasses, neither will your Father forgive your trespasses."[55] This verse is often misunderstood and generates differing points of view. Here is mine: it does not mean that faithful Christians will lose their salvation if they fail to forgive others. Once we become a child of God, having confessed our sinful nature, repented of our sinful life, and been baptized, I believe nothing can separate us from our salvation.[56] Jesus died so that we would be forgiven of our sins.[57] Therefore, when God looks at us, He does not see us as sinners but as His children, redeemed through the atoning sacrifice of Christ's death and resurrection. What, then, does Jesus's statement in Matthew 6 mean? "If you do not forgive others their trespasses, neither will your Father forgive your trespasses" suggests that our unforgiveness corrupts our ability to enjoy fellowship with God. Not because God's love changes, but because unforgiveness poisons the ability of the heart and mind to be in union with God: it stunts our spiritual growth. Being in a right relationship with God requires that we also be in a right relationship with our fellowship of believers and with non-believers who live in our ecosystem.

Adam and Eve provide a clear example of this truth. When Adam and Eve sinned, God cast them out of the garden of Eden. He still loved them and looked out for their welfare, going so far as to kill an animal to make clothes to cover their nakedness. He continued to bless them in other ways as well, but they paid the consequences for their sin, one of which was the loss of the deep, direct interpersonal fellowship they had enjoyed with God in the garden. In the same way, when we do not forgive others, we hinder ourselves from enjoying a deep experience with God.

King David of Israel, described as a man after God's own heart,[58] provides another example of the effect of sin on our relationship with God. After David sinned against Bathsheba and her husband Uriah, he asked God not to hide His face from him because of his iniquities.[59] There is no indication that David lost his salvation, but David's relationship with God was forever changed, and the consequences of his sin continued to haunt him for the rest of his life. Similarly, when we fall out of fellowship with God, our sense of the Holy Spirit can go cold, forcing us to operate from a place of darkness and vulnerability to evil.[60] Instead, when we love God and keep His commandments, we are blessed. Jesus specifically told us that we are blessed when we make peace with others and are merciful.[61]

Forgiving others may seem like an unreasonable or even impossible task. When we are hurt, it is difficult to see the transgressor in a loving way. However, Jesus said that His yoke is easy, and His burden is light. He said if we come to Him, He will lighten our burdens, and He sent the Holy Spirit to help us with these tasks. God, as our Creator, knows what is ultimately best for us. Forgiving someone is in our best interest, as well as in the best interests of the offender. As we shall see later, a strong, loving relationship with God can aid in terminating the vicious cycle of unforgiveness. The following journal exercise will help set the tone for the remainder of the work you do in *Forty Days to Forgiveness*.

Journal Exercise 2: Prayer for Guidance

A Personal Prayer for Strength and Guidance

Almighty God, grant me the serenity to accept the things I cannot change about the transgression I have experienced. The things I cannot change include:

I am calling out for Your loving hand to endow me with the courage to change the things I can. The things about the transgression that make me fearful are:

Wisdom is a gift You grant us. Wisdom is the ability to look at this situation from Your perspective. Help me to know what I can do in this situation that will glorify You. The things I feel I need courage to do include:

I pray that You will hear my prayer and that You will guide me and be by my side as I learn the meaning of forgiveness from Your perspective.

In Your Son's name I pray all these things. Amen.

DAY 3

Reasons to Forgive

As disciples of Christ, we are commanded to forgive. But why? Ideally, we forgive out of a sense of compassion for others and not out of a sense of duty. I would suggest that when we forgive, we contribute to the building of the kingdom of God. Our primary motivators for forgiving are our well-being; our love for fellow disciples of Christ; our love for our enemies, neighbors, and persecutors; and our desire to have a deep relationship with God. These motivators are the source of Christians' four primary reasons to forgive:

Reason #1: Forgiveness is a means for God's grace, mercy, and love to be conveyed to the world through us.

As disciples of Christ, we know that God's will for us is that we reflect His love for others.[62] Jesus left the church behind to continue His mission to build the kingdom. As members of His church, we endeavor to emulate Christ in our actions toward the world and toward other disciples of Christ.

Jesus said that our love for others would directly identify us as His followers.[63] As previously stated, forgiving others is also necessary to maintain a relationship with the Father.[64] In the course of Jesus's ministry, He specifically mentioned the concept of interpersonal forgiveness eight times. Three of those times occur when he was teaching the disciples to pray.[65] In these passages, He told us to forgive others as the Father has forgiven us. In order to emulate God's divine forgiveness properly, we adopt five characteristics of His forgiveness:[66]

1. Since God *forgives us even before we ask*, we emulate His forgiveness when we forgive before it is required.[67]
2. Since God's forgiveness is freely given and *requires no prior payment or restitution,* we forgive before the offender makes a request for forgiveness, attempts to apologize, or performs acts of repentance and restitution. In so doing, we become the means through which

God's grace is extended to others.[68] So often I hear people say that the other person must apologize before they'll forgive. I would ask such a person, "Why?" How does the other person's apology serve you? Does God expect you to apologize before He forgives you? We will address this idea more later.

3. God freely grants His forgiveness, requiring only that we be born again and follow the Savior. *God would have us freely grant our forgiveness to others.* This provides us with opportunities to be a conduit to pass along God's grace, freely, to others.[69]

4. *God wants to minister to those who are most in need of His love and forgiveness.* Jesus focused our attention in this world on the marginalized, the spiritually depraved, and those most in need of our love and mercy.[70]

5. God's forgiveness is *an opportunity for His disciples to grow the kingdom by transmitting His grace to others.* Jesus told His disciples to go into the entire world and preach the gospel, bringing others to a saving knowledge of Christ. Forgiving others is a way of going into the world to spread the gospel and to bring others to Christ through our reflection of God's grace and mercy. Some will never experience the love of God except by first interacting with His disciples. When we forgive others, we are behaving in a way that is countercultural and that reflects God's nature to transgressors and to others who may be observers of the situation. I would like to introduce a key concept that is a central theme throughout this journey: In a sense, forgiveness is a missionary practice.[71]

In the Gospel of Matthew,[72] Jesus told Peter to forgive his brother a seemingly infinite number of times (seventy times seven), and in the Gospel of Luke, He told us to forgive a brother if he repents.[73] Jesus's commands, however, do not suggest that the Christian condones offensive behavior. The very act of deciding to forgive implies regarding the offensive act as sin. Followers of Christ understand that the sin is not the person but, rather, the actions of the person. As we will discuss later in detail, forgiveness is not reconciling with an abusive person who will continue to take advantage of you, nor is forgiveness condoning or excusing sinful behavior. While we are commanded to forgive the *person*, we often find it necessary to set boundaries for the relationship to discourage continuation of sinful acts and to encourage the offender to seek help with controlling future displays of the transgression.[74]

Reason #2: Forgiving others is a way to express our concern for their eternal welfare.

While hanging on the cross, the greatest offense He experienced in His time on earth, Jesus demonstrated concern for His tormentors' eternal welfare by asking the Father to forgive them and not hold their sins against them. Jesus asked, "Father, forgive them; for they know not what they do."[75] Two interesting points come from this short prayer. First, it is the only example of Jesus mentioning forgiveness in the context of a transgression against Him. Second, Jesus did not actually forgive those who instigated His suffering. Instead, He asked the Father to forgive them and not to hold the sin against them. As He was dying, Jesus was thinking about the kingdom. When the criminal on the cross next to Him asked to be remembered when He came into His kingdom, Jesus told him that he would be ushered into paradise that very day. Even under the extenuating circumstances of His own death, He thought about the eternal welfare of another and the mission He had been sent to fulfill.[76]

We see a similar situation with Stephen, an early disciple of Christ, in the book of Acts. When Stephen was being brutally stoned, he prayed, "Lord, do not hold this sin against them."[77] The examples of Jesus and Stephen are both instances of the victims not directly forgiving their offenders; instead, they asked the Lord to show the offenders mercy. We can learn two things from these examples. First, even in the most extreme circumstances, we can be concerned primarily about the transgressor and not the transgression.[78] Yet, in the heat of a transgression, such grace is practically impossible without our prayer and help from the Holy Spirit.[79] Second, there will be times when we simply cannot bring ourselves to forgive someone of their trespass against us. Calling out to God to forgive in our place connects us with the divine mission of God: He wills that all should be saved and come to a knowledge of His love and mercy, regardless of whether they are sinners or not. Those who trespass against us fall under the same category we do: sinners who fall short of God's expectations of us.

Reason #3: We are commanded to forgive others in order to live peacefully with all people.

The inspiring words of Paul to the Roman church speak for themselves:

> *Bless those who persecute you; bless and do not curse them. Rejoice with those who rejoice, weep with those who weep. Live in harmony with one another. Do not be haughty, but associate with the lowly. Never be conceited. Repay no one evil for evil, but give thought to do what is honorable in the sight of all. If possible, so far as it depends on you, live peaceably with all. Beloved, never avenge yourselves, but leave it to the wrath of God, for it is written, "Vengeance is mine, I will repay, says the Lord." To the contrary, "If your enemy is hungry, feed him; if he is thirsty, give him something to drink; for by so doing you will heap burning coals on his head." Do not be overcome by evil, but overcome evil with good.[80]*

In my view, this passage tells us more about the essence of forgiveness than any other single passage in the New Testament. Let's take it apart to identify what we are expected to do.
We are to:

- Bless our persecutors, which means to give good things to them.
- Lift the names of our transgressors to God, ask Him to bless them, and put the situation in His hands.

- Empathize with the feelings of others, regardless of their emotions and state of mind.
- Live in harmony with everyone to the extent that is within our control.
- Be humble toward others, especially those less fortunate.
- Never take revenge against offenders; rather, treat them honorably.

Of course, we could study these behaviors and attitudes in detail, which would require another book. Here I have simplified these points to make this illustration: if these six points were easy, you would not be reading *Forty Days to Forgiveness*. To be frank, this passage seems to make forgiveness appear simpler than it really is. Paul's message may seem absurd to you right now in light of the hurt you have experienced. But as you work through the exercises in *Forty Days to Forgiveness*, God will bless you and soften your heart to find joy in His will for you and His will for your transgressor.

You might be asking yourself, *Why would I want to forgive someone anyway? I can seek justice in other ways that would even the score.* This may be true. But be honest with yourself. Do you truly believe justice will bring you the emotional peace that forgiveness will? Do not confuse justice with forgiveness. Justice and forgiveness can go hand in hand, but they are not the same thing. Justice occurs independently from forgiveness, and forgiveness does not absolve anyone from the consequences of their actions. Just bear in mind that Jesus and Stephen did not demand justice for their brutal executions.

Let's digress here for a moment to understand what stoning is. I always thought of it as someone just throwing rocks at a transgressor. But there's more to it. Webster's dictionary describes stoning is a method of capital punishment where a group throws *stones* at a person until the subject dies from blunt trauma. It has been attested as a form of punishment for grave misdeeds since ancient times. In short: stoning is death by torture. While there are varieties of ways stoning is done, here's an example of how it works.

The victim is buried in a hole and covered with soil (men up to their waists; women to a line above their breasts). Some accounts from more ancient times indicate a person is staked out on the ground in a laying position with arms and legs outstretched. In other words, the victim is immobilized. A selected group then executes the alleged victim using rocks and sticks. It is often done slowly and methodically to inflict as much pain as possible. In essence, the blunt trauma of stones breaks down bodily functioning to the point of organ failure. As a chaplain, I have witnessed the last days of patients who are living with progressive organ failure: it's a horrible way to go. So Paul and Steven were tortured mercilessly until taken for dead.

How do you feel now about forgiveness? I imagine myself in that experience . . . . could I ask God to forgive my aggressors? While some people blame themselves for the misdeeds of others, most people blame the offending person. Others also blame auxiliary people, those indirectly involved in the offense, such as parents, teachers, and/or former friends or enemies who may have contributed to the transgression. Any kind of blame, however, inhibits the forgiveness process. When we blame others, we set ourselves up, at worst to seek revenge. At best, we distance ourselves from and ignore the transgressor(s). These reactions are the tip of an iceberg that we call "unforgiveness."

And now, here is the central theme of the ACTION approach to forgiveness, and the key points upon which *Forty Days to Forgiveness* is based: Unforgiveness is a state of mind wherein we maintain thoughts of harming or repaying transgressors to teach them a lesson or to even the score. Forgiveness, on the other hand, is replacing those feelings of retaliation, bitterness, contempt, and deserved restitution with feelings of empathy, compassion, and love for the offender. Sound difficult? From my own personal experience with unforgiveness, I answer an emphatic yes. I'm in the boat with you. If unforgiveness were not a struggle for me, I would not be able to write *Forty Days to Forgiveness*. It's out of my own pain and struggle that I join you on this journey. We will talk more about what forgiveness is and is not in chapter 3.

It is also common for people to blame God for not protecting us from all harm. Yet in scripture we are continually reminded that we will experience—and can even expect—suffering, tribulation, persecution, betrayal, pain, and rejection. The apostle Paul taught that God works all things—good and bad—together for the good of those who love Him.[81] Though Satan can certainly influence the actions of our offenders toward us, in reality our transgressors are seldom as maleficent as they seem. In the Old Testament, Satan intervened in the life of a man named Job, coming to God and daring Him to allow him to tempt Job, one of God's righteous servants, to sin. Satan wanted to show God that people only serve Him when their lives are going well, claiming that if God did not provide protection for Job, then Job would turn his back on God. God allowed Satan to torment Job as long as he did not take his life. After a number of intense calamities, Job sustained his love for God, even while not understanding why God would allow such suffering to happen to him.

Job shows both that we can love God in spite of feeling that we are not receiving His complete protection and that we can have favor with God even in our suffering. We might later be allowed to see the positive effects of our suffering, how it often results in building hope in others and strengthening our own faith. And we can find God in our wounds, as Job did: "Then Job arose and tore his robe and shaved his head and fell on the ground and worshiped. And he said, 'Naked I came from my mother's womb, and naked shall I return. The Lord gave, and the Lord has taken away; blessed be the name of the Lord.' In all this Job did not sin or charge God with wrong."[82]

When Job chose to view God as the source of both his blessings and his losses, he could keep focus and place blame properly. Job could have focused instead on God's failure to protect his possessions or his family, but he chose wisely, acknowledging God's hand in all his circumstances. Eventually, God blessed Job by returning all that he had lost.[83] After all these intervening centuries, Job continues to serve as a prototype for us today as we progress in our journey toward forgiveness.

Reason #4: There are benefits to you when you forgive.

I will cover the benefits of forgiveness in the next section. However, before you can realize any of the benefits of forgiving a transgressor, it is important to decide whether or not you want to try to forgive. When people offend us, it is hard to imagine treating them with anything other than contempt. We want to get even, teach them a lesson, and/or avoid them altogether. We often live in the illusion that getting back at an offender will make us feel better—and it may for a while. However, the long-term emotional peace that we are looking for will not be realized simply by the act of getting even. We are hardwired to protect ourselves from offenses. But God tells us to forgive others, particularly our enemies. He tells us this in a very straightforward manner, without any exceptions, and His Words are repeated by several New Testament writers.

Although we usually speak of forgiveness as a singular idea, there are actually three different types of interpersonal forgiveness that can be identified. The first is decisional—simply the making of the decision to try to forgive the person who has wronged you. The second is the granting of forgiveness, which is the release of negative thoughts and actions toward your offender. Third is "emotional forgiveness," which is judged by the extent to which you feel emotional peace following your decision to forgive and grant forgiveness. In the following journal exercise, you will be asked to rate yourself on each of these three types of forgiveness. Whether you are ready to forgive or not, it is important that you come to a decision to try to forgive with an open heart, knowing why you are making your choice. Check your motivation to forgive in the next journal exercise.

Journal Exercise 3a: Letter to Self

Write a short letter to yourself about how you feel forgiveness will help you begin the journey of putting the offense behind you and moving on to emotional peace.

Dear _____ [your name],

When I think about the offense I've experienced, it makes me feel … [list all the ways you feel about the offense]

I want to forgive this person because …

❏ I want to begin to reconcile my relationship with him or her.
❏ I want to stop thinking about the situation.
❏ I want relief from these feelings of hurt.
❏ I want to experience peace of mind and put the matter behind me.
❏ Other:

_____

_____

As I journey through Forty Days to Forgiveness, I am committed to … [what are you willing and not willing to do?]

Journal Exercise 3b: Forgiveness Readiness Survey

Thinking of the person and the situation you have chosen, rate how you currently feel about each of the three types of forgiveness:

Type 1: Decisional forgiveness. How ready are you to make a decision to work toward forgiveness in your chosen situation?

Not ready [1] [2] [3] [4] [5] [6] [7] [8] [9] [10] Ready

What would it take for you to move to the next-higher number?

Type 2: Granting forgiveness. How ready are you not to seek retaliation, vengeance, or apology?

Not ready [1] [2] [3] [4] [5] [6] [7] [8] [9] [10] Ready

How ready are you not to talk/think negatively about your offender?

Not ready [1] [2] [3] [4] [5] [6] [7] [8] [9] [10] Ready

How ready are you to seek to live peacefully with your offender?

Not ready [1] [2] [3] [4] [5] [6] [7] [8] [9] [10] Ready

What would it take for you to move to the next-higher number?

Type 3: Emotional forgiveness. To what degree are you experiencing less negative emotion about the offense; to what degree are you feeling at peace about granting forgiveness; to what degree are you willing to restore your relationship with the offender (if a restored relationship does not make you vulnerable to additional harm)?

Low [1] [2] [3] [4] [5] [6] [7] [8] [9] [10] High

What would it take for you to move to the next-higher number?

Once you have completed the survey, add your scores together and then divide by 10. This number is your readiness quotient. It will serve as your starting point and a baseline to help you see your progress in your forgiveness journey.

My totals for all questions: _____

Divide by 10.

My current forgiveness readiness quotient: _____

DAY 4

The Core of the Matter

All three types of forgiveness are difficult. So why does God command us to act in ways that are difficult and counterintuitive to how He hardwired our minds? Despite our inherent doubts about it, forgiveness brings many benefits. In the following section, we will explore some of them.

We experience physical and mental benefits when we forgive.

One's ability to forgive has a demonstrable influence on the mental and physical health of both the forgiver and the forgiven. God's desire for us to forgive is much more than a difficult commandment: it is for our good. In recent decades, the behavioral sciences have determined from research that forgiveness has many benefits:

- Forgiveness leads to improved emotions and feelings.[84]
- Individuals who forgive have a lower rate of psychiatric illness.[85]
- People who forgive have a lower physiological stress response, thereby improving their physical well-being.[86]
- Forgiveness leads to a greater sense of personal control.[87]
- Forgiveness helps to facilitate the restoration of relationship closeness.[88]
- Forgiveness helps to cure disease such as cancer, heart disease, and fibromyalgia, among others.[89]

These and other positive benefits have led researchers to look for and create resources to promote the process of learning to forgive others. Self-improvement books such as this one,[90] as well as workshops with a similar theme, are resources that play an important role in helping people learn the forgiveness process in order to improve their health and well-being. As a health-care chaplain, I have found that unforgiveness is often coupled with a patient's reason for being in the hospital.

Forgiveness has been shown to release the emotional pain that patients carry with them, opening the door for their bodies and minds to better heal. Forgiveness is free and it is teachable, and the resources to accomplish the process are accessible.

Forgiveness builds a deeper relationship with God.[91]

Jesus emphasized the importance of interpersonal forgiveness. When the disciples asked Jesus to teach them to pray, Jesus offered what is frequently referred to as the Lord's Prayer, the Our Father, or the Disciples' Prayer.[92] In this template for prayer, Jesus made clear that we are to ask God for forgiveness *as we forgive others who have trespassed against us.* The way He worded this part of the prayer does not imply that we automatically forgive others, but it does imply that we can make the choice to forgive. The remainder of the prayer focuses on our devotion to God and His provision for our most basic needs. This point about forgiveness is so important, however, that it is the only part of the prayer that Jesus reiterated in the verse that follows: "If you forgive those who sin against you, your heavenly Father will forgive you. But if you refuse to forgive others, you Father will not forgive you."[93]

Jesus also made several other statements that could be construed as directives to forgive although forgiveness is not specifically mentioned. He taught us all of the following:

- To be merciful toward others.[94]
- To reconcile with a brother or sister who sins against us.[95]
- To love our neighbor as ourselves.[96]
- To treat others as we would like to be treated if we were in their shoes.[97]
- To withhold our judgment of others.[98]
- To love our enemies.[99]

Forgiveness releases us from the negative thoughts that hold us emotionally captive.

Some transgressions may be major offenses that can change the course of our lives forever, even if the transgression is resolved. Other transgressions may be relatively minor, but they may happen repeatedly. These repeated hurts accumulate and can create incredible anxiety, depression, and anger, which, if not resolved, can lead to decreased physical, mental, or spiritual health and well-being. We can become desensitized to these relatively minor infractions to the point that we do not consciously realize that they are happening. As with entering a room with an odor, in time we become desensitized to the odor and the room does not seem to smell anymore. However, the odor is still there and, if toxic, continues to harm us without our conscious awareness. Similarly, over time we become desensitized to ongoing transgressions against us, and we may make concessions to try to cope with the offense. We may deny it is happening, negotiate to resolve it, repress it, or react in passive anger or hostility. Eventually, these small transgressions will reach a tipping point where our health and relationships suffer.

Whether we are conscious of it or not, the transgression bonds us to the transgressor. Until the matter is resolved (and in some cases, even after resolution), we think about the offender and what he or she has done. We hold a grudge, or we begin to plot ways to get even or to escape without resolving the offense. These are all examples of "reducing unforgiveness,"[100] but they do not release us from the emotional bond we have with our transgressors. Instead, these thoughts form a story that takes on a life of its own. Before we know it, the story promotes our unforgiveness more than the actual transgression does. As we continue through life, we look for signs to confirm or discredit the story. As these thoughts go around and around in our heads, we enter a state called rumination. These ruminating thoughts about the transgression keep us locked to the transgressor. Forgiveness is a means of unlocking our bond to the transgressor by rewriting our story and reframing what happened so that we can cope with it.[101]

In some cases, however, the transgression continues. During the ups and downs of good times and bad with our transgressors, we develop a dysfunctional connection and/or relationship that bonds us to them through a sense of purpose, commitment, or loyalty. We can begin to feel we need them, as if something would be missing without them. In fact, something would be missing: the transgression. But since we have become desensitized to the transgression, we forget what it is like to function in its absence. The thought of being without the transgressor becomes bittersweet. Although this concept is counterintuitive, research shows that we want to be connected to our transgressors, believing that they will eventually care about us in return. The following are signs that an unhealthy bond exists:[102]

- You are excessively preoccupied with the offender(s) even though you may not want such preoccupation.
- You continue to seek contact with people who cause you further pain.
- You go overboard to help people who have been destructive to you.
- You continue being a team member even though the situation has obviously become destructive.
- Even though they are clearly using you, you continue attempts to get certain people to like you.
- You again and again trust people who have proved to be unreliable.
- You are unable to distance yourself from unhealthy relationships.
- You want to be understood by those who clearly do not care.
- You choose to stay in conflict with others when it would cost you nothing to walk away.
- You persist in trying to convince people that there is a problem, and they are not willing to listen.

- You are loyal to people who have betrayed you.
- You are attracted to untrustworthy people.
- You keep damaging secrets about exploitation or abuse.
- You maintain contact with an abuser who acknowledges no responsibility.

If you see yourself in any of these scenarios, you may need help with setting boundaries before forgiveness is possible.[103] I recommend two books in the resource list that may be helpful: *The Betrayal Bond* by Patrick Carnes and *Boundaries: When to Say Yes, When to Say No to Take Control of Your Life* by Henry Cloud and John Townsend. If you are not sure whether you are experiencing an emotional bond with your transgressor, then you might consider seeing a professional Christian counselor, which may also be helpful.

Knowing When to Forgive

Is forgiving always right? I offer a qualified yes. Some circumstances may require you to avoid reconciliation with an offender, as in the case of an abusive person, yet forgiveness is always beneficial for you, and in some cases it is beneficial for the transgressor. As I pointed out earlier, both Jesus and Stephen turned the forgiveness of their transgressors over to God, suggesting that they were pained beyond an ability to forgive. However, as they turned over their pain to God, they did it in a spirit of God's intervention in the salvation of their souls. A whole book could be written on this topic alone with many more details than we can cover here. Still, we will examine a few typical instances that can occur in various forgiveness scenarios.

✓ When We Feel We Cannot Forgive

A significant concern for Christians is that we feel guilty when we do not or cannot forgive. When this happens, we have God and the Holy Spirit to help us. Through our relationship with Christ, we are able to deal with difficult feelings that arise when we are transgressed. Feelings of anger, disgust, fear, and resentment are normal and are part of God's design because these feelings allow us to adapt to prevent or defeat future offenses that threaten our well-being.

How you respond to offenses has already been heavily determined by the habits and practices you developed before the transgression. Even a baby learns to cope with "transgressions," that is, conditions that present pain or discomfort, such as hunger, a wet diaper, heat, cold, or sleepiness. Later in childhood, the coping mechanisms grow or shrink as they are either reinforced or reduced. Our coping mechanisms continue to be molded and shaped by how the world responds to our reactions to pain and discomfort. Eventually, we develop positive or dysfunctional ways to cope with transgressions. Whether our coping mechanisms are good or bad depends upon how they affect our well-being and how the society around us responds to us. (More on coping mechanisms later.) In the case of disciples of Christ, coping mechanisms are also determined to be good or bad by how well they are aligned with the Word of God and our Christian community.

If we deny our feelings and reject our programming to react, we cut ourselves off from our anger or fear, both of which serve as important warning mechanisms designed by God to help us avoid being hurt. As we will discuss further in later chapters, these feelings of anger and fear trigger a response: to cope, resolve, hide from, or demolish the source of the transgression. When these responses do not work, we begin to think excessively about the scenario (rumination) and formulate thoughts about getting revenge or holding a grudge (negative intentions). It is at this point that we enter a state of unforgiveness. On the other hand, the first responses of coping, negotiating resolution, and getting justice are reasonable but are "non-forgiving" responses to a hurt. They can be employed by Christians to relieve the hurt of a transgression, but they only serve to reduce our unforgiveness. They do not bring the emotional peace that forgiveness does.

✓ When We Have Been Treated Unjustly or Unfairly

We all have some idea of how the world should be and how it should treat us. You might say we have a "justice meter" hardwired into our brains that is similar to a smoke detector. When some harm or threat comes our way, it goes off to warn us that we are in danger. When someone treats us in a way we feel is harmful, in a way that is different from how we ideally want to be treated, a gap forms between how we think we should be treated and what is actually happening. Our instinctive initial response is to see all threats as the same, but once our justice meter goes off, we size up the situation to decide just how dangerous the threat is.

✓ When We Are Angry

Being angry is another symptom that may signal our need to forgive someone. Anger is our reaction to our justice meter's going off but we're not receiving a quick resolution. Anger is a way of coping with a transgression to ward off the offender. Our Lord demonstrated anger at least three times. The first time was when He made a whip to drive illicit merchants and their livestock from the temple.[104] Another was when He confronted the scribes and Pharisees for their hypocrisy.[105] The third was when He was criticized for healing a man with a withered hand.[106] In all three cases, His anger was targeted at hardness of heart and offenses against the kingdom of God. Does this mean that Jesus did not forgive these offenses? If He did, it is not recorded in scripture. Expressing anger, though, is not necessarily unforgiveness, but if the anger is not resolved, it may lead to rumination and unforgiveness. As we will explore in chapter 3, anger can also be the first stepping-stone on the path to forgiveness.

Jesus did not come to minister to the spiritually healthy, but to the sick.[107] Furthermore, Jesus willed that no one should perish but that all should come to Him.[108] Clearly, the people in the temple were spiritually sick for misusing God's house of prayer. Moreover, the Pharisees were spiritually sick for their hypocrisy, claiming to be spiritually superior while they exhibited sinful attitudes. Jesus had good reason to be angry; however, Jesus checked His anger, not letting it get out of control, and He kept Himself from seeking vengeance or retaliation. Jesus's behavior demonstrates where the boundary lies between righteous anger and sinful anger. As His followers, we need to know when our anger crosses the line and becomes sin.

Jesus's examples of justified anger were in response to offenses against the kingdom of God, not against Him. Yet for us, He commanded that we forgive people who have trespassed against us. When we do not feel forgiveness in our hearts but instead harbor malice and hatred, we do not imitate Christ's example; however, when we repay evil with kindness, we are blessed.[109]

Similarly, Paul refused to become bitter, hateful, and unforgiving when he was wrongly accused and beaten, but neither did he blindly accept harsh treatment. Instead, he chose the acceptable alternatives of defending himself and challenging the Jewish leaders to disprove their claims against him. In fact, the Lord endorsed his defense by appearing to him and saying, "Take courage, for as you have testified to the facts about me in Jerusalem, so you must testify also in Rome."[110]

✓ **When We Need to Live in Peace with Others**

In addition to Jesus's statements about interpersonal forgiveness, the New Testament writers give much helpful counsel about how to treat others and the importance of being reconciled to one another within the faith.[111]

- Eight passages discuss forgiveness in an interpersonal context (more if you count redundant passages throughout the gospels).[112] New Testament authors describe five examples by Christ and three by other New Testament writers.[113]
- Jesus talked about being merciful twice, and James mentioned it once.[114]
- More than one hundred ten passages of scripture[115] discuss our treatment of one another. These include treating one another with love, without judgment, as peacemakers, and with justice, patience, kindness, tenderness, etc.

While most of these passages do not specifically mention forgiveness, they do clearly state that we are to love other disciples, our neighbors, evildoers, and persecutors. The apostle Paul wrote one of the most explicit passages about forgiveness of a brother in Christ in his letter to the church at Colossae:

Put on then, as God's chosen ones, holy and beloved, compassion, kindness, humility, meekness, and patience, bearing with one another and, if one has a complaint against another, forgiving each other. As the Lord has forgiven you, so you also must forgive. And above all these put on love, which binds everything together in perfect harmony. And let the peace of Christ rule in your hearts, to which indeed you were called in one body.[116]

A similar passage in Ephesians could be construed as commands for how to treat everyone, not just fellow Christians: "Let all bitterness and wrath and anger and clamor and slander be put away from you, along with all malice. Be kind to one another, tenderhearted, forgiving one another, as God in Christ forgave you."[117]

The apostle's directive to forgive is always in one of three contexts: (1) creating unity in the body of Christ, (2) doing good to those who transgress against us, or (3) divine forgiveness of our sin and our relationship with God. Paul also emphasized being reconciled to fellow Christians who have transgressed against us after we have forgiven them and they have repented. Even though there are no specific references to being reconciled with a transgressor who is not in the body of Christ, such reconciliation may be beneficial to the transgressor, as well as to us. While *Forty Days to Forgiveness* and the ACTION process are not targeted at reconciliation, I have a section in chapter 7 that talks briefly about it. We are urged to have a loving spirit toward those who commit evil against us, persecute us, and spitefully use us. Clearly, love and forgiveness go hand in hand.[118]

Three Contexts for Transgressions

When you are in a relationship with someone who is mistreating or abusing you, what do you do about ongoing anger or fear that seemingly cannot be resolved? In some cases, anger can be directed at the transgression and not at the transgressor. In other cases, the transgression may continue even after you have forgiven the offender. Ongoing transgressions, and possibly abuse, may occur in three contexts. The first is where there is a personal relationship with the transgressor, such as a spouse or other family member. The second is an ongoing relationship with a casual acquaintance such as a work colleague or another disciple of Christ. The third context is when the transgressor is no longer available.

Ongoing transgressions often become abuse, which may be defined as a pattern of coercive behavior used by one person (or group) who has the power to subordinate and control another person. An abuser is one who seeks physical, sexual, psychological, spiritual, emotional, or economic control over another. The tactics of coercion may include terrorism, degradation, exploitation, bullying, and violence to provoke fear in a victim in order to gain compliance. In situations of ongoing transgressions, the victim must plan a way of escape to ensure his or her safety. While doing so, however, the victim needs to forgive the transgressor but not necessarily the transgression. We will deal with this topic more in chapter 3.

Concerning the third context, you may be experiencing ongoing unforgiveness toward a person who has died, has moved away, or is no longer available. This is often a difficult type of unforgiveness because the negative feelings it generates can be misplaced and your unforgiveness for a missing person is directed toward others who have not harmed you. There are, however, some approaches to finding forgiveness under these conditions. While I am recommending that you select a forgiveness issue with someone who is still available, *Forty Days to Forgiveness* is also designed to address situations where the transgressor either is not or should not be available to you. This situation will be addressed in later chapters.

Journal Exercise 4a: What Do You Need?

Write a brief letter to God describing what you need from Him to lighten the burden of the unforgiveness you are experiencing.

Dear God,

When I think of the way I have been treated … [describe the offense].

I know that Your hand can guide me to forgive _____ [name of transgressor].

I will need You to help me overcome my … [describe the negative feelings you are having toward your offender].

Thank You for Your grace and power to help me reach a state of peace.

Sincerely,

Journal Exercise 4b: Getting a New Perspective

Are you in a state of unforgiveness? Here are some questions to ask yourself regarding the transgression you selected in the day 2 journal exercise.

1. Describe a time when you behaved in a way that made others feel unforgiveness toward you.	
A transgression or offense I once committed was ...	I caused someone else to feel ...

2.   Briefly describe a time when someone committed an offense against you or treated you unfairly in a hurtful way, but you later realized that you misunderstood the situation.

3. What would you like to see happen to the one who trespassed against you for how he or she treated you?

4. Have you had any of the following negative thoughts about the offense that you cannot seem to get out of your head? Check all that apply.

    ❑ Retaliation   ❑ Resentment
    ❑ Revenge   ❑ Negative judgment
    ❑ Indifference   ❑ Hostility
    ❑ Estrangement   ❑ Bitterness
    ❑ Verbal aggression   ❑ Hatred
    ❑ Promoting justice   ❑ Anger
    ❑ Demanding restitution   ❑ Fearfulness
    ❑ Mercilessness   ❑ Grudges
    ❑ Demanding an apology   ❑ Envy

PRAYER FOR STRENGTH AND GUIDANCE

Lord Jesus, You have said that we all have sinned and have fallen short of reflecting Your love and light to others. I pray, Lord, that You will help me to soften my heart and cause me to know that I, too, am capable of harming others, whether intentionally or unintentionally. I pray for Your grace as I seek wisdom and insight to know how to live with others in peace and harmony.

In Your precious name I pray. Amen.

Chapter 1 Summary

This chapter provides an introduction to forgiveness from Jewish, Christian, and behavioral science perspectives. Write your impressions of each point in your journal.

We noted several key points:

- Forgiveness is a means for God's grace, mercy, and love to be reflected through us to the world.
- Forgiving others is a way we express concern for their eternal welfare.
- We are commanded to forgive others in order to live peacefully with all people, to the extent that peace is within our control.

We also explored reasons to forgive, as follows:

- We can experience physical and mental benefits.
- It builds a deeper relationship with God.
- It releases us from negative thoughts that hold us captive.

Through journal exercises, we assessed the following:

- your current level of forgiveness
- your readiness to forgive the transgressor you selected
- your readiness for three types of forgiveness: decisional, granting forgiveness, and emotional forgiveness

You also wrote two letters: one to yourself about how forgiveness would help you and one to God describing what you need from Him.

Finally, we talked about when to forgive:

- When we feel we cannot forgive.
- When we are angry.
- When we need to live at peace with others.
- When there are ongoing transgressions.

Drawing Strength from Scripture

"Come to me, all who labor and are heavy laden, and I will give you rest. Take my yoke upon you, and learn from me, for I am gentle and lowly in heart, and you will find rest for your souls. For my yoke is easy, and my burden is light" (Matthew 11:28–30).

Devotional Prayer

My Father in heaven, great is Your name. I know You are all-powerful to help me in this time of need.

I want Your kingdom to be real to me and to those around me. Help me to be a blessing to reflect Your light to others by ... [describe how you would like to reflect Christ's light to the people around you].

Thank You for continuing to supply my daily needs of ... [describe how God supplies for your daily needs].

Forgive me for the ways I have fallen short of following You ... [describe some ways that you feel you have stepped away from following Christ].

And help me as I try to forgive _____ [the person's name] for the way that he or she has treated me. [Describe the offense you have experienced.]

Protect me from the fiery darts of the evil one and the temptation to conform to this world.

I pray these things in the name of Jesus Christ as I start my forgiveness journey.

Amen.

Resources for Further Study

Carnes, Patrick. *The Betrayal Bond: Breaking Free of Exploitive Relationships.* Deerfield Beach, FL: Health Communications, Inc., 1997.

Cloud, Henry, and John Townsend. *Boundaries: When to Say Yes, When to Say No to Take Control of Your Life.* Grand Rapids, MI: Zondervan, 1992.

Enright, Robert. *Forgiveness is a Choice: A Step by Step Process for Resolving Anger and Restoring Hope.* Washington, DC: APA Life Tools, 2001.

Smedes, Lewis. *Forgive and Forget: Healing the Hurts We Do Not Deserve.* New York: Harper Collins, 1996.

Worthington, Everett. *Steps to Reach Forgiveness and to Reconcile.* Boston: Pearson Custom, 2008.

Chapter 1 Endnotes

1 Matthew 5:43–45.

2 Rye, Pargament Rye, Ali, Beck, Dorff, and Hallisey, "Religious Perspectives on Forgiveness," in *Forgiveness: Theory, Research, and Practice*, ed. M. McCullough, K. Pargament, and C. Thorenson (New York: Guilford Press, 2001).

3 Proverbs 3:1–9.

4 *Note to the reader:* I have searched for examples but have found none. If any readers have a different view, I invite you to enter into a dialogue with me to help open my eyes. I deal with this point in more detail later in *Forty Days to Forgiveness*. Please read all of my assessment of this point before drawing conclusions.

5 Colossians 3:12–13.

6 Enright and Fitzgibbons, *Helping Clients Forgive: An Empirical Guide for Resolving Anger and Restoring Hope* (Washington, DC: American Psychological Association, 2000). See also Matthew 5:43–48 and Romans 12:14–15.

7 L. G. Jones, *Embodying Forgiveness: A Theological Analysis* (Grand Rapids, MI: Eerdmans, 1995), pp. 231–33.

8 Romans 8:16–17.

9 Romans 5:3–5.

10 Romans 8:18–21.

11 2 Corinthians 1:5.

12 Philippians 1:29.

13 2 Timothy 1:8–9.

14 James 5:13.

15 1 Peter 2:19–23.

16 1 Peter 3:17.

17 1 Peter 4:19.

18 1 Peter 5:10–11.

19 Romans 8:16–17.

20 1 Corinthians 10:13.

21 Romans 12:1–2.

22 Matthew 5:39, 15:12; John 15:1–8.

23 Matthew 5:23; John 4:23, 15:1–2; Galatians 5:22; Mark 7:21.

24 Mark 16:15; John 15:9–10, 12–13.

25 Acts 2:42; Galatians 5:16–25; 1 Thessalonians 5:17; Hebrews 4:1–2; 1 Timothy 4:7–8.

26 Genesis 32–33.

27 Genesis 44–50.

28 1 Samuel 24:8–22, 26:13–25.

29 2 Samuel 19; 1 Kings 2:8–9, 36–46.

30 Genesis 50:17.

31 E. Dorff, "The Elements of Forgiveness: A Jewish Approach," in *Dimensions of Forgiveness: Psychological Research and Theological Perspectives*, ed. Everett Worthington Jr. (Philadelphia: Templeton Foundation Press, 1998), pp. 29–53. Elliot Dorf, PhD, is a rabbi, visiting professor of law at UCLA School of Law, and distinguished professor of philosophy at the American Jewish University (formerly the University of Judaism). At UCLA, he teaches a course titled Religious Legal Systems: Jewish Law.

32 Leviticus 19:17–18.

33 Remorse may include crying and making entreaties for forgiveness. In the most serious cases, offenders may have changed their names to show that they were no longer the same person. Interestingly, this may be the tradition on which the Lord based His renaming of Simon to Peter and Saul to Paul.

34 Dorf, "The Elements of Forgiveness."

35 Colossians 3:13 (NIV).

36 Matthew 18:15–20.

37 Matthew 18:17.

38 Acts 26:20.

39 Romans 12:16–18; Galatians 6:10; Colossians 3:11; Ephesians 4:1–3.

40 Romans 12:18–19.

41 Ephesians 4:31–32.

42 Matthew 18:21–21.

43 Galatians 6:1; 1 Thessalonians 5:12–15; 2 Thessalonians 3:13–15.

44 Matthew 18:17.

45 Romans 2:1, 14:10–12.

46 Matthew 7:1–5.

47 Mark 11:25; Matthew 5:43–48; Luke 6:27–31, 35.

48 Colossians 3:13.

49 Leviticus 19:18; Matthew 22:39.

50 Romans 12:17.

51 Luke 6:27–35; Romans 12:14–21.

52 Matthew 7:1; Romans 12:19.

53 James 5:19–20.

54 1 Corinthians 10:13.

55 Matthew 6:14–15; cf. Luke 6:37; Mark 11:25.

56 Romans 8:38.

57 Colossians 2:12–15.

58 1 Samuel 13:14; Acts 13:22.

59 Psalms 13:1–7, 31:9, 102:2.

60 Ephesians 1:13, 4:29–31, 15:9–10.

61 John 5:45, 14:21, 15:10.

62 Matthew 22:37–40.

63 John 13:34; Matthew 5:16.

64 Matthew 6:14–15; Mark 11:25–26; Luke 6:37, 11:4; John 15:10.

65 Matthew 6:9–15; Luke 11:2–4.

66 J. Voiss, *Rethinking Christian Forgiveness: Theological, Philosophical, and Psychological Exploration* (Collegeville, MN: Liturgical Press, 2015).

67 Ephesians 4:32.

68 Romans 5:8; 1 Corinthians 2:12–16; Luke 5:31–32.

69 Matthew 5:16, 10:8; Romans 5:6–11, 15–17; 2 Corinthians 4:15; Ephesians 2:8, 4:29.

70 Matthew 25:35–40; Luke 5:31–32.

71 Matthew 5:13–16, 18:12–14, 28:19–20.

72 Matthew 18:21.

73 Luke 17:3–4.

74 See Henry Cloud and John Townsend's book *Boundaries* for suggested readings on this issue.

75 Luke 23:34.

76 Luke 23:39–43.

77 Acts 7:60.

78 Chapter 3 will discuss God's intentions for victims of abuse.

79 The role of prayer in the forgiveness process is covered more thoroughly in chapter 6.

80 Romans 12:14–21.

81 Romans 8:28.

82 Job 1:21.

83 Job 42:10–17.

84 Hebl and Enright, "Forgiveness as a Psychotherapeutic Goal with Elderly Females," *Psychotherapy: Theory, Research, Practice, Training* 30 (1993): 658–67.

85 Karremans, Van Lange, Ouwerkerk, and Kluwer, "When Forgiving Enhances Psychological Well-Being: The Role of Interpersonal Commitment," *Journal of Personality and Social Psychology* 84, no. 5 (2003): 1011–26; Stein, Mbanga, and Zungu-Dirwayi, "Forgiveness: Toward an Integration of Theoretical Models," *Psychiatry* 63, no. 4 (Winter 2000): 344–57; Toussaint and Webb, "Theoretical and Empirical Connections between Forgiveness, Mental Health, and Well-Being," in *Handbook of Forgiveness*, ed. E. L. Worthington Jr. (New York: Routledge, 2005), p. 358.

86 Berry and Worthington, "Forgiveness, Relationship Quality, Stress while Imagining Relationship Events, and Physical and Mental Health," *Journal of Counseling Psychology* 48, no. 4 (2001): 447–55; Kaminer, Stein, Mbanga, and Zungu-Dirwayi, "Forgiveness: Toward an Integration of Theoretical Models, 2000; VanOyen, Ludwig, and Vander Laan, "Granting Forgiveness or Harboring Grudges: Implications for Emotion, Physiology, and Health," *Psychological Science*, 12, no. 2 (March 2001): 117–23.

87 Ibid.

88 Fincham, Hope, and Beach, "Transgression Severity and Forgiveness: Moderators for Objective and Subjective Severity," *Journal of Social and Clinical Psychology* 24 (2005): 860–75.

89 M. Barry, *The Forgiveness Project: The Startling Discovery of How to Overcome Cancer, Find Health, and Achieve Peace* (Grand Rapids, MI: Kregel, 2001); L. Toussaint, E. Worthington, and D. Williams, eds., *Forgiveness and Health: Scientific Evidence and Theories Relating Forgiveness to Better Health* (New York: Springer Dordrecht, 2015).

90 See suggested readings at the end of this chapter.

91 John 15:10.

92 Matthew 6:9–13; Luke 11:2–4.

93 Matthew 6:14–15.

94 Matthew 5:7; Luke 6:35.

95 Matthew 18:15–20.

96 Matthew 22:39.

97 Luke 6:31.

98 Luke 6:37; Matthew 7:1–5.

99 Luke 6:27, 35.

100 We will talk about reducing unforgiveness in a later chapter.

101 We talk more about this in the following chapters.

102 P. Carnes, *The Betrayal Bond: Breaking Free of Exploitive Relationships* (Deerfield Beach, FL: Health Communications, Inc., 1997).

103 H. Cloud and J. Townsend, *Boundaries: When to Say Yes, When to Say No to Take Control of Your Life* (Grand Rapids, MI: Zondervan, 1992).

104 John 2:13–16.

105 Matthew 23:13–33.

106 Mark 3:1–5.

107 Matthew 9:12–13.

108 John 3:16–17.

109 Matthew 5:11, 44; Luke 6:27–35; Romans 12:20–21.

110 Acts 23:11.

111 Galatians 5:22–16, 6:2; Romans 12:10, 13:8, 14:10; 1 Corinthians 13:1–7; 2 Corinthians 2:5–8; Galatians 5:13; Ephesians 4:2, 32; 1 Thessalonians 3:12, 5:13; 1 Peter 1:17, 1:22, 3:8; 1 John 3:11, 4:7; 2 John 5; Hebrews 10:24.

112 Matthew 6:9–15, 18:21–22, 35; Mark 11:25; Luke 6:37, 11:2–4, 17:3–4.

113 1 Corinthians 2:5–11; Ephesians 4:32; Colossians 3:13.

114 Matthew 5:7; Luke 6:35; James 2:13.

115 By my count, at least sixteen passages of scripture pertain to how we treat others, but these do not explicitly refer to forgiveness. The Greek word for "one another" is found 110 times in the New Testament, as in "comfort one another," "help one another," "confess to one another," "exhort one another," "pray for one another," and so forth. See https://www.biblegateway.com/ and enter as keywords "one another."

116 Colossians 3:12–15.

117 Ephesians 4:32.

118 An oft-cited passage is 1 Corinthians 13. See also Romans 12:21 and Luke 6:27–31.

CHAPTER 2

Acknowledging the Hurt

Then He said, "Go out, and stand on the mountain before the Lord." And behold, the Lord passed by, and a great and strong wind tore into the mountains and broke the rocks in pieces before the Lord, but the Lord was not in the wind; and after the wind an earthquake, but the Lord was not in the earthquake; and after the earthquake a fire, but the Lord was not in the fire; and after the fire a still small voice.

—1 KINGS 19:11–12

DAY 5

Acknowledging the Unforgiveness Life Cycle—Introduction

As a hospital palliative care chaplain, I work with people who are more seriously ill than the average patient. Many of the patients I work with die, transfer to hospice care or an extended care facility, or are so seriously ill that they remain in the hospital for weeks. I have also encountered patients immediately after finding out that they have a terminal illness. I frequently encounter patients who wonder, *Why is God doing this to me?*[1]

I often wonder, *Is God using the pain in this person's life to get their attention? What does He want to show them?* Like the story of Elijah in the verse quoted at the beginning of this chapter, when patients have been struggling with their faith, they often come to realize that their illness provides a way to turn their attention to God. Families often ask me to pray for a miracle, and I have seen people at death's door recover and go home. Like a treacherous wind, earthquake, or fire, serious illness is a time when we look for God's voice, still and small, like a whisper. I would suggest that transgressions are the same. Within the hurt and pain, we look for God's voice.

One of my roles is to help patients and families uncover the feelings they are experiencing and then help them to acknowledge the illness and the underlying effect it is having on them. I often pray for God's mercy on pain and discomfort, and at a patient's request I pray for healing if it be God's will. Some patients with unfinished business ask God to grant them more time for closure. Prayers for healing, miraculous or not, are often misguided because they put too much emphasis on *what we want* and leave out an important element of faith: *what God wants*. Prayers like these ask God to intervene in our plans, as opposed to prayer that asks God how we can enter into His plan. We are here to glorify God. Disciples of Christ are immortal beings in the sense that when we accept Christ as our Savior and repent of our sins, we walk through this life with one foot on the earth and the other in the paradise of heaven. If only we could see what God sees.

As patients who know they are sick but have not fully explored and understood the effects of the illness have to do, this chapter is about acknowledging the effect the transgression is having on you and on the people in your life. In this chapter we will explore, in depth, how the transgression is affecting you and how God can use your experience to glorify Him and build His kingdom.

Chapter 1 provided an acronym to help you remember the steps in the forgiveness process: the word ACTION. This chapter focuses on *A*, acknowledging the transgression, an idea that may seem absurd since you have already acknowledged that someone has committed a transgression against you. What more need be said?

As a counselor, one of my hardest tasks is helping clients, usually couples, to acknowledge what the underlying issue is that brings them to my couch. They know they are struggling to "get along," and they often have a sense of why: finances, communication struggles, addictions, parenting, family loyalties. These, however, are not core issues; they are symptoms. The core issue behind almost all marital discord is one thing: self-centeredness. We think of selfishness as a bad thing, and when it causes us to put our needs before others', at the expense of others, it is. But selfishness is not quite the same as self-centeredness. Selfishness is an attitude that influences us to act like a petulant child. Self-centeredness is different.

Self-centeredness is when we see the world through a lens of our own expectations for how we should be treated. We look for the world around us to meet *our* needs, and that perspective eclipses the needs of others around us. Our needs let us off the hook from targeting the needs of those we encounter. For example, when a married person has a relationship with someone other than a legitimate spouse, that person is looking for the expectations he or she has of the spouse to be met by someone other than the spouse. Most of the time, my clients feel entitled to have affairs because they feel that they have a right to have their needs met. Whether their needs are emotional, physical, or sexual, it does not matter: "I'm entitled to have my needs met, if not by you then by someone. After all, God created me with these needs, so if He brings someone across my path who can satisfy me, then I say, the sooner the better." *Yikes.* Where does that principle come from?

When you are moving toward forgiveness, acknowledging the transgression goes well beyond simply noting that someone has offended or hurt you. It means exploring, reflecting on, and synthesizing the various ways the offense has affected you—before you act upon your anger or disappointment. With that in mind, let's dig deeper into understanding your condition in order to help you take a detour from your unforgiveness.

Forgiveness Step 1:
Acknowledging How the Hurt Is Affecting You

The following are important first steps in the forgiveness journey:

- Reflecting on the transgression to gain greater insight into its specific impact on you.
- Seeking to understand how the transgression has compromised your ability to think positive thoughts about your transgressor.
- Identifying ways your life is different because of the effects of the transgression.
- Reflecting on how the transgression has distracted you from intimacy with God.

Things that Inhibit Acknowledging the Transgression

Number the following inhibitors 1–8, with 1 being most like you and 8 being the least like you.

_____ I am mad about what happened.

_____ I am bitter about what he or she did to me.

_____ I try to avoid him or her.

_____ I want to withdraw from him or her.

_____ I ought to just forget what happened and move on. What happened was not really that bad.

_____ I want to restart my relationship with the person who hurt me, acting as if nothing happened.

_____ I have accepted an excuse or explanation for what someone did, and I have tried to move on.

_____ I tolerate what my transgressor has done to me, and I accept him or her despite his or her flaws.

(Ask, out loud, for God to hear you as you read aloud the top three inhibitors most like you.)

This chapter will help you assess the offense you experienced so that you may better understand what you are trying to forgive and how the offense is affecting you. Research shows that forgiveness happens more readily when victims clearly understand, on a deep emotional level, how the transgression affects them.[2] Sure, you have a general idea of the offense and can probably talk at length about what happened. That's good. This section, however, breaks the transgression into its basic parts so you may understand the effects of each.

Day 5: Acknowledging the Unforgiveness Life Cycle—Introduction

Day 6: Acknowledging the Type of Transgression

Day 7: Acknowledging Your Emotions and Feelings

Day 8: Acknowledging Unenforceable Rules

Day 9: Acknowledging How You Are Coping with the Transgression

Day 10: Acknowledging the Vicious Cycle

Day 5: Acknowledging the Unforgiveness Life Cycle–Introduction

Unforgiveness is a process, as is forgiveness, except unforgiveness is mostly an automatic response we instinctively direct toward the transgressor. In fact, unforgiveness is the way we are naturally wired to respond to unresolvable situations that threaten our well-being. Some people think of forgiveness as how we *feel* about (1) someone who has hurt us, (2) restoring a relationship with someone who has committed a transgression against us, or (3) exacting justice or restitution from someone who has hurt us. Forgiveness is *not a feeling*; rather, forgiveness is an intentional process that requires initiative and effort. Feelings are associated with both forgiveness and unforgiveness, but we can learn to control those feelings, resulting in a more positive well-being. Paul told the Christians in Rome not to avenge themselves when mistreated but to leave the offense to the wrath of God. Staying in a relationship with someone who continually repeats an offense is not required,[3] yet we are required to do good to such a person without subjecting ourselves to mistreatment. In fact in some cases, to keep us from further or more serious harm, reconciliation is ill-advised.

Unforgiveness is a process that may happen quickly, in a matter of minutes, or it may smolder over a long period. Regardless of the length of time you have experienced unforgiveness, the forgiveness process cannot be rushed, but it can be learned and applied to the transgression you want to work on. The old adage "time heals all wounds" is a myth. As stated in chapter 1, research has repeatedly shown that time is an important factor in forgiveness; however, time in itself is insufficient to result in the forgiveness that brings emotional freedom and peace. Time is most likely to nurture forgiveness and heal wounds when accompanied by a process to achieve both decisional and emotional forgiveness. In our case, that process is ACTION.[4]

We often think of forgiveness as an event that is as simple as gritting our teeth and saying, "I forgive you." If you have tried this approach, you have probably learned that a simple "I forgive you" does not bring the peace of mind and sense of well-being that you desire. You may also have thought that if the transgressor would just say "I'm sorry" and ask for forgiveness, everything would return to how it was. But I am sure you have discovered that long-term peace is not to be found in expecting (or even receiving) an apology. And then you sometimes find yourself saying, "It wasn't all that bad; I just need to let go and move on." This is another shallow response that will not result in emotional peace and wellness. There is more to forgiveness than can be experienced in a few uttered phrases.

From a big picture perspective, we have two ways to respond to a transgression: reducing unforgiveness and promoting forgiveness. We will talk more about promoting forgiveness in chapter 3. In this chapter, we will unpack the meaning of unforgiveness and how it affects our well-being. To understand forgiveness fully, we first need a working knowledge of the cycle of actions that lead to unforgiveness. We will refer to this as the "unforgiveness life cycle." It begins with a transgression and progresses through emotions and feelings that lead to a state of unforgiveness. We will examine each step of the life cycle and see how each leads to another. The following chart provides a graphic overview of events that result in unforgiveness. The experiences in this chart may happen suddenly, in the blink of an eye, or these elements of the unforgiveness process may percolate and emerge after reflection and thought over a longer period of time. It is not uncommon for us to freeze in the face of a transgression and not be able to fully comprehend its scope and impact right away. Whether your transgression experience happened in an instant or over time, the pieces of the puzzle remain the same.

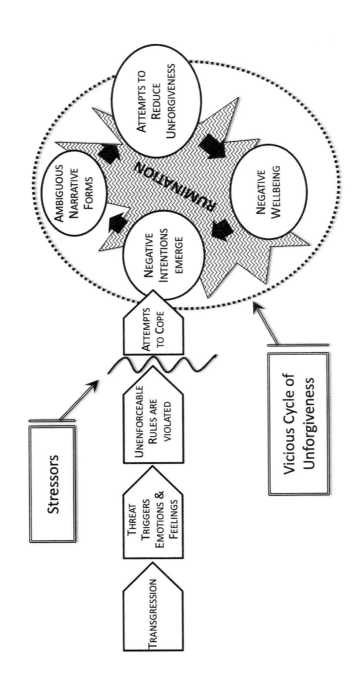

Unforgiveness Lifecycl

1. **The transgression** is an action that the victim perceives as a threat. A threat is any behavior that we believe will negatively affect our physical, mental, spiritual, financial, or social well-being. In some cases we may assume the unforgiveness is associated with a threat made to someone we care for, not to us.

2. **Triggers: emotions and feelings.** A transgression stimulates a combination of emotions such as fear, sadness, anger, surprise, and disgust. These emotions are not unforgiveness; rather, they are the primary emotions that give rise to feelings such as disappointment, jealousy, envy, shame, guilt, residual fear, and anger. We could say that emotions come as standard equipment when we are born: emotions are the body's preconscious automatic physical reactions to a threat. They are hardwired into our brains: they are instinctive. Feelings, in contrast, arise as we think about and interpret our emotions based on past experiences with similar situations. Feelings, then, affect our moods, behaviors, and reactions to a threat. In other words, emotions happen before we think about them, and feelings happen as a result of thinking about emotions. Our emotions, giving way to feelings, affect the intensity with which we experience transgressions.

3. **Unenforceable rules.** We all carry around a set of cherished ideas about how we should be treated. When emotions and feelings surface to our consciousness and begin to replay in our minds, we begin to think about the transgressor's motives, the consequences of his or her actions, and how those actions challenge our cherished ideas of how things "should" be.[5] If we have not developed the ability to cope with our awareness of the offense, then we become stressed and fixated on reviewing and evaluating the experience.

4. **Coping and stress.** We desire, at this point, to try to cope with the mistreatment by looking for ways to enforce our rules for how we want to be treated, when in reality these cherished ideas, or rules, are unenforceable. The stress of coping is amplified by emotions and feelings, especially anger and fear. When we cope effectively, we are able to avoid the vicious cycle of negative thoughts that lead to unforgiveness. When we are unable to cope with the stress that results from the unenforceable rules, we enter a state of unforgiveness.

5. **Negative intentions.** As stories about the unenforceable rules continue to swirl in our minds, they begin to give way to thoughts about actions that we believe will correct the situation. When our expectations of how things should be are shattered and revealed to be untrue, the result, according to E. L. Worthington, is "delayed emotions and feelings such as resentment, bitterness, residual anger, residual fear, hostility, and amplified stress, which motivates [us] to reduce or eliminate the threat."[6] These thoughts may continue without our acting on them, or they may result in delayed reactions that have the potential to lead us to act in negative ways. However, negative intentions are *not* unforgiveness; they are the stepping-stones that lead to unforgiveness.

6. **Rumination.** Negative intentions add more fuel to the stories we tell ourselves repeatedly about the hurt. Rumination is the recurring mental fixation on the transgression and the negative feelings we cannot get out of our conscious or unconscious minds. When we try to repress or ignore our ruminating thoughts, the ruminations filter through our unconscious and show up as misplaced negative actions toward the transgressor or other people. The more we think about the stories, the more they become the problem, fueling our negative intentions more than the actual transgression. In other words, our formulation of the story about the offense may become the problem as we begin to see it as the transgression and lose sight of the facts associated with the actual transgression. This vicious cycle also increases the intensity of our stories, making us even unhappier. The cycle continues to the point where the thoughts become automatic, and we tell ourselves the stories over and over. Eventually, we realize from these stories that the rules we impose on the world cannot be enforced; they are unenforceable. The story about the transgression fans the flames of our emotions and feelings and go round and round in our heads. This rumination creates a vicious cycle of thinking that amplifies the creation of negative intentions toward the transgressor.

7. **Unforgiveness.** Finally, when we cannot cope with an offense, our ruminations lead us to enter a state of unforgiveness. We cannot stop thinking about the offense because it is a threat to a cherished idea of how we should be treated, but that cherished idea is a rule that we cannot enforce. In order to minimize the stress caused by the threat of harm, we attempt to get rid of negative emotions and feelings by thinking about how to reduce the unforgiveness. We may attempt to reduce unforgiveness by acting upon our negative intentions through insisting on an apology or restitution; trying to get revenge; giving the offender reciprocal treatment; retaliating; holding a grudge; criticizing; stonewalling; being defensive; or displaying contempt. (We will discuss these concepts later.) Alternatively, we can promote forgiveness. Remember that reducing unforgiveness and promoting forgiveness are not the same thing. We promote forgiveness by replacing our negative intentions toward the transgressor with positive intentions such as grace, empathy, and love. In doing so, we also begin to rewrite the story to create a new narrative about the situation.

In summary, the chart detailing the life cycle of unforgiveness shows that unforgiveness occurs when we are not able to cope effectively with a transgression and we begin to think about negative ways to respond to a transgressor. Those negative thoughts go around in our minds (rumination) until we enter a vicious cycle of demonizing the transgressor. In chapter 3, we will talk about the forgiveness life cycle, and in chapter 4, we will talk about how the forgiveness life cycle can be altered to fit a Christian worldview. For now, we will further examine each step in the unforgiveness life cycle and discuss the importance of acknowledging each one.

Journal Exercise 5: Your Forgiveness GPS

Where are you on the unforgiveness life cycle? Use the following exercise to help you locate your godly perspective on the situation (GPS).

The transgression			
Put a check next to any of the following emotions the transgression brings up for you:			
❏ Fear	❏ Surprise	❏ Jealousy	❏ Guilt
❏ Sadness	❏ Disgust	❏ Envy	❏ Indifference
❏ Anger	❏ Disappointment	❏ Shame	

Unenforceable rules
What rules about how you feel you should be treated have been violated?

Coping
How have you reacted to the stress imposed on you by the transgression?

Negative intentions
List any actions that you think might correct the transgression.

Rumination

Pretend we are on an elevator and you have six floors until I get off. Tell me the story about what happened. Write your story on a separate piece of paper.

Unforgiveness

Put a check next to any of the following actions that you believe will help reduce your unforgiveness:

❏ Apology	❏ Revenge	❏ Retaliation	❏ Criticism
❏ Restitution	❏ Reciprocation	❏ Holding a grudge	❏ Stonewalling
❏ Defensiveness	❏ Contempt	❏ Avoidance	❏ Contempt

Interpreting Your Results

In this assessment activity, I challenged you to think about where you find yourself in the unforgiveness life cycle. You may find that some of the elements are a little foreign to you. Others may seem very familiar. Not to worry. We will be discovering more about what each part of the unforgiveness life cycle is and how each affects your ability to be forgiving. In the next chapter I will ask you to think about how ready you are to *try* to forgive. We will talk about how the first step in the forgiveness journey, after a deep dive into acknowledging the details of the situation, is to make a commitment. It may be helpful to come back and review the activity you just completed when you get to that section of chapter 3.

DAY 6

Acknowledging the Type of Transgression

Understanding the transgression helps us to focus on the details of what happened and to clarify the facts. Sometimes other factors, such as similar previous experiences or details that we may be overlooking, color our initial understanding of the transgression.

With every transgression, there is a transgressor, a victim, and an event or action. Transgressors are the ones who commit acts that are hurtful toward others—acts that threaten our sense of well-being. While there is no consensus for a single definition of well-being, there is general agreement that two kinds of well-being exist, affective and cognitive. Affective well-being includes the presence of positive emotions and moods (e.g., contentment, joy, happiness) and the absence of negative emotions (e.g., depression, anxiety, guilt, shame, sadness, anger, fear), resulting in a state of balance and satisfaction with life, a sense of fulfillment, and positive functioning. Cognitive well-being is the result of evaluating one's life and thinking that it measures up to predetermined expectations of what a satisfied life should be.[7] In simple terms, cognitive well-being can be described as judging life positively and having balanced thoughts about the transgression.

Once a transgression is committed, our well-being is affected. The harm cannot be undone, so we try to cope with it in whatever way we can since we are wired to "survive" the hurt. Initially, "survival" is conceived of as coping with the transgression in ways that eliminate the threat and protect our well-being from further damage.

In the famous Sermon on the Mount and the Sermon on the Plain,[8] Jesus said that we are blessed when we mourn, are meek, are hungry for righteousness, are merciful, are pure in heart, are peacemakers, and are persecuted for righteousness' sake. These attributes are active behaviors that bring us in closer relationship with God's favor and goodness.[9] The Greek word for blessed is sometimes translated as "happy" or "fortunate." In that sense, these attributes describe a pathway to a state of well-being, both in this life and the next.[10]

Paul discussed what could be considered well-being in his letter to the Galatians. He said that when we are led by the Spirit, we experience the fruit of the Spirit, which is love, joy, peace, patience, kindness, goodness, faithfulness, gentleness, and self-control. These are attributes of well-being.[11] Jesus also said that His followers would be given the Holy Spirit, who would strengthen them to withstand adversity and bring them peace.[12] Thus, a Spirit-filled person experiences well-being through a closer relationship with God.

Transgressions that threaten our well-being come in many shapes and sizes. A transgression is personal: what is offensive or hurtful to one person might not be to another. Encountering harm is also a personal experience of disruption because it is based on individual interpretations of what well-being means and how things should be from each person's individual point of view. Expectations of how things should be affect all aspects of our well-being—physical, mental, spiritual, economic, and social—and differ from one person to another.[13]

Transgressions range from an inconvenience or situational offense, such as being cut off in traffic, to traumatic abuse and life-altering crimes, whether a single episode or ongoing. Everett Worthington Jr., a prominent researcher of forgiveness behaviors, classifies transgressions into five types, any of which may be accidental, deliberate, or retaliatory:[14]

- *hurting someone's feelings* through criticism and/or teasing, which causes emotional and possibly physical pain
- *betrayals*, usually between close friends, work associates, or romantic partners, which makes the one who is betrayed feel rejected
- *active dissociation*, an action that explicitly rejects a person, such as ostracizing him or her from a group or abandoning him or her in a time of need
- *passive dissociation*, a subtle, unclear attempt at rejection that makes the individual feel unwanted
- *being unappreciated* with a heightened sense of rejection and dismissiveness from someone or a group.

Think about the transgression you are working on and try to determine which of these five categories it aligns with.

All five types of transgressions elicit a sense of injustice or unfair treatment. To be treated with injustice is to be treated in violation of a law, rule, or commonly accepted standard. To be subjected to unfair treatment is to be treated differently from how others are treated in a similar situation or different from the reasonable treatment one expects. Worthington, who is a Christian, a retired professor, and a researcher into forgiveness behaviors, calls this the "injustice gap," defined as the distance between how a person believes he or she should be treated and the actual treatment received. The greater the distance, the more intense the reaction. A large gap, Worthington says, can lead to "poor mental, physical, relational, and spiritual health."[15] In other words, the transgression is not what leads to negative emotions, feelings, and thoughts. Instead, the negative emotions, feelings, and thoughts are caused by our expectations for how we want to be treated by the transgressor. The extent to which we believe our well-being has been affected determines how threatening the transgression seems and the severity of our injustice gap. The following are examples of transgressions that fall into the five categories:

- Behaviors that threaten the stability of a relationship
- Interactions that are demeaning or insulting
- Lying and deception
- Unwanted physical or intimate contact
- Threats to our physical safety
- Something being taken that the transgressor has no right to take
- Being manipulated or coerced to conform in unhealthy ways
- Being treated unjustly or unfairly

These types of transgressions are only a sampling. Is the transgression you experienced listed? If not, what would you add to this list? Some types of transgressions, for example, disturb our well-being without actually occurring. In such cases, the threat of a transgression is sufficient to cause anger or fear and affect our sense of well-being.

Jesus said, "Whatever you wish that others would do to you, do also to them, for this is the Law and the Prophets."[16] I believe this is an often misquoted and misunderstood passage. It does not mean "treat people how you think they should be treated." Nor does it mean treating someone how you want to be treated; doing so may not be consistent with what the other person believes is acceptable. What Jesus is saying is to treat people how they need or want to be treated. When others do not treat us as we want to be treated, we feel rejected or unappreciated. The reality is that we are not always treated the way we wish to be treated, and we do not always treat others how they expect to be treated. We are all capable of being transgressors.

These truths may be upsetting because we want to know that we are able to love others and that we are able to be loved; we want to feel we are worthwhile to ourselves and to others. When we feel unloved or believe that others do not value us, we may protest in some way to convince the other that we actually are lovable and worthwhile. When the actions of someone else suggest that we are not worthwhile, or when we commit an act that makes us feel that we are not worthwhile, then our well-being is challenged, prompting us to right the wrong in order to restore balance and regain a sense that we are okay in the eyes of others and ourselves. When our own image of our self-worth is challenged, our sense of well-being is threatened. We will explore how our relationship with Christ protects us from these challenges in chapter 5.

Degrees of Transgressions

Slight variations occur from person to person, but most transgressions can be placed into one of six levels.

- Level 1: Simple offense
  A simple offense is an action by another person that irritates us or creates some inconvenience, such as someone cutting in line or making a distracting noise. It has no life-altering effect.

- Level 2: Complex offense
  A complex offense is a transgression that challenges our well-being with longer-term implications, such as being the victim of gossip, lies, or deceit, or seeing another person receiving preferential treatment over us. This type of transgression has minimal life-altering effect.

- Level 3: Relational offense
  A relational offense is a transgression that threatens to negatively alter an ongoing relationship with the offender. Such offenses include demeaning comments, deceitfulness, lying, infidelity, or betrayal. Relational offenses have a moderate life-altering effect and, worst case, a permanent effect on the relationship.

- Level 4: Malicious offense
  A malicious offense is when someone commits an injustice or unfair act with the intention of being harmful, such as theft, extortion, slander, or defacement of another's property. Malicious offenses often have a strong life-altering effect.

- Level 5: Abuse
  Abuse may be a onetime episode or an ongoing state of intimidation, coercion, or manipulation by a person who seeks dominance, such as controlling what another can do, inflicting physical harm, making threats, being purposefully intimidating, or using another for one's own gain. The perpetrator may try to isolate the victim, exert economic control, or demand sexual behaviors. Abuse always has a life-altering effect, sometimes severe.

- Level 6: Trauma
  Trauma is a onetime or ongoing severe and harmful transgression that violates one's rights and is abusive, unexpected, and life-altering. Trauma creates in the mind a lingering replaying of the event, which seems as real as the actual transgression. Trauma is not always caused by other people. It can be brought on by significant harm coming from a nonspecific

source, such as being in a car accident. It may also include our experience of being harmed, being controlled by another, being harmed sexually, or experiencing extreme ongoing abusive behaviors. Trauma has a severe and sometimes debilitating life-altering effect.

While all levels of transgressions have some effect on our lives, levels 2–4 temporarily affect our well-being, but we can overcome them on our own, either directly with the transgressor or with the help of friends and community. Levels 5 and 6, however, typically have a longer-term severe effect on our lives. Recovering from these levels may require help from a mental health professional or a pastor who is trained to counsel.

Regardless of the level, any transgression changes our experience with life. A life-altering event, however, threatens our sense of well-being and creates a loss of freedom, dignity, justice, equitable treatment, physical functioning, and emotional and/or spiritual health. A life-altering event causes us to change our patterns of functioning in order to divert the event(s) and return to a state of well-being.

In summary, transgressions are actions committed against an individual or group that involve injustice or unfair treatment. The following journal exercise will help you identify the parts of the transgression you have chosen to work on and how it is affecting you.

Journal Exercise 6a: Acknowledging How You Are Affected

Complete the following sentences to describe how are you thinking about the transgression you experienced.

I FEEL …	BECAUSE THE OTHER PERSON [DID WHAT?] …
❏ Unloved by others	
❏ That my love is not accepted by others	
❏ That I am not worthwhile to myself	
❏ That I am not worthwhile to others	

MY PRIMARY GRIEVANCE IS …	BECAUSE THE OTHER PERSON [DID WHAT?] …
❏ Hurt feelings (which may arise from being criticized or teased in a hurtful way)	
❏ Betrayal (which made you feel rejected. This usually happens between close friends, work associates, or romantic partners)	
❏ Active dissociation (an act that explicitly rejected you)	
❏ Passive dissociation (subtle, unclear attempts to make you feel unwanted)	
❏ Being unappreciated (experiencing a heightened sense of rejection and dismissiveness)	
❏ Unfair treatment (receiving different treatment than others)	

☐ Unjust treatment (treatment that violates some law or common rule)

☐ Abuse (being intimidated, manipulated, or controlled for the personal gain of the transgressor)

☐ Other

MY WELL-BEING IS AFFECTED BY THIS THREAT IN WAYS THAT ARE …	THE OFFENSE IS AFFECTING ME BY CAUSING ME TO EXPERIENCE …
☐ Physical	☐ Embarrassment ☐ Sleeplessness
☐ Mental	☐ Preoccupied thoughts ☐ Irritability
☐ Social	☐ Anger ☐ Fearfulness
☐ Spiritual	☐ Suspiciousness ☐ Protectiveness
☐ Economic	☐ Other
I WANT TO RESPOND TO THE TRANSGRESSION BY …	**I WOULD DO THAT BEST BY …**
☐ Fighting back	
☐ Avoiding or ignoring the transgressor	
☐ Calming down	
☐ Finding a peaceful resolution	

Journal Exercise 6b: Acknowledging Degrees of Transgression

Use the ratings that follow to describe the degree of transgression against you. In the left column, put a check mark in front of the level that applies to you. In the right column, check the type of transgression that applies.

I AM EXPERIENCING THIS LEVEL OF TRANSGRESSION …	BECAUSE MY TRANSGRESSOR HAS …
Level 1—Simple offense: something that irritates you or creates some inconvenience	☐ demonstrated behaviors that threaten the stability of my relationship with him or her or someone else. ☐ interacted in ways that are demeaning or insulting to me.
Level 2—Complex offense: a transgression that challenges your well-being for a longer term	☐ lied to or deceived me. ☐ made onetime or persistent unwanted physical or intimate contact. ☐ threatened me physically or has inflicted actual physical harm.
Level 3—Relational offense: a transgression that threatens to alter in a negative way an ongoing relationship with the offender	☐ has taken from me things that he or she had no right to take. ☐ been manipulative or has coerced me to conform in unhealthy ways.
Level 4—Malicious offense: someone committed an injustice or unfair act that was intended to be harmful	☐ treated me unjustly or unfairly. ☐ other: _____
Level 5—Abuse: an ongoing state of coercion and manipulation by someone seeking dominance over you	
Level 6—Trauma: experiencing a severe harmful transgression that was unexpected and life-altering, creating a lingering replaying of the event in your mind	

DAY 7

Acknowledging Your Emotions and Feelings

Science has shown that our brains are programmed to survive an attack or a threat to our quality of life or our well-being.[17] We are hardwired to survive. When we experience a transgression that threatens our well-being, we respond instinctively to protect ourselves. Our instinct to protect ourselves, which is part of human nature, has developed over millennia. A throwback to caveman days, our instincts are likely patterns that are imprinted on our nature as a result of constant danger from animal attacks or as a result of protecting our territory from other humans or predators. In any case, we learned to react instinctively to certain experiences that presented real harm.

Even though dinosaurs and wild animals no longer chase us, a part of our primitive brain (the amygdala) does not distinguish between threats from a dinosaur and a person cutting in line in front of us at the coffee shop. This part of the human brain is programmed to react quickly to anything considered a threat, thus treating all threats the same. We might say that this primitive part of our brains represents one way that our sinful nature hijacks our behavior, since it is the emotional reaction of the body responding without regard for the morality or consequences of our actions.

Emotions, as stated earlier, are not feelings. Emotions come as standard equipment, like the behaviors of babies who have not yet learned how to respond to their environment, yet they react to pain, discomfort, or pleasure through the emotions of anger, fear, sadness, surprise, disgust, and joy. When their behavior results in their needs being met, they repeat those behaviors when similar threats occur. Anger, fear, sadness, disgust, surprise, and joy are our primary emotions.

Primary emotions, then, are the body's immediate unconscious physiological reactions to a threat, occurring before we have time to think about what is happening, preparing us to address impending harm. We become aware of our emotions from our bodies' reactions, which vary from person to person: pupil dilation, adrenaline rush, increased heart rate, tensing of the shoulders and neck, a light feeling in the legs and arms, gut tightening, and other responses.[18]

Primary emotions give rise to feelings; feelings, as explained in chapter 1, are the meanings consciously assigned to emotions after we have had time (an instant, hours, or days) to think about them and compare them to similar previous experiences. In other words, emotions are automatic, but feelings require thought. Humans experience numerous combinations of feelings, some of which are more prominent than others. Feelings that lead to unforgiveness include jealousy, envy, embarrassment, shame, and guilt, to name a few. Feelings have a logic all their own, varying from one individual to the next,[19] with specific emotions resulting in feelings that we associate with the triggering experience (such as a transgression).

In short, emotions are our bodies' physical reaction to threats; our feelings determine how we choose to respond to threats. When we are very young, we begin to test different feelings in response to our emotions. When those feelings are acknowledged positively, we learn to associate them with the emotions that triggered them. Consequently, we are likely to reexperience those feelings in response to similar future situations. When a feeling is not acknowledged or is discouraged, we learn to avoid that feeling in the future. In some cases, when our feelings are repeatedly discouraged, our ability to accurately identify how we feel becomes disabled.

The previous journal exercises gave you an opportunity to think about what emotions and feelings have been triggered by the offense committed against you. The two most common emotions that fuel unforgiveness are fear and anger. An examination of these two emotions will help to determine which affects you the most.

Acknowledging Fear

Fear can be a healthy response in that it is the body's way of alerting us to avoid hurt, whether physical or emotional. Fear is the body's emotional response to an imminent threat, real or imagined. It can even occur before a threat, anticipating that a transgression may happen or escalate. Fear leads us to protect ourselves by preparing to fight off the threat or avoid it. The residual effect of fear may continue once a transgression actually does occur, but fear usually smolders under the emotion of anger. Since fear occurs before or concurrently with a transgression, it is less likely to fuel unforgiveness unless we believe that someone is purposely trying to evoke fear. In that case, our fear becomes what we ruminate about, which may lead to unforgiveness toward the transgressor for putting us in a fearful emotional state.

As explained earlier, our natural inclination is to compare a transgression with similar situations from the past. Based on the outcome of previous similar situations, we respond in a way that either copes with or wards off the threat. Usually our fears are based on a hurtful experience that we encountered personally or witnessed someone else encounter. When people have had more than their share of transgressions in the past, however, they have their antennae up to detect threats before they occur. When we constantly suspect that nonthreatening situations may become transgressions, we often respond in negative ways: anxiety, negative sentiment override, depression, and avoidance.

Anxiety is an ongoing conscious or unconscious state of real or imagined concern that something bad is *going* to happen. It triggers worry, anticipation, and chronic thoughts of worst-case scenarios.

Negative sentiment override is when we experience repeated negative behaviors from others to the point that we believe they will always behave that way, overriding our ability to recognize different, nonnegative behaviors.

Depression is an ongoing conscious or unconscious sadness or sense of hopelessness or despair. It is the result of feeling that we cannot escape real or imagined threats and that we are captives to the hurtful actions of others.

Avoidance is an attempt to remove ourselves from the real or imagined hurtful actions of others to prevent confronting or interacting with them.

The most effective antidote to fear is to (1) determine the feelings created by it and then (2) realize that not all encounters with similar threats have identical results.[20] Fear affects the life cycle of unforgiveness by feeding into negative feelings and the vicious cycle of rumination. While it would be wonderful if we could say that Christians have nothing to fear, the truth is that fear is a preconscious primary emotion. Chapter 5 will address in more detail how to control fear.

Acknowledging Anger

Anger is not an event or thing; it is a primary emotion that reflects how we see and interpret the world around us. Initially, it is experienced unconsciously in the body, and then, after we become consciously aware of it, anger may be a feeling that triggers a conscious stress response in the body. Anger is a healthy emotion that God built into us to help us face danger or injustice. To deny our anger is not healthy; instead, we must acknowledge it and control it or look to God for help.[21]

Anger is an instinctive response to threats and to the frustration of our goals and desires. It can arise when our rules for how things should be are unjustly or unfairly violated. We sometimes try to cope with transgression by believing that we can influence the people making us angry. We assume that they can behave differently: if we just inform them of the offending behavior, we think, then they will stop. We might even think that we can teach them a lesson so that they will not commit the transgression again. Such assumptions are usually wrong.

We generally believe that anger is inappropriate and unacceptable. However, the Bible tells us that anger is an acceptable emotion, as long as it does not lead us to sin.[22] As discussed in chapter 1, we can look to Christ as one example of anger without sin. Christ was angry on at least three occasions, yet He was angry without sinning.[23] The first example is when He saw the Jews' hardness of heart when He healed someone on the Sabbath, the Jewish day of rest.

"And they watched Jesus, to see whether he would heal him on the Sabbath, so that they might accuse him. And he said to the man with the withered hand, 'Come here.' And he said to them, 'Is it lawful on the Sabbath to do good or to do harm, to save life or to kill?' But they were silent. And he looked around at them with anger, grieved at their hardness of heart."[24]

In the second example, Jesus's anger was caused by people using the temple as a place for monetary gain, profiting from worshippers who came to make sacrifices.

"And he entered the temple and began to drive out those who sold and those who bought in the temple, and he overturned the tables of the money changers and the seats of those who sold pigeons. And he would not allow anyone to carry anything through the temple. And he was teaching them and saying to them, 'Is it not written, "My house shall be called a house of prayer for all the nations"? But you have made it a den of robbers.'"[25]

The third example of Jesus's anger is His denouncing the Pharisees for their hypocrisy. They were keeping minute aspects of the law without paying attention to more important matters such as justice, mercy, and faithfulness. They publicly displayed piety while being corrupt in their hearts, claiming to be different from their forefathers who killed the prophets, when in fact, they were just the same. Jesus reprimanded them without mincing words:

> *Woe to you, scribes and Pharisees, hypocrites! For you tithe mint and dill and cumin and have neglected the weightier matters of the law: justice and mercy and faithfulness. These you ought to have done, without neglecting the others. You blind guides, straining out a gnat and swallowing a camel!*
>
> *Woe to you, scribes and Pharisees, hypocrites! For you clean the outside of the cup and the plate, but inside they are full of greed and self-indulgence. You blind Pharisees! First clean the inside of the cup and the plate, that the outside also may be clean.*
>
> *Woe to you, scribes and Pharisees, hypocrites! For you are like whitewashed tombs, which outwardly appear beautiful, but within are full of dead people's bones and all uncleanness. So you also outwardly appear righteous to others, but within you are full of hypocrisy and lawlessness.*
>
> *Woe to you, scribes and Pharisees, hypocrites! For you build the tombs of the prophets and decorate the monuments of the righteous, saying, "If we had lived in the days of our fathers, we would not have taken part with them in shedding the blood of the prophets." Thus you witness against yourselves that you are sons of those who murdered the prophets. Fill up, then, the measure of your fathers. You serpents, you brood of vipers, how are you to escape being sentenced to hell?*[26]

Although many view anger as a completely negative emotion, these episodes illustrate that we can be angry for appropriate reasons. Jesus's anger was prompted by ungodly attitudes and actions toward the kingdom of God, not toward Him. We can learn six lessons from His anger:

1. *His anger had the proper motivation.* In other words, Jesus was angry for the right reasons. Jesus's anger did not arise from petty arguments or personal slights against Him. His anger

was against people mistreating the kingdom of God and sinning against God. No self-centeredness was involved.

2. *His anger had the proper focus.* He was not angry at God or at the weaknesses of others. His anger targeted sinful behavior and true injustice.

3. *His anger had the proper sentiment,* namely, it was accompanied by grief over the Pharisees' hardness of heart.[27] Jesus's anger stemmed from His love for the Pharisees and His concern for their spiritual condition; it had nothing to do with hatred or ill will toward them.

4. *His anger had the proper control.* Jesus was never out of control. The temple leaders resented His cleansing of the temple,[28] but He did nothing sinful. He controlled His emotions; His emotions did not control Him.

5. *His anger had the proper duration.* Jesus did not allow His anger to turn into bitterness, nor did He hold grudges. He dealt with each situation properly, and He handled anger in good time.

6. *His anger had the proper result.* Jesus's anger resulted in His taking godly action. As with all His emotions, Jesus always sought to accomplish God's will.

When we are angry, we can easily lose our control or focus, but following four requirements will ensure, instead, that our anger is based on Christ's example:

❑ First, our anger must not be motivated by an occasion when we do not get our way. Some examples of proper and godly reasons to become angry are religious hypocrisy, sinful acts of others, or the injustice of poverty or oppression.

❑ A second requirement when we are angry is to act appropriately. Jesus healed a man even when He was angry, revealing that we are called to do good even when we are upset. When Jesus overturned the tables in the temple, he removed people who were breaking God's expectations for the use of the temple (a house of prayer) by making a profit from those coming to present sacrifices. He then proceeded to teach in the temple.

❑ Third, we must not exhibit the anger of humankind but the righteous indignation of God. When angry, we must not spew vile language, do damage, or be violent. If we are to be angry like Jesus, then our anger must be a controlled expression of concern.

❑ Finally, the anger of Jesus did not result in a long-term grudge. Instead, His anger was brief and appropriate. When His angry response was completed, he moved on. The apostle Paul said it well: "Be angry and do not sin; do not let the sun go down on your anger and give no opportunity to the devil."[29]

When we handle our anger in productive ways, we are then able to better cope with transgressions and chart a path to forgiveness. We will come back to examples of how to deal with anger in chapter 5. For now, it is important to acknowledge our anger and to identify the type we have.

Three Types of Anger

Aggressive, passive-aggressive, and assertive are three ways that anger expresses itself. Aggressive and passive-aggressive anger are intended to return hurt to an offender. *Aggressive* anger is outwardly directed toward the offender or things that the offender values and often includes threatening behaviors such as hitting, yelling, or other forms of intimidation. Aggressive anger usually seeks to eliminate the threat by intimidating the other person and transferring accountability for a problem back onto the transgressor. *Passive-aggressive* anger is also intended to be hurtful, but in an indirect way. Its goal is to express anger, hurt, or frustration subtly to avoid major conflict. While acting aggressively may escalate the transgressor's response, a passive-aggressive approach will be hurtful without detection. The victim's anger stays under the radar, so to speak.

An *assertive anger* style, in contrast, is akin to negotiating with the transgressor to resolve the offense in an acceptable and appropriate way. The dictionary defines assertiveness as the quality of being self-assured and confident without being aggressive. It is a form of behavior characterized by a confident respect for the boundaries of oneself and others; it presumes an interest in the fulfillment of needs and wants through cooperation.[30] Assertiveness is communicating in a way that another person's point of view is heard without threatening his or her rights.

Assertive people do not shy away from defending their point of view or from trying to influence others. Instead, they respond to both positive and negative emotions without resorting to aggression or passive aggression. Assertiveness does not mean being a doormat for others. As Paul said, "If possible, so far as it depends on you, live peaceably with all,"[31] but the truth is that we cannot live peacefully with some people. We can try, but at some point we have to release them to God.[32] Our role is to continue to model the light of Christ,[33] even when others are difficult and refuse to live in peace with us.[34]

When an unwanted event occurs to us, you may create a picture of what happened that causes you to respond with undue anger, fear, or negative emotions. However, you are the only person who can choose how you will think and behave in response to that picture. Please consider the story or picture you created to explain the transgression you experienced. Both aggressive and passive-aggressive anger can be hurtful unless they are under control, and any type of anger that is intended to return hurt is sin. To keep yourself from a sinful response, ask three questions when you feel angry:

1. "Will I be in control of my actions?"
2. "How long will my anger last?"
3. "Do I have hurtful intentions?"

Journal Exercise 7: Acknowledging Emotions and Feelings

As discussed, anger is only one of many emotions. In chapter 1, you thought about a person who hurt you in some way. The questions below will help you determine the nature and extent of the emotions you are experiencing from this hurt. You may want to refer back to the journal exercises in chapter 1 as you think about these questions.

1. What emotions and feelings are you experiencing about the transgression?	**Fear**	**Anger**	**Disgust**	**Sadness**	**Surprise**
	❏ Alert ❏ Afraid ❏ Cautious ❏ Uneasy ❏ Terrorized ❏ Shocked	❏ Annoyed ❏ Contemptuous ❏ Indifferent ❏ Frustrated ❏ Mad ❏ Outraged	❏ Revulsion ❏ Repugnance ❏ Distaste ❏ Loathing ❏ Sickness ❏ Avoidance	❏ Regretful ❏ Bitter ❏ Mournful ❏ Sorrowful ❏ Despairing ❏ Depressed	❏ Disappointment ❏ Amazement ❏ Outrage ❏ Uncertainty ❏ Anticipation ❏ Numbness
	Examples of other emotions/feelings:				
2. What are you experiencing in your body that confirms how you are feeling?					
3. How are you responding to your emotions and feelings?	❏ Contempt ❏ Defensiveness ❏ Stonewalling ❏ Criticism ❏ Other	Will you give an example?			

DAY 8

Acknowledging Unenforceable Rules

As stated earlier, babies begin very early to learn acceptable and unacceptable responses to their emotions. They sense what their culture and their caregivers expect as a reasonable response, and then they store that information so that it becomes an automatic or instinctive way of responding in the future, a rule that they believe will always have an acceptable result. Over time, we develop cherished ideas about appropriate reactions to our experiences.

Since we learn to respond in certain ways to the world around us, we hold expectations for others to respond similarly. As explained previously, we all have rules for how the world should work and treat us, but we cannot enforce these rules.[35] When we come into contact with people whose behavior is unacceptable to us and whose "misbehavior" inflicts harm on us (or represents a threat to us), our human nature is to change something.

In 1954, Leon Festinger, a behavioral scientist, proposed the concept of cognitive dissonance to describe how we interpret the world around us. According to this theory, individuals tend to compare the actions and attitudes of others to their own beliefs or attitudes to see if they are in agreement. Since we are instinctively wired to create harmony in the world around us, when the two do not align, we experience a tension. We all have an instinctive desire to make the tension go away; in other words, we desire to make the world around us match our own cherished ideas of how the world should be and how we should be treated. When our beliefs about how we should be treated do not align with what we actually experience from others, we try to resolve the mismatch in one of three ways:

1. We reduce the importance of the transgressor's attitude or actions and our own beliefs. When we do this, we are analyzing the impact of the transgression on us and deciding whether it is important enough to get worked up about.
2. We strengthen the resolve of our own beliefs to outweigh what we are experiencing in order to try to influence a change in the actions and attitudes of others to align with how we believe the world should be.

3. We change our beliefs about how we should be treated so that they are no longer inconsistent with what we are experiencing from others. This may happen when we realize that what we experienced is actually different from how we see it.

Let's apply these ideas to our study of unforgiveness. When we experience a transgression, we are experiencing an action or attitude that does not align with our cherished ideas of how we should be treated. This creates a tension, or stress, in our emotions and our thinking. By nature, we try to minimize stress; therefore, we might minimize the importance of the transgression to us. Or we can dig in our heels, deny that the transgression is okay, and try to influence the transgressor to change. In some cases, however, we cannot influence the other to change. Another option is to change how we believe we should be treated.

When a transgression violates our expectations of how we should be treated, we perceive it as a violation of the rules we carry for how we should be treated. However, it is seldom that we can enforce our rules or cherished ideas of how we expect to be treated. When we cannot control how we are treated, we may interpret the behaviors of others as a form of adversity that can threaten our well-being. In other words, adversity is the result of our emotional reaction to a transgression that we cannot control. The process begins when we recognize that we are experiencing some form of unwanted treatment, which is a perception that our well-being is being challenged. We then respond to adversity with emotions and feelings. Positive emotional responses can lead to coping in a productive way, but negative emotional responses such as fear, anger, sadness, and disgust may ultimately lead to unforgiveness if we allow ourselves to ruminate on these emotions. On the other hand, if we do not see the transgression as a threat, we may respond positively with an emotion of joy or happiness or just maintain our status quo.

Beliefs are rules that we hold as true or real. They govern how we see the world and respond to the world. When our beliefs are disputed, we are challenged to pass judgment on whether or not they are correct. If, on the other hand, we find that our beliefs are true and that we have been violated by a transgressor, we respond in a way to protect ourselves, which may be assertive or aggressive. If, however, we find that our belief that some rule has been violated is not true, we may return to a state of calmness and well-being.

Another way to look at being treated unjustly or unfairly is to consider our possible responses: fighting back, running away (or other avoidance), resolving the situation (positive coping), or freezing (not responding or else numbing out by avoidance or through substance abuse). Fighting can be literal or figurative: it can mean becoming argumentative, belligerent, intimidating, defensive, or combative. Running away means that we literally avoid the transgressor or refuse to acknowledge him or her. Resolving is a form of coping that involves problem-solving with the transgressor. When we freeze, we are stunned and do not know how to respond in that moment, so we do not respond at all. Yet, no response is also a response.

Sometimes our desire to resolve the tension created by the transgression leads to playing internal dialogues: find the bad guy, protest the threat, freeze, and reframe. Find-the-bad-guy is saying, "I am not the problem; you are." It is a form of self-protection that attacks the other and deflects the blame from us to them; it kicks in when we feel hurt by someone or when we transfer control of our situation to a person who hurt us. When we feel threatened, we use any strategy to regain control. We can do this by seeing the other person in a negative way, by attacking him or her with belligerence, or by being threatening in return. These offensive moves turn the tables; instead of being threatened, we become the ones issuing the threats. Our hope is that the other person will back off or shut down the threatening behavior. Or, as the one posing the threat, we retaliate and pay back the transgressor for his or her offensive behavior.

The second internal dialogue, protesting the threat, is a way of seeking a response that connects with the offender in a positive way. By protesting against his or her actions, we adopt more acceptable behavior in an attempt to show the offender the error of his or her actions. When the transgressor does not respond, however, the protest can get more intense, potentially creating confusion and disconnection. This distress can lead to the next response: avoiding the transgressor. The more our protest is ignored, the more we feel devalued, rejected, and dismissed by the transgressor. This can lead to a number of negative emotional responses:[36]

- shutting down or numbing out in order to repress or deny the transgression
- avoiding the transgression by employing rational problem-solving to avert the offense
- feeling hopeless and lacking confidence to act appropriately to resolve the situation
- seeing oneself as a failure and as inadequate to resolve the situation
- feeling judged and unaccepted by the transgressor.

Freezing in the face of a transgression, the third internal dialogue, is a form of avoidance. We freeze or get out of the way when we feel helpless to do anything about the transgression, even while we fear its impact on our well-being. Freezing often happens in response to a surprise. Getting out of the way is a form of ducking, either physically, emotionally, or socially, in order to avoid the transgression. When we freeze, it is often because we do not know what else to do, and we believe that doing nothing is better than doing something that worsens the situation. When avoidance or doing nothing does not restore our sense of peace, we often resort to one of the other strategies in an attempt to protect our sense of well-being.

These four ways of responding to a transgression—finding the bad guy, protesting the threat, resolving the discord, and freezing—are attempts to cope with the transgression and restore peace. These tactics show the offender that he or she has violated our idea of how things should be. The offender may respond positively and acknowledge our attempt to restore peace. If so, we then successfully engage with the transgressor and find resolution before our response escalates into fear and anger. These emotions can lead to a state of unforgiveness and prompt us to act in some negative, vengeful, or retaliatory way, such as having negative intentions, which are ways that we intend to act toward our offender when the opportunity presents itself.

A fifth way of responding to a transgression is to reframe it. The key question here is, has our perception of the offense been clouded by our past experiences? Your initial response to this question may be, "Of course not." But bear with me. Sometimes our beliefs about how we should be treated may be so dogmatic and judgmental that we see what we are programmed to see instead of what is really happening. Let's look at an example of how this could happen. Observe this image.[37] What do you see? Do you see an old woman or a beautiful young woman? If you do not see both, cover one eye and stare at the center. Now do you see something different? Our perception of how others treat us is like this drawing. Sometimes, when we turn the situation around and look at it from different points of view, we gain a new perspective. We may determine that our view of the situation is indeed accurate, which prompts a different course of action than if we determine that our view is inaccurate. To reframe the situation is to look at it from different perspectives. Most situations can be viewed in different ways, and sometimes there are shades of ray.

Ambiguous Image

Reframing your point of view

Journal Exercise 8: Unenforceable Rules

In this exercise, think about your rules for how you should be treated. Assess how they are being violated and how you would like to enforce them.

1. What rules for how you should be treated were violated?		
2. Which internal dialogue have you used to respond to your transgressor?	☐ Find the bad guy ☐ Freeze or avoid ☐ Protest the actions of the transgressor ☐ Resolve the discord ☐ Reframe ☐ ☐	What response did you get?
3. Is there a way to enforce the rules that have been violated?		

DAY 9

Acknowledging How You Are Coping with the Transgression[38]

As discussed in the previous section, when we encounter a transgression that challenges our cherished ideas of how the world should treat us, we become stressed. Stress is the body's response to a threat that puts us on alert to avoid harm. The onset of stress usually starts as a gut reaction that occurs before we even have time to think about the stressful situation. Chemicals rush through our bodies, triggering what scientists call "allostasis." Allostasis is characterized by increases in respiration, blood pressure, heart rate, and energy release, along with decreases in digestion, growth hormones, and sexual hormones.[39] Allostasis puts the body in a state of readiness to fight, run away, or freeze in the face of a threat.

When we realize that the body is having a physical reaction to some event, we quickly try to assess the danger of being hurt and begin to decide how to respond. Each of us responds to stressors in different ways, and each way has different consequences for our mental and physical health. Initially, the offense triggers an emotional response, the most common of which is fear or anger or both. Stressors may result in hostility, depression, anxiety, paranoia, etc. When stressors are repeatedly caused by the same person, they may trigger negative sentiment override, the belief that repeated offenses will continue. Eventually, our anticipation of the offense overrides our ability to accept a change to positive or neutral behavior from the transgressor.[40] In close relationships, negative sentiment override leads to a breakdown in friendship and a general state of unforgiveness that affects every aspect of the relationship, regardless of whether the same offense occurs.

Coping is the use of cognitive and behavioral strategies to reduce transgression-induced stress and to return to a state of well-being. The first step in coping is to be aware of how we see and interpret the situation.[41] When we do not see an experience accurately and do not correctly assess how it is affecting us, our coping strategies may not be effective.[42] Coping begins with an attempt to gain a better understanding of an offense; its goal is to respond in ways that reduce stress and restore our sense of well-being. We may initially respond by tolerating or minimizing our reaction to a transgression, but these are short-term solutions that often do not have a lasting effect on our stress. There are three types of coping strategies:

- **Problem-solving** strategies, which are efforts to alleviate stressful circumstances by clarifying the problem and finding acceptable, appropriate, and positive solutions that are in our best interest and the best interests of our transgressors.
- **Emotion-focused** coping strategies, which seek to regulate the emotional consequences of stressful or potentially stressful events.
- **Meaning-focused** coping strategies, which attempt to reduce stress by changing our interpretation or point of view of the stressor or our response to the stress.[43]

Each of these coping strategies can be active (positive) or avoidant (negative).[44] Positive coping strategies are the ones that result in a reduction of stress in a way that does not create new tensions or compound existing tensions. Negative coping is the use of strategies that have a collateral effect on you or others. Action-oriented coping, whether problem-focused, emotion-focused, or meaning-focused, may be the most effective way to minimize stress and return to a state of well-being.

On the other hand, avoidant coping strategies can also be focused on problem-solving, emotions, or meaning; in most cases, however, avoidant coping leads to unproductive negative behaviors that may reduce unforgiveness yet not produce the peace and well-being that positive coping brings. Negative avoidant behaviors run the gamut from busywork, to withdrawal, to diversions such as substance abuse or other behaviors that prevent directly addressing stressful events. In most cases, negative avoidant coping strategies ultimately result in negative intentions, rumination, and a vicious cycle of unforgiveness. However, avoidant strategies are not always negative, and in some cases they may be needed. When a transgression threatens abuse or traumatic harm, some avoidant strategies, such as setting appropriate boundaries, are the best way to react, followed by emotional regulation and problem-solving to eliminate the abuse. These are all necessary steps to forgiveness and peace. Simply ignoring abuse will not result in positive well-being.

The following chart summarizes how coping mechanisms work. In this chart, active strategies are considered positive coping strategies, meaning that they promote productive coping. Avoidant strategies are considered negative, meaning that they inhibit coping productively with your transgression.

	PROBLEM FOCUSED	EMOTIONAL REGULATION	MEANING FOCUSED
Active Coping	• Problem solving • Research solutions • Idea generating • Reframing situation • Reviewing concerns • Negotiation • Setting boundaries • Reappraise situation • Prayer	• Humor • Seeking Support • Crying • Empathizing • Prayer • Relaxation, Yoga	• Adjusting expectations • Writing about transgression • Prayer/meditation • Bible study • Read inspirational quotes • List life's blessings
Avoidant Coping	• Disregarding threat • Talking with others • Trivializing threat • Argue about solutions • Express hostility • Rationalizing • Ladder of inference	• Self blame, Venting • Fear & anger • Diversions: movies, hobbies, recreation • Express hostility • Ladder of inference • Busy work • Substance abuse	• Denial • Post on social media • List their shortcomings • Telling story to others

Coping Strategies

Avoidant emotion-focused coping becomes a problem when, instead of taking action to resolve a transgression peacefully, we let our emotions and feelings lead us to ongoing resentment, a desire for revenge, or other negative intentions. Effective emotion-focused coping seeks to regulate our reactions to a transgression by controlling our negative thoughts to prevent them from escalating. As we do this, we begin to collect new information that changes our interpretation of the transgression. Instead of ruminating on our negative interpretation of the transgression, we can improve our ability to resolve the matter peacefully. Some examples of emotion-focused coping include seeking support from others, using relaxation techniques, doing yoga, and crying.

Although problem-focused coping generally has a positive effect on emotions,[45] it can also cause collateral problems. When we take matters into our own hands to resolve a problem, we can make our transgressors feel worse about what they have done or we can appear to be retaliating against them, stimulating their threat response and producing stress for them, both of which exacerbate the conflict. Positive problem-solving is best done when we can involve the transgressor in agreeing that a problem exists and then when we collaborate to find mutually acceptable solutions. Collaborating with the transgressor, however, may not always be possible. Sometimes it is necessary to think of positive solutions by ourselves, such as when we are in a hostile or abusive relationship. Problem-focused coping includes such actions as researching solutions, reappraising the situation, and negotiating.

A meaning-focused approach involves reappraising the transgression to determine whether it was truly harmful or whether it might lead to a beneficial outcome. For example, we might view the stress as beneficial to our spiritual growth or moral character or as an opportunity to learn something new about ourselves or others. In this way, meaning-focused coping can transform an unforgiving posture into a forgiving one. Some examples of positive meaning-focused coping include adjusting expectations, writing about the transgression, praying, and meditating. This type of coping, however, may have negative effects. For example, an individual might not hold the transgressor accountable for his or her behavior and thereby will open the door to repeated offenses.[46]

Research indicates that people use all three types of coping strategies to combat their most stressful events.[47] Our preference for a type of coping strategy is determined by learned patterns from our early childhood, our personal style (some people are wired to cope more actively than others), and the type of stressful event. People typically employ problem-focused coping to deal with potentially controllable problems, such as work or family-related problems, but stressors perceived as less controllable, such as certain kinds of physical health problems or transgressions by people who are no longer accessible, may prompt emotion-focused coping. A meaning-focused coping strategy would be used to change your perception of the nature of the stressor itself or to decide to forgive the transgressor.[48]

Coping is more than a behavior, feeling, or process. In most cases, how we cope involves unlearning behaviors and ways of thinking that harm our ability to live with others peacefully. That is to say, how we cope is based on what has worked in similar situations in the past. Our experiences contribute to the formation of coping habits that ultimately lead to a way of life. When we are spiritually mature, a Christlike lifestyle influences our coping strategy and its effectiveness. A Christlike lifestyle cultivates any of the coping disciplines that reduce our stress and nurture a compassion for a transgressor's soul and well-being,[49] ideas that will be discussed in chapter 4.

Coping involves how we respond both internally and externally to the transgressor. When our internal and external responses are not balanced, we create more stress for ourselves. For example, when we are thinking of ways to get even with transgressors (an internal response) but our behavior toward them is kind and friendly (an external response), we are likely to feel the inauthentic and hypocritical conflict between the two responses, which sustains or increases stress. The ultimate goal of coping is to bring our internal feelings in line with positive external behaviors. Successful coping creates balance.

Trying to control the transgressor is an inadvisable form of coping that can negatively affect our health. Attempts to control others almost always results in resistance; it is a train wreck looking for a place to happen. Responding to transgressors by demanding that they treat us differently or by imposing our will on them is likely to fuel anger, fear, vengeance, or retaliation.

On the other hand, trying to address the transgression by totally controlling our own emotions and keeping our experience to ourselves also increases the likelihood of a negative impact on our health. Keeping a lid on our emotions can result in any of the following disorders:[50]

- Denial—acting as if some injustice or act of unfairness did not happen
- Repression—burying the memory in the unconscious
- Displacement—targeting people other than the transgressor with our anger
- Regression—having a childlike response to the offense
- Identification—imitating the behavior of the transgressor
- Depression—an intense internal state of sadness

Yet even when our coping strategy is effective, we still have no guarantee that we will not ruminate on negative intentions. We can accept the best explanation—one that is most in harmony with our preconceptions about the transgressor, with our desire to be treated a certain way, with our history with the transgressor, and with what is culturally acceptable—but if we believe that the offender was malicious or intentionally harmful, or if we believe that the offense may happen again, we may remain in a state of anger and fear. Remaining in a state of anger and fear fuels unforgiveness. In other words, coping is sometimes not effective or possible, so we have to make a choice: to go down the path of forgiveness or unforgiveness.

At this stage in your forgiveness journey, it is important for you to think about how you have tried to cope with your transgressor.[51] The following exercises are designed help you to think about your situation with the transgressor.

Journal Exercise 9: Coping with Offenders

The following is a list of ways that we try to cope with offenders. Look at the list and put a check by any of the coping methods you have tried.[52]

☐ *1. What happened was not really that bad. I ought to just forget what happened and move on.*

☐ *2. I have tried to restart my relationship with the person who hurt me, acting as if nothing happened.*

☐ *3. I have accepted an excuse or explanation for what someone did, and I have tried to move on.*

☐ *4. I've done what I can to smooth over conflict and restore my relationship.*

☐ *5. I have voluntarily released my right to condemn the person who hurt me and to get revenge against him or her.*

☐ *6. I tolerate the negative things my transgressor has done to me, and I accept my transgressor despite his or her flaws.*

☐ *7. To clear the air, I blamed and confronted the person who hurt me, and I demanded that he or she apologize, express regret, or beg forgiveness.*

☐ *8. I have tried getting even with the person who hurt me.*

☐ *9. I have made a voluntary decision to give up the right to revenge, and I have released the offender from any interpersonal debt to me.*

Interpreting Your Results

In the previous exercise, only two of the coping examples (5 and 9) replace negative thoughts with positive ones and lead to successful coping and forgiveness. These positive thoughts, feelings, and behaviors do not mean that we condone or accept the offender's actions. Effective coping requires that we understand offenders while holding them accountable for their actions. The other coping examples (1–4 and 6–8) are myths about forgiveness that are not effective coping styles; they do not lead to a reduction in stress or to genuine forgiveness. They may reduce our unforgiveness, but they will not provide the peace that comes from *actual* forgiveness. As seen below, the seven examples that do not lead to forgiveness are also not biblically based. Following is an overview of why each approach does or does not qualify as an effective coping strategy:

1. *What happened really was not that bad. I ought to just forget what happened and move on.*

This is rationalizing, which is an avoidant problem-solving form of coping. Denying that we have been hurt almost never works. When the hurt keeps resurfacing, we may begin to ruminate on it and respond negatively.[53] Forgetting about a transgression is also a form of denial. Once a memory has been formed, it can shift and change with time, but it cannot be erased. The harder we try to just forget what happened, the more we think about it. Trying to forget might even fuel more resentment and anger and lead us to take out our anger on people other than the offender.

2. *I have tried to restart my relationship with the person who hurt me, acting as if nothing happened.*

This is an example of denial, which is an avoidant meaning-focused form of coping. While restarting a relationship might actually smooth things out and elicit a positive response from the transgressor, you might continue to harbor unforgiveness. While this approach may make it possible for you (the injured person) and the transgressor to live peacefully with each other, it also runs the risk that the transgressor will think it is okay to be hurtful in the same way again.[54]

3. *I have accepted an excuse or explanation for what someone did to me, and I have tried to move on.*

This could be considered disregarding the threat, an avoidant problem-solving coping mechanism. Understanding why the transgressor caused the hurt or accepting an excuse may help to reduce unforgiveness, and it may even lead to a desire to forgive, but it is not forgiveness. Accepting the offender's excuse without his or her repentance may open the door for hurtful behavior to occur again.[55]

4. *I've done what I can to smooth over the conflict and restore my relationship.*

This might be an example of trivializing the transgression, thinking of it as being less serious than it is, a form of avoidant problem-focused coping. The Old Testament contains a number of stories about reconciliation without explicitly mentioning forgiveness.[56] A relationship can be restored through reconciliation. For example, Joseph reconciled with his brothers, but their father, Jacob, still urged the brothers to seek forgiveness from Joseph.[57] When smoothing over a transgression and reconciling with an offender, it is necessary to replace our thoughts of negative intentions with positive thoughts toward the transgressor as Esau demonstrated toward his brother Jacob.[58]

5. *I have voluntarily released my right to condemn the person who hurt me and to get revenge on him or her, and I have decided to treat him or her with kindness.*

This is an example of adjusting expectations for the transgressor, which is an active meaning-focused form of coping. This is an example of emotional forgiveness, discussed earlier in this chapter. It acknowledges a wrong and changes the negative thoughts directed at the transgressor to positive thoughts. When this coping approach is activated, the offended person no longer seeks revenge and does not condemn the person who caused the hurt. In short, the hurt person experiences different feelings toward the offender. This effective approach is best characterized as a meaning-focused coping strategy.[59]

6. *I tolerate negative things my transgressor has done to me, and I accept my transgressor despite his or her flaws.*

This is an example of disregarding the transgression and its effect on you, an avoidant form of problem-solving coping. Smoothing over conflict and recognizing the offender's flaws can be done whether or not negative thoughts are exchanged for positive ones. However, this will not remove the possibility of a repeat offense. Tolerating negative actions and words does not usually stop the negative behavior and will likely keep the hurt person in an angry and unforgiving state. This is an avoidant coping strategy, a path of least resistance taken because positive coping through problem-solving, emotional regulation, or meaning-focused strategies may not be comfortable.

7. *To clear the air, I blamed and confronted the person who hurt me, and I demanded that he or she apologize, express regret, or ask forgiveness.*

Blaming can be an avoidant problem-solving or emotionally focused form of coping with a transgression. Playing the blame game acknowledges the person's guilt, but blame keeps the hurt on the front burner for both the transgressor and the victim. While confrontation with the transgressor may make the injured person feel better, it is unlikely to get a positive response from the transgressor. Blaming can be used as a form of suggesting that the transgressor is the problem and that your willingness to forgive is the responsibility of the transgressor. Blame might also be an avoidant emotional regulation coping strategy when blaming is used to shift the focus of the problem totally onto the transgressor as a way to feel superior to him or her. Confronting the transgressor might also cause further damage to the relationship. Confronting is not forgiving.[60]

8. *I have tried getting even with the person who hurt me.*

Revenge and expressing hostility are avoidant forms of emotional regulation coping. Getting even is revenge. It may reduce stress in the short term, but it leads to negative intentions and unforgiveness. While revenge may feel good briefly, it can later create shame or guilt within the injured person. Revenge may also raise a concern that the wrongdoer will retaliate, creating an ongoing one-upmanship cycle of offenses that has no end.[61]

9. *I have made a voluntary decision to give up the right to revenge, and I have released the offender from any interpersonal debt to me.*

This is an example of a problem-focused coping strategy; it leads to decisional forgiveness. It involves the injured person's pledge that his or her behavior will not be aimed at revenge or unforgiving thoughts and behaviors; rather, the offended person tries to behave with empathy, compassion, and gentleness that glorifies God.[62]

DAY 10

Acknowledging the Vicious Cycle

As illustrated in the diagram of the life cycle of unforgiveness, when we are not able to cope with a transgression, we begin thinking about how we *want* to respond to our offenders, based on our rules and expectations about how we should be treated. Eventually, we realize that we cannot enforce our rules; therefore, these unenforceable rules and their associated feelings lead us to think about how we *intend* to respond given the opportunity. Responses can range from ignoring or justifying the transgression to launching a full-scale retaliatory attack. Instead of resolving the transgression through effective coping, negative intentions lead to unforgiveness. Once we begin to consider negative actions, a story about the transgression forms in our heads and we begin to ruminate on it, getting locked into a vicious cycle of unforgiveness. Rumination, behavioral scientists tell us, is at the core of unforgiveness; it fuels unforgiveness.[63] Rumination is the process of continually going over something in our minds. *Webster's Dictionary* suggests that rumination is similar to a cow bringing up and chewing again what has already been chewed and swallowed. Continually thinking about a transgression does not resolve it, nor does it bring peace of mind.

Forgiveness does not occur until we get a grip on our negative feelings and intentions. Following are examples of negative intentions that inhibit forgiveness:

- Retaliation
- Revenge
- Indifference
- Estrangement
- Verbal aggression
- Promoting justice
- Demanding restitution
- Mercilessness
- Demanding an apology

- Resentment
- Negative judgment
- Hostility
- Bitterness
- Hatred
- Anger
- Fearfulness
- Holding grudges
- Envy

The feelings in the first column are directed toward the transgressor; they are negative intentions. The feelings in the second column are directed inward; they fuel our negative intentions and make us miserable. Two antidotes for these unforgiving thoughts are available to us: reducing unforgiveness and promoting forgiveness. Reducing unforgiveness involves exacting a form of restitution or judgment on the offender, which will help us feel less stressed temporarily. Forgiveness, in contrast, is an effort to reduce hurt feelings by deliberately substituting, abandoning, letting go of, and denying our legitimate right to negative feelings, thoughts, and behaviors.[64] With forgiveness, we seek to replace negative emotions with positive ones such as empathy, sympathy, compassion, or love. Forgiveness involves acknowledging that someone has harmed us and then working through the hurt to the degree that we can abandon both the hurt and the desire for retaliation. When that happens, we feel goodwill toward the offender and, when possible, restore relations.[65]

Negative intentions fall into three categories: (1) retribution, the desire to return the harm through resentment or vengeance; (2) withdrawal, a self-protection strategy that may cut off the relationship; and (3) conditional continuation of the relationship that is usually shallow and at a distance. We will talk more about these responses in chapter 5.

As explained earlier, a transgression is a threat to our well-being, and threats trigger emotions that are experienced preconsciously in our bodies. Emotions lead to feelings, and when not coped with effectively, feelings may ignite negative intentions toward the transgressor. The details of the transgression, the feelings, and the negative intentions stick in our minds. We rethink the offense, replaying it in our minds to see whether we fully understand it and to allow ourselves the opportunity to consider how we want to respond. We might ruminate about the transgressor, the conditions that led to the transgression, how the transgression occurred, the response of the transgressor, seeking revenge, devaluing and villainizing the wrongdoer, how the transgression negatively affects us, and so on.[66]

Rumination is fixating our thoughts on the feelings and negative intentions associated with the transgression. Either we cannot get them out of our conscious minds, or we push them out of our minds into our unconscious (repression). Repressed ruminations filter through our unconscious and can show up as misplaced negative actions toward people other than the wrongdoer. Ultimately, the negative intentions give rise to stories about the hurt, stories that we tell ourselves or others about what happened. These takes become our internal "truth" about what happened and how it affects us, which then becomes the focus of our rumination. The stories eventually take on a life of their own and often continue even after some resolution occurs. After a while, we accept the stories as the truth even when they may not contain all the facts or consider all perspectives.

Remember how we reframed our perception of the drawing of the old woman? Rumination is an unproductive response that inhibits our ability to see the transgression from another perspective, that is, to reframe our perception. Some people call this "awfulizing," making things seem totally awful regardless of the facts. One of the more common ways we ruminate is with a process that I call a "ladder of inference": inferring or interpreting what has happened without checking all the facts. It is also a thought process that gradually stacks up worst-case scenarios of how things may turn out if we do not react to the threat. We talk ourselves into believing that the situation is negative and that it can only have a negative result. The ladder of inference has five imaginary rungs:

Rung 1.   We selectively collect and believe information about the transgression that may not contain all the facts.

Rung 2.   We create a theory or untested interpretation about the transgression, and we begin to associate feelings with this interpretation. This step repeats as we think about our experience in ways that distort details and embellish its meaning.

Rung 3.   We construct a problem from the inferences we have made, determine what needs fixing, and decide what actions are available to us. As we begin to formulate a story about our experience, our feelings intensify.

Rung 4.   We draw conclusions that are worst-case scenarios, based on faulty data, and we make decisions about how to solve the problems that we have constructed in our story. These decisions are fueled by the feelings we attach to these scenarios. Rungs 3 and 4 often repeat.

Rung 5.   We react. We have created what we believe to be a plausible interpretation of the experience without checking to confirm it fully or without seeking to apply positive coping strategies. We react to this created story more than to the facts.

As our negative thoughts escalate, we begin to speculate on the potential consequences of the transgression, which stimulates belief that another transgression may occur, such as unfair treatment or being skewered with a demeaning remark. Continued thoughts about our feelings feed more and more into our ladder of inference, fanning the flames of rumination. The longer we ruminate, the more likely we are to develop a state of unforgiveness.[67] On the other hand, at any point in the ladder of inference, we may choose to collect new information that may confirm our interpretation or reveal that our interpretation is false. Instead of ruminating over a fabricated negative story, we may resolve the matter peacefully by using positive coping mechanisms.

Unforgiveness occurs as a response to the stories we have created about the transgression, stories that may be based on inaccurate, incomplete, or misunderstood information. The more we think about our story, the more we ruminate, and the more we ruminate, the more we contemplate negative intentions toward the offender. We become stuck in a vicious cycle. One way to break this cycle is by reducing unforgiveness, which is done by demanding restitution, ensuring that the transgressor is brought to justice, or addressing his or her unfair actions in some manner. While these approaches may temporarily help us feel better and may be important consequences for an offender, they are not forgiveness. Following are ways to reduce unforgiveness, but as you will see, they do not lead to forgiveness:

- Compare yourself to your offender to show that you are better, righter, or stronger.
- Rehearse schemes of revenge in your mind.
- Entertain thoughts of life being unkind to the offender.
- Tell numerous people about the rotten character of the offender.
- Mention the offense to people who are not involved.
- Do unto the wrongdoer as he or she has done unto you.
- Ruminate on the offense to avoid the hard work of addressing the hurt productively.
- Demand an apology, justice, and atonement.
- Ignore the offense and act as if it did not happen.
- Excuse the behavior and let the transgressor off the hook.

Reducing unforgiveness may provide temporary relief, but it does not provide lasting peace or lead to reconciliation. However, just letting go of negative thoughts and feelings aimed at the offender is difficult. In fact, the more we think about letting go of negative thoughts, the more they become automatic and ingrained. The thoughts create something similar to tire ruts in our minds. It is like saying, "Do not think of red cars." Guess what cars we are most likely to notice? The more we think negative thoughts, the deeper the ruts get.

If you recognize such ruts in your mind, do not despair: there is nothing wrong with you. Negative feelings and behaviors are a natural reaction to a threat; they are attempts to protect yourself. However, the *most* effective strategy is to replace the negative thoughts with positive ones, which we will talk more about later. But for now, complete the following exercise while considering your negative thoughts.

Journal Exercise 10a: Acknowledging Your Negative Intentions

Answer the following questions to assess your negative intentions toward your transgressor. As you think about these negative behaviors, you may want to refer back to the journal exercise "Acknowledging Your Emotions and Feelings."

1. What negative intentions do you have toward the wrongdoer?	Check all that you are experiencing toward your transgressor	
	❏ Retaliation ❏ Revenge ❏ Indifference ❏ Estrangement ❏ Verbal aggression ❏ Promoting justice ❏ Demanding restitution ❏ Mercilessness ❏ Demanding an apology ❏ Find the bad guy ❏ Protesting	❏ Resentment ❏ Negative judgment ❏ Hostility ❏ Bitterness ❏ Hatred ❏ Anger ❏ Fearfulness ❏ Holding grudges ❏ Envy ❏ Avoidance
2. What would be the results if you were to carry out these negative intentions?		
3. Do you believe that taking these actions would reduce your stress?		

Journal Exercise 10b: Acknowledging Your Rumination

In column 1, make a chronological list of the facts of what happened when your transgressor committed the offense. The facts are descriptions that you would see if you had videotaped the offense. List each fact separately. Then, in column 2, describe how you would use those facts to tell the story to someone else. Any other information that may help others to understand your narrative should be listed in column 3.

List the facts—what a video camera would see if it were recording the transgression	How would you tell the story about the offense based on the facts?	What other information would help you understand these observations better?
1.		
2.		
3.		
4.		

Journal Exercise 10c: Reducing Unforgiveness

Read the statements below and put a check mark beside those that describe your efforts to reduce your unforgiveness. Next, rate each on this scale: 1 = not like me; 2 = a little like me; 3 = a lot like me.

❐ Comparing yourself to your offender to show that you are better, righter, or stronger.	[1] [2] [3]
❐ Rehearsing schemes of revenge in your mind.	[1] [2] [3]
❐ Entertaining thoughts of life being unkind to the offender.	[1] [2] [3]
❐ Telling numerous people about the rotten character of the offender.	[1] [2] [3]
❐ Mentioning the offense to people who are not involved.	[1] [2] [3]
❐ Doing unto the wrongdoer as he or she has done unto you.	[1] [2] [3]
❐ Ruminating on the offense to avoid the hard work of addressing the hurt productively.	[1] [2] [3]
❐ Demanding an apology, justice, and atonement.	[1] [2] [3]
❐ Ignoring the offense and acting as if it did not happen.	[1] [2] [3]
❐ Excusing the behavior and letting the transgressor off the hook.	[1] [2] [3]

Journal Exercise 10d: My State of Unforgiveness

In the space below, write a letter to your transgressor, a letter that no one will see except you. In it, tell the transgressor the things indicated by the writing prompts.

Dear _____,

I want you to know that you hurt me when you …

The way I see it, what happened was …

Because of this hurt, I have been feeling …

How I would really like to resolve this matter is to …

Chapter 2 Summary

This chapter focuses on the first step in taking action: acknowledging the transgression. We noted several key points:

- Transgressions against us make us feel threatened. When we feel threatened, we develop thoughts of taking negative actions toward the offender, which begins the process of unforgiveness.
- Our negative thoughts often arise from our rules of how we think the world should be, yet we cannot enforce these expectations on others.
- Our negative thoughts give rise to negative intentions toward the transgressor, resulting in rumination, thinking about the offense over and over until we create a story about what happened and how it is unjust.
- Rumination leads to feelings of unforgiveness, which is a combination of our fabricated story about the transgression and what we think must be done to fix the situation.

  We examined the following concepts:

  - emotions (the body's physical reactions to threats) and feelings (which arise after thought)
  - types of anger (aggressive, passive-aggressive, and assertive)
  - types of coping (problem-solving, emotion-focused, and meaning-focused).

In the journal exercises, you assessed the following:

- your GPS (godly perspective on the situation)
- the degree of the transgression
- your anger temperament
- your emotions and feelings
- your unenforceable rules
- the ways in which you are trying to cope with unforgiveness.

  I appeal to you therefore, brothers, by the mercies of God, to present your bodies as a living sacrifice, holy and acceptable to God, which is your spiritual worship. Do not be conformed to this world, but be transformed by the renewal of your mind, that by testing you may discern what is the will of God, what is good and acceptable and perfect. For by the grace given to me I say to everyone among you not to think of himself more highly than he ought to think, but to think with sober judgment, each according to the measure of faith that God has assigned. (Romans 12:1–3)

Devotional Prayer

Dear Father in Heaven,

In response to Your many mercies to me, I want to present myself to You as a holy and acceptable sacrifice. To do so, I must ensure that my thoughts no longer conform to the ways of this world. Please help me, Lord God, to release ungodly thoughts about _____, particularly my intentions toward him or her to say or do ... [add your description(s) here].

Instead, Father, please help my thoughts about _____ to be good and acceptable. Turn them into thoughts of how I can show empathy, compassion, and gentleness to [the transgressor] by ... [list your ideas here].

Finally, Father, please help me not to think too highly of myself but to use sober judgment, especially as I consider whether I have been trapped in a vicious cycle of unforgiveness toward _____.

Lord God, I love You, and I want my thoughts and my actions to please You.

In Jesus's name, amen.

Chapter 2 Endnotes

1   I will not go into the theology of whether or not God brings illness and pain upon His children.

2   E. Worthington, "The Pyramid Model of Forgiveness: Some Interdisciplinary Speculations about Unforgiveness and the Promotion of Forgiveness," in *Dimensions of Forgiveness: Psychological Research and Theological Perspectives*, ed. Everett Worthington Jr. (Philadelphia: Templeton Foundation, 1998), pp. 114–18.

3   Matthew 18:15–18.

4   R. D. Enright and C. T. Coyle, "Researching the Process Model of Forgiveness within Psychological Interventions," in *Dimensions of Forgiveness*, p. 157; E. L. Worthington Jr., *Forgiveness and Reconciliation: Theory and Application* (New York: Routledge, 2006), pp. 58–60.

5   F. Luskin, *Forgive for Good: A Proven Prescription for Health and Happiness* (New York: HarperCollins, 2002), p. 125.

6   E. L. Worthington, *Steps to Reach Forgiveness and to Reconcile* (Boston: Pearson Custom, 2008), pp. 23–30.

7   B. B. Caza and A. Wrzesniewski, "How Work Shapes Well-Being," in *The Oxford Handbook of Happiness*, eds. I. Boniwell and A. C. Ayer (Oxford: Oxford University Press, 2014), p. 694.

8   Matthew 5:2–11; Luke 6:20–22

9   G. A. Buttrick, T. S. Kepler, J. Knox, H. G. May, S. Terrien, and E. S. Bucke, *The Interpreter's Dictionary of the Bible: An Illustrated Encyclopedia* (Nashville, TN: Abingdon, 1962), p. 445.

10 H. D. Betz, *The Sermon on the Mount: A Critical and Historical Commentary on the Bible* (Minneapolis: Fortress, 1995), p. 97. The role of the beatitudes in our well-being is discussed more in chapter 6.

11 Galatians 5:22–23.

12 John 14:25–27.

13 F. Luskin, Forgive for Good Workshop, Ann Arbor, MI, 2016; C. Tavris, *Anger: The Misunderstood Emotion* (New York: Touchstone, 1982), p. 49.

14 Worthington, *Forgiveness and Reconciliation*, pp. 35–36.

15 Ibid., pp. 7–8.

16 Matthew 7:12.

17 B. Van der Kolk, *The Body Keeps the Score: Brain, Mind, and Body in the Healing of Trauma* (New York: Penguin, 2014), pp. 54–62; J. Orloff, *Emotional Freedom: Liberate Yourself from Negative Emotions and Transform Your Life* (New York: Harmony Books, 2009), p. 35.

18 Tavris, *Anger: The Misunderstood Emotion*, pp. 91–100.

19 R. Lazarus and B. Lazarus, *Passion and Reason* (Oxford: Oxford University Press, 1994), pp. 5–10.

20 For our purposes, we are considering fear from the perspective of unforgiveness. For a more detailed description of how to combat fear, see J. Orloff, *Emotional Freedom*, pp. 145–72.

21 Ephesians 4:26.

22 Ibid.

23 Hebrews 4:15; 2 Corinthians 5:21.

24 Mark 3:1–6.

25 Mark 11:15–17.

26 Matthew 23:23–33.

27 Mark 3:5.

28 Luke 19:47.

29 Ephesians 4:26–27.

30 J. M. Gottman, *The Seven Principles for Making Marriage Work* (London: Orion House, 2000).

31 Romans 12:18.

32 Romans 12:19.

33 Matthew 5:14–16; 2 Corinthians 4:4–6.

34 Luke 9:5.

35 F. Luskin, *Forgive for Good* (New York: HarperCollins, 2002), pp. 49–51; P. F. Cioni, "Forgiveness, Cognitive Restructuring, and Object Transformation," *Journal of Religion and Health* 46, no. 3 (2006): 386.

36 S. Johnson, *Hold Me Tight: Seven Conversations for a Lifetime of Love* (New York: Little Brown and Co., 2008).

37 The Young Woman, Old Woman Ambiguous Figure (also known as My Wife and My Mother-in-Law) was created by an anonymous illustrator in late nineteenth-century Germany and was reproduced on a postcard. William Ely Hill (1887–1962), a British cartoonist, produced a later, well-known version. The later, well-known version was first published in the magazine *Puck* in 1915 (W. E. Hill, "My Wife and My Mother-in-Law [Puck, Puck Press, 1915]).

38   In this chapter, we will work on acknowledging *what* coping is in order to assess how you are coping with your transgression. We will address *how* we cope in chapter 4.

39   E. Worthington, *Forgiveness and Reconciliation*, p. 63.

40   R. L. Weiss and M. C. Cerreto, "Development of a Measure of Dissolution Potential," *American Journal of Family Therapy* 8 (1980): 80–85.

41   You worked on observation and assessment of the effects of your transgression on days 7 and 8.

42   R. Lazarus and S. Folkman, *Stress, Appraisal, and Coping* (New York: Springer, 1984), pp. 142–43.

43   Worthington, *Forgiveness and Reconciliation*, pp. 50–53.

44   J. Haidt, *The Happiness Hypothesis: Finding Modern Truth in Ancient Wisdom* (New York: Basic Books, 2006), p. 146.

45   Ben-Zur, "Coping Styles and Affect," *International Journal of Stress Management* 16, no. 2 (May 2009): 87–101.

46   E. Worthington and S. Sandage, *Forgiveness and Spirituality in Psychotherapy: A Relational Approach* (Washington, DC: American Psychological Association, 2015), p. 28.

47   S. Folkman and R. S. Lazarus, "An Analysis of Coping in a Middle-Aged Community Sample," *Journal of Health and Social Behavior* 21 (1980): 219–39.

48   C. J. Holahan and R. H. Moos, "Risk, Resistance, and Psychological Distress: A Longitudinal Analysis with Adults and Children," *Journal of Abnormal Psychology* 96 (1987): 3–13.

49   G. L. Jones, *Embodying Forgiveness: A Theological Analysis* (Grand Rapids, MI: Eerdmans, 1995), p. 163.

50   R. D. Enright, *Forgiveness Is a Choice: A Step-by-Step Process for Resolving Anger and Restoring Hope* (Washington, DC: American Psychological Association, 2001), pp. 93–100.

51   More about coping in chapter 4.

52   Adapted from Everett Worthington Jr.'s workbook *The Path to Forgiveness: Six Practical Sections for Becoming a More Forgiving Person*, pp. 27–28. See his website at http://www.evworthington-forgiveness.com/.

53   Galatians 6:1–2.

54   Proverbs 22:24.

55   Proverbs 17:15, 24:24–25; Matthew 18:15–17.

56   This was discussed in chapter 1. See those footnotes for scripture references.

57   Genesis 50:17.

58   Genesis 33:4–17.

59   Romans 12:20–21.

60   Proverbs 15:4, 14, 16:24; Matthew 5:5–7; Romans 12:17–18.

61   Proverbs 20:22; Matthew 7:12; 1 Thessalonians 5:15.

62   Proverbs; 21:21 24:17–18; Ephesians 4:2–3.

63   Worthington, *Steps to Reach Forgiveness and to Reconcile*, pp. 23–30). See also Enright, *Forgiveness Is a Choice*.

64   R. D. Enright and R. Fitzgibbons, *Forgiveness Therapy: An Empirical Guide for Resolving Anger and Restoring Hope* (Washington, DC: American Psychological Association), pp. 35–36.

65   E. Worthington, ed., *Handbook of Forgiveness* (New York: Routledge, 2005), pp. 4, 247.

66   Worthington, *Forgiveness and Spirituality in Psychotherapy*.

67   Worthington, *Dimensions of Forgiveness*, pp. 114–18.

CHAPTER 3

Commitment to Forgive

Then Peter came up and said to him, "Lord, how often will my brother sin against me, and I forgive him? As many as seven times?" Jesus said to him, "I do not say to you seven times, but seventy times seven."

—MATTHEW 18:21–22

DAY 11

Why Commitment Is Critical—Introduction

In chapter 1, we talked about why forgiveness is a good idea. Chapter 2 helped you to acknowledge the effects of the transgression on you. In this chapter, we will explore why making a commitment to *try* to forgive is an important step toward achieving the long-term goal of emotional well-being. In our ACTION model, this chapter addresses C, committing. Forgiveness follows the act of making a commitment to try to forgive,[1] which means trying to replace unforgiving thoughts with positive, prosocial thoughts and trying to see the transgression from a godly perspective. Go through the following checklist to get an idea of what this chapter will focus on and to assess your readiness to proceed.

Forgiveness Step 2: Committing to Trying to Forgive

Things that inhibit one from committing to trying to forgive the transgression

Number the following inhibitors (1–10) from the most (1) to the least (10) like you.

_____ I do not like the person who transgressed against me.

_____ I cannot forgive a friend for just anything.

_____ I will keep as much distance between me and the transgressor as possible.

_____ I teach him or her a lesson by not acting in the same way I did before he or she hurt me.

_____ I will not try to forgive, even when the person feels guilty for what he or she did, until he or she apologizes.

_____ I will live as if he or she does not exist or is not around.

_____ I believe there are some things I could never forgive anyone, even a loved one.

_____	I rehearse schemes of revenge in my mind.
_____	I try to let the transgressor's behavior roll off my back and get on with life.
_____	I tell numerous people about the rotten character of the offender.

This list outlines a few typical responses toward a person who has hurt us. While any of these actions may make you feel good temporarily, your probability of reaching long-term emotional peace is very small if you continue in this vein.

When we are hurt or offended, our emotions and feelings lead us to determine whether the transgression violates cherished rules about how the world should treat us. We experience an alert from our emotions and feelings to the stress caused by the transgression. At this point, we have three choices:

1. **Active positive coping.** We can try to resolve the offense by actively coping through positive, assertive means such as problem-solving, regulating our emotional response, or rethinking what the transgression means to us. When we are able to cope with the offense, we sidestep entering a state of forgiveness.

2. **Ruminating.** When we are not able to cope with an offense, we may begin to ruminate about how we have been treated, which leads to a vicious cycle of negative intentions and unforgiveness. We can attempt to reduce our unforgiveness by seeking justice or fairness and by responding to the transgressor in nonforgiving ways such as revenge, avoidance, or making demands of him or her. All these actions fuel the vicious cycle of unforgiveness. The unforgiveness cycle is an unbalanced state of mind that harms our well-being, our relationships with others, and our relationship with God.

3. **Forgiveness.** When we are not able to cope effectively, we can avoid the cycle of rumination and unforgiveness by letting go of our right to act upon our negative intentions toward the offender. When we commit to trying to forgive, which includes nurturing empathy and beneficence toward our transgressor, forgiveness can follow. Forgiveness leads to an internal state of peace and balance, which paves a path to physical, spiritual, social, and emotional well-being.

It is common to believe that the only way to regain peace of mind is to require something of the transgressor: an apology, restitution, punishment, repentance, etc. Resolving unforgiveness, however, requires nothing from the transgressor. Forgiveness is an internal process that requires only a change of mind and heart on the part of the victim. In the ideal situation, a transgressor is available and is willing to work with you to reach a peaceful state. But this is more closely akin to reconciliation than forgiveness. In reality, transgressors are often not willing to admit their wrongdoing or to work with the person they hurt to reach a satisfying and amiable solution. Approaching transgressors to let them know they must perform some act that you require of them may even leave you feeling worse. In cases where a transgressor has died or is otherwise no longer available, many of the common ways of coping with a transgression are not possible.

In order to pursue emotional freedom through forgiveness, we must short-circuit our negative intentions toward the person who hurt us with a conscious decision to cope with the offense internally in a positive way. When we decide to forgive, we replace negative intentions and rumination with empathy, beneficence, and love. These positive intentions, however, do not necessarily require that we interact with the offender, except in two situations: when we desire reconciliation and when we actively seek to reflect the love of Christ for the offender. This brings us to the next step of making a commitment to try to forgive the offender. In this chapter we will review the following points:

Day 11: Why Commitment Is Critical—Introduction
Day 12: Alternatives to Trying to Forgive
Day 13: Justice, Fairness, and Safety
Day 14: What Forgiveness Looks Like
Day 15: Commitment to Trying to Forgive

Before continuing on to day 11, take a few moments to meditate on this prayer:

Lord Jesus, soften my heart so I may be willing to try to make a commitment to forgive people who have transgressed against me.

Help me recognize the thoughts that inhibit my ability to see the transgression from Your perspective.

Send Your Spirit to fill me with Your love and compassion and to find refuge and comfort in knowing You are my fortress and strength.

I ask these things in Your name, amen.

Forgiveness Is Critical for Emotional Peace

Before we talk further about making a commitment to trying to forgive, let's revisit what we mean by forgiveness and the reasons for forgiveness that we covered in chapter 1. First, we discussed how God expects us to forgive. In some cases, Christians are also required to reconcile with fellow believers, even though the two processes are not dependent on each other. We also talked about the need to forgive enemies and people who are not fellow Christians. Furthermore, forgiveness is required if we are to have a deeper relationship with God. However, going through the motions and forgiving out of a sense of duty is not likely to reap the ultimate benefits of peace of mind and positive well-being. (In chapter 5, we will work on forgiving out of a sense of love rather than a sense of duty.) The following statements summarize some benefits of forgiveness:

- Forgiveness is a way to express concern for the eternal welfare of others.
- Forgiveness is a stepping-stone to living peacefully with others.
- Forgiveness releases us from negative thoughts that hold us captive.
- Forgiveness leads to physical and mental health benefits.
- Forgiveness builds a deeper relationship with God.

In the journal entry on day 3, other reasons to forgive were suggested:

- a desire to begin to reconcile one's relationship with the offender
- to be able to stop thinking about the situation
- to be relieved from feelings of hurt
- to experience peace of mind and put the matter in the past
- reasons of a more personal nature.

Biblical Reasons to Forgive

When we do not short-circuit the vicious cycle of unforgiveness, we are yielding to the temptation to disobey our Lord's commandment to forgive,[2] and in doing so, we separate ourselves from an intimate relationship with God. When we do not commit to trying to forgive, we are not following Christ's principles. Without His abiding light in us, we follow the works of the flesh and walk in the darkness of this world. When we walk in darkness, we ultimately harm our well-being, the well-being of the offender, and in some cases, the well-being of others.

By forgiving others, we walk in the light of Christ's love and enjoy a more intimate relationship with the Father. Jesus said that He is the light of the world;[3] as imitators of Christ,[4] we reflect His light to the world.[5] One way we reflect His light is through an overt or covert love for others. Forgiveness is an outward and inward expression of Christ's love for us.[6] Our desire to forgive others springs from God's forgiveness of us, which is a reflection of His love for us.[7] Christ clearly stated that our relationship with God is affected by our willingness to forgive those who have wronged us. The apostle Paul encourages us to show love through the absence of vengeance,[8] not repaying evil with evil,[9] and living peacefully with others.[10] When we transform and renew our minds by loving and forgiving others, we transform our relationship with God.[11]

Transgressions against us may bring suffering but forgiving others despite our suffering brings comfort to us and potentially to our transgressors. Forgiveness of others demonstrates our joy in the grace and mercy Christ has shown us for our shortcomings. It also demonstrates that same grace and mercy to another. In some cases, our reflection of God's mercy may influence a wrongdoer to come to know Christ as Savior. In other words, forgiveness is a type of mission work. All Christians can use forgiveness to advance the kingdom of God, acting as missionaries to the people around them.[12]

Paul had some specific ideas about what love is. He penned the well-known chapter on love in his first letter to the church at Corinth. He describes love as being patient, kind, not envious or boastful, and not arrogant or rude. Love does not insist on its own way and is not irritable or resentful. It does not rejoice at wrongdoing but rejoices in the truth. Love bears the burden of a transgression, hopes and believes that forgiveness will reflect Christ's light, and endures the long process of demonstrating forgiveness to an offender.[13] If Paul were writing this book now, he might also say that love forgives all things.

Jesus proposed this same idea when He was asked, "What is the greatest commandment?" He replied that we are to love the Lord our God with all our hearts, souls, and minds and to love our neighbor as ourselves.[14] Unforgiveness cannot exist where there is love; the two are mutually exclusive.

When we choose unforgiveness, we reject Christ's teachings, which puts us in jeopardy of never reaching the joy of emotional peace and well-being that God desires for us. In Paul's letter to the churches of Galatia, he enumerates both internal and external sins and contrasts the sinful life to life in Christ:

Now the works of the flesh are evident: sexual immorality, impurity, sensuality, idolatry, sorcery, enmity, strife, jealousy, fits of anger, rivalries, dissensions, divisions, envy, drunkenness, orgies, and things like these. I warn you, as I warned you before, that those who do such things will not inherit the kingdom of God.

But the fruit of the Spirit is love, joy, peace, patience, kindness, goodness, faithfulness, gentleness, self-control; against such things there is no law. And those who belong to Christ Jesus have crucified the flesh with its passions and desires.[15]

Deciding to forgive is counterintuitive to our desire to protect ourselves from harm; it is deciding to put on a new self. As we avoid the works of the flesh and put on the new self, we practice spiritual maturity, which comes through prayer, fellowship, meditation, and study of the Word.[16] As we grow in our spiritual maturity, our behavior toward others changes to reflect Christlikeness, which sows seeds of kindness; in return, we reap blessings from God.[17]

Put on then, as God's chosen ones, holy and beloved, compassion, kindness, humility, meekness, and patience, bearing with one another and, if one has a complaint against another, forgiving each other. As the Lord has forgiven you, so you also must forgive. And above all these put on love, which binds everything together in perfect harmony. And let the peace of Christ rule in your hearts, to which indeed you were called in one body. And be thankful. Let the word of Christ dwell in you richly, teaching and admonishing one another in all wisdom, singing psalms and hymns and spiritual songs, with thankfulness in your hearts to God. And whatever you do, in word or deed, do everything in the name of the Lord Jesus, giving thanks to God the Father through him.[18]

Forgiveness allows us to put away the desire to harm another and to sow compassion, kindness, humility, patience, and tolerance, restoring harmony in a Christlike way. When we sow these character traits in ourselves and introduce them to the hearts of others, we reap love, which is manifested in our lives as joy, peace, patience, kindness, goodness, faithfulness, gentleness, and self-control. These qualities are the fruit that blossom from the Holy Spirit living within us.[19] Acting with a Christlike heart, we teach others by our example about the love, grace, and mercy shown us by God as we exhibit the grace and mercy of God. Forgiving others, when it is done in the name of God, is not a burden but an opportunity for joyfulness and thankfulness.

Varieties of Forgiveness Situations

You may not feel ready to forgive yet. That's understandable. Forgiveness is a process that takes time, and everyone moves through the process at a different speed. In addition, people can forgive in multiple situations, such as the following:[20]

- Forgiving a *transgressor* who is an ongoing part of your life. Forgiving such a person can be a stepping-stone to reconciliation, but this can be difficult because continued contact with your transgressor repeatedly reminds you of the offense or may open up the possibility of repeat encounters of the same or similar transgressions.
- Forgiving an *absent transgressor*, someone who has died, has moved away, or is not a regular part of your daily life. Forgiving an absent transgressor also has challenges.
- Forgiveness of *oneself*, which is needed when you are consumed by negative feelings toward another person such as guilt, remorse, shame, or disappointment. In this situation, letting go of your past misdeeds lubricates your ability to forgive others.
- Forgiving *God*, which may be necessary when you believe that God has let you down or has not met your expectations.
- Forgiving a *nonspecific transgression*, which is for cases where no single person or event is responsible for an offense. It may be related to such experiences as general abuses in one's childhood (e.g., from other children) or an unjust penalty from civic authorities.[21]

Kenneth Pargament and Mark Rye, two behavioral researchers, provide a framework for thinking about forgiveness.[22] They have found that forgiveness is a way of responding to stressors. Stress occurs when a set of circumstances alerts our bodies to deal with a situation by escaping, fighting back, or freezing. Stress can trigger emotions of anger, fear, anxiety, or worry. How we cope with these emotions determines whether our stress level is high or low. We can better cope with stressors by transforming our thinking. For example, here are a few strategies:

- looking at the transgression from different points of view
- realizing the transgressor is human and capable of making a mistake or performing a hurtful action, just as we all are
- showing empathy or compassion for the transgressor (but not for his or her behavior) by trying to understand what makes him or her tick
- reappraising the situation to determine whether it was actually intended as a transgression or whether one's perception is based on misperception, misinformation, or similar past experiences
- facilitating resolution by interacting with the transgressor, such as checking for understanding, negotiating a solution, or educating him or her.

Initially, these coping strategies may seem ridiculous. After all, you are the victim, and someone stepped out of line by committing a transgression against you. If you are the victim of a life-altering injustice, the very thought of offering your persecutor compassion, beneficence, empathy, and love may seem absurd. Thinking this way is natural, and finding peace, especially while dealing with rumination and unforgiveness, takes time. Forgiveness starts with acknowledging the way the transgression has affected you, followed by a decision to try to forgive; however, trying may be all you are ever able to do. Forgiveness is a journey that takes time, not time to forget, but time to reprogram your mind to reduce, or eliminate, feelings of bitterness and the desire to seek vengeance. In some cases, the transgression is so heinous that you simply cannot forgive, and the suggestion of forgiving seems like a transgression in itself, such as indicated in the following story told by Corrie ten Boom in her book *The Hiding Place*.[23]

Forgiveness: A Difficult Journey

Corrie ten Boom, along with all her family, was imprisoned by the Nazis at the Ravensbrück concentration camp during the Second World War. Her family was treated with brutality and were ultimately killed during their incarceration. Corrie, however, survived and was eventually released to freedom.

After her release, Corrie became a disciple of Christ and forgave her transgressors. She traveled from place to place to speak about her experience with God's love and forgiveness. At one of those speaking events, she was approached by a former prison guard who had treated her and her sister brutally. The man extended his hand and thanked Corrie for her talk about forgiveness of sins, telling her that he was glad to know that he had been forgiven by God for his crimes. He said to her, "I have become a Christian, and I know that God has forgiven me for the cruel things I did [at Ravensbrück], but I would like to hear it from your lips as well. Fräulein, will you forgive me?" Corrie froze in a rush of thoughts; a coldness clutched her heart. She knew she had to forgive, but how could she? The cruel and unspeakable things she had witnessed this man do seemed beyond the scope of what was forgivable. In that moment, she turned to God and silently cried out, *God I cannot forgive. Help me in my unforgiveness.* The book records her thoughts:

> *"Jesus, help me!" I prayed silently. "I can lift my hand. I can do that much. You supply the feeling." And so woodenly, mechanically, I thrust my hand into the one stretched out to me. And as I did, an incredible thing took place. The current started in my shoulder, raced down my arm, sprang into our joined hands. And then this healing warmth seemed to flood my whole being, bringing tears to my eyes.*
>
> *"I forgive you, brother!" I cried. "With all my heart!"*[24]

Despite our resistance, God always meets us where we are, moves us where He wants us to be, and loves us throughout the process.[25] In a time of regret, pain, emotion, and fear, we can reach out to our God for help. But why would we? As explained in chapter 1, Jesus wants everyone to be saved and to know the grace and mercy of God. Jesus demonstrated that grace and mercy on the cross when He was more concerned about the salvation of the criminal next to him and the sins of His persecutors than His own situation. He wants us to follow in His footsteps because *forgiveness is our attempt to play a role in God's plan of salvation for others by sowing seeds of love and mercy.*

As stated earlier, forgiveness should not be confused with reconciliation. Yes, people have forgiven murderers who took the life of a family member. Such people have gone to the prison to attend to the murder's spiritual needs. The Old Testament also has examples of reconciliation without mention of forgiveness, such as the case of Joseph reconciling with his brothers[26] and Jacob reconciling with Esau.[27] Forgiveness, however, does not require personal contact with the person you are forgiving. Rather, forgiveness is an internal journey to benefit you and sometimes the offender, if he or she is available and willing. Over time, you can learn to think about your offender from a perspective that is larger than the offense. After all, is not the person more than one act? Hating the offense does not mean we have to hate the offender. Forgiveness sows spiritual seeds for shade trees under which you and your transgressor may one day sit.

Let's expand on your readiness to try to forgive. In the following journal exercise, you will once again (as you did in chapter 1) gauge your readiness for forgiveness:

Journal Exercise 11: Readiness to Forgive

Go back to the journal exercise earlier in chapter 1 and review your readiness for the three types of forgiveness. Use the prompts below to write a letter to yourself describing your readiness (or lack of readiness) to forgive. Be honest with yourself. This exercise is for *your* journey and will help you along the way. Unless you wish to share it, it is for your eyes only.

I acknowledge that my unforgiveness is triggering feelings of …

Forgiving my offender will lead me to feel …

I have great [difficulty] / [optimism] with the idea of trying to commit to forgive because …

I [do] / [do not] feel that I am ready to forgive. So my next step is to …

DAY 12

Alternatives to Trying to Forgive

Coping with the stress produced by our emotional response to a transgression is a key to avoiding unforgiveness, but there are alternatives to committing to trying to forgive a transgressor. When we fail to cope with the stress of a transgression, we resort to the vicious cycle of ruminating over the story of the transgression, which leads to unforgiveness. Yet even when we are stuck in this vicious cycle, we have the choice to seek forgiveness or seek ways to reduce our unforgiveness. We will talk about some of the positive coping strategies in chapter 4; here we will talk about the coping strategy of reducing unforgiveness.

As explained in chapter 2, reducing unforgiveness and promoting forgiveness are not the same thing. We attempt to reduce unforgiveness in two ways: by seeking justice or by developing negative intentions. We will talk about seeking justice in the section on day 17. For now, we will look at how acting on our negative intentions is not forgiveness but is something that only helps to *reduce* our unforgiveness.

Seventeen Negative Responses

Unforgiveness is created when we think about negative ways to respond to a transgressor or ways that we want to see a transgressor treated. Thinking about insisting on an apology, seeking restitution, exacting revenge, or treating the transgressor as he or she treated us is an act of mental gymnastics. These thoughts rattle around in our heads as we attempt to cope with the transgression. The thought process of mulling over how we want to treat our transgressor is what produces an emotional state of unforgiveness. Unforgiveness is a state of thinking about how we will respond to an offender if given an opportunity to take action. Taking action on our negative intentions, however, does not bring the long-term emotional peace that comes with forgiveness. In fact, acting on our negative thoughts will often make matters worse.

The following list describes the kinds of negative thoughts that, if acted upon, may reduce how unforgiving we feel, but they are not thoughts that will prompt the lasting emotional peace that comes from forgiveness. The first eight are thoughts directed outward toward the transgressor as displays of punishment. The second nine are thoughts directed inward that fuel our painful emotions and feelings. While ruminating on all these negative intentions may help us cope temporarily with the transgression, in the final analysis they are unsatisfactory since they serve to launch us into a vicious cycle of rumination that prolongs our pain and suffering.

Negative thoughts directed outward toward our offenders:

1. *Retaliation*
   Thoughts about taking action to harm others in return for how they harmed you.

2. *Revenge*
   Thinking about taking action to repay someone with the same (or worse) harmful act that was committed against you.

3. *Indifference*
   Thinking about treating offenders as if what they did does not matter and that they are too unimportant to make a difference in how you feel.

4. *Estrangement*
   Thinking about attempting to eliminate contact with offenders and considering disregarding their attempts to reconnect.

5. *Verbal aggression*
   Rehearsing verbally lashing out toward offenders with offensive or hurtful words, seeking to make them feel bad for their offenses.

6. *Demanding restitution*
   Planning to withhold some resource or relationship previously available to transgressors until they restore what was lost or damaged because of their transgressions.

7. *Mercilessness*
   Thinking about applying the results of negative intentions without regard for how they affect the transgressor.

8. *Demanding an apology*
   Deciding that requiring the transgressor to apologize will make things right and help you feel less unforgiving.

Negative thoughts directed inward:

9. *Resentment*
   Harboring bitter anger or annoyance at having been treated unjustly or unfairly.

10. *Negative judgment*
    Convincing yourself that a transgressor's behavior violates some commonly accepted norm or rule without considering all the facts.

11. *Hostility*
    Formulating and rehearsing thoughts about physical or verbal aggression toward a transgressor.

12. *Bitterness*
    Holding on to negative feelings toward a transgressor despite attempted resolution on his or her part.

13. *Hatred*
    An intense dislike and disdain for a transgressor that may trigger an extreme rumination of negative intentions and aggressive reactions to the offense.

14. *Anger*
    A strong feeling of annoyance, displeasure, or hostility directed toward a transgressor that results in a desire to respond in a negative way.

15. *Fearfulness*
    An intense concern that something harmful will happen to you unless measures are taken to stop the course of events.

16. *Grudges*
    An ongoing feeling of dislike, distrust, or disdain for a transgressor.

17. *Envy*
    Desire for another's possessions that are not available to you, but you feel they should be.

While these ways of thinking may make you feel better briefly, they do not improve your overall sense of well-being. They create a state of anticipation for an opportunity to act on these thoughts; then the anticipation fuels a contaminated story about transgressors that leads down a dark path. Punishment or thinking negatively about your offender brings its own set of problems. When you punish your offender, you cripple your own feelings of empathy and make it difficult, if not impossible, to unlock the door to emotional freedom. Acting on your negative intentions may also backfire by offending your own sense of morality and/or triggering fear of the offender's retaliation toward you. Most importantly, harboring these negative intentions and acting on them grieves the Holy Spirit and distances you from God.[28]

When we ruminate about responding negatively toward an offender, we enter a vicious cycle of awfulizing and demonizing the transgressor. Once we place labels on our transgressors, describing (in our own minds or to others) how terrible they are, it is nearly impossible to shift from negative to positive thoughts about them. As mentioned, these repeating thoughts fuel the vicious cycle of rumination and may lead us to take actions that we later regret. Obsession with getting satisfaction can also lead to depression and/or anxiety and, ultimately, may wreak havoc on our health. When satisfaction does not come quickly enough, we may even become obsessed with trying to intervene to make justice, fairness, or safety happen sooner. These seventeen forms of non-forgiving responses are most likely motivated by one of four reasons:

1. **Vindication**
   "I, the offended one, am not to blame because the transgressor deserves what is coming to him or her: an equal (or greater) share of the pain that was inflicted on me. Then the scales of injustice or unfairness will be balanced."

2. **A lesson has been served**
   "Transgressors need to know that they cannot treat people this way, so I am going to teach a lesson for their own good."

3. **Safety from future episodes**
   "How I treat my transgressors will prevent them from committing the same infraction toward me or others in the future."

4. **Reduced anger and resentment**
   If I get my feelings of anger or resentment off my chest, I will feel relieved.

Journal Exercise 12: Motivations for Unforgiveness

Have you thought about any of these seventeen negative responses? What motivates you to consider these responses? In the list below, place a check next to the statements that apply to you:

Motivations for Not Forgiving

- ☐ Vindication
- ☐ A lesson has been served
- ☐ Safety from future repeat episodes
- ☐ Reduce anger and resentment

Rate Your Current Motivations:

- ☐ I am not thinking of any of these behaviors.
- ☐ Some of these behaviors appeal to me (the ones checked, above.)
- ☐ I have already done some of these things and feel good about it. (Put a + in front of those motivations.)
- ☐ I have already done some of these things and feel bad about it. (Put an *x* in front of those motivations.)

I would like to do some of these things, but I am holding back because:

- ☐ I tend to feel bad when I see others in pain.
- ☐ It challenges my sense of morality.
- ☐ I fear that the other person will retaliate.
- ☐ Truthfully, these behaviors are not something I would seriously think of doing.

What is your motivation for how you would like to respond?	How do you see the situation playing out if you act on your negative intentions?
Vindication	
To teach the other person a lesson	
To ensure safety from future episodes	
To have a reduced amount of anger and resentment	

DAY 13

Justice, Fairness, and Safety

Not all alternatives to forgiveness are negative. Seeking justice, fairness, and safety from further transgressions may be a positive attempt to hold the transgressor accountable for the offensive behavior. Typically, justice, fairness, and safety go hand in hand with forgiveness, but they are not forgiveness. While justice and fairness are means to reducing unforgiveness, they do not produce the peace of mind that comes with forgiveness. Additionally, they can become negative if we become obsessed with thoughts of bringing the transgressor to justice.

What exactly is justice? Why do we sometimes think we will feel better when we know that justice has been served to our transgressor? From our societal perspective, there are two contexts for justice: criminal and civil. Criminal justice applies to people who are found to have committed a crime by breaking some law. Civil justice applies to individuals who have committed a damaging act toward another member of society but have not broken a law. Both contexts set the ground rules for how a transgressor will be treated when found guilty of violating some commonly accepted standard and suffers consequences for the violation.

There are six types of justice:

- Distributive justice seeks to allocate resources equitably among the parties involved in some wrong-doing.
- Retributive justice seeks to mete out punishment that will equalize suffering between victim and transgressor and will demand fair payment for the crime.
- Restorative justice seeks to find equitable and fair solutions by involving victims in determining what action would bring satisfactory change without removing the transgressor from society.
- Procedural justice attempts to specify fair processes for dealing with matters of conflict of potential conflict.

- Social justice movement is one in which a transgression is assessed in light of a socially just world in which human rights is weighed agains equality.
- Revenge and retaliation are actions that seek to get even with a transgressor either by the victim or those sympathetic to the victim's treatment.

While each type of justice is unique, they share some common features. Justice is concerned with the responsibilities of all who are involved in a transgression to restore equality and fair treatment to the victim and transgressor when a wrong doing occurs. Except for revenge, each type of justice involves a dispassionate third party to intervene in sorting out the facts to bring a conclusion to the actions that are to be taken to bring about justice. Our individual feelings of being transgressed against triggers our motivation for justice that often come from a need to protect ourselves, even at the expense of evil reactions toward the transgressor. In other words, seeking justice comes out of our primitive urge for survival.

As individuals, we all develop a spirit of fair treatment very early in life. This early formative perspective is built on what we feel is important to us (our values), what will disrupt our comfort and satisfaction (homeostasis), what is right vs. wrong (our moral compass), and just what makes rational common sense (rational reasoning). We develop a preference for beliefs about how we "should" be treated that formulates a cognitive schema, or a pattern of thinking that becomes imprinted on our minds. While some of our preferences for treatment find their origin in community truth, some preferences for how we are treated are formed at a very personal level. In either case, when we are treated in a way that is in contrast to our preferred way of being, we develop a reaction to execute whatever actions are required to return us to a status quo.

It's important to point out that once we have experienced an in justice, or transgression, we cannot *unexperience* it. Our thoughts and emotions in reaction to our memory of the treatment will be with us always. Attached to those memories is our reaction to the transgression. The intensity of how we reexperience the injustice depends on our perception of the size of the gap between what we see as unjust treatment and what we consider just treatment. The bigger the gap the stronger the justice motive. The perception we have of the injustice gap will influence the amplitude of our anger, bitterness, hostility, and resentment. These feelings and thoughts lead to an intention to respond to the transgression, which we make seek to act upon, or we may merely ruminate on what we would like to do in order to "make things right." I refer to this later as "negative intentions," which are the hurtful ways we intend to respond to a transgression. Responding to a transgressor in a negative way may temporarily reduce our feelings of unforgiveness, negative intentions do not bring the long-term emotional peace forgiveness can.

Michael McCullough, a prominent behavioral scientist who has studied forgiveness behaviors extensively provides this perspective. Revenge might seem appropriate, and restorative, for four reasons: It can balance a moral ledger, it can teach a transgressor a lesson, it can feel good, and it can raise the self-esteem of the punisher.[29]

As Christians, we are not called to reduce our feelings of unforgiveness in revengeful or retaliatory ways. While we cannot reconcile justice and love perfectly, we are called by God to be responsible for trying to bring about God-informed justice without taking ultimate responsibility for justice out of God's hands. While God has instilled His sense of justice in each of us, we are ill-prepared to mete out justice without His help: without the indwelling of the Holy Spirit, which I talk about more extensively later.

Receiving Comfort from Justice

For a number of reasons, we often find comfort in knowing that justice, in either form, has been served to the transgressor. First, justice provides some level of assurance that the transgression will not be repeated toward us or anyone else. Second, justice shows that another entity (society, the court system, or a person who administers consequences for the judgment) cares about our feelings of hurt and pain. Finally, justice reassures us that we are not making up our pain: our suffering is real, acknowledged, and to some extent substantiated.

Finding safety from our transgressors is different from seeking justice and fairness. Wanting our offenders to be prevented from repeating the offense is reasonable and often necessary. When our safety is in jeopardy, it is important to establish boundaries that prevent further exposure to harm. Boundaries are our conditions or rules that limit how and when we interact with another person. Like justice and fairness, however, these boundaries are not an alternative to forgiveness. People in abusive relationships need to find shelter from further abuse, but they can still find emotional peace through an internal state of forgiveness toward their abusers. Later in this chapter we will discuss how boundaries may or may not be expressed to the transgressor.

As explained previously, unfair treatment is treatment that is not equal to what those around us are receiving, or treatment that is not in alignment with what we legitimately deserve. When we receive unfair treatment, we often seek to regain equality with the standards that we are entitled to receive. Once experienced it cannot be unexperienced. Restoring equality may come from a third party making a judgment that confirms the unequal treatment, or it may come from you and your transgressor negotiating to make things right.

We need to keep in mind that *the transgression is not the transgressor*. We might legitimately see a transgression as a malicious attempt to harm us or an attempt by transgressors to protect themselves from some perceived attack. But forgiveness separates transgressors from their behavior in our minds, thus imitating the love of Jesus for all. When we treat transgressors with positive intentions, however, they are not absolved from responsibility for their offenses. Justice and fairness may need to happen despite our willingness to forgive.[30]

David: The Consequence of Offenses

A story involving King David contains a good example of justice and fairness. While David's army was off fighting the enemies of the Hebrew people, David was walking on the outdoor terrace of his palace when he saw a beautiful woman, Bathsheba, bathing on a nearby terrace. She was the wife of Uriah, one of his generals who was away in battle. David sent for her, and when she was brought to him, he had sexual relations with her.

Following his transgression, David learned that Bathsheba was pregnant with his child. In an attempt to cover up his sin, he sent for Uriah to come home, expecting that Uriah would sleep with his wife, making the honorable Uriah believe that the child was his. But Uriah would not take pleasure in the comfort of his home or wife while his men were fighting. To "solve" his problem, David gave secret orders for his men to withdraw from Uriah during battle, which led to Uriah's death.

Nathan, the prophet, confronted David with his sins of adultery and murder, and David repented before God. David took responsibility for Bathsheba by making her one of his wives. Bathsheba lost that child, but eventually God blessed them with Solomon, who became king after David's death.[31] While David is referred to by Paul as a man after God's own heart,[32] he still suffered the consequences of his sin: unremitting conflict in his family and not being allowed to build the temple of God.[33]

Paul tells us that a man reaps what he sows[34] because God holds people accountable for their sins; in fact, God clearly states that He will punish transgressions. Sometimes His punishment is direct, and sometimes punishment comes another way, such as through the judicial system. The question for you, then, is whether you will find comfort in knowing that a transgressor has been brought to justice or has "learned a lesson." Will justice restore your sense of emotional peace? As discussed earlier, we might feel comforted by justice or fairness, but we might instead feel guilt for the transgressor's pain or live in fear of retaliation if the transgressor believes that we are the source of his or her consequences. If we do actually find comfort in knowing that the transgressor received what he or she had coming, that comfort will not restore a sense of peace and well-being. Only forgiveness can do that. Regardless of how we respond to injustice, the transgressor is still another human being whom God values. God wills that none should perish but that all should come to repentance.[35]

Journal Exercise 13a: Justice, Fairness, Safety

Which, if any, of the following do you feel is needed for your transgressor?

☐ Criminal justice, administered by a court of law

☐ Civil justice, administered either by direct restitution or by a court of law

☐ Fairness by restoring a balance of equal treatment to me based on agreed upon or preestablished expectations

☐ Boundaries put in place to ensure that no further harm comes to me

☐ That my transgressor will not benefit from any of these actions

---

Would your pain be relieved if your transgression received the response you checked in the previous list?

1 = no relief; 10 = great relief

[1] [2] [3] [4] [5] [6] [7] [8] [9] [10]

If your transgressor were to receive some sort of justice, what consequences for him or her would help you feel less pain about the transgression?

How do you think your transgressor would react to those consequences?

Journal Exercise 13b: Knowing When You Have Forgiven

Forgiveness is a process, not a onetime event. It is not some priestly incantation that you say as you wave your hand over the transgressor. When we decide that we are going to try to forgive, we are signing up for a journey, and the journey itself is important, not just the end state. In fact, there is a chance that you will never feel 100 percent forgiving of a transgression. Furthermore, forgiveness often ebbs and flows like tides coming in and out. At some point, you may feel that you have achieved forgiveness, but then something reminds you of the transgression, and you must work again to neutralize its effect on you. (We will address how to sustain forgiveness in chapter 7.)

Making a decision *to try* to forgive does not mean *granting* forgiveness; rather, it means you are willing to go through the action steps that may lead to forgiveness. Before we discuss knowing when you have forgiven, let's first assess some statements about forgiveness. What are your thoughts about forgiveness? Rate how much you agree or disagree with each of the following statements:

COMMON IDEAS ABOUT FORGIVENESS	YOUR RATINGS
1 = STRONGLY DISAGREE; 5 = STRONGLY AGREE	
Forgiveness is an emotional reaction to a transgression.	[1] [2] [3] [4] [5]
Forgiveness is an outward action directed at another person.	[1] [2] [3] [4] [5]
Forgiveness is a religious act.	[1] [2] [3] [4] [5]
Forgiveness affects only one's mental state.	[1] [2] [3] [4] [5]
Some people are more capable of forgiving than others.	[1] [2] [3] [4] [5]
Forgiveness means letting the transgressor off the hook.	[1] [2] [3] [4] [5]

Interpreting Your Results

In reality, all the above are misunderstandings about forgiveness. We will review what research shows about each one.

Forgiveness is not an emotional reaction to a transgression. Behavioral scientists have categorized forgiveness into two types: decisional and emotional. Decisional forgiveness is the step in the forgiveness process when an individual commits to trying to forgive someone for an offense.[36] Emotional forgiveness comes sometime after a commitment to forgive has been made, and it involves actions to replace hard, negative emotions with softer, positive ones.[37] The old adage that time heals all wounds will be proved untrue unless one makes a conscious commitment to engage in an intentional process to heal the wounds over time, such as the ACTION process.[38]

Forgiveness is not an outward action directed at another person. The acronym for our forgiveness model is ACTION, yet the only action required is that you walk through the process of discovering that you are more like those who hurt you than different from them.[39] In other words, forgiveness is an action directed inwardly; it benefits the forgiver and is not dependent on the actions of the transgressor.

Forgiveness is not a religious act. Forgiveness can have religious connotations as illustrated by *Forty Days to Forgiveness*, but research shows that nonreligious and spiritual people are more likely to be forgiving than religious people.[40] Forgiveness is taught in disciplines ranging from Buddhism to international relations. While some people visit their clergy for help with forgiveness, others seek the help of counselors. Both can be effective. It would be more accurate to classify forgiveness as a spiritual act.

Forgiveness affects more than one's mental state. Some people think of forgiveness as a mental activity only. However, we also know from research that forgiveness benefits every part of a person's being, including his or her physical, mental, and spiritual health, as well as his or her relationships with others.[41]

Some people may be more naturally forgiving than others, but everyone is capable of forgiving. What we know about forgiveness is that it can be learned.[42] Some people may have a forgiving disposition in the face of offenses, but forgiveness can be learned by anyone.

Forgiveness does not mean letting the transgressor off the hook. We know that excusing a transgression does not result in happiness or a better mood. Turning a blind eye or letting the transgression roll like water off a duck's back may reduce unforgiveness, but it does not relieve emotional pain; it simply hides the pain deep into our repressed minds. In fact, merely excusing a wrong simply increases negative feelings and unforgiveness. When we repress our feelings toward a transgressor, those feelings often become displaced and then negatively influence how we act toward others.

DAY 14

What Forgiveness Looks Like

A commitment to forgive is vitally important as a first step in the forgiveness process. Therefore, understanding the dynamics of what is happening when we try to forgive is helpful.

- **We begin to short-circuit the vicious cycle of negative intentions, rumination, and unforgiveness.** Once negative intentions and rumination begin to formulate repeating stories, forgiving becomes very difficult, particularly when the transgressor is unrepentant. The most critical time to think about forgiveness is when your coping with a transgression is not leading to a positive resolution.

- **We begin to replace negative intentions with positive ones.** When your attempts to cope with a transgression do not bring resolution and you dwell on the negative impact of the transgression, it is important to make a conscious decision to replace negative thoughts with thoughts of tolerance, patience, and benefit of the doubt, and eventually with empathy, beneficence, and love.

- **We set boundaries to avoid repeat offenses.** One question that often arises is, "If I forgive this person [or persons], will I not have to continue my relationship with them?" The simple answer is no. Paul told the church in Rome to live in harmony with everyone "if possible, so far as it depends on you"[43] and to leave vengeance to the Lord.[44] It may not be possible to live in harmony with your transgressor. When you must continue in a relationship with your transgressor, he or she must demonstrate repentance and humility and have a willingness to live in harmony. Although your positive intentions will help you live in harmony, you have no guarantee that the offender will do the same.

- **Accept that an apology is not repentance and is not required.** Another common question is, "What if they apologize and say that they will not do it again? Will I have to continue my relationship with them?" The answer is still no. Forgiving someone does not require you to reconcile the relationship, nor does it condone the actions of the transgressor or absolve him or her of consequences. An apology can be a pseudo-attempt at reconciling; the transgressor may still be unwilling to repent and face the offense in a productive way. A dysfunctional and potentially unsafe response is to try to redeem a relationship with someone who continues the offensive behavior or denies that the transgression occurred.

- **We are more likely to react to our transgressors with mercy.** Christian principles urge us to treat aggressors with kindness and love. This can be done in several ways,[45] with or without the transgressors knowing what we are doing. We can privately pray that God will soften their hearts and that they will repent and restore the relationship. We can change our negative thoughts to positive thoughts, which will be revealed when we cross paths with offenders again, and we can behave in kind and loving ways, repaying evil with good.[46] These are ways that we can reflect the love of Christ for our transgressors.[47] Note that Christian principles do not require that a relationship be reconciled before the kindnesses are extended. If a Christian brother repents, we must forgive.[48] We are told to live in harmony as far as it depends on us. As discussed in chapter 1, in the Jewish culture of Jesus's time, repentance required a display of penance by a transgressor. Similarly, the New Testament passages go far beyond a simple apology and also require demonstrable acts of penance.

- **We open the door for the relationship to be reconciled.** This is a thorny characteristic of forgiveness. In the Old Testament, reconciliation sometimes occurred before forgiveness and, in some cases, instead of forgiveness. However, reconciliation may not be possible if the transgressor is not willing or unavailable, and sometimes reconciliation is not in the interests of the victim's safety. Only you, with the Lord's help, can decide whether reconciliation is possible and desired. On the other hand, reconciliation can be an indicator that you have succeeded in forgiving the offender. It can be the final nail in the coffin of anger, bitterness, and unrest, especially when reconciling is the goal of your efforts to forgive.

To be very clear, I am not suggesting that a commitment to forgive a transgressor requires that you stay in the line of fire for future offenses. Instead, I am suggesting that the offender be separated in your mind from the offense. Although the transgressor is to be forgiven, Christians are *not* required to stay in relationships characterized by abuse and persecution. This is a controversial point. As a counselor and chaplain I have witnessed cases where pastors and clerics have encouraged a partner to stay in a relationship where they are experiencing abusive treatment. By the way, it is not always the wife who experiences the abuse. I have had numerous men who feared for their life, or who were under oppressive power and control treatment. My daughter is a social work for a shelter for intimate partner abuse. She routinely sees men flee with their children seeking asylum from their abuser.

Certainly we are told by Christ to pray for our enemies and do good to those who persecute us.

I believe however, we can do so without continuing to be harmed. I will address this briefly here, but I'll go into greater detail in chapter 4.

In the Gospel of Matthew, as mentioned earlier, Jesus describes what we are to do when a brother in Christ transgresses against us.[49] We first go to the brother and tell him his fault. If he listens (that is, if he repents), then we can reconcile. However, if the brother does not listen, then we are to take one or two others with us to speak to him again. If the offender still refuses to listen, the matter is to be presented to the church. If the brother still does not listen and repent, then we are to treat him as an outsider. These instructions in Matthew make clear that we do not have to continue subjecting ourselves to the hurtful behaviors of others, but before we break ties with offenders, our responsibility as followers of Christ is first to seek resolution with them.

A common question through Christian fellowships is, "Should a spouse stay in a relationship where there is abuse? If the victim forgives the abusing spouse, or if the abusing spouse asks for forgiveness, shouldn't the transgressed spouse be tolerant and forgiving?" The answer is no and yes.[50] That is, the victim can forgive the abuser without tolerating the abuse. From my study of the Word, I believe God does not expect us to stay in relationships where our safety or well-being is threatened or harmed or where we are tempted to sin.[51] The following are some situations where God made provisions for His people to escape abuse:

- The Israelites were in an abusive relationship with Pharaoh. God tormented Pharaoh until he allowed the Israelites to flee the abusive situation.
- Paul was secretly taken out of Damascus in order to avoid being arrested and possibly killed by the king.[52]
- Rahab hid Israelite spies and then helped them sneak out of the city, avoiding certain harm.[53]
- God made provisions for Joseph to be rescued and kept out of harm's way so that Pharaoh could eventually promote him.[54]
- The disciples hid behind a locked door after Christ's resurrection in order to avoid being persecuted by the Jews.[55]
- The captain of the Roman guard saved Paul from an angry Jewish mob of people who threatened to beat him.[56] Although Paul was not always rescued, in this case protecting Paul suited God's purpose to give him the opportunity to witness before the Roman governor.
- When Jesus said, "I and the Father are one," the Jews in the temple picked up stones to attack Him, but He slipped away, escaping and going across the Jordan to continue His ministry.[57]
- When Jesus was speaking at the synagogue, He incited anger when He said that He is the fulfillment of the prophecy for the coming of the Messiah. The people "rose up and drove him out of the town and brought him to the brow of the hill on which their town

DAY 14: WHAT FORGIVENESS LOOKS LIKE

was built, so that they could throw him down the cliff. But passing through their midst, he went away."[58]

- "'You are not yet fifty years old,' they said to him [Jesus], 'and you have seen Abraham!' 'Very truly I tell you,' Jesus answered, 'before Abraham was born, I am!' At this, they picked up stones to stone him, but Jesus hid himself, slipping away from the temple grounds."[59]
- Paul said to the church in Corinth, "No temptation has overtaken you that is not common to man. God is faithful, and he will not let you be tempted beyond your ability, but with the temptation he will also provide the way of escape, that you may be able to endure it."[60]

These scriptures describe acts of self-preservation; they are not acts of anger, unforgiveness, or (for that matter) forgiveness. God often provides a way of escape from danger, and He will inflict vengeance upon offenders in His own way, in His own time. These examples illustrate God making a way of escape in circumstances of impending persecution or harm. As for abusive husbands, Paul instructed husbands to love their wives as Christ loves the church and not to be harsh with them.[61] Christ has never used physical or emotional force to get the church, His bride, to bend to His will. In like manner, a husband (spouse) should not act in an unloving way to force (emotionally or physically) his wife to bend to his will. Nowhere in his description of love in 1 Corinthians 13 does Paul mention the use of force, intimidation, control, yelling and screaming, or abuse of any kind. Instead, love is described as an act of service and unconditional care for another.

Journal Exercise 14: What Forgiveness Looks Like

How difficult would each of these actions be for you? Rate each statement on a scale from 1 to 5 with a rating of 1 being not difficult and 5 being very difficult. Then, describe briefly what it would take to move to the next number.

COMPONENTS OF THE FORGIVENESS PROCESS	YOUR RATINGS
I will begin to short-circuit the vicious cycle of negative intentions, rumination, and unforgiveness.	[1] [2] [3] [4] [5]
What would increase your rating?	
I will begin to replace negative intentions with positive ones.	[1] [2] [3] [4] [5]
What would increase your rating?	
I will set boundaries to avoid repeat offenses.	[1] [2] [3] [4] [5]
What would increase your rating?	
I will react to my transgressor with mercy.	[1] [2] [3] [4] [5]
What would increase your rating?	
I will open the door to reconciling our relationship.	[1] [2] [3] [4] [5]
What would increase your rating?	

DAY 15

Committing to Trying to Forgive

Committing to trying to forgive is not easy. At this point, you may be entertaining reasons why you do not want to try to forgive, which would be understandable. The following are some common reasons why people feel this way (some of which overlap with the motivations for responding negatively that were discussed earlier in this chapter):

Reasons for Not Trying to Forgive

- **"I will not forgive until the transgressor approaches me and takes responsibility for the transgression."**

  Since scripture teaches us to be the first to address unforgiveness, this approach is not a good building block for achieving forgiveness. Forgiveness is not dependent on the behavior of the other person. In many cases, the other person is not even available to apologize to you or ask for forgiveness. When you require action from the transgressor, you give him or her control of the situation.

  Unforgiveness poisons our well-being and our peace of mind. Only we can take control of the decision to try to forgive, and this decision must be independent of what the transgressor does.

- **"Forgiving means having to talk with the transgressor, and I want nothing to do with him or her."**

Talking with the transgressor is not necessary before you forgive, but talking with him or her will be easier once you have made a decision to try to forgive. The scriptures teach us to seek out our transgressors to clear up misunderstandings and to discuss how their behavior has affected us.[62] However, the alternatives of criticism, defensiveness, stonewalling, and contempt are like poisonous gases that cloud our minds and make it difficult to think about anything other than holding a grudge and not forgiving.

- **"Forgiving the transgressor means that I would be condoning his or her actions, which may lead him or her to repeat the transgression."**

Forgiveness is not a replacement for justice, fairness, accountability, or safety. In fact, forgiveness will make it easier to attempt to reach justice and will remove negative feelings that could raise doubts in the justice process.

- **"The transgressor owes me, and if I extend forgiveness, he or she will not repay the debt."**

This may be true. Some offenders will see forgiveness as permission to withhold taking responsibility for justice and fairness. However, justice is separate from forgiveness. In fact, transgressors do not need to know that forgiveness has occurred. Furthermore, a display of negative intentions actually reduces the potential of the transgressor to own up to his or her behavior. We need to remember that in Jesus's model prayer, He specifically says that we are to ask God to forgive our trespasses as we forgive those who have trespassed against us.

Six Styles of Forgiveness

On the one hand, Jesus wants us to forgive as the Father has forgiven us. What we know from behavioral science, however, is that forgiveness comes in various varieties: one size does not fit all. Forgiveness researcher Robert Enright has identified six styles of forgiveness:[63]

Style 1 **Revengeful forgiveness.** "I forgive someone who wrongs me only if I can punish him or her to experience pain similar to my own."

Style 2 **Restitution or compensational forgiveness.** "If I get back what was taken away from me, then I forgive. Or if I feel guilty about withholding forgiveness, I forgive to relieve my guilt."

Style 3 **Expectational forgiveness.** "I forgive if others put pressure on me to forgive. It is easier to forgive when other people expect it."

Style 4 **Lawful expectational forgiveness.** "I forgive when my religion demands it."

Style 5 **Forgiveness as social harmony.** "I forgive when it restores harmony or good relations in society. Forgiveness decreases friction and outright conflict in society."

Style 6 **Forgiveness as love.** "I forgive unconditionally because it promotes a true sense of love. Because I must truly care for each person, unconditional forgiveness keeps open the possibility of reconciliation and closes the door on revenge."

Despite the style of forgiveness, forgiveness is not a substitute for the consequences of justice, fairness, accountability, or safety from further abuse. At the same time, while the offender has no right to receive the kindness of forgiveness, our decision to forgive is what brings us peace.

Review of What Forgiveness Is and Is Not

In order to clarify what forgiveness is and is not, the following review of major concepts includes biblical examples to illustrate each:

- Forgiveness is not pardon and lenience for hurtful behavior, nor is it absolution from the consequences of hurtful actions.

  David suffered ongoing consequences when he sinned against Uriah and Bathsheba. After the prophet Nathan brought David's sin to his attention, David and his household were in turmoil for the remainder of his life.[64]

- Forgiveness is not condoning, excusing, tolerating, or justifying the behavior.

  When the mob brought the adulterous woman to Jesus to see whether He would follow the Mosaic law and have her stoned, He told her to sin no more.[65]

- Forgiveness is not merely the offended person's accepting an apology or the offender's receiving reconciliation. Even after the offender offers an apology or the offended person has reconciled with the offender, the offended one may still have to work to forgive completely.

Jesus told of a servant who begged a king to forgive his massive debt. When the king showed him mercy, the servant turned around and demanded full payment of a very small debt from a fellow servant. Hearing of this offense, the king reinstated the unforgiving servant's debt and had him thrown into prison for not giving the same compassion he had received.[66]

- Forgiveness is not just forgetting about the offense with the notion that time heals all wounds. You may come to accept what happened and become less disappointed, but this approach will leave you open to reexperiencing the offense.

We can surmise that Joseph delayed forgiving his brothers until their father, Jacob, encouraged the brothers to seek his forgiveness years after the offense.[67]

- Forgiveness is not getting even, retaliating, getting vengeance, or punishing the offender.

Joseph did not inflict vengeance against his brothers for selling him into slavery. Instead, he took care of them and gave them food and land in a time of famine.[68]

Anger and Grudges

As you consider trying to forgive, you may feel lingering bitterness and anger, or you may feel that the transgression is unforgivable. The offender, however, may not even realize the extent of the offense since victims and transgressors do not usually see the offense in the same way. Each person is motivated to see the transgression from a perspective that best serves him or her.

Victims tend to exaggerate the severity of a transgression, while transgressors tend to minimize it. Additionally, the victim usually expects the transgressor to provide some restitution that is greater than the original offense dictates. The transgressor, on the other hand, may expect the victim to move on after a simple apology has been offered. After taking a closer look at the incident, victims may find that they overreacted and wrongly felt victimized. Forgiveness requires the offended person to reject the role of victim and decide to return to a state of peace. The alternative is to hold a grudge against the transgressor, thereby continuing to play the role of victim.

An alternative to holding a grudge is to hold onto anger, another poor choice. Anger is a form of pride, which stirs up clamor and evil speaking and is part of our old sinful nature. Anger causes strife, further transgressions, and harsh words, leading to sin and evil. Often anger brings its own punishment as confirmed by research and common sense. It has an adverse effect on our health, causing elevation of blood pressure, production of ulcers, and an increase in stress and the production of cortisol.

Is anger always bad? Are we sinning when we feel angry? Anger is not necessarily a sin. As Paul says, "Be angry and do not sin." Denying your anger can actually fuel bitterness and grudges that block your ability to forgive. Paul, though, adds, "Do not let the sun go down on your anger," meaning that dealing with anger in an authentic yet loving way is necessary to forgive. When, instead, we allow our anger to fuel negative intentions to harm the transgressor, we cross the line from righteous anger to sinful anger.

You may be thinking, *That's all easier said than done.* In later chapters, we will explore some processes to help you reach forgiving behaviors. For now, let's identify what you must decide at this point in the ACTION process. At this stage, your task is only to decide that you will try to forgive. The exercises in the remainder of *Forty Days to Forgiveness* will help you move in that direction. (We will examine how to overcome objections to forgiveness later.)

Journal Exercise 15a: Deciding to Commit to Trying to Forgive

Think about the offense as you answer these questions. You may want to refer back to the journal exercises for days 3 and 4.

1. Describe the transgression. What was said or done to hurt you?	
2. What triggered the transgression?	
3. Is there evidence that the transgressor might have been justified?	[Yes] [No]
4. Is there an alternative way to view the transgression?	
5. What is the worst that could happen now?	
6. What is the best that could happen now?	
7. What outcome would you like to see?	
8. If the transgressor had the same thoughts that you are having, what advice would you give him or her?	

Journal Exercise 15b: Committing to Trying to Forgive

This exercise requires you to think about the transgression. Although you do not yet know exactly how to proceed, are you able to step out in faith and commit to *try to forgive*? Here are some things to consider:

- Contemplate your desire to imitate the heart of God toward forgiveness. Read Exodus 34:6–7.
- Do you want to *try* to derail the unforgiveness life cycle?
- Do you want to *try* to experience the freedom of forgiveness?

If you answered no to either of these questions, you may not be ready to work on the forgiveness process. That's perfectly normal.

JOURNAL LOG

Commitment to Try to Forgive

I declare to myself that on this date, ____/____/____, I intend to use these experiences to try to forgive_____
for the offense of _____

I want to be open to God's work in my life to become a more forgiving person in general.

Name: _____

Prayer partner: _____

Chapter 3 Summary

The focus of this chapter is on making the commitment to try to forgive, a crucial aspect of positively coping with a transgression. The following are key points:

- Because transgressions make us feel threatened, we develop negative thoughts and intentions against our transgressors, which deny *us* peace of mind and the ability to restore our well-being.
- Forgiveness means replacing negative thoughts and intentions toward our transgressors with positive intentions, which promotes peace and well-being within us.
- Justice achieved in a court may hold the transgressor accountable, but it does not necessarily bring us peace of mind.
- While justice, fairness, and safety are necessary in many cases, they do not replace our need to develop positive intentions toward the transgressor.
- Forgiveness does not require us to stay in an abusive relationship. When we forgive a person, we can also set boundaries that prevent further harm.
- Making a commitment to try to forgive is the first step on the journey toward forgiveness.

Journal exercises assessed your forgiveness readiness; possible current negative responses toward your transgressor; your desire for justice, fairness, and safety; and your understanding of the meaning vs. the myths regarding forgiveness. Finally, several journal exercises helped you to make the commitment to try to forgive.

Scripture for Strength

There is therefore now no condemnation for those who are in Christ Jesus. For the law of the Spirit of life has set you free in Christ Jesus from the law of sin and death. For God has done what the law, weakened by the flesh, could not do. By sending his own Son in the likeness of sinful flesh and for sin, he condemned sin in the flesh, in order that the righteous requirement of the law might be fulfilled in us, who walk not according to the flesh but according to the Spirit. For those who live according to the flesh set their minds on the things of the flesh, but those who live according to the Spirit set their minds on the things of the Spirit. To set the mind on the flesh is death, but to set the mind on the Spirit is life and peace. For the mind that is set on the flesh is hostile to God, for it does not submit to God's law; indeed, it cannot. Those who are in the flesh cannot please God.

You, however, are not in the flesh but in the Spirit, if in fact the Spirit of God dwells in you. Anyone who does not have the Spirit of Christ does not belong to him. But if Christ is in you, although the body is dead because of sin, the Spirit is life because of righteousness. If the Spirit of him who raised Jesus from the dead dwells in you, he who raised Christ Jesus from the dead will also give life to your mortal bodies through his Spirit who dwells in you. (Romans 8:1–10)

Devotional Prayer

Gracious Father in Heaven,

This scripture tells me that the mind set on the flesh is hostile to You and that it leads to death. The mind set on the Spirit, in contrast, experiences life and peace and pleases You.

Lord, I see now that harboring negative intentions toward _____ means that my mind is set on the flesh. Father, this is not the place I want to be, so I humbly beg You to cleanse my mind and Spirit of _____, _____, and _____. Lord God, I also humbly ask that You help me fill my mind with positive thoughts and intentions toward _____, so the Spirit of Christ will live in me and I can begin to have peace and well-being.

God, I believe that the Spirit that raised Jesus from the dead can raise my thoughts and cleanse my mind. Please strengthen me as I commit to doing Your will.

In the holy and powerful name of Your Son Jesus. Amen.

Chapter 3 Endnotes

1   R. D. Enright, *Forgiveness Is a Choice: A Step-by-Step Process for Resolving Anger and Restoring Hope* (Washington, DC: APA Life Tools, 2001), pp. 125–37. R. D. Enright and R. P. Fitzgibbons, Forgiveness Therapy: An Empirical Guide for Resolving Anger and Restoring Hope (Washington, DC: APA Press, 2015), pp. 69–73.

2   Matthew 6:14–15.

3   John 8:12.

4   1 Corinthians 11:1.

5   Matthew 5:14.

6   Ephesians 4:20, 5:2.

7   1 John 4:19; Colossians 3:13.

8   Romans 12:19.

9   1 Thessalonians 5:15.

10   1 Thessalonians 5:13; Hebrews 12:14–15.

11   Romans 12:1–2.

12   John 15:4–5, 8; 2 Corinthians 5:18–20.

13   Paraphrased from 1 Corinthians 13:4–7.

14   Matthew 22:37–40.

15   Galatians 5:19–24.

16   1 Peter 2:1–3; Hebrews 5:12–14, 6:1; Colossians 1:10.

17   Galatians 6:1–10.

18   Colossians 3:12–17. We will talk more about spiritual maturity in chapter 6.

19   Galatians 5:22–23.

20   L. Toussaint and J. R. Webb, "Theoretical and Empirical Connections between Forgiveness, Mental Health, and Well-Being," in *Handbook for Forgiveness*, ed. E. Worthington Jr. (New York: Routledge, 2005), p. 358.

21   These last three types of forgiveness are not discussed in *Forty Days to Forgiveness*, yet they may affect your ability to forgive in some situations.

22   K. Pargament and M. Rye, "Forgiveness as a Method of Religious Coping," in *Dimensions of Forgiveness: Psychological Research and Theological Perspectives*, ed. E. Worthington Jr. (Radnor, PA: Templeton Foundation Press, 1998) p. 62.

23   Corrie ten Boom, *The Hiding Place* (Grand Rapids, MI: Chosen Books, 1984), pp. 247–48.

24   Ibid.

25   Romans 5:6–10.

26   Genesis 45.

27   Genesis 32–33.

28   Ephesians 4:30–32.

29   Michael McCullough, *Beyond Revenge: The Evaluation of the Forgiveness Instinct.* (San Francisco:Josey-Bass, 2008).

30   For a more in depth review of the role justice plays in the forgiveness process, I suggest reading Everitt Worthington, Jr's book *A Just Forgiveness: Responsible Healing Without Excusing Injustice* (Intervarsity Press:Downers Grove, Il., pages 54-72)

31   2 Samuel 12:1–24.

32   Acts 13:22.

33   2 Samuel 7:13; Psalms 31:9–13.

34   Galatians 6:7.

35   2 Peter 3:9.

36   Enright and Fitzgibbons, *Forgiveness Therapy*.

37   E. Worthington, *Reach for Forgiveness* (Boston: Pearson Custom, 2013), pp. 32–36.

38   R. Enright, *Forgiveness Is a Choice*, pp. 28–29.

39   S. Pattison, *Shame: Theory, Therapy, Theology* (Cambridge, UK: Cambridge University Press, 2000), p. 198.

40   E. Worthington, "More Questions about Forgiveness: Research Agenda for 2005–2015," in E. Worthington, ed., *Handbook of Forgiveness* (New York: Routledge, 2005); E. Worthington, D. E. Davis, J. N. Hook, and P. C. Hill, "Research on Religion, Spirituality and Forgiveness: A Meta-Analytic Review," *Psychology of Religion and Spirituality* 5, no. 4 (2013): 239.

41   Berry and E. Worthington, "Forgiveness, Relationship Quality, Stress while Imagining Relationship Events, and Physical and Mental Health," *Journal of Counseling Psychology* 48, no. 4 (2001): 447–55; Kaminer, Stein, Mbanga, and Zungu-Dirwayi, "Forgiveness: Toward an Integration of Theoretical Models," *Psychiatry* 63, no. 4 (Winter 2000): 344–57; VanOyen, Ludwig, and Vander Laan, "Granting Forgiveness or Harboring Grudges: Implications for Emotion, Physiology, and Health," *Psychological Science* 12, no. 2 (March 2001): 117–23.

42   R. Enright and R. Fitzgibbons, *Helping Clients Forgive: An Empirical Guide for Resolving Anger and Restoring Hope* (Washington, DC: APA Press, 2000).

43   Romans 12:17.

44   Romans 12:19.

45   This will be covered in more detail in chapter 5.

46   Romans 12:20–21; Luke 6:35.

47   John 20:23.

48   Luke 17:3–4.

49   Matthew 18:15–17.

50   This is a much-debated issue, one that goes beyond the scope of *Forty Days to Forgiveness*. For more information, see Barbara Roberts, *Not Under Bondage: Biblical Divorce for Abuse, Adultery, and Desertion* (Maschil Press, 2008); Ron Clark, *Setting the Captives Free: A Christian Theology for Domestic Violence* (Eugene, OR: Cascade Books, 2005); Catherine Clark Kroeger and James R. Beck, eds., *Women, Abuse, and the Bible: How Scripture Can Be Used to Hurt or Heal* (Grand Rapids, MI: Baker Books, 1996).

51   See Matthew 18:15–20; 1 Corinthians 10:13.

52   2 Corinthians 11:32–33.

53   Joshua 2:1–6.

54   Acts 7:9–10.

55   John 20:19.

56   Acts 21:30–36.

57   John 10:22–42.

58   Luke 4:29–30.

59   John 8:57–58.

60   1 Corinthians 10:13.

61   Colossians 3:19.

62   Matthew 18:15–17.

63   Enright and Fitzgibbons, *Helping Clients Forgive*, p. 55.

64   2 Samuel 12:13–18.

65   John 8:1–11.

66   Matthew 18:23–35.

67   Genesis 44:1–45:15.

68   Genesis 45:16–22.

CHAPTER 4

Transitioning to a Godly Perspective

Therefore, I urge you, brethren, by the mercies of God, to present your bodies a living and holy sacrifice, acceptable to God, which is your spiritual service of worship. And do not be conformed to this world, but be transformed by the renewing of your mind, so that you may prove what the will of God is, that which is good and acceptable and perfect. For through the grace given to me I say to everyone among you not to think more highly of himself than he ought to think; but to think so as to have sound judgment, as God has allotted to each a measure of faith.

—ROMANS 12:2

DAY 16

A Christian View of Forgiveness—Introduction

This chapter focuses on the third step in the forgiveness process, *transitioning* to a godly perspective, represented by the letter *T* in the ACTION model. The challenging steps and strategies discussed in this chapter will help you to transition your vicious cycle of negative feelings to a state of positive intentions. We will also revisit the unforgiveness life cycle (chapter 2) and consider a Christ-centered approach to promoting forgiveness.

Forgiveness Step 3: Transitioning to a Godly Perspective

Unforgiveness fuels a vicious cycle of negative thoughts about the transgressor and what you would like to see happen to him or her. Transitioning to a state of positive intentions includes the following:

- Transferring the negative thoughts about the transgression that are going around in your head into positive thoughts.
- Looking at the transgression from a different point of view.
- Transitioning from intending for bad things to happen to your transgressor to showing love, empathy, and compassion toward him or her.
- Transitioning from seeing the transgressor as a villain to seeing him or her as a child of God.

Use the following checklist to help you think about your current state of transitional thinking and to make the journey from negative intentions to positive, prosocial thoughts.

Things that inhibit transitioning to positive thoughts. Number the following inhibitors (1–6) with 1 being most like you and 6 being least like you.

_____	I seek revenge and ways to make the transgressor pay.
_____	I contemplate ways to hurt him or her in the same way he or she hurt me.
_____	I want to see him or her miserable. I wish that something bad would happen to him or her.
_____	I would find it difficult to act warmly toward him or her.
_____	I resent what he or she did to me.
_____	I keep thinking about the offense to avoid working on the hurt productively.

Prayer for God's Guidance

> *My brother and Savior Lord Jesus Christ, change sometimes comes hard for me, especially when I feel that I will be harmed by the changes.*
>
> *Help me to accept the changes needed for me to grow a forgiving heart. I know I am … [name the top three things inhibiting your ability and desire to transition from unforgiveness to forgiveness].*
>
> *I want to find the peace that comes from forgiving others as You have forgiven me.*
>
> *I pray these things in Your name, amen.*

Overview of the Chapter

Day 16: A Christian View of Forgiveness—Introduction
Day 17: Coping with the Stress of Unenforceable Rules
Day 18: Short-Circuiting the Vicious Cycle
Day 19: Positive Intentions
Day 20: Forgiveness Outcomes
Day 21: Empathy

In Paul's letter to the church in Rome, he speaks to the concept of transitioning: "Do not be conformed to this world, but be transformed by the renewal of your mind, that by testing you may discern what is the will of God, what is good and acceptable and perfect."[1] Paul uses the term *transformed* in the powerful sense to indicate that we change the way we think, no longer thinking about forgiveness as the world does. This action of renewing one's mind in order to know the will of God is what sets Christian forgiveness apart from non-Christian or secular forgiveness. This passage implies a transition from thinking about a transgressor from the world's point of view to thinking about him or her from a Christlike point of view. You started the change process when you made the decision to try to forgive in chapter 3. But here Paul is raising the bar. Can people truly change from unforgiveness to forgiveness? Yes, with the help of the Holy Spirit. In this chapter we will talk about the conditions that, when brought to bear on your mind and heart, will help you move from an unforgiving to a forgiving position.

Description of the Christian's Forgiveness Life Cycle

In chapter 3, we talked about your making a commitment to try to forgive your transgressor. The following diagram, "The Christian Forgiveness Life Cycle," illustrates what you are committing to. Chapter 2 presented the top half of this chart and called it "The Unforgiveness Life Cycle." The focus of the new diagram is on changing our thoughts from unforgiveness to the forgiveness process from a Christlike

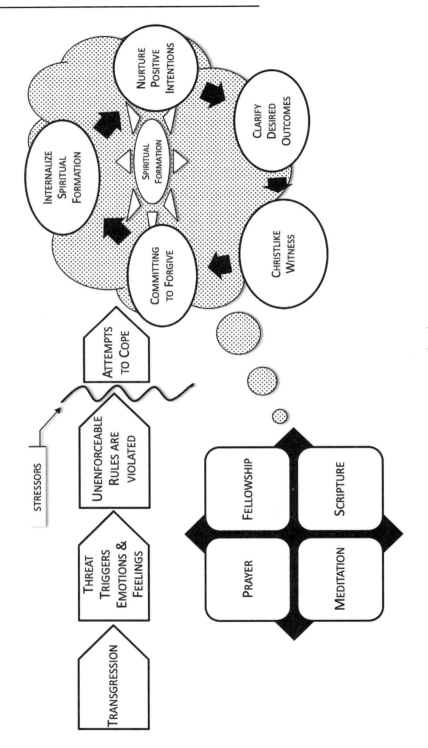

Forgiveness Lifecycle

worldview. Our goal is to "short-circuit" the unforgiveness process, a disruption that begins at the coping stage by our deciding to forgive. In this chapter we will revisit this process from a Christ-centered approach to spiritual maturity and forgiveness. Let's start by looking at each element of the Christian forgiveness life cycle:

1. **Committing to forgive.** Making a decision to forgive is called "decisional forgiveness." Deciding to pursue forgiveness is a stepping-stone to emotional freedom, peace of mind, and a Christlike spirit. Without this decision, attempts at forgiveness will be superficial and, most likely, will not lead to a state of peace. Without a decision to forgive, our thoughts toggle back and forth between rumination about the transgression and taking a Christlike approach to forgiveness. Committing to forgive sets a firm foundation that leads to emotional freedom from our transgressors. Without making a decision to forgive, emotional forgiveness is not achievable.[2] Deciding to try to forgive disrupts the vicious cycle of unforgiveness by reversing our plunge into negative intentions and rumination. (Although *emotional forgiveness* and *decisional forgiveness* are terms used in the behavioral sciences, in this chapter they are primarily explored from a Christian worldview.)

Acknowledging the Transgression

As explained in chapter 2, a transgression stimulates a combination of emotions such as fear, sadness, anger, surprise, and disgust. Without a reliance on Christ's example of love for others, our natural response to a transgression is to protect ourselves from hurts that destabilize our well-being. These emotions are not unforgiveness; rather, they are the primary emotions that give rise to feelings such as disappointment, jealousy, envy, shame, guilt, and residual fear and anger. These emotions become a lens through which we look at the hurt, and they lead us to take control of how we protect ourselves.

We and *ourselves* are keywords here. When we acknowledge a transgression from the perspective of how *we* can cope with it and address it, we are proceeding without the help of the Holy Spirit. In the Christian life cycle of forgiveness, however, the transgression is viewed through a different lens. In the Christian life cycle, we are reflecting, synthesizing, and evaluating the effect of the transgression on us from a godly perspective, which is fueled by our spiritual formation. In other words, by the indwelling of the Holy Spirit we eclipse our natural instinct to protect and defend ourselves. We are looking at the transgression through the lens of the fruit of the Spirit, as described by the apostle Paul:

The fruit of the Spirit is love, joy, peace, patience, kindness, goodness, faithfulness, gentleness, self-control; against such things there is no law. And those who belong to Christ Jesus have crucified the flesh with its passions and desires. If we live by the Spirit, let us also keep in step with the Spirit. Let us not become conceited, provoking one another, envying one another.

Brothers, if anyone is caught in any transgression, you who are spiritual should restore him in a Spirit of gentleness. Keep watch on yourself, lest you too be tempted. Bear one another's burdens, and so fulfill the law of Christ.[3]

Paul uses this metaphor to suggest that disciples of Christ are like a fruit tree. When we nourish, prune, and tend to the tree, it bears fruit. Paul explains further: "Walk by the Spirit, and you will not gratify the desires of the flesh [such as our instinct to protect ourselves]. For the desires of the flesh are against the Spirit, and the desires of the Spirit are against the flesh, for these are opposed to each other, to keep you from doing the things you want to do."[4]

When we subordinate our instincts to protect ourselves to a Christlike spirit, the Holy Spirit helps us[5] to respond in ways that are in contradistinction to our human instincts to survive. In other words, to have the instinct to react negatively toward our transgressors is to be like a dead branch on our tree. Instincts are not of themselves wrong; they are God-given aids in our survival. However, when our instinct leads us to allow our self-centered nature to dominate our spiritual nature, instincts are like dead branches. Just as pruning a tree is sometimes necessary to prevent unproductive branches from receiving the nourishment needed by fruit-bearing branches, it is necessary for us to prune the instincts that lead our flesh to sap spiritual nourishment from our hearts and minds. When we prune negative instincts, we allow the Holy Spirit to nourish our hearts to bear the fruit of the Spirit.

2. **Internalizing spiritual formation.** Spiritual formation is like an act of pruning: it redirects nourishment to the branches of our lives that bear fruit. Spiritual formation is an antidote to rumination. Without a Christlike spirit and the help of the Holy Spirit, it is almost impossible to internalize our desire to forgive. When we filter our perception of the transgression through the mind of Christ, which is living in our hearts, the Holy Spirit intercedes and leads us to see our transgression from a godly perspective. Spiritual formation, also referred to as spiritual maturity, is comprised of adopting the disciplines of understanding the Word of God, meditating on the Lord and His Word, praying, and enjoying fellowship with like-minded disciples of Christ.[6]

Nurturing Positive Intentions

Nurturing positive intentions is the antidote to the negative intentions that keep us locked in the vicious cycle of unforgiveness. Transitioning from a mind that seeks to protect and defend to a mind of worship is critical if we are to avoid the vicious cycle of unforgiveness. When the Word of God blooms in our hearts and minds, we have a different vocabulary for describing what has happened to us. That vocabulary helps us to set our minds on the experience from a godly perspective.

> *"If then you have been raised with Christ, seek the things that are above, where Christ is, seated at the right hand of God. Set your minds on things that are above, not on things that are on earth. For you have died, and your life is hidden with Christ in God. When Christ who is your life appears, then you also will appear with him in glory."[7]*

Our initial interpretation of this passage may be to think that to "appear with Him in glory" is a reference to our position in the next life. It also suggests, however, that His glory will shine through us to the transgressor and to others, such as bystanders familiar with the transgression. When He shines through us, people see Christ; when they see our behavior, then we are appearing with Him in glory. One of my favorite verses speaks to this principle:

Put on then, as God's chosen ones, holy and beloved, compassionate hearts, kindness, humility, meekness, and patience, bearing with one another and, if one has a complaint against another, forgiving each other. As the Lord has forgiven you, so you also must forgive. And above all these put on love, which binds everything together in perfect harmony. And let the peace of Christ rule in your hearts, to which indeed you were called in one body. And be thankful. Let the word of Christ dwell in you richly, teaching and admonishing one another in all wisdom, singing psalms and hymns and spiritual songs, with thankfulness in your hearts to God. And whatever you do, in word or deed, do everything in the name of the Lord Jesus, giving thanks to God the Father through him.[8]

I believe these verses are the best summary of the essence of forgiveness in the Bible. Love is what makes the clock of forgiveness tick. Let's pull out the key themes in this passage and apply them to forgiveness:

- Love is an action that we adopt, based not on how we feel about someone but on how we choose to act toward him or her.
- A compassionate heart, humility, meekness, and patience are the foundation upon which forgiveness is formulated.[9]
- We are all capable of committing acts that render us in need of forgiveness.
- Our pattern for forgiveness is based on our understanding of how we have been forgiven by the Lord.
- Christ's Spirit in us powers our ability to forgive others.

- Learning God's Word from like-minded believers, singing to the Lord and edifying one another through singing, and developing a spirit of gratitude all lubricate the transition from our natural instinct to a spirit of grace to love.

What the Word of God describes as forgiveness, behavioral scientists refer to as empathy and altruism. Simply put, empathy happens when we are able to look at a situation from the point of view of another person. This does not mean looking at the other person's situation from what we *think* is his or her point of view or looking at the situation from the perspective of how *we* would act in the same set of circumstances that led that person to transgress against us. Instead, empathy is looking at the other person's situation from his or her perspective. We find this difficult because we are programmed to evaluate another's point of view rather than to simply understand it. We want to discredit the other person's motivations and actions based on his or her faulty reasoning or poor choices. We want to say "See? See? He (or she) is at fault" as if we want to drop the person from a tall building and listen for his or her cries of remorse all the way down. When we transfer blame to another person, we feel that we are more righteous than the other person is, along with being better and more beloved than he or she is. This is inappropriate and misguided pride.

It is necessary that we suspend judgment of another person's actions in order to see the transgression from his or her point of view, whether we agree with it or not. Robert Enright, a prominent researcher of forgiveness, refers to the process of transitioning as "reframing." Remember our picture of the old woman / young woman? Recall how you saw the picture initially shift when you reframed your perspective of the drawing? In the same vein, it is difficult to step into the transgressor's shoes and see his or her actions from his or her point of view. Instead, we see either the old woman or the young woman.

As Enright explains, "Empathy cannot be engineered or simply willed into existence. Its emergence takes time, sometimes a great deal of time."[10] He goes on to say that when we reframe our understanding of a transgressor's point of view, we seek to understand the individual's motivations to act as he or she did. In my graduate program, one professor impressed on us students that "all behavior makes sense—in context." The goal of reframing is to see transgressors as separate from their actions—to see them as members of the human race: "Is he or she a child of God? Might he or she be granted salvation? Will I see him or her in heaven some day? Is he or she loved by God to the same extent that I am loved?"[11]

As we ask these questions, we are engaging in a process of reframing our understanding of the transgressor from our natural point of view to God's point of view of the transgressor as someone worthy of salvation. We are seeking to expand our view of the context in which the person committed the offense. In addition to Enright, numerous other researchers have come to the same conclusion: It is *only* when we reframe our experience with the transgressor that we can show empathy and have compassion. Empathy and compassion fuel the transition of our negative intentions into positive ones.[12] This is the core principle in our ability to forgive.

In other words, when you implement all the steps in the forgiveness process without God in the picture, you have a point of view that is limited to your programing as a person in a fallen world, a person motivated by the instinct to survive. Without empathy, there is a hole in our ability to forgive. In the final analysis, *it is Christ in us, with the help of the Holy Spirit, that enables us to forgive others and binds us to the glory of Christ!* I am going to go out a limb here and ask the question, can anyone ever truly forgive, forgive with a truly compassionate heart, without the indwelling of the Holy Spirit? Can you? I cannot. I've proven that to myself so many times that it has prompted me to spend the latter years of my life researching, contemplating, and reflecting on forgiveness in order to share these thoughts with you in *Forty Days to Forgiveness.*

3. **Clarifying forgiveness outcomes.** In my previous profession of organizational development, I designed leadership training programs and processes for achieving sustainable change in the cultures of large organizations. One principle was behind almost everything I did in that job: begin with the end in mind. Similarly, in the Christian forgiveness life cycle, it is important that we ask ourselves, "What end result am I reaching for? How do I know when I have forgiven my transgressor?" Certainly, peace and well-being for ourselves is important, but we are also reaching for another outcome.

Is not our ultimate goal to minister to the pain and suffering of others through the power of Jesus Christ? Is not our job to be a light in a world of darkness? The positive well-being, happiness, and godly result we are seeking is to bring the light of Christ to a troubled world, and the work of forgiveness helps us accomplish this goal. Christians are motivated to forgive for reasons that go beyond the secular approach. Christians forgive first because they are emulating God's forgiveness[13] and, in turn, are reflecting the light of Christ's forgiveness to others. Second, Christians forgive because they have been encouraged to do so by Christ Himself,[14] though His encouragement is not intended to make us feel guilty if we do not forgive. Third, struggling to forgive unites us with the Holy Spirit and strengthens our bond with God.

When we approach forgiveness based on the indwelling of the Spirit of the Lord, we are being obedient to God's will and we achieve joy,[15] a life in balance, positive well-being, and the fruit of the Spirit.[16] In addition to peace and a life in balance for the person transgressed against, Christian forgiveness provides a gateway to salvation for all people, particularly for those who wronged us.[17] Christian forgiveness takes place in relationship with God and, because of this, is a means to project God's love for us to the people who have harmed us.[18]

Biblical Characteristics of Forgiveness

Scriptural discussions of forgiveness and its associated behaviors help us understand Christian forgiveness more fully. The scriptural references to forgiveness expand when we consider that forgiveness is part of God's loving nature and His grace toward us through the atoning blood of Christ. When we broaden our view of Christlike forgiveness to include God's love and grace in forgiving us, we get a better picture of what a forgiving follower of Christ looks like. The following table provides a summary of some of the characteristics of forgiveness from a biblical perspective:

FORGIVENESS IS …	FORGIVENESS IS NOT …
• long-suffering and patient[19] • ongoing and repetitive[20] • an awareness of one's own shortcomings • merciful and beneficent[21] • loving [22] • a reflection of Christ[23] • prayerful[24] • reliant on God for strength • repaying evil with good[25] • offered to all people[26] • a blessing to the offender • a provision of comfort[27] • kindness and gentleness[28] • imitating God's grace and thus transmitting it to others[29]	• judgmental[30] • continuing association with unrepentant, unsafe offenders • retaliatory and vengeful[31] • malicious, deceitful, or hypocritical[32] • a onetime action[33] • reconciliation[34]

These descriptors shed light on Christ's commandment to "forgive others their trespasses as our Father has forgiven us."[35] When Christ says to forgive, He is telling us to assume all the behaviors in the "Forgiveness is …" column and to put aside the characteristics in the "Forgiveness is not …" column. The list of positive attributes makes clear that, from a godly perspective, forgiveness is not a feeling; it is a set of cognitive and behavioral actions one takes, rooted in a relationship with Christ, in order to put aside thoughts of vengeance, retaliation, and bitterness.[36] Forgiveness is not repaying evil with evil; instead, forgiveness requires blessing offenders by being merciful, loving, beneficent, and prayerful.[37] Since reflecting the behaviors of forgiveness is a conscious choice, we find it easier to respond in a Christlike manner when we have nourished our hearts and our lives with spiritual formation.

Once we enter into unforgiveness, the vicious cycle of rumination and negative intentions (the right column of the foregoing chart) can, like a bad habit, lead us to walk in darkness. If you have ever tried to stop a bad habit, you know it is not easy. It seems the more you think about the habit, the more you engage in it. Paul commented on this when he said, "I do not understand my own actions. For I do not do what I want, but I do the very thing I hate."[38] Once we progress in the unforgiveness life cycle to the point where we ruminate on the transgression, the story about our transgressor forms a rut in our neural pathways just as habits do. Neurons that fire together become wired together, which may be the path to creating what Paul refers to as a "stronghold."[39] In the behavioral sciences, this phenomenon is known as "conditioning." We learn the story we are telling ourselves (and possibly others) to the point that it becomes our reality regardless of whether we have weighed all the facts. As with breaking a bad habit, once our minds begin this vicious cycle of rumination, it is difficult for us to eliminate the story that is fueling our unforgiveness.

In a state of unforgiveness, we compare a current threat to similar past experiences in order to decide whether the transgression is a legitimate threat and what to do about it. If our past experiences include a study of the Word of God, however, the Word guides how we transition from a negative to a positive response to the threat. Through His Word, Christ sends the Holy Spirit to dwell within us to give us an alternative to acting upon our instinct to protect ourselves from a threat. When the Word of God is living in us, the more rational part of the brain responds to threats in ways that glorify God, trusting Him for protection and judgment.[40] Without the Word of God, the tendency of our rational brain is to respond to threats from our sin nature, and the results here are self-serving.

As explained previously, forgiveness is a process whereby we renew our minds by transitioning from negative emotions and feelings to positive ones and, in doing so, begin to let go of our negative intentions toward the transgressor. It is virtually impossible, however, to eliminate negative feelings altogether since emotions and feelings are part of the standard programming that we receive at birth. As discussed in chapter 2, Paul tells us that we can be angry as long as our anger does not lead us to sin. Anger turns into sin when it leads us to negative intentions toward another person[41] and to rumination about the cause of anger. The key to controlling our anger and fear is to develop effective habits for coping with the difficult emotions and feelings that are triggered by transgressions.

Journal Exercise 16: Finding Your Forgiveness Strengths

Rate yourself on each of the Christian attributes of forgiveness listed in the following table. A rating of 1 means not at all like you, and a rating of 5 means very much like you.

CHRISTIAN FORGIVENESS ATTRIBUTES	RATINGS
❏ I am long-suffering and patient with transgressors.	[1] [2] [3] [4] [5]
❏ My forgiveness is ongoing and repetitive.	[1] [2] [3] [4] [5]
❏ I am aware of my own shortcomings.	[1] [2] [3] [4] [5]
❏ I am merciful and beneficent toward others.	[1] [2] [3] [4] [5]
❏ I believe I am a loving person with transgressors.	[1] [2] [3] [4] [5]
❏ I am a reflection of Christ for transgressors.	[1] [2] [3] [4] [5]
❏ I am prayerful about transgressions toward me.	[1] [2] [3] [4] [5]
❏ I rely on God for strength when facing an offense.	[1] [2] [3] [4] [5]
❏ I repay evil and offenses toward me with goodness.	[1] [2] [3] [4] [5]
❏ I offer forgiveness to all people who transgress against me.	[1] [2] [3] [4] [5]
❏ My behavior is a blessing to a transgressor.	[1] [2] [3] [4] [5]
❏ I give comfort and reassurance of love to transgressors.	[1] [2] [3] [4] [5]
❏ I show kindness and gentleness toward transgressors.	[1] [2] [3] [4] [5]
❏ I transmit God's grace to others who transgress against me.	[1] [2] [3] [4] [5]

Interpreting Your Results

Look over your forgiveness attributes and put a check in front of the top five that you rated most like you. These are your Christian forgiveness strengths. In the following exercise, you will think about how you can lean on these strengths to help you forgive the transgressor you chose to work on in chapter 1. Write each of your top five strengths in the spaces provided in the following chart, and then give an example of how your strongest forgiveness attributes can shape your behavior toward your transgressor.

Strength 1:
Describe how you can you use this strength to shape your response to your transgressor:

Strength 2:
Describe how you can you use this strength to shape your response to your transgressor:

Strength 3:

Describe how you can you use this strength to shape your response to your transgressor:

Strength 4:

Describe how you can you use this strength to shape your response to your transgressor:

Strength 5:

Describe how you can you use this strength to shape your response to your transgressor:

DAY 17

Coping with the Stress of Unenforceable Rules

Wouldn't it be nice if we did not have to choose between reducing unforgiveness and promoting forgiveness? The key to making the right choice is to have effective coping skills. Notice in the life cycle of forgiveness chart (day 16) that "coping" sits at the crossroads of the processes that lead to unforgiveness or forgiveness. The manner and the effectiveness with which we cope with a transgression directly affects our ability to transition away from the vicious cycle of negative intentions and rumination that keep us locked in a state of unforgiveness. In other words, our coping skill is an alternative to the vicious cycle of unforgiveness. In this section we will talk about how positive coping mechanisms can help us address transgressions without entering a state of either forgiveness or unforgiveness.

How we cope with transgressions is determined in part by what triggers our emotions. Triggers are learned automatic responses to offenses that we have previously experienced. Our triggers are like antennae that are constantly scanning our environment for things that can harm us; we scan the world based on what has harmed us in the past. When we operate with rules about how we should be treated in order not to be harmed, we look for cases of those rules not being observed. Then, when we cannot enforce the rules by which we judge right from wrong, our emotions go into protection mode, triggering us to respond in ways that may prevent us from coping with the situation in positive ways. Although we may hope that we will create a win-win resolution to a transgression, when our emotions are triggered, our natural response is first to protect and second to resolve the transgression.

Another perspective is that coping is more than a behavior performed, feeling felt, or process experienced. In most cases, how we cope involves unlearning things that divide us and destroy our ability to live with others in temperance, peace, and community. In other words, how we cope with a situation is the embodiment of specific habits that lead to a way of life. Learning to forgive involves a commitment to cultivating coping habits and spiritual disciplines that grow and nurture a compassion for the soul and the well-being of a transgressor.[42] By coping in a positive and effective way, we avoid the need for forgiveness, and we avoid the vicious cycle of unforgiveness. Unfortunately, our emotional natural instinct to protect ourselves often overpowers our desire to cope effectively with a transgression. Paul explains this truth clearly:

> So I find it to be a law that when I want to do right, evil lies close at hand. For I delight in the law of God, in my inner being, but I see in my members another law waging war against the law of my mind and making me captive to the law of sin that dwells in my members. Wretched man that I am! Who will deliver me from this body of death? Thanks be to God through Jesus Christ our Lord! So then, I myself serve the law of God with my mind, but with my flesh I serve the law of sin.[43]

I cannot imagine a better description of what happens after a transgression leads one to a state of unforgiveness. Satan with his evil schemes is constantly looking for opportunities to tempt us to behave in ways that ruin our intimacy with God and our ability to reflect God's grace and mercy toward our transgressors. If our goal is to turn a transgression into an opportunity to reflect God's grace, what better way for Satan to trip us up than to trigger a negative emotional response to the transgression? Satan is firing arrows at us and watching us destroy our testimony by acting on our negative intentions toward our offenders.

So what is the alternative? Positive coping. Just to reiterate what I have said in previous chapters, we can cope with transgressions in both positive and negative ways. Negative coping may reduce unforgiveness, but it does not release us from the vicious cycle of rumination and negative intentions. Positive coping processes, in contrast, allow us to resolve a transgression or the threat of a transgression.[44] Positive coping *is* the transition point between status quo and unforgiveness.

As shown in our Unforgiveness Life Cycle chart (chapter 2, day 6), stress is the body's response to a threat to our well-being. Coping is a response to reduce stress from a transgression and return to a state of well-being. The first step in positive coping is to be aware of how we see and interpret the situation we are encountering and its effect on us, because how we observe and assess a transgression sets the stage for how we see the overall conditions surrounding our transgression experience. Like the old woman / young woman illustration, what we observe about our transgression sets up the perspective through which our coping strategies are carried out. The more specific and accurate our understanding of the overall situation, the better we will be able to adapt and respond in effective and productive ways.

As our stress evolves, our thoughts regarding how to cope change as well. As we respond to our stress, our coping strategies need to change. Coping is a shifting process; there is no perfect style or response. Therefore, our coping strategy and coping style both adapt as the situation changes. For this reason, it is important that we stay clear on what is triggering us and how we are interpreting the transgression.

Coping positively with our belief that some unenforceable rule has been broken is our best defense against the vicious cycle of ruminating over negative intentions toward our transgressors. Consequently, our first commitment to break the vicious cycle is to learn new ways to cope with a transgression. We need to change the pattern of how we respond to our emotional triggers.

As a reminder, to tolerate a transgression or to reduce or minimize our reaction to one, we can cope actively or avoid the situation altogether. The three general coping strategies, introduced in chapter 2 (day 9), are reviewed as follows:

- **Problem-solving**, which are strategies and efforts to actively alleviate stressful circumstances by clarifying the problem that is creating the stress and finding win-win solutions.
- **Emotion-focused** coping strategies, which involve efforts to regulate the emotional consequences of stressful or potentially stressful events.
- **Meaning-focused** coping, which tries to reduce stress by changing one's interpretation of the stressor or one's response to the stress.[45]

Research indicates that people use all three types of strategies to combat their most stressful events.[46] At this point we are considering the strategies from a positive perspective, but as you will see shortly, each can be the basis of a negative coping strategy as well. Generally speaking, as explained earlier, coping strategies are of two types: active (positive) and avoidant (negative).[47] Action-oriented coping—whether problem-solving, emotion-focused, or meaning-focused—is thought to be the most effective way to deal with stressful events. Similarly, avoidant coping strategies can also be problem-, emotion-, or meaning-focused, but they lead us into unproductive behaviors that keep us from directly addressing stressful events.

In the chart in chapter 2 (day 9), we see that active coping mechanisms are seen as positive and that avoidant coping mechanisms are seen as negative. Briefly, active problem-focused coping strategies include researching solutions, generating ideas, reviewing concerns, and negotiating; active emotion-focused strategies include humor, crying, relaxation, and finding emotional support; and active meaning-focused coping strategies include prayer, meditation, Bible study, and adjusting expectations.

In contrast, avoidant problem-focused coping strategies involve disregarding or trivializing the threat, talking about it inappropriately to others, or arguing and expressing hostility; avoidant emotion-focused strategies involve self-blame, fear, substance abuse, and immersion in movies, music, television, doodling, or hobbies; and avoidant meaning-focused strategies include denial, telling others the story, or posting about the transgression on social media.

The predominance of one type of coping strategy over another is determined, in part, by personal style (that is, some people cope more actively than others) and also by the type of stressful event. For example, people typically employ problem-focused coping to deal with potentially controllable problems such as those related to work or family, whereas stressors perceived as less controllable, such as physical health problems or transgressions committed by people no longer accessible, prompt more emotion-focused coping. A meaning-focused response would be drawn upon to change our perception of the nature of the stressor itself, to adjust how we think about it, or to make the decision to forgive the transgressor.[48]

So if coping effectively derails unforgiveness, why don't we cope better all the time? Mostly we don't because the stressors that affect our ability to maintain a state of well-being take control of our emotions and feelings. Our feelings and emotions are connected to patterns of behaving that we engaged to deal with similar stressors in the past. The emotions that make coping with a transgression most difficult and that prevent our navigating away from unforgiveness are anger and fear. Anger typically leads to hostile actions, while fear often leads to avoidant reactions. If not addressed productively, our anger or fear may propel us to a state of unforgiveness.

When we commit to forgive, we are committing first to trying to cope in positive ways. Productive scriptural ways to deal with our emotions include self-control;[49] prayer;[50] wisdom; calmness and meekness;[51] avoiding angry people;[52] and slowing down and thinking.[53] If we cannot control our anger, then we definitely will not cope with a transgression in a positive way. Here are four simple techniques to keep anger from eroding your ability to cope positively:

1. Pause and slowly and quietly count to ten. (You learned this strategy in kindergarten.)
2. Cool off; take a time-out by going for a walk or practicing deep breathing.
3. Do not be in a hurry; put the situation on hold until you have time to think and prepare to cope in a positive way.
4. Be alert and not tired. Revisit the matter after you have had some rest.

Fear and anger, however, are not our only emotional responses. At times we respond out of other emotions and feelings such as disgust, hostility, and avoidance, which can also fuel unproductive conversations with, or verbal responses to, the transgressor. Listening to transgressors is difficult when we are busy thinking of what we will say to them or how we intend to address their offenses when they are through talking. The apostle James tells us, instead, to be swift to hear and slow to speak because anger never produces the righteousness of God.[54] Being slow to speak means controlling the tongue, which is often used to reflect our anger. I believe it also means being fully present when listening to another person's point of view. This aids with empathy and reframing.

At the same time, it is important to remind ourselves that anger is not a sin. The initial emotional response of anger is helpful because it alerts us to legitimate wrongdoing, injustice, or unfair treatment that we need to be concerned about. As seen in chapter 1, the Bible includes examples of Christ's anger, and Paul gives us permission to be angry as long as our anger does not lead to sin. The anger itself is not a sin, but how we respond to our anger can lead to sin and the vicious cycle of unforgiveness. Anger can morph into thoughts of gaining vengeance or shunning the transgressor. When anger or any coping mechanism becomes distorted, our view of productive ways to address the transgression becomes clouded. Distorted anger can manifest in many different ways, such as antagonism, revenge, and verbal lashing out. When we respond to a transgression with distorted anger, we are giving in to temptation and our sinful nature.

Do you know how you tend to cope with the stress of a transgression? The next exercise will help you determine your preferred coping style.

Journal Exercise 17a: Coping Style

Think about the offender you are working on during these exercises, and answer as honestly as you can. Only you decide who sees your answers.

When you feel stressed by a transgression that occurred to you, how true is each of the following behaviors for you?

SCORING

1. Completely untrue of me
2. Mostly untrue of me
3. Moderately true of me
4. Mostly true of me
5. Describes me perfectly

SCORE	PRODUCTIVE BEHAVIORS	SCORE	AVOIDANT BEHAVIORS
	I try to research solutions to the problem.		I tend to disregard or trivialize the threat.
	I generate alternative ideas to the problem.		I talk with others about the offense to get their viewpoint.
	I reframe the situation from other perspectives.		I tend to argue about solutions with the offender.
	I objectively review my concerns.		I tend to express anger and hostility toward the offender.
	I try to negotiate a solution with the offender.		I rationalize why the offense is not an issue for me.
	I set boundaries to avoid further transgressions.		I think about how awful the offender is without all facts.
	Other:		Other:
	Total of all scores for active problem-solving		**Total of all scores for avoidant problem-solving**
	I try to use humor to lighten up the situation.		I tend to blame myself and to vent how I feel.
	I seek support from others to help me deal with my emotions.		I use hobbies, movies, or diversions instead of thinking.
	I employ relaxation techniques to help me deal with emotions.		I express hostility toward the offender to deflect my feelings.
	I have a good cry.		I abuse drugs, food, or alcohol to avoid painful thoughts.
	Other:		Other:
	Total of all scores for active emotional focus		**Total of all scores for avoidant emotional focus**

Think about the offender you are working on during these exercises, and answer as honestly as you can. Only you decide who sees your answers.

When you feel stressed by a transgression that occurred to you, how true is each of the following behaviors for you?

SCORING

1. Completely untrue of me
2. Mostly untrue of me
3. Moderately true of me
4. Mostly true of me
5. Describes me perfectly

SCORE	PRODUCTIVE BEHAVIORS	SCORE	AVOIDANT BEHAVIORS
	I tend to adjust my expectations of the offender or the situation.		I deny that the offense is important to me or that it affects me negatively.
	I write about the transgression in a journal.		I post about the offense on social media to get comments from others.
	I pray or mediate for guidance and for a new meaning of the offense.		I make a list of the shortcomings of the offender to explain the situation.
	I study the Bible to help me better understand God's will in the situation.		I tell the story about the offense to others, looking for new insight.
	I read inspirational quotes to help me look at different points of view.		I talk with the offender to try to get him or her to see my point of view.
	I make a list of blessings and things I am grateful for.		I compare my experience to others with similar transgressions.
	Other:		Other:
	Total of all scores for active meaning-focused coping		**Total of all scores for avoidant meaning-focused coping**

Interpreting Your Scores

	Active problem-solving		Avoidant problem-solving
	Total for active emotion-focused coping		Total for avoidant emotion-focused coping
	Total for active meaning-focused coping		Total for avoidant meaning-focused coping
	Total of all positive scores		Total of all negative scores

Interpretation of the Coping Survey

After compiling your scores, consider which coping mechanisms have the highest scores. Overall, are the scores on the active (positive) or avoidant (negative) side higher? This survey is intended to give you a general idea of your coping style, though the coping mechanisms listed are by no means complete. You should also have written any other ways that you try to cope with the transgression you are experiencing in the "Other" spots.

You may find that your overall scores for positive coping mechanisms are higher than the negative scores. If this is the case, then go back over your negative scores and identify which is ranked the highest. Sometimes a negative coping style can overshadow one's positive attempts to control one's stress. Take note of the negative coping mechanisms and think of how you can work to improve the positive mechanisms in order to reduce the impact of any negative coping styles.

It is beyond the scope of *Forty Days to Forgiveness* to provide coaching on improving coping style, but I have provided references to resources that can be helpful in developing coping skills. It is important for your forgiveness journey to know what your style is in order to understand the effect it may be having on your ability to control your stress related to the transgression. Knowing about your coping style may also help you better understand why the transgression is having a negative effect on your ability to reduce your vicious cycle of unforgiveness and to move on with a peaceful spirit.

Now go back and circle the top five highest scores in the active/positive coping column. These coping strategies are your strengths in challenging situations. The following activity will help you think about how your coping style can lead either to resolving your unforgiveness or moving you toward a more forgiving state:

Journal Exercise 17b: Coping Action Planner

Coping strength 1:
Have you used this strength in response to your transgressor? [Yes] [No]
If so, what result did you get?
Describe how and when this strength could be used to have a positive effect on your ability to forgive:

Coping strength 2:
Have you used this strength in response to your transgressor? [Yes] [No]
If so, what result did you get?
Describe how and when this strength could be used to have a positive effect on your ability to forgive:

Coping strength 3:

Have you used this strength in response to your transgressor? [Yes] [No]

If so, what result did you get?

Describe how and when this strength could be used to have a positive effect on your ability to forgive:

Coping strength 4:

Have you used this strength in response to your transgressor? [Yes] [No]

If so, what result did you get?

Describe how and when this strength could be used to have a positive effect on your ability to forgive:

Coping strength 5:
Have you used this strength in response to your transgressor? [Yes] [No]
If so, what result did you get?
Describe how and when this strength could be used to have a positive effect on your ability to forgive:

DAY 18

Short-Circuiting the Vicious Cycle

When you are unable to cope with a transgression, the alternative is to break away from the anger and fear associated with the vicious cycle of unforgiveness in order to gain a more forgiving spirit. In chapter 3, we saw that making a commitment to try to forgive is the first step toward breaking the vicious cycle of negative feelings that lead to negative intentions, rumination, and unforgiveness. This commitment begins the journey that leads to emotional freedom, which in turn leads to happiness, a balanced life, and positive well-being. However, more than the mental activity of committing to forgive must be done to derail unforgiveness.

As stated before, when we commit to try to forgive from a Christian perspective, the concerns prompting our anger can be averted by self-control; prayer; wisdom;[55] calm and meekness;[56] avoiding angry people;[57] and slowing down and thinking.[58] The apostle James tells us to be swift to hear and slow to speak because anger never produces the righteousness of God. While misuse of the tongue often fuels our anger, effective listening can aid in the control of emotional anger.

The reality is that punishing others out of anger or fear—whether through vengeance, a cold shoulder, or other typical negative reactions—does not improve our situation, nor does it deter others from continuing in transgressive behaviors.[59] When we commit to try to forgive as Christians, we model, instead, a way of functioning that shows love and does good to our transgressors.[60] As Christ disciples us in love, we reflect more Christlike behaviors to transmit Christ's love to others. We are to function first in the best interests of the offender's salvation. In some cases, we may no longer have access to the offender, but our loving response may still lift up the name of the offender to God for restoration and salvation.

As discussed, we can choose productive ways to cope with anger over a transgression before it elevates into unforgiveness. We do this by renewal of our minds, which is accomplished by an ongoing study of the Word, prayer, meditation, and fellowship with believers. We can summarize the biblical approach to anger like this:

1. demonstrating self-control through calmness and meekness, a tender heart, a humble mind, sympathy, brotherly love, and mercy[61]
2. repaying the transgressions of others with blessings and goodness[62]
3. praying for our enemies and praying without ceasing[63]
4. gaining wisdom by continually searching the Word for God's will in our lives[64]
5. as much as we can, avoiding angry people and evildoers[65]
6. being careful not to think of ourselves as better than others[66]
7. slowing down to listen accurately and preparing our response only *after* we think about and understand what we have heard[67]
8. not judging others for their shortcomings, but looking inwardly at our own shortcomings.[68]

Only when we disconnect from anger and fear can we change our response to transgressions from unforgiveness to forgiveness. A lack of these Christlike characteristics allows our negative feelings to become inflamed.

Review of Three Types of Anger

Aggressive, passive-aggressive, and assertive are three types of anger discussed earlier. Aggressive anger and passive-aggressive anger are intended to return hurt to an offender. **Aggressive anger** is outwardly directed toward the offender or things that the offender values, and often includes threatening behaviors such as hitting or yelling or other forms of intimidation. Aggressive anger usually seeks to eliminate the threat by intimidating the other person and transferring accountability for a problem back onto the transgressor. **Passive-aggressive anger** is also intended to be hurtful, but in an indirect way. Its goal is to express anger, hurt, or frustration subtly to avoid major conflict. While acting aggressively may escalate the transgressor's response, a passive-aggressive approach will be hurtful without detection. The victim's anger stays under the radar, so to speak.

An **assertive anger** style, in contrast, is akin to negotiating with the transgressor to resolve the offense in an acceptable and appropriate way. The dictionary defines assertiveness as the quality of being self-assured and confident without being aggressive. It is a form of behavior characterized by a confident respect for the boundaries of oneself and others; it presumes an interest in the fulfillment of needs and desires through cooperation.[69] Assertiveness communicates in a way that another person's point of view is heard without threatening his or her rights.

Assertive people do not shy away from defending their points of view or from trying to influence others, but they respond to both positive and negative emotions without resorting to aggression or passive-aggression. Assertiveness does not mean being a doormat for others. As Paul said, "If possible, so far as it depends on you, live peaceably with all,"[70] but the truth is that we cannot live peacefully with some people. We can try, but at some point, we have to release these people to God.[71] Our role is to continue to model the light of Christ,[72] even when others are difficult and refuse to live in peace with us.[73]

Use the following journal activity to assess what your primary anger style is:

Journal Exercise 18: Your Anger Style

Where is anger controlling your thoughts and actions? This short survey will measure your current level of anger.[74] We can all behave in a way reflective of any of these three styles of anger. Circle "T" (true) if the statement reflects how you most commonly respond in situations similar to the ones described, or circle "F" (false) if the statement does not reflect how you most commonly respond in those situations. Each true answer counts as 1 point; false answers counts as 0 points.[75]

1. T F When people do not respect my feelings, I do not respect theirs.
2. T F I lash out instantly when I am angry.
3. T F When I get mad, I get even.
4. T F When I get angry, I yell and scream.
5. T F When someone is rude to me, I get right in their face and let them have it.
6. T F When someone pressures me to do something I do not want, I usually agree to do it but often take my time or do it incorrectly.
7. T F When I am angry with someone, I laugh and pretend to be joking.
8. T F During most arguments, I usually keep the conflict from escalating by just dropping the subject and walking away.
9. T F When I get angry at someone, I do not say anything for fear of arousing their anger.
10. T F I tend to sulk or brood when someone hurts my feelings.
11. T F I can usually express my anger without repercussions. I let people know I am angry without hurting their feelings.
12. T F When I am angry with someone, I try to share my feelings respectfully.
13. T F When I get angry with someone, I usually wait to say anything until we've both had a little time to cool off.
14. T F When I am angry with somebody, I usually say something about it in a firm yet calm manner.
15. T F When I am angry with somebody and other people are around, I generally wait for the right time and place before I confront the person.

Total score for questions 1–5   _____   Aggressive style of expressing anger
Total score for questions 6–10   _____   Passive-aggressive style of expressing anger
Total score for questions 11–15   _____   Assertive style of expressing anger

Interpreting Your Scores

The highest score for each anger style is 5 and the lowest is 0. We can all show any of these styles, depending on the situation and the emotional state we are in at the time. Think of these styles as a hierarchy, ranking them from the style with your highest score to the one with your lowest score. Your highest score may be thought of as your go-to or default way of responding to situations you find threatening. As with Corrie ten Boom, being aware of your default style can help you recognize when to call upon the Lord to give you guidance and intervene in your emotions. Reflect on the forgiveness issue that you have chosen to work on throughout *Forty Days to Forgiveness*. Have you shown any of these anger styles outwardly? inwardly? toward the transgressor?

DAY 19

Positive Intentions

Anger and fear are our natural traits, and like any trait, they are virtually impossible to stop. We can, however, replace anger and fear with more constructive behaviors. In the forgiveness life cycle, we are seeking to terminate the vicious cycle by replacing negative intentions with positive thoughts and intentions toward the transgressor. For example, review the following chart:

FORGIVENESS SEEKS TO REPLACE NEGATIVE THOUGHTS AND INTENTIONS OF ...	... WITH PROSOCIAL, POSITIVE THOUGHTS AND INTENTIONS OF ...
• retaliation and revenge	• empathy
• resentment and bitterness	• compassion
• negative judgment and emotions	• generosity
• hatred and verbal aggression	• love
• hostility and anger	• beneficence
• fear and avoidance	• humility
• shame and guilt	• unconditional regard
• indifference	• reflecting Christ's light

Both the transgressor and the transgressed experience positive, prosocial outcomes when the offended person exchanges negative thoughts for those listed in the foregoing chart. In essence, forgiveness is another word for loving others; forgiveness is a means of being faithful to the life to which God has called us. When we forgive a transgression, we reflect the light of Christ and allow God's grace to flow through us to the offender. In that sense, forgiveness helps us to experience gratitude to God as we remember that we are passing to another person the same love God has shown to us by forgiving our transgressions.[76]

Shifting from negative to positive thoughts may seem difficult. In fact, thinking positive thoughts about your transgressor may seem like a form of persecution. Thinking this way now, while you are still on your forgiveness journey, is all right. (You still have twenty-one days to go.)

Although Paul said that being persecuted for the cause of Christ is a blessing,[77] we will discuss how to overcome feelings of persecution in chapter 5.

In our model of the forgiveness life cycle, four key actions derail us from ruminating over negative intentions: praying, meditating, studying the Word of God, and fellowshipping with other disciples of Christ.[78] These four actions transition us from negative to positive intentions, which in turn leads to forgiveness. This transformation is called "spiritual formation." Research by Berthold and Ruch bears out the efficacy of spiritual formation:

> People with a religious affiliation that also practice their religion were found to be more satisfied with their life and scored higher on instruments that measure "life of meaning" than those who do not practice their religion and non-religious people. Also, religious people who practice their religion differed significantly from those who do not practice their religion and non-religious people regarding several character strengths; they scored higher on surveys measuring kindness, love, gratitude, hope, forgiveness, and on spirituality.[79]

The vicious cycle of rumination and negative intentions is destined to make us unhappy and threaten our state of well-being; in an ever-downward spiral, unhappy people are less likely to be forgiving.[80] In contrast, research reveals that forgiveness makes a positive impact on life satisfaction.[81] The alternative is to become stuck in a state of anger and fear, which fuels the vicious cycle of unforgiveness.

In preparation to transition to a forgiving state, you will take inventory of how prepared you are for the next step: replacing negative intentions with positive ones. Replacing your negative intentions toward your offender with positive thoughts is no simple task, especially without the assistance of a loving and merciful God. Holding anger and grudges in our hearts is much easier than wishing a transgressor well. The following journal activity builds on our commitment to try to forgive by replacing thoughts of vengeance, retribution, anger, hostility, and the like with empathy, compassion, mercy, and love.

Journal Exercise 19a: Negative to Positive Intentions

In the following chart, put a check next to all the negative thoughts you have toward the offender you are focusing on. Next, draw a line to a positive thought that you believe would be an antidote to the negative thought. Then, rate on a scale of 1 to 5 how difficult each positive thought/feeling would be for you to learn with 1 being the least difficult and 5 being the most difficult.

FORGIVENESS SEEKS TO REPLACE NEGATIVE INTENTIONS AND BEHAVIORS SUCH AS ...	... WITH POSITIVE, PROSOCIAL FEELINGS, THOUGHTS, AND BEHAVIORS SUCH AS ...	
❏ retaliation and revenge	❏ empathy	[1] [2] [3] [4] [5]
❏ resentment and bitterness	❏ compassion	[1] [2] [3] [4] [5]
❏ negative judgment and emotions	❏ generosity	[1] [2] [3] [4] [5]
❏ hatred and verbal aggression	❏ love	[1] [2] [3] [4] [5]
❏ hostility and anger	❏ beneficence	[1] [2] [3] [4] [5]
❏ fear and avoidance	❏ humility	[1] [2] [3] [4] [5]
❏ shame and guilt	❏ unconditional worth	[1] [2] [3] [4] [5]
❏ indifference	❏ reflecting Christ	[1] [2] [3] [4] [5]
other _____	other _____	

Journal Exercise 19b: Visualization Activity

Step 1: Choose one negative intention from the list in journal exercise 19a and write it here:

Close your eyes and visualize acting out that negative intention toward your offender. Think about how he or she would respond and about your own reaction to that response.

Step 2: Choose a positive intention that you believe could replace the negative action that you just visualized. Write it here:

Close your eyes again. Now think about how and when you could display that action toward your offender. Think about how he or she would respond and about your own reaction to that response.

Step 3: Pray for strength using the following prayer template.

Heavenly Father, thank You for the blessing of grace that You have shown to me when I have transgressed against You. I pray now that You give me the strength to stop thinking about [write the negative intention here]

Also, please grant me the desire to show [write the positive intention here]

I pray that You show me how to reflect Your light toward _____ [transgressor].

I bring these requests before You in hopes that I will reflect Your light in all that I do and find peace and well-being for myself as I bring peace and well-being to my offender.

I pray these petitions in Jesus's name, our brother and Savior through whom all good things come. Amen.

DAY 20

Forgiveness Outcomes

In the final analysis, forgiving another person has two outcomes. First, it produces within the forgiver a state of positive well-being and puts his or her life in balance. Second, since it is an empathic response toward a transgressor, it sets the stage to reflect to him or her the love and grace Christ has shown us. In short, forgiveness removes stress and leads to a state of happiness and harmony with both God and the transgressor.

In chapter 3, the terms *happiness* and *well-being* were used interchangeably. Although they are similar, happiness is actually one aspect of our overall well-being. Well-being is defined as the emotional state of being comfortable; being physically, spiritually, and mentally healthy; and being happy. Humans are programmed to keep a balance between being comfortable and uncomfortable, healthy and unhealthy, and happy and unhappy because being too far one way or the other creates stress; too much stress then makes human beings uneasy, unhealthy, and unwise. In short, stress unattended affects our well-being.[82] Forgiveness is the means to be at peace after experiencing the stress that is induced by unforgiveness.

Well-being and happiness are, of course, relative and are defined differently by every person. A transgression that makes one person unhappy may have no effect on another. Consider Sam Berns, for example. How many of us would be happy if we were faced with his challenges? Sam was born with a debilitating condition known as progeria, a disease that causes premature rapid aging and death at an early age. Despite his condition, in a recent TedX Talk, Sam Berns shared his philosophy for a happy life:[83]

- Be okay with what you cannot do because there is so much you can do.
- Surround yourself with people you want to be around.
- Keep moving forward, having something to strive for to make your life richer.
- Never miss a party if you can help it.

How does Sam's advice influence your view of your unforgiveness? At the least, we can say that happiness is a choice. A Gallup poll[84] identified five factors that make up well-being: success with one's career, positive social relationships, achieving financial goals, having community connection, and being physically healthy. As Sam Berns said, social and community well-being are created by surrounding ourselves with people who show interest and encouragement to us—people whom we like and to whom we can relate in positive ways. When career, physical health, and financial health are all goal-oriented and we focus on what we can achieve instead of what is missing from our lives, we increase our sense of well-being.

Each of us determines in our own mind what we see as well-being in each of these five categories of life. As stated in chapter 1, we have ideas about how the world should be, and when those ideas are violated, we become stressed. In response to our stress, we try to cope in ways that will restore our well-being to what it was before the transgression. This hope, however, is an illusion. Our lives can never be fully restored to how they were before a transgression. It is like stepping into a river: even though you step into the same spot, the river has changed because it is always moving. Trying to recreate a relationship to be what it was before a transgression creates more stress. Once a transgression has occurred, we have to visualize what we want our new situation to look like; we also have to visualize how the transgression has changed us. If our goal is for things to be as they were before, we are setting ourselves up for more anger and unhappiness because we cannot reach that goal. Anger and unhappiness create frustration and more stress. Our unhappiness is then reinforced and maintained by the vicious cycle of unforgiveness.

Transitioning from unforgiveness to forgiveness requires three actions on our part. First, we must be aware of what is challenging or attacking our sense of well-being (chapter 2) and how that challenge is changing us. Second, we must be willing to consider making a choice to forgive (chapter 3). Finally, we must visualize what life will be like for us after we forgive so that we are clear about what happiness will look like for us (the fruit of the Spirit) and understand the steps of spiritual formation that are required to move us from an unhappy to a happy state.

We cannot become happy by thinking about changing our feelings. Instead, when we change our spiritual state, we overcome transgressions and injustices that cause feelings of unhappiness. Then with the help of the Holy Spirit, we move toward restoring our state of well-being. Our spiritual formation is nurtured through a rich prayer life, gratitude, an indwelling knowledge of the Word, and our relationships with other followers of Christ. We will cover each of these elements of spiritual formation in more depth in chapter 5.

Journal Exercise 20: Activity to Assess Well-Being[85]

Rate how much you agree or disagree with the statements about each element of well-being: 1 = highly disagree and 5 = highly agree.

CAREER WELL-BEING	RATING
Regarding where I work to earn an income to support myself and those dependent on me:	
1. I look forward to working, and I like the work I do.	[1] [2] [3] [4] [5]
2. My work fits my strengths and interests.	[1] [2] [3] [4] [5]
3. I feel a deep sense purpose for my life.	[1] [2] [3] [4] [5]
4. I have a plan to attain my life goals.	[1] [2] [3] [4] [5]
5. I am motivated by a key leader in my life.	[1] [2] [3] [4] [5]
6. I am enthusiastic about my future.	[1] [2] [3] [4] [5]
7. I take time to enjoy life.	[1] [2] [3] [4] [5]
	Total score:___

SOCIAL WELL-BEING	RATING
Regarding those I spend time with (family, coworkers, and community members):	
8. I have several close relationships.	[1] [2] [3] [4] [5]
9. Close relationships help me achieve my goals.	[1] [2] [3] [4] [5]
10. My close relationships help me enjoy life.	[1] [2] [3] [4] [5]
11. My close relationships help me to be healthy.	[1] [2] [3] [4] [5]
12. I am surrounded by people who encourage me.	[1] [2] [3] [4] [5]
13. I am surrounded by people who accept me.	[1] [2] [3] [4] [5]
14. I invest time in developing relationships.	[1] [2] [3] [4] [5]
	Total score:___

FINANCIAL WELL-BEING	RATING
Regarding how I make and manage money and the economic resources I rely on to support my lifestyle:	
15. I manage my finances well.	[1] [2] [3] [4] [5]
16. I spend my money wisely.	[1] [2] [3] [4] [5]
17. I buy experiences as well as material things.	[1] [2] [3] [4] [5]
18. I give generously to others.	[1] [2] [3] [4] [5]
19. I am satisfied with my overall living standard.	[1] [2] [3] [4] [5]
20. I am financially secure.	[1] [2] [3] [4] [5]
21. I am free to spend leisure and social time as I wish.	[1] [2] [3] [4] [5]
	Total score:___

PHYSICAL WELL-BEING	RATING
Regarding my physical body, including energy level, capabilities to do what I want, and appearance:	
22. I have healthy lifestyle habits.	[1] [2] [3] [4] [5]
23. I make smart choices about diet.	[1] [2] [3] [4] [5]
24. I exercise regularly and like to exercise.	[1] [2] [3] [4] [5]
25. I get a full night's sleep and feel rested daily.	[1] [2] [3] [4] [5]
26. I am able to do physical activities that most people my age can do.	[1] [2] [3] [4] [5]
27. I am satisfied with my outward physical appearance.	[1] [2] [3] [4] [5]
	Total score:____

COMMUNITY WELL-BEING	RATING
Regarding the people, activities, and organizations with whom and on which I spend time:	
28. I feel safe and secure where I live.	[1] [2] [3] [4] [5]
29. I trust that my basic needs will be met.	[1] [2] [3] [4] [5]
30. I give time, effort, and money to my community.	[1] [2] [3] [4] [5]
31. I receive benefits from the community I am part of.	[1] [2] [3] [4] [5]
32. I feel engaged with the community around me.	[1] [2] [3] [4] [5]
33. My beliefs and interests match those of others in my community around me.	[1] [2] [3] [4] [5]
	Total score:____

Interpreting Your Results

Your scores from the foregoing questions draw a profile of wellness. Use each of your total scores from the foregoing chart to put an X on the line corresponding to score number on each spoke of the chart. Next, connect each of the X marks with a straight line. This line forms an inner circle of well-being. The larger your circle, the greater you perceive that your behaviors, thoughts, and feelings are attuned to promote your well-being. Answer the questions following the spider chart to assess how you feel your state of well-being influences your ability and willingness to forgive.

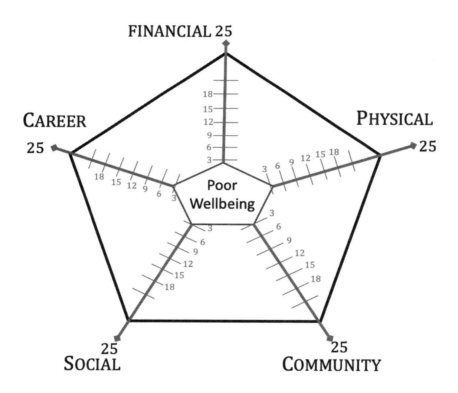

Wellbeing Summary

WHICH OF YOUR WELL-BEING FACTORS DO YOU FEEL WILL BE MOST AFFECTED BY THE TRANSGRESSION YOU EXPERIENCED?

WHAT WILL YOUR WELL-BEING BE LIKE ONE YEAR FROM NOW IF YOU DO NOT FORGIVE THE TRANSGRESSION?

WHAT OTHER EVENTS IN YOUR LIFE WILL AFFECT YOUR WELL-BEING OVER THE NEXT TWELVE MONTHS?

Financial	
Physical	
Community	
Social	
Career	

DAY 21

Empathy

Forgiveness is a broad concept that embraces more than our well-being. One way to examine forgiveness is to consider what is absent from it as well as what is present within it. Absent from forgiveness are the negative thoughts that we entertain about our transgressor and our desire to retaliate, avenge ourselves, or defame him or her to others. Also absent is the fight for our own justice and fairness, as well as our rumination on the story we have created in our minds about the transgression. Present in forgiveness is beneficence, empathy, mercy, and compassion for the soul of our transgressor. When our forgiveness life cycle includes these attributes, we have a powerful ability to short-circuit the vicious cycle of negative intentions and rumination, reduce stress, and restore well-being.

Empathy has been found to be the pivotal behavior that stands between negative and positive intentions.[86] Although there are a variety of definitions for empathy, all include the following components: seeing things from another person's perspective; understanding the other's point of view of a situation; and using that understanding to guide one's behavior toward another person. Empathy is also characterized by asking the transgressor questions to clarify his or her perspective on the transgression, but empathy does not mean having to accept that explanation as accurate or sufficient. Instead, empathy is gaining insight in order to separate the person from his or her behavior. One author explains empathy as "a social and emotional skill that helps us feel and understand the emotions, circumstances, intentions, thoughts, and needs of others, such that we can offer sensitive, perceptive, and appropriate communication and support."[87]

The key is that empathy is a coping skill that is not unique to any particular group of people; it is a skill that can be learned by men and women, children and the aged, rich and poor. In our chart of coping skills, empathy is an active "meaning making" strategy: it is an approach to comparing our ideas of how the world should be to another person's views of the world, regardless of our relationship to such person. Another author defines empathy as "a constant awareness of the fact that your concerns are not everyone's concerns and that your needs are not everyone's needs, and that some compromise has to be achieved moment by moment."[88] This writer goes on to say that empathy is not self-sacrifice but is an ongoing, ever-evolving way of living. Empathy pushes us into new worlds of understanding what others deem important, which may differ from what we feel is important. Like forgiveness, empathy requires repeated effort to remove the barriers created by our unenforceable rules. Fortunately, we are wired to be empathic. Empathy goes back to the days when humans lived in packs and had to rely on one another for survival. Getting along with and relying on others was crucial to working as a group to overcome challenges to survival. Researchers have found that a portion of the human brain is dedicated to empathy.[89] We can nurture and develop that part of the brain to reclaim a skill that was once common among humankind.

Empathy is a response to your own emotions and the emotions of others. As explained in chapter 2, emotions differ from feelings. Emotions are the body's reaction to situations that alert us to demonstrate anger, fear, disgust, surprise, or joy. Emotions are the reactions that we are born with. We do not learn emotions; they are innate. Feelings are, in contrast, our responses to emotions after we have thought about their meaning. For example, I may experience the emotion of fear when I am standing at a crosswalk and a car honks. After thinking about my fear, feelings of relief arise when I realize that the honking is aimed at another car, not at me. When we interpret our emotions, we can then channel them productively with sensitivity and authenticity. Empathy is foremost a social and emotional skill that helps us understand our own and others' emotions, circumstances, intentions, thoughts, and needs so that we can offer sensitive, perceptive, and appropriate communication and support.

Being empathic means accepting that all emotions are good when expressed appropriately. Unfortunately, many of us learn in early childhood to distrust our emotions, to categorize them as positive or negative, and to be suspicious of them. For some, emotions have been portrayed as unwelcome, irrational, and even dangerous. Emotions, however, always truly reflect the internal experiences of the person experiencing them even though the person may not be expressing them appropriately.

If we can decipher emotions, intentions, nuances, social space, and nonverbal language, we can see deeply into people's lives. We can see the issues others think they are hiding and understand how they approach life and relationships. We then can become skilled at getting to the essence of who people are. Skilled empathy is the bridge to understanding the perspectives of others and imagining what life feels like for them: how they approach a situation, what their intentions are, how they will respond to others. The point is not to ask yourself what you would do in the other person's place but to understand what that person would do. Empathy has six essential aspects:[90]

1. **Emotion awareness**—a sense that an emotion is occurring in you or another person or that a particular emotion is expected of you.

2. **Emotional accuracy**—the ability to identify accurately and understand emotional states, thoughts, and intentions in yourself and others, drawing upon a rich vocabulary to identify the emotions.

3. **Emotion regulation**—the ability to understand, regulate, and work with your own emotions; to be self-aware.

4. **Perspective taking**—imaginatively putting yourself in the place of others, seeing situations through their eyes, and accurately sensing what they are feeling and thinking so you can understand what they want or need.

5. **Concern for others**—connecting with others in a way that demonstrates an ability to care about them.

6. **Perceptive engagement**—making thoughtful decisions about the emotions another person is experiencing and taking appropriate action based on perception of his or her emotional state from facts and insight.

Empathy is the essence of forgiveness. Without empathy toward a transgressor, forgiveness is not likely. Being empathic is a process that seeks to accurately understand others' behaviors, whether the people are present or not. By actively understanding their perspectives, we can find ways to regulate our own reactions to them and show concern for them. Then, through our concern, we can engage with them in ways that help us break the vicious cycle of unforgiveness and begin to formulate positive intentions. In other words, empathy is the doorway to loving others and treating them with goodness despite their transgressions. In the next chapter we will talk about how spiritual formation leads to empathy. For now, the following two exercises will help you nourish your empathy for the person who offended you:

Journal Exercise 21a: Activity to Build Empathy

1. For this activity, you will need three chairs and a close friend, prayer partner, or sympathetic family member who takes notes throughout the process. Set three chairs as shown in this diagram:

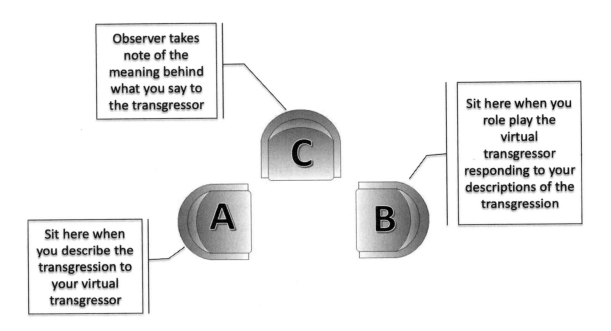

Empathy Exercise

2. To begin, sit in chair A and pretend that your transgressor is in chair B. Describe the transgression as if the person is actually in the chair. You can go back to chapter 2 and use your journal logs to help you do this.

3. Next, sit in chair B and face the chair you were just in, chair A. Verbalize aloud what you think the transgressor would say in answer to your description of the transgression and its effect on you. Here are some questions you can consider from the perspective of the transgressor:

    a. What was life like for the transgressor while he or she was growing up?
    b. What wounds did he or she suffer from others that could have made him or her more likely to hurt you?
    c. What extra pressures or stresses were in this person's life at the time he or she offended you?

d.   What is he or she like when not embroiled in a situation such as the one that hurt you?

e.   What is this person like from a spiritual perspective? Does he or she need God's grace and salvation?

Note: These questions are not meant to excuse or condone; rather, they are intended to help you better understand the other person's areas of pain, those areas that make him or her vulnerable and human.

Now go back to chair A and continue your conversation with the transgressor, responding to the reaction that you just created for him or her.

4.   Return to chair B and respond to what you just said from the point of view of the transgressor.

5.   Repeat this process until you have a better understanding of the transgression from your transgressor's point of view.

6.   Ask your partner (who has been observing this process from chair C) to give his or her reaction. This person might ask what you meant by something you said or may help clarify the transgressor's responses to your descriptions of what happened.

7.   When the observer is through, take a few moments to pray before going on to the next step.

8.   For the final step, you need paper and a pencil/pen. Write a letter from the transgressor to you, describing what happened (or is happening) from his or her point of view. Read the letter to your partner and ask him or her to reflect on whether you have accurately and completely described what happened from the transgressor's perspective.

Journal Exercise 21b: Mindful Empathy

Beginning the Mindfulness Meditation Practice

- Find a comfortable place to sit where you will not be interrupted for twenty minutes.
- Let your insides relax and feel your breathing as your lungs expand your diaphragm for ten breaths. Breathe in slowly and deeply through your nose; exhale slowly through your mouth. Do not rush.
- As you focus on the sensation of breathing, your body and mind will begin to relax; the chronic tension that comes with suffering will loosen; and you will be able to think more clearly and creatively.
- When your mind wanders off and you are no longer simply feeling yourself breathing, just come back to the breath without judgment of yourself.

Gratitude Meditation Practice

- As you continue to sit, begin to extend thoughts of well-being, peace, happiness, and love to yourself. What are you thankful for? What is going well in your life? How could the transgression you experienced have been worse? Think about your thankfulness for the transgression's not having been worse than it was.
- Look within yourself and consider the ways God has gifted you and enabled you in your life.
- Look into your past to remember how God has used events to shape you and prepare you for something greater.
- Think of your own life or the lives of others to find examples of how people have responded to adversity.
- Look ahead into your future to think about where God is leading you and how this transgression will strengthen you to move toward His will for you.

Loving-Kindness Meditation Practice

- As you continue to sit, begin to extend thoughts of thankfulness toward God for the person who offended you.
- Look into his or her past and consider events that shaped the transgressor and brought him or her to the point of committing the transgression against you.
- Think of your own life and ways that you and your transgressor are similar and dissimilar. Remember that to a greater or lesser extent, you both share a relationship with God.
- Consider where God is leading your transgressor and how His grace will be part of the transgressor's future through you (if only through your prayers for him or her).

Closing the Mindfulness Meditation Practice

- As you continue to sit, let your insides relax and feel yourself breathing deeply as your lungs push against your diaphragm for ten breaths.
- When your mind wanders into negative thoughts, bring it back to thoughts of what you are thankful for and come back to the breath without judgment of yourself.
- Pray the prayer of Saint Francis of Assisi:

  Lord, make me an instrument of your peace:
  where there is hatred, let me sow love;
  where there is injury, pardon;
  where there is doubt, faith;
  where there is despair, hope;
  where there is darkness, light;
  where there is sadness, joy.

  O divine Master, grant that I may not so much seek
  to be consoled as to console,
  to be understood as to understand,
  to be loved as to love.
  For it is in giving that we receive,
  it is in pardoning that we are pardoned,
  and it is in dying that we are born to eternal life.
  In the name of Christ, from whom all good things come,
  amen.

- Slowly let yourself rest in the peace of your meditation, and then resume your activities.

Chapter 4 Summary

This chapter focused on the third step in the ACTION model, transitioning out of the vicious cycle of negative thoughts about your transgressor to a state of positive intentions toward him or her. Elements of this process include the following:

- replacing the unforgiveness life cycle with a Christ-centered approach to forgiveness
- looking at the transgression from a different point of view
- embracing love, empathy, and compassion for the transgressor in order to reflect the light of Christ
- reestablishing balance and peace of mind in your own life.

We also explored key concepts:

- biblical characteristics of forgiveness
- coping positively with stress
- short-circuiting the vicious cycle of rumination and negative intentions
- empathy and its role in forgiveness.

In the journal exercises, you considered the following:

- your forgiveness strengths
- your preferred coping style (active/positive or avoidant/negative)
- your plan to cope positively (problem-solving, emotion-focused, meaning-focused)
- your anger style (aggressive, passive-aggressive, assertive)
- your commitment to replace negative intentions with positive ones
- your current state of well-being (career, social, financial, physical, community)
- how to extend empathy to your transgressor.

Scripture for Strength

Put on then, as God's chosen ones, holy and beloved, compassionate hearts, kindness, humility, meekness, and patience, bearing with one another and, if one has a complaint against another, forgiving each other. As the Lord has forgiven you, so you also must forgive. And above all these, put on love, which binds everything together in perfect harmony. And let the peace of Christ rule in your hearts, to which indeed you were called in one body. And be thankful. (Colossians 3:12–15)

Devotional Prayer

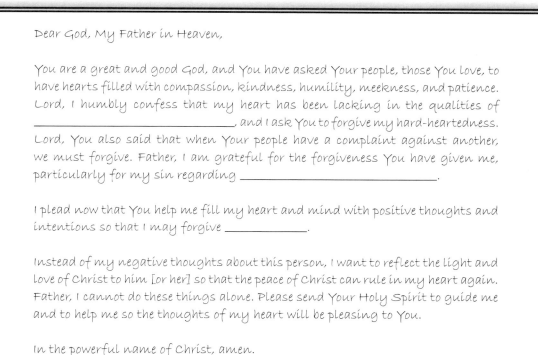

Dear God, My Father in Heaven,

You are a great and good God, and You have asked Your people, those You love, to have hearts filled with compassion, kindness, humility, meekness, and patience. Lord, I humbly confess that my heart has been lacking in the qualities of _____, and I ask You to forgive my hard-heartedness. Lord, You also said that when Your people have a complaint against another, we must forgive. Father, I am grateful for the forgiveness You have given me, particularly for my sin regarding _____.

I plead now that You help me fill my heart and mind with positive thoughts and intentions so that I may forgive _____.

Instead of my negative thoughts about this person, I want to reflect the light and love of Christ to him [or her] so that the peace of Christ can rule in my heart again. Father, I cannot do these things alone. Please send Your Holy Spirit to guide me and to help me so the thoughts of my heart will be pleasing to You.

In the powerful name of Christ, amen.

Resources to Help with Coping

Hankins, G., and C. Hankins. *Prescription for Anger: Coping with Angry Feelings and Angry People.* Newberg, OR: Barclay Press, 2000.

Orloff, J. *Emotional Freedom: Liberate Yourself from Negative Emotions and Transform Your Life.* New York: Harmony Books, 2009.

Sande, K. *Peacemaker: A Biblical Guide to Resolving Personal Conflict.* Grand Rapids, MI: Baker Books, 2004.

Smith, J. C. *Stress and Coping: The eye of Mindfulness.* Dubuque, IA: Kendall Hunt, 2016.

Chapter 4 Endnotes

1   Romans 12:1–2.
2   In E. L. Worthington, *Dimensions of Forgiveness* (Philadelphia: Templeton Foundation Press, 1998), p. 157; E. L. Worthington, *Forgiveness and Reconciliation: Theory and Application* (New York: Routledge, 2006), pp. 58–60.
3   Galatians 5:22–6:2.
4   Galatians 5:16–17.
5   Romans 8:13, 26.
6   The process of internalization and spiritual formation will be dealt with more in chapter 5.
7   Colossians 3:1–4.
8   Colossians 3:12–17.
9   Do these first two bullets ring any bells? Read 1 Corinthians 13.
10 R. D. Enright, *Forgiveness Is a Choice: A Step-by-Step Process for Resolving Anger and Restoring Hope* (Washington, DC: APA Life Tools, 2001), pp. 157–59.
11 R. D. Enright and R. P. Fitzgibbons, *Helping Clients Forgive: An Empirical Guide for Resolving Anger and Restoring Hope* (Washington, DC: APA Press, 2000), p. 81.
12 Worthington, *Forgiveness and Reconciliation*, pp. 100–3.
13 Ephesians 4:32.
14 Ephesians 4:14–15.
15 John 15:11; 1 Thessalonians 1:6.
16 Galatians 5:22, 25.
17 Matthew 5:44.
18 Ephesians 4:32; Colossians 3:12–15.
19 1 Corinthians 13; Galatians 5:22; Ephesians 4:1–3.
20 Matthew 18:21–22; Luke 17:4.
21 Matthew 5:38–42.
22 Matthew 5:44; Ephesians 5:1–2.
23 Ephesians 5:1–2.
24 Mark 11:25.
25 Romans 12:21.
26 Luke 11:4; 1 Timothy 2:3–4; John 20:23.
27 2 Corinthians 1:3–7.
28 Galatians 6:1–3.
29 Ephesians 4:32.
30 Matthew 7:1–3.
31 Matthew 5:38; Romans 12:21.
32 1 Peter 2:1–3.
33 Matthew 18:21–22.
34 2 Corinthians 2:7; Ephesians 4:31–32.
35 Matthew 6:14–15.
36 Ephesians 4:22–32.
37 Matthew 5:39–48; Luke 6:27–36.

38 Romans 7:15–20.

39 2 Corinthians 10:3–6. We will talk more about strongholds in chapter 6.

40 Matthew 7:1–3.

41 Ephesians 4:25–27.

42 L. G. Jones, *Embodying Forgiveness: A Theological Analysis* (Grand Rapids, MI: William B. Eerdmans, 1995), p. 163.

43 Romans 7:21.

44 R. Lazarus and S. Folkman, *Stress, Appraisal, and Coping* (New York: Springer, 1984), pp. 142–43.

45 Worthington, *Forgiveness and Reconciliation*, pp. 50–53.

46 S. Folkman and R. S. Lazarus, "An Analysis of Coping in a Middle-Aged Community Sample," *Journal of Health and Social Behavior* 21 (1980): 219–39.

47 J. Haidt, *The Happiness Hypothesis: Finding Modern Truth in Ancient Wisdom* (New York: Basic Books, 2006), p. 146.

48 C. J. Holahan and R. H. Moos, "Risk, Resistance, and Psychological Distress: A Longitudinal Analysis with Adults and Children," *Journal of Abnormal Psychology* 96 (1987): 3–13.

49 Proverbs 25:28.

50 1 Timothy 2:8.

51 Proverbs 15:1; Ecclesiastes 10:4.

52 Proverbs 22:24–25.

53 Proverbs 15:18, 16:32, 19:11; James 1:19.

54 James 1:19–20.

55 Proverbs 29:8.

56 Proverbs 15:1; Ecclesiastes 10:4.

57 Proverbs 22:24–25.

58 Proverbs 15:18, 16:32, 19:11; Titus 1:7; James 1:19.

59 Jones, *Embodying Forgiveness*, pp. 270–78.

60 Romans 12:14–21; Martin Luther King Jr., "Loving Your Enemies," in *Strength to Love* (Philadelphia: Fortress, 1963).

61 Proverbs 15:1, 25:28; Ecclesiastes 10:4.

62 1 Peter 2:15, 3:9; Romans 12:20–21.

63 Matthew 5:44; Luke 6:35; 1 Thessalonians 5:17; Ephesians 6:18.

64 Proverbs 29:8.

65 Proverbs 22:24–25.

66 Romans 12:3; 2 Peter 2:17.

67 Proverbs 15:18, 16:32, 19:11; James 1:19, 4:11.

68 Matthew 7:1–5; James 4:11, 5:9.

69 J. M. Gottman, *The Seven Principles for Making Marriage Work* (London: Orion House (2000).

70 Romans 12:18.

71 Romans 12:19.

72 Matthew 5:14–16; 2 Corinthians 4:4–6.

73 Luke 9:5.

74 Adapted from G. Hankins and C. Hankins, *Prescription for Anger: Coping with Angry Feelings and Angry People* (Newberg, OR: Barclay, 2000). Used with permission.

75 For more information, see the workbook by Hankins and Hankins: Info@Barclaypress.com, (800) 962-4014.

76 Ephesians 4:32; Colossians 3:13.

77 1 Peter 4.

78 These four features of Christian forgiveness will be covered in more detail in Chapter 5: Internalizing Spiritual Formation.

79 A. Berthold and W. Ruch, "Satisfaction with Life and Character Strengths of Non-Religious and Religious People: It Is Practicing One's Religion that Makes the Difference," *Frontiers in Psychology* 5 (August 14 2014), Article 876.

80 F. Jiang, X. Yue, S. Lu, and G. Yu, "Can You Forgive? It Depends on How Happy You Are," *Scandinavian Journal of Psychology* 56, no. 2 (2015): 182–88; R. D. Carlisle and J. Tsang, "The Virtues: Gratitude and Forgiveness," in *APA Handbook of Psychology, Religion, and Spirituality*, i (2013).

81 J. Eldeleklioğlu, "Predictive Effects of Subjective Happiness, Forgiveness, and Rumination on Life Satisfaction," *Social Behavior and Personality* 43, no. 9 (2015): 1563–74.

82 T. Rath and J. Harter, *Well-Being: The Five Essential Elements* (Toronto, Canada: Gallup Press, 2010).

83 S. Berns, "My Philosophy for a Happy Life," TEDxMidAtlantic, YouTube video, 12:44, December 13, 2013, https://www.youtube.com/watch?v=36m1o-tM05g. I highly recommend watching "Remembering Sam Berns" on YouTube.

84 This data, based on Gallup research collected in an international survey in 2010, is presented by Tom Rath and Jim Harter in *Well-Being: The Five Essential Elements*.

85 This survey is based on Gallup data collected in an international survey reported in 2010. The data is presented by Tom Rath and Jim Harter in *Well-Being: The Five Essential Elements*.

86 There is more research on the role of empathy in mediating forgiveness than can be cited here. Three of the more significant findings are as follows: M. E. McCullough, E. L. Worthington, and K. C. Rachel, "Interpersonal Forgiving in Close Relationships, in E. Worthington, ed., *Dimensions of Forgiveness* (1979), pp. 259–61; Enright and Fitzgibbons, *Forgiveness Therapy*; N. Wade and E. Worthington, "In Search of a Common Core: A Content Analysis of Interventions to Promote Forgiveness, *Psychotherapy: Theory, Research, Practice, Training* 42, no. 2 (2005): 167.

87 K. McLaren, *The Art of Empathy: A Complete Guide to Life's Most Essential Skill* (Boulder: Sounds True, 2013), p. 10.

88 R. Krznaric, *Empathy: Why It Matters and How to Get It* (New York: Perigee, 2014), p. xxi.

89 Ibid.

90 Adapted from McLaren, *The Art of Empathy*.

CHAPTER 5

Internalizing Forgiveness through Spiritual Maturity

The good person out of the good treasure of his heart produces good, and the evil person out of his evil treasure produces evil, for out of the abundance of the heart his mouth speaks. For God, who said, 'Let light shine out of darkness,' has shone in our hearts to give the light of the knowledge of the glory of God in the face of Jesus Christ.

—2 CORINTHIANS 4:6

DAY 22

The Condition of the Heart–Introduction

Forgiveness comes from the heart. When our hearts are filled with the light of Christ, His light shines through us to glorify Him to everyone we come in contact with. Chapter 4 describes forgiveness as coming from a heart of compassion and empathy. Our tendency, however, is to approach unforgiveness with rational thought. When we internalize our story about the transgression, we become consumed with thoughts about what happened to us and how we would like to get relief from the hurt. The more we think about the transgression we experienced, the more we run the risk of a hardened heart. When the heart is hard and closed off, it becomes difficult for the heart to express compassion and empathy. The antidote for a hardened heart is the fourth step in the ACTION model, internalizing forgiveness through spiritual maturity.

Forgiveness Step 4: Internalizing Forgiveness through Spiritual Maturity

Positive thoughts about your transgressor stir up a different set of emotions from the negative ones you initially felt. Internalizing your experience and viewing it through a godly lens promotes the development of Christlike behaviors, thoughts, and feelings. The following are the key goals for internalizing your forgiveness process:

- Beginning to practice the disciplines that lead to ongoing spiritual maturity.
- Developing feelings, thoughts, and actions so that others will see Christ in you.
- Nurturing a preference for prayer and meditation in all things.
- Building a stronger knowledge of God's Word.
- Nurturing fellowship with like-minded disciples of Christ in whom you can confide your forgiveness journey.

Things that inhibit nurturing spiritual maturity. Rank the following inhibitors from the most (1) to the least (8) like you.

_____ I hold onto grudges, and that distracts me from nurturing my spiritual maturity.

_____ I withhold my help from my transgressor if he or she needs something.

_____ I want him or her to get what he or she deserves.

_____ If I see him or her, I will not act friendly.

_____ I am going to get even.

_____ I will try to get back at him or her.

_____ I want to cut off the relationship with him or her.

_____ I want to demand an apology and receive justice and atonement.

This chapter will examine (1) how the condition of the heart determines how we internalize the transgression we have experienced, (2) how our hearts influence our ability to forgive, and (3) how to create a spiritually mature heart that pleases God and brings us peace.

Day 22: The Condition of the Heart—Introduction

Day 23: Internalizing Forgiveness through Spiritual Formation

Day 24: Internalizing Forgiveness through Scripture Study

Day 25: Internalizing Forgiveness through Meditation

Day 26: Internalizing Forgiveness through Prayer

Day 27: Internalizing Forgiveness through Fellowship

Even though the transgression we experienced may seem insurmountable, the Lord promises that forgiveness is possible. Even when the hurt seems to have turned our hearts to stone, God tells us, "I will remove from them their heart of stone and give them a heart of flesh."[1] Paul told the church at Corinth, "No temptation has overtaken you that is not common to man. God is faithful, and He will not let you be tempted beyond your ability, but with the temptation He will also provide the way of escape, that you may be able to endure it."[2]

The use of the word *temptation* in this passage is interesting. A transgression becomes a temptation only if it seduces us to entertain the negative intentions that come with unforgiveness. The temptation to respond negatively to the transgressor is what ensnares us. The passage just quoted tells us that the temptation to respond negatively is not beyond what we can endure: we can overcome our negative intentions. The transgression itself is not a "trial"; rather, the trial is the temptation to respond to the transgression in a way that does not mirror the love of Christ. James tells us, "Count it all joy, my brothers when you meet trials of various kinds, for you know that the testing of your faith produces steadfastness."[3] In other words, demonic forces in the world instigate acts of transgression, *but God uses transgressions in our lives to perfect our faith.* In his letter to the church in Corinth, Paul spoke about how the devil leads us astray by false teachings. Paul says, "I am afraid that as the serpent deceived Eve by his cunning, your thoughts will be led astray from a sincere and pure devotion to Christ."[4] One way Satan pulls us from a pure devotion to Christ is through our unforgiveness. One author referred to this as "the bait of satin."

God, on the other hand, takes advantage of a transgression as a "teachable moment." Peter puts it this way:

> *Be sober-minded; be watchful. Your adversary the devil prowls around like a roaring lion, seeking someone to devour. Resist him, firm in your faith, knowing that the same kinds of suffering are being experienced by your brotherhood throughout the world. And after you have suffered a little while, the God of all grace, who has called you to his eternal glory in Christ, will himself restore, confirm, strengthen, and establish you.*[5]

When we experience suffering or other challenging situations, we sometimes wonder, *Why is God letting this happen to me?* Although thinking of transgressions as personal affronts that threaten our well-being is natural, we must understand that God is not orchestrating these events: Satan is hoping to convince believers that God's strength is not sufficient to sustain His followers. Satan wants to turn us away from God to live by our own will rather than God's will. The suffering created by a transgression, however, is a critical part of how God uses circumstances in our lives to make us strong in our faith. James explains that we are to "let steadfastness have its full effect that [we] may be perfect and complete, lacking in nothing."[6] Without God's might in our lives, we would crumble, and Satan would, in fact, use transgressions to drive a wedge between us and God.

As Peter admitted (as quoted earlier), we may suffer for a little while.[7] God never promised us lives without suffering; rather, He promised that He would be there to help us get through suffering, trials, and temptations. As God told Paul when he complained about his thorn in the flesh, "My grace is sufficient for you, for my power is made perfect in weakness."[8] Paul's response to this promise is our response as well: "Therefore, I will boast all the more gladly of my weaknesses, so that the power of Christ may rest upon me."[9] In short, we choose how we respond to a transgression: we can choose to have God's help, or we can allow Satan to use transgressions to drive us farther from God.

One way help comes from the Lord is through the comfort and direction we receive through His Word, but we have to ask God for help in order to receive His strength. The psalmist implores the Lord to fill his heart with His Word: "With my whole heart I seek you; let me not wander from your commandments! I have stored up your word in my heart that I might not sin against you."[10] You may remember from an earlier chapter the story of how Corrie ten Boom could not forgive the German soldier who inflicted great pain on her and her family. She ultimately cried out to the Lord for help, and He provided her with the strength to accept the soldier's plea for forgiveness. Other examples of victims asking God to forgive their persecutors are Christ on the cross and Stephen as he was stoned. They both cried out to God to forgive their transgressors and not hold their sin against them because the transgressors did not know what they were doing.[11] We have a hard time emulating Christ and Stephen, however, when we are frozen in our anger and resentment. Negative intentions build up like strongholds around our hearts, preventing our behavior from reflecting the love of Christ.[12] With God's help, we can take back control of our thoughts, break down the walls that trap our hearts, and respond to transgressors with compassion and empathy.

> *A heart that seeks God displaces the unrighteous thoughts that lead to unrighteous actions. A heart that seeks God leads to righteous behaviors such as love, joy, peace, patience, kindness, goodness, faithfulness, gentleness, and self-control.[13] Our willingness to keep God's commandments equips us to trade negative intentions for compassion and empathy. During Old Testament times when the Hebrews, God's chosen people, had been conquered and forced to live in exile, God spoke to them through the prophet Jeremiah, saying, "For I know the plans I have for you … plans for welfare and not for evil, to give you a future and a hope. Then you will call upon me and come and pray to me, and I will hear you. You will seek me and find me when you seek me with all your heart."[14]*

Seventy years later, God delivered the Israelites from exile. Today, this verse still encourages people to seek God in difficult times and to have hope and patience amid seemingly insurmountable circumstances. It reminds us that God uses our circumstances for His purposes, a fact we often overlook when we internalize a transgression and ruminate on negative intentions. But we have to ask Him for His help. As Jesus said, "Ask, and it will be given to you; seek, and you will find; knock, and it will be opened to you. For everyone who asks receives, and the one who seeks finds, and to the one who knocks it will be opened."[15] Not only is Jesus saying that prayer is available to every child of God, but also He is expressing an expectation that we will ask for what we need. God answers prayer. Unfortunately, when we do not get an immediate response, we have a tendency to become disappointed and give up.

Paul, in his letter to the church in Thessalonica, also offers helpful instruction: "Rejoice always, pray without ceasing, give thanks in all circumstances; for this is the will of God in Christ Jesus for you."[16] If we were to look at this passage in the original language, we might interpret it as saying, "As you are going, pray." In other words, we are to pray at all times, for all things, in every time of need, in every time of blessing, giving thanks and praise and making supplication for ourselves and others. Note that we are instructed to pray continually and to rejoice in what we are praying for. This means that as we pray for God's strength to overcome a transgression and the temptation to harbor negative intentions, we also rejoice that the transgression occurred since it perfects us and strengthens our faith in Jesus.

Before working as a chaplain, I believed that frequent brief prayers made me seem needy and selfish. Such prayers seemed like a child saying, "Gimme, gimme, gimme." Frequent prayer made me feel like I was whining to God and not presenting my best self. Since becoming a health-care chaplain, however, my view has changed drastically. My job is to go from room to room, and when the patient desires, I help to create a connection with God. But every patient is as different as night and day from all the others. Preoccupation with a previous experience taints my ability to offer spiritual comfort in the next room. Without prayer in between rooms, I don't know how I would get through the day. I've found that prayer is not something that we *do*. Instead, it is a way of living, a lifestyle; it is who we are at every point of every day.

The Condition of the Heart Influences How We Respond to Transgressions

Before Jesus said "My yoke is easy and my burden is light," He said, "Take my yoke upon you and learn of me."[17] How can learning more about Christ lighten the burden of unforgiveness? As mentioned earlier, Jesus never demonstrated personally how to resolve an interpersonal transgression, so how are we to learn from Him? Actually, we have at least three ways to learn how to forgive from Christ.

First, when we learn the mind of Christ and develop a heart like His, our yoke of unforgiveness is lightened by our ability to forgive as God has forgiven us.[18] As we synchronize our hearts with Christ, we build our strength to forgive others the same way the Father forgives us: totally and without regret.

Second, Jesus told parables that illustrate one person forgiving another of an interpersonal transgression. In one, He told about a rich ruler who forgave a man a large debt,[19] and in another He told of a father who forgave his son who had squandered his inheritance.[20]

Third, Jesus gave specific commandments about forgiveness:

- To forgive an unlimited number of times, illustrated in the concept of forgiving seventy times seven.[21]
- To bless those who curse you and pray for those who abuse you.[22]
- To do good to those who hate you.[23]
- To treat others as you wish to be treated.[24]

I suspect there are no instances of Christ forgiving interpersonal transgressions, because those examples would distract us from the truest and best forgiveness ever offered: His death on the cross. In essence, the entire Bible is about God's forgiveness of humankind. Paul tells us that God wants us to forgive others as He has forgiven us.[25] Our pattern for how to forgive was given by God in the sacrifice of Jesus, His Son. Forgiveness requires us, similarly, to sacrifice some part of ourselves, to be replaced with the light of Christ.

The Heart Is the Emotional and Psychological Center of Who We Are

What does "the heart" actually mean? The Bible uses *heart* to refer to the center of something. In the case of humans, the center of our being is the collection of values that influence how we think, behave, and feel. We will call this the spiritual heart. Let's examine how the spiritual heart is formed and sustained:

When the brain receives information from the senses, the unconscious part of the brain immediately classifies the experience as dangerous/harmful or pleasant/beautiful. The experience is then almost instantaneously conveyed to the conscious part of the brain, where we interpret whether or not action is required (movement, thinking, responding). This is called cognitive processing. Next, the brain turns the experience into a memory. Once our senses send information about an experience into our minds, we cannot "unexperience" it, and memories of the event remain permanently in our brains. New experiences trigger our brains to search our memories for similar experiences in the past and compare those with new information being received by our senses.

The spiritual heart is a collection of memories about how our experiences have been beneficial to us or not. The heart evaluates these memories to determine what we like/dislike; believe/disbelieve; value/reject; find pleasurable / find uncomfortable; and so on. Through a study of many passages of scripture, we can be certain that the heart is more than a center for emotions. Because it is composed of our mind, our will, our emotions, and our conscience, the heart does much more than simply provide feelings; the heart also thinks, decides, and places a value on things and events by sensing right from wrong. The following chart lists some of the key verses that describe the characteristics of the heart. The columns to the right suggest which of the four functions of the heart each scripture relates to. Look it over to see if you agree with the functions assigned to each scripture.

	FUNCTIONS OF THE HEART			
SCRIPTURES DESCRIBING THE HEART	VALUES	THINKING	FEELING	DECIDING
1. Our will comes from our heart.[26]	X			X
2. Our emotions are part of our heart. [27]			X	
3. Our conscience is part of our heart.[28]	X			X
4. Our heart influences what we value.[29]	X			X
5. Our heart influences what and whom we trust.[30]	X			X
6. Our heart is the source of all our actions.[31]		X		X
7. Our heart is strengthened by God.[32]	X			
8. Our heart gains peace through Christ, not through the world.[33]	X		X	
9. Our heart helps us overcome fear.[34]			X	
10. Our heart is where our desires come from.[35]			X	X
11. Our heart may be either pure or corrupt.[36]	X			X

Scriptures Describing the Heart	Functions of the Heart			
	Values	Thinking	Feeling	Deciding
12. Our heart is a source of meditation.[37]		X	X	
13. Our heart can be hidden by a stubborn will.[38]			X	X
14. Our heart can be cleaned and made new.[39]	X			
15. Our heart is naturally deceitful, sick, and difficult to understand.[40]	X			
16. Springs of life flow from the heart.[41]	X			
17. Our heart is where what we say comes from.[42]				X
18. What we value in our heart affects good or evil actions.[43]	X			X
19. God's Word dwells in our hearts.[44]	X	X	X	X

The Heart Places a Value on Our Experiences from Either a Worldly or Godly Point of View

From the foregoing list, we can see that the heart has four capacities: to think (or believe), to make choices, to assign value, and to influence how we feel. The heart is the "innermost part" of us that David refers to in Psalms 51:6: "Behold, you delight in truth in the inward being, and you teach me wisdom in the secret heart."[45] Later in this psalm, he says something apropos to our discussion about transgressions. After imploring God to remediate him from his sin, David says, "Then I will teach transgressors your ways, and sinners will return to you."[46]

David's words are a powerful endorsement of the role forgiveness plays in God's plan for humankind. Jesus tells us that what we value determines where our hearts lie.[47] If we value a pure heart, God will bless that. If we value being blameless in God's sight, He will bless that. If we desire to be close to God, He will bless that. When we make a decision to forgive our transgressor, we are seeking resolution, peace of mind, and reduction of our feelings of hurt. But have you also thought, as David did, that forgiving demonstrates God's ways to transgressors and teaches them so they can turn (or return) to Him? If that is a motivation for your decision to forgive, God will bless that too. Our values, therefore, are the basis of our decisions, and when taken together, our values make up our worldview. This means that the heart places a value on our experiences from either a worldly or a godly point of view.

We Make Decisions about How We Behave Based on Our Hearts

Jesus tells us that what we place value on will determine where our heart lies. People walk either by their own personal desires or in the Spirit. Anything related to the fleshly or worldly appetites and desires, rather than to godly and spiritual desires, is referred to as a carnal nature. The carnal person is hostile to God and unable to please God.[48] A carnal mind has active hatred toward righteousness and against God.[49] In addition, we can be open to ourselves and those around us, or we can be concealed and known only to ourselves. One way to visualize this truth is to think about two types of balloons:

Let's suppose we are going to a party, and we decide to take some balloons. If we want the balloons to float in the air, we fill them with helium. If we do not have any helium, we can blow the balloons up with air, but they will not float. In order to create a more festive feeling, the balloons need to float high enough to be visible to everyone. The balloons with air can be hung from the furniture, taped to a wall, or strung to a line that stretches across the room, but since the balloons do not float on their own, they do not create the same atmosphere as helium-filled balloons. If we put a mixture of helium and air in the balloons, they will only hover and will not rise to the height of the room. Such balloons would get bumped into as guests walked around, quickly become annoying.

Our hearts are like these balloons: righteous thoughts are like helium, and worldly thoughts are like air. If we fill our hearts with godly thoughts, they rise above everything else, and we view the world from a godly perspective. If our hearts are filled with worldly thoughts, however, they will not rise above our circumstances. We can artificially prop up our hearts to create some sense of happiness, but this is a limited approach. In the case of forgiveness, we prop up our hearts by doing things to reduce our unforgiveness, but with half measures, our hearts will never float to where we can see our transgressors from a godly perspective. As for the notion of filling our hearts half with worldly thoughts and half with godly thoughts, the result is that our hearts hover close to the ground. Most people throw away balloons that are losing their helium. Jesus had something to say about this half-in, half-out condition. In the book of Revelation, Jesus told the church in Laodicea that they were like lukewarm water, not hot or cold, not against God but not totally for God. Like balloons half full of helium, the people of the church of Laodicea were hovering between their desire for worldly things and their desire for God. They were so distasteful to Christ that He told them, "I will spit you out of my mouth."[50] A heart not totally devoted to Christ will never please Him, but a totally devoted heart will cause us to behave in ways that rise above the expectations of the world. I would suggest that forgiveness is evidence of the condition of a devoted heart.

The condition of our hearts sets the stage for how we respond to the world around us. When our heart is like Christ's, goodness comes out of us. "The good person out of the good treasure of his heart produces good."[51] By the same token, when a heart is filled with worldly thoughts and desires, evil results. "The evil person out of his evil treasure produces evil."[52]

As the foregoing verse attests, a strong relationship exists between the heart and what we think about. Paul told the church in Philippi to think about whatever is true, honorable, just, pure, lovely, and commendable.[53] These are the kinds of thoughts Paul meant when he urged Christians "not [to] be conformed to this world, but [to] be transformed by the renewal of your mind, that by testing you may discern what is the will of God, what is good and acceptable and perfect."[54] As explained in the previous chapter, forgiveness cannot be achieved until we replace the negative intentions toward our transgressor with Christlike thoughts. Thinking about whatever is true, honorable, just, pure, lovely, and commendable conditions the heart to produce Christlike behavior. So just do it, right? Unfortunately, as Jeremiah the prophet tells us, the heart is not naturally conditioned to think and react this way; he says, "The heart is deceitful above all things and desperately sick; who can understand it?"[55]

The heart forms the attitudes that shape our behavior; in other words, our behavior is driven by the condition of the heart. The two are inseparably linked. The heart stores up our attitudes, feelings, beliefs, and values, all of which are the lenses through which we look at a transgression. Our hearts place value on responding to transgressions in ways that yield us to God or in ways that yield us to forces of evil. Without the intervention of Christ, scripture makes clear, our hearts store up attitudes and beliefs that are evil. The heart either provides pure thoughts and attitudes to guide our words and behavior or prompts us to harbor negative intentions and unrighteousness,[56] to devise evil acts,[57] and to invent evil deeds[58] such as murder, saying hurtful things,[59] adultery, sexual immorality, theft, false witness, slander, strife, deceit, gossip, hatred of God, insolence, haughtiness, boastfulness, disobedience to parents, foolishness, faithlessness, heartlessness, ruthlessness,[60] worshipping idols, the practice of homosexuality, greed, drunkenness, reviling, swindling, covetousness, malice,[61] impurity, sensuality, sorcery, enmity, jealousy, fits of anger, rivalries, dissensions, divisions, envy, orgies,[62] bitterness, wrath, clamor,[63] obscene talk,[64] an unhealthy craving for controversy and quarrels about words, evil suspicions, constant friction among people who are depraved in mind and deprived of the truth,[65] and judging with evil thoughts.[66]

Most of the acts of unrighteousness listed in the foregoing paragraph involve, to some extent, what we say: false witness, slander, strife, deceit, gossip, insolence, haughtiness, boastfulness, malice, enmity, fits of anger and wrath, clamor, obscene talk, unhealthy cravings for controversy and quarrels about words, and constant friction among people. And what is the source of all this destructive speech?[67] Jesus, speaking to Peter, said, "What comes out of the mouth proceeds from the heart, and this defiles a person. For out of the heart come evil thoughts." [68]

According to the New Testament writer James, the brother of Jesus, the heart's influence on what we say is too great for us to control consciously. The heart's inability to fully control what we say results in great harm, as we see in this scripture:

The tongue is a fire, a world of unrighteousness. The tongue is set among our members, staining the whole body, setting on fire the entire course of life, and set on fire by hell. For every kind of beast and bird, reptile and sea creature, can be tamed and has been tamed by mankind, but no human being can tame the tongue. It is a restless evil, full of deadly poison. With it we bless our Lord and Father, and with it we curse people who are made in the likeness of God. From the same mouth come blessing and cursing.[69]

I would suggest, furthermore, that the words the heart endorses do not have to be spoken aloud to transgressors to be harmful. We can also speak words to other people to gain their affirmation of our hurt feelings, and those words can negatively affect the transgressor. Even when we merely think harmful words about the transgressor, we are filling our hearts with air instead of helium; we are being worldly rather than Christlike. In various ways, our tongues reflect what our hearts value, resulting in harm for us and our transgressors. Since the heart, the place from which evil comes, can then lead us to respond to transgressions with negative intentions, it stands to reason that in order to treat our transgressors instead with love and empathy, we must have love and empathy in our hearts to eclipse the evil thoughts and deeds that the heart naturally creates.

The Heart Influences What We Are

Just as the physical heart is the center of the body and bodily functions, the spiritual heart is the center of each person's attitudes, beliefs, knowledge, and values and, therefore, is the dwelling place of Christ[70] and the peace of God.[71] Some say that the heart is best understood with an emphasis on reason and will, and others say that the heart is best understood with an emphasis on emotions and temperament, but the Bible uses the term *heart* to designate the whole personality that influences our behavior and how we present ourselves to others. The heart, however, is more than personality. The heart and personality influence each other, yet they are formed in different ways and have separate and distinct influences on our behavior. A simple way to think of the distinction between heart and personality is to know that heart *influences* what we are, whereas the personality *is* what we are.

The heart influences how we feel about things. Jesus said that "from within, out of men's hearts, come evil thoughts" (Mark 7:21). Because the human heart is deceitful above all things (Jeremiah 17:9) and folly is bound up in the heart of a child (Proverbs 22:15), the Spirit of God must give humans a new heart (Jeremiah 31:33; Ezekiel 36:26) that is purified through faith (Acts 15:9; cf. Ephesians 3:17). While we may like to think of the heart as the spiritual part of us that aligns us with the will of Christ, we are inherently human, and therefore we build both spiritual and worldly dispositions. In other words, the heart can never be 100 percent worldly or 100 percent godly. In reality, every decision we make about how we interpret and respond to our experiences is a mixture of our carnal (worldly) nature and our commitment to serve our Lord. So what distinguishes a godly heart from a worldly heart? The worldly heart has a tendency to keep the harm of transgressions in the forefront of the mind.

Anytime we suffer a transgression, we have a strong tendency to ruminate about what happened to us. Sometimes our thoughts about a transgression are so vivid that we actually reexperience the event in our minds as if we were going through the transgression all over again. In extreme cases, this is called posttraumatic stress disorder (PTSD). Transgressions do not usually render us incapable of going on with our lives, but to some degree, we all reexperience transgressions in the form of rumination. The tendency of our minds is to keep the harm in the forefront of our thoughts, creating within us a state of continuing turmoil. Having a heart and mind like Christ is the only way to end this turmoil and create emotional peace. Our minds stay in perfect peace only when they are fixed on our Lord.[72]

Having a heart for God, however, requires more than going to church on Sundays. While coming together in fellowship is important,[73] simply "being religious" is not enough to achieve lasting emotional peace as we attempt to forgive. Nor are casual efforts to serve God enough to fill our hearts with loving words and behaviors. Sunday morning acts of service—welcoming guests, running a soundboard, teaching a Bible class—are not enough to put God at the center of our lives. While these are legitimate forms of service, they are not sufficient to transform our hearts. You can no more become a Christ-centered believer by going to church on Sundays than you can become a car by sleeping in your garage. If your Christian life is limited to Sunday mornings, you will likely struggle to forgive your transgressor and gain emotional peace.

Having a transformative walk with God can be compared to being an Olympic skier: medals are not won by joining a ski club and having fun on the slopes with friends on Sunday mornings. Nor do skiers become champions by carrying other people's skis to the top of the hill or setting up gates on a slalom course. Champions ski as much as they can. When there is no snow, they do not wait for it to fall; they go where the snow is, or the exercise to build their strength and agility. Neither do they eat just anything set before them. They create a diet that nourishes their minds and bodies so they can perform at optimal levels. Furthermore, championship skiers do not rely solely on their own knowledge; rather, they seek out coaches who teach them, correct them, and urge them to excel. Skiing becomes the center of their lives; it dominates their thoughts and activities every minute of every day. Their desire to be Olympians is at the heart of who they are.

We often hear that all we need to do to be happy is to make God the center of our lives. This statement is an empty cliché. Living a life with Christ at the center requires no less of us than the life practices of an Olympic skier. The apostle Paul equated the Christian faith with athletic achievement: "I have fought the good fight, I have finished the race, I have kept the faith. Henceforth there is laid up for me the crown of righteousness, which the Lord, the righteous judge, will award to me on that day, and not only to me but also to all who have loved his appearing."[74] If life is like an athletic competition, then our success as children of God relies on practice and conditioning. Like the skier, our practicing the disciplines of a godly life with dedication is the only way to make Christ the center of our hearts, not going to church on Sunday mornings. Do you have a "club" religion, or do you have an "Olympic" religion?

We also do not keep the faith by desiring harm to befall our transgressors or expecting them to meet our requirements for their penance. Such approaches to forgiveness are like preparing for an Olympic event by hoping that the competition will fail by becoming sick or breaking a leg. Successful athletes do not win by making their competitors less capable, nor is this the approach of God's people. We cannot make God the center of our lives by expecting the transgressor to take responsibility for our emotional peace. It is not up to our transgressors to earn our forgiveness, nor is expecting transgressors to assuage our unrest reasonable. It is up to us, and us alone, to build our strength and maturity, develop a mind like Christ's, and become the vehicle through which God reaches others. Scripture calls God's people the "earthen vessels" through which Christ reaches the world today.[75] The only way we can have a Christlike mind and heart is to fill ourselves with thoughts that are honest, just, pure, lovely, and of good report.

A heart that is corrupted by unrighteousness will foil our attempts to show love and compassion. When we draw near to God by knowing and keeping His Word, meditating on His Word, praying for His strength to help us, and fellowshipping with like-minded disciples, we establish a relationship with Him. Then we can show love and compassion to others, even our transgressors. When our relationship with Him is defined by how we seek to know, understand, and obey His commandments, our hearts are filled with love for God; that love, in turn, influences our behavior to others. Like a skier who goes in search of snow so she can practice her craft, each of us must go in search of God. Jesus said that the person who hungers and thirsts for righteousness will be filled.[76] A heart filled with the helium of God's love will float above evil desires for harm to befall our transgressors. When our hearts are filled with love for God, we find psychological and emotional peace from the pain of the transgression we experienced,[77] not because we are trying harder to be forgiving but because the Lord "keep[s] him in perfect peace whose mind is stayed on [Him] because he trusts in [Him]. Trust in the Lord forever, for the Lord God is an everlasting rock."[78]

In the next section, we will focus on what it means to have a heart like Christ's, a heart that reflects Him as the central empowering factor in our lives. His empowerment will guide us to overcome the pain of the transgression we experienced. Simply put, making God the center of our lives means engaging in behaviors, every hour of every day, that fill our minds with thoughts that praise Him and seeking His guidance in prayer, in scripture, and in living in harmony with other disciples of Christ. As much as I wish I could say that I engage in these kinds of thoughts all day, every day, I am a dismal failure on all counts. I am writing this next section for me, and I invite you along for the journey.

A Relationship with Christ Is Fundamental to Spiritual Maturity and Is an Ongoing Process

Jesus said that if we love Him, we will keep His commandments.[79] While all the commandments are important, Jesus said that the two greatest are to love God with all our hearts, souls, and minds and to love our neighbors—and our neighbors include our enemies—as ourselves.[80] Loving God is not a casual endeavor: it is a vocation and a lifestyle. Loving God requires that we constantly resist evil, which is done through prayer, meditation, study of the Word, and fellowship with other believers.[81] Loving God also requires that we hold in check our love for this world, meaning that we suppress our lusts and pride. We do this by imprinting into our minds a knowledge of God's Word, praying for God to strengthen us, nurturing the indwelling of the Holy Spirit, and living in peace and harmony within our Christian fellowship and our corner of the world.

If I am building a relationship with Christ, then His love is projected through my life. But when I think of people who have treated me unjustly or unfairly, I realize that some are easy to love, some are difficult to love, and some are impossible to love. Without a heart that is filled with His light, it is impossible to make ourselves love someone toward whom we feel unforgiveness.[82] I know that I am in Him and that God is working in my life when I begin to love those who are impossible for me to love naturally. Another personal quality that shows Christ in my life is empathy, the mental process of looking at a transgression from the transgressor's point of view. As stated earlier, looking at the situation from another's point of view does not mean we approve of or accept his or her behavior. Instead, empathy gives us insights that allow God's love to flow through us to the transgressor.

Research into forgiveness has shown that empathy is pivotal to gaining emotional freedom from a transgressor.[83] With Christ, we show empathy that is deeper and more genuine than can be gained without His presence in our hearts. In other words, with the supernatural power of Christ in our hearts, we can overcome our instinct to protect ourselves with unforgiveness and, instead, love those whom we could never love on our own. We cannot by our own will force ourselves to love someone. Only God through the divine working of the Holy Spirit can prepare our minds to love those we deem unlovable.[84]

Loving those who have transgressed us means that we are being guided by the principles and commandments found in the New Testament, that is, the teachings and examples that Christ gave us during His time on earth.[85] We control the world's influence on us by taking every thought captive[86] and by continually renewing our minds.[87] Rejecting the world's standards of right and wrong also includes disassociating ourselves from the world's value system and its preoccupation with pleasure, wealth, and power. Rejecting the world's standards includes resisting close relationships with people whose values could weaken our ability to resist the things of the world. To cultivate intimacy with worldly people is dangerous to the soul.

Our rejection of worldly standards means that we have a willingness to confess Christ openly and not be ashamed to let others know that we are committed to God. Being engaged in spiritual warfare means standing firmly for what is right in God's eyes, habitually ready to let others see that we are guided by principles higher than those that govern our society. Paul told the church at Colossae to "set their minds on things above."[88] Setting our minds on things above includes loving and praying for our enemies;[89] it also requires devotion to filling our hearts with God's Word, asking God for what we need, meditating on how God's Word should influence our lives, and fellowshipping with like-minded believers beyond our Sunday morning rituals.

How well do you set your mind on things above? Is spiritual maturity evident in your thoughts and behaviors? The following exercise will help you answer these crucial questions:

Journal Exercise Part 22a: Setting Your Mind on Things Above

How well are you showing spiritual maturity? Do you feast on the meat of the Word or only on the milk? Use this survey to assess the degree to which you are showing spiritual maturity and growing in spiritual maturity. For each of the signs of spiritual maturity, rate how often and how well you behave that way.

SIGNS OF SPIRITUAL MATURITY	SATISFACTION WITH HOW WELL I DO THIS
1. Generosity	1. [1] [2] [3] [4] [5]
2. Love	2. [1] [2] [3] [4] [5]
3. Beneficence	3. [1] [2] [3] [4] [5]
4. Humility	4. [1] [2] [3] [4] [5]
5. Recognizing others' unconditional worth	5. [1] [2] [3] [4] [5]
6. Reflecting Christ's light	6. [1] [2] [3] [4] [5]
7. Showing self-control through calmness and meekness	7. [1] [2] [3] [4] [5]
8. Having a tender heart and humble mind	8. [1] [2] [3] [4] [5]
9. Showing sympathy, brotherly love, mercy, and compassion	9. [1] [2] [3] [4] [5]
10. Wishing blessings and goodness even on the undeserving	10. [1] [2] [3] [4] [5]
11. Praying for my enemy	11. [1] [2] [3] [4] [5]
12. Praying for strength to overcome my unforgiveness	12. [1] [2] [3] [4] [5]
13. Seeking wisdom by searching the Word for God's will	13. [1] [2] [3] [4] [5]
14. Avoiding angry people and evildoers, but praying for them	14. [1] [2] [3] [4] [5]
15. Not thinking of myself as better than others	15. [1] [2] [3] [4] [5]
16. Listening accurately to what my transgressor says and thinking about my response from a Christlike perspective	16. [1] [2] [3] [4] [5]
17. Choosing godly ways to cope with my feelings about my offender	17. [1] [2] [3] [4] [5]
18. Not judging others for their shortcomings	18. [1] [2] [3] [4] [5]

Journal Exercise 22b: Inhibitors to Spiritual Maturity

Next, complete the following chart to identify the things that get in the way of or inhibit your forward progress in building spiritual maturity. Think of this exercise as a prayer to God.

Dear Lord, I hunger and thirst to build my strength and maturity as Your child. I humbly ask the following of You that I may become closer to You so Your light will shine through me to glorify You in all that I do, particularly as I learn to be more forgiving.	
Dear Lord, the signs of spiritual maturity that I do not embody well because I do not know how to do them are …	With Your help, I can improve each of these signs of spiritual maturity by …
The signs of spiritual maturity that I do not do well because feel I have a better way include …	With Your help, I can improve each of these signs of spiritual maturity by …
You know my heart, Father, and You know that the signs of spiritual maturity that I do not do well because I do not want to include …	Help me to know what You can do to improve each of these signs of spiritual maturity by …

Lord, the signs of spiritual maturity I do not do well because I get discouraged when I try but keep failing include …	I know I must rely on Your strength to improve each of these signs of spiritual maturity, including …
Father, I get distracted from building my spiritual maturity because I struggle with …	Help me to keep my mind focused on You and to overcome distractions by …

Father, I release all these requests into Your loving hands of grace. I ask that You give me insight to know how I can love You more, wisdom to fill my heart with Your light, and the strength and courage to live in Your mighty power. In the name of Your Son Jesus, my brother and Savior, amen.

DAY 23

Internalizing Forgiveness through Spiritual Formation[90]

[90]Prominent researchers have shown that "for the forgiveness process to be helped, an individual must engage their religious or spiritual beliefs when thinking and processing the transgression (i.e., imbuing the transgression with religious or sacred meaning) which may be one way for a highly religious or spiritual person to engage their beliefs when processing the transgression."[91] In other words, seeing the transgression from God's point of view through the spiritual lens of faith, and understanding the transgression from a spiritual perspective, are both key components of achieving lasting emotional peace.

It is not enough to simply be religious, however. As stated earlier in this chapter, going to church on Sunday, participating in mission trips, and performing other acts of piety and goodness will not produce a heart that is softened toward a transgressor. We gain emotional peace when our thoughts about a transgression are filtered through a heart committed to God. A heart committed to God and full of His love, reflecting His grace and mercy, is one that engages with Him through prayer, study of the Word, meditation, and fellowship with like-minded believers. The heart is the central spiritual resource that is nurtured through our commitment to growth in the Lord.

The heart is the part of us that God flows through for others to see. Such a heart understands that, while we are feeling pain from a transgression, the transgressor may also be hurting. As mentioned in chapter 1, a transgression is a doorway through which God can attend to the hurt in others that led them to commit a transgression against us.

It is true that people need to be held accountable for their actions, but practicing patience with others and holding onto the vision of God's relationship with them through us is a true act of compassion, one that takes the eternal view into account. Peter instructs Christians, "Therefore, preparing your minds for action, and being sober-minded, set your hope fully on the grace that will be brought to you at the revelation of Jesus Christ."[92] In this verse, we can think of the word *revelation*, not in the sense of end times, but in the sense of an awareness or understanding. It is quite natural to let our thoughts build a barrier against our ability to allow the love of God to be expressed toward others, especially if they have transgressed against us. As both Peter and Paul have said, we must *prepare* ourselves to be able to stand firm in the face of being taken advantage of and hurt. Just as we can internalize our anger and resentment toward a transgressor, we can also internalize the love of God and the mind of Christ. When we think upon things above, such as the grace God has shown us and His covenant to bless us, we can tear down the wall of thoughts that prevents us from showing God's love to others.

Internalizing the forgiveness process requires first that you nurture the positive intentions you committed to for your offender (chapter 4). Nurturing positive intentions means replacing negative intentions, one by one, with positive Christlike thoughts of behaviors that you visualize yourself showing toward your transgressor. In some cases, these positive thoughts may never be spoken to the transgressor. However, attaching these thoughts to your memory of the offense will help to release the rumination that holds you captive.

Nurturing is like gardening. Jesus told a parable about how rocky ground, ground with weeds, and ground that is hard all prevent the Word of God from taking root. Gardeners prepare the soil for planting by removing the rocks, tilling and softening the soil, and pulling the weeds that would choke out a new crop. Nurturing Christlike behaviors requires planting the seeds of His Word in our hearts after first removing the rocks of doubts and the weeds of worldly distractions that choke out our desire for God's Word. Instead, we must cultivate the soil of our minds with a constant commitment to prayer and meditation on God's Word so that the evil in this world does not snatch the Word from us.[93]

But this is easier said than done. Negative intentions are weeds in the garden of our minds: they choke out Christlike thoughts that are working in us to reach transgressors and show them how they may turn to Him.[94] In fact, I believe that we are *not capable* of replacing negative intentions with positive ones without a heart that seeks to draw close to God through Jesus Christ. To aid us, God has sent a helper: the Holy Spirit. Jesus said, "But the Helper, the Holy Spirit, whom the Father will send in my name, he will teach you all things and bring to your remembrance all that I have said to you."[95] As you grow in spiritual maturity, the forgiveness process will flow from you with the help of the Holy Spirit, and you will gain a greater sense of well-being and become a more forgiving person.

The Christlike qualities of empathy, altruism, compassion, and mercy are fostered through spiritual maturity. Although there are many disciplines that help us mature our character toward Christlikeness, for the purposes of navigating from the darkness of unforgiveness to the light of Christlikeness, we will focus on meditation,[96] prayer,[97] studying the Word of God,[98] and fellowship.[99]

Spiritual formation refers to practicing *the Spirit-driven disciplines through which people are inwardly transformed in such a way that the personality and deeds of Jesus Christ naturally flow from them wherever they are and in whatever situation they find themselves.* Through the process of spiritual formation, true Christlikeness is established in the very depths of our inward being. Our Christlikeness is comprised of thoughts (images, concepts, judgments, inferences), feelings (sensations, responses to emotions, mood), will (desires, choices, decisions, character), and heart or soul (where feelings, thoughts, will, and choices are integrated).

A prominent Christian philosopher and theologian, Dallas Willard, suggests that spiritual formation is influenced by disciplines of abstinence—solitude, fasting, chastity—and disciplines of engagement, such as study, worship, prayer, and fellowship.[100] Another theologian, Richard Foster, is best known for his 1978 book *Celebration of Discipline*. He refines Willard's thoughts by suggesting thirteen spiritual disciplines, which he divides into three categories: inward disciplines, outward disciplines, and corporate disciplines.[101] The inward disciplines include prayer, fasting, meditation, and studying the Christian life; the outward disciplines are simplicity, solitude, submission, and service; and the corporate disciplines include confession, worship, guidance, and celebration.

Willard and Foster agree that these disciplines provide a purposeful way to put ourselves before God so He can transform us into Christlikeness. In trying to simplify these disciplines into a practical approach to spiritual formation, I have distilled them into four processes to till the soil of our hearts to promote spiritual maturity and forgiveness:

- **Prayer**—an upward discipline that connects with God.
- **Meditation**—an inward and upward discipline that cultivates the infusion of God's presence into our lives.
- **Scripture study**—an inward discipline that nourishes what the heart values, thinks, feels, and decides.
- **Fellowship**—an outward discipline that engages God through His children.

These four disciplines engage us with our offender and are the most direct route to enhance our ability to forgive. These practices of spiritual formation are a progression that lead to your reflecting Christlikeness from your inner being and into all you do. In other words, you do not just start these practices and—*bam!*—you're a forgiver. Like athletes practice their sports in order to improve their performances in competition, Christians practice spiritual disciplines to improve their readiness and ability to forgive.

If you are like me, then you look for ways to incorporate the spiritual disciplines into the schedule you have already established. I have not found this approach to work. As the *Star Wars* character Yoda would say, "Up to us, it is. Build spiritual disciplines into our lives, we must." We need to get creative and innovative in order to shape our lives around these spiritual disciplines (processes) in order to actively set the stage for cultivating positive intentions. The four methods we will focus on are prayer, study, meditation, and fellowship, which are in an order of progression. Through them, we succeed in becoming forgiving people. As Paul says to the church in Rome, spiritual maturity is nurtured by "yielding ourselves unto God as those that are alive from the dead, and our members as instruments of righteousness unto God."[102]

We can all become more spiritually mature regardless of where we are on our journey. We cannot give to others what we do not have, but in the fellowship of Christ, we have a great deal to share: a vision of love, the example of Christ, and the impetus to form positive intentions toward all our offenders. Think about it: when we are spiritually mature, the fruit of the Spirit flows from us. How can we harbor negative intentions when we are showing love, joy, peace, patience, kindness, goodness, faithfulness, gentleness, and self-control?[103]

Ask yourself the question, "What good can come from my negative intentions toward my transgressor?" The honest answer is, "None at all." Naturally, you want to do something to relieve your pain and suffering, but the best way to find relief, indeed the only way, is through forgiveness. Unforgiveness is a battleground of spiritual warfare because Satan is attacking us. In fact, he is seeking to devour us when we take his bait and ruminate about our transgression, focusing our thoughts on negative intentions toward our offenders. Our rumination, ironically, becomes a prison that holds *us* hostage: we are hostages to our ungodly desires. Yes, forgiveness is a difficult journey because any transgression that requires forgiveness is a form of suffering. We need to remember, however, that our suffering is bigger than us: it is for the cause of Christ since forgiveness sets the stage for the offender to see and experience Christ's love. When we return unfair or unjust treatment with goodness, we glorify and honor our Savior because we are following in His steps, showing others the mercy He has shown us. As a result, God will restore, confirm, and strengthen us and establish us as His disciples.[104]

Even though others may not see Christ in our forgiveness, the Holy Spirit is a witness to our suffering and goodness, and He brings us comfort. Through our attitude of forgiveness, we witness to anyone who may be taken aback by our Christlike attitude toward our transgressors, a situation that can give us an opportunity to share the faith that is working in us as explained by the apostle Peter:

> But even if you should suffer for righteousness' sake, you will be blessed. Have no fear of them, nor be troubled, but in your hearts regard Christ the Lord as holy, always being prepared to make a defense to anyone who asks you for a reason for the hope that is in you; yet do it with gentleness and respect, having a good conscience, so that, when you are slandered, those who revile your good behavior in Christ may be put to shame. For it is better to suffer for doing good, if that should be God's will, than for doing evil.[105]

At this point, you may be wondering whether forgiveness is truly your best option. To solidify your understanding that it is, the following paragraphs will review key points about forgiveness, followed by pertinent scripture. As you read the biblical texts, please keep in mind that they were written with the inspiration of the Holy Spirit for our guidance.

First, to review some basic facts, forgiveness is an internal process where we replace negative emotions and feelings with positive ones and, in so doing, begin to let go of our negative intentions toward our transgressor. It is virtually impossible, however, to eliminate negative feelings altogether. As Paul tells us, we can be angry as long as we do not sin. Anger turns into sin when it leads us to negative intentions, the desire to do evil toward another person, and rumination about the cause of the anger.

But now you must put them all away: anger, wrath, malice, slander, and obscene talk from your mouth. Do not lie to one another, seeing that you have put off the old self with its practices and have put on the new self, which is being renewed in knowledge after the image of its creator.[106]

Second, as described by the Christian Forgiveness Life Cycle in chapter 4, a major distinction between a secular and Christian view of forgiveness is that we followers of Christ can derail the rise of negative intentions, rumination, and unforgiveness by relying on our relationship with Christ. We do this by deepening our relationship with Christ through spiritual maturation as described by Paul in his letter to Titus:

For we ourselves were once foolish, disobedient, led astray, slaves to various passions and pleasures, passing our days in malice and envy, hated by others and hating one another. But when the goodness and loving-kindness of God our Savior appeared, he saved us, not because of works done by us in righteousness, but according to his own mercy, by the washing of regeneration and renewal of the Holy Spirit, whom he poured out on us richly through Jesus Christ our Savior, so that being justified by his grace we might become heirs according to the hope of eternal life.[107]

If we hold a grudge or unleash our instinctive drive to get even with a transgressor, we limit our relationship with Christ.[108] However, with the development of spiritual maturity, which comes through a study of the Word, prayer, meditation, and fellowship with believers,[109] our behavior toward others begins to change. In sowing seeds of kindness, we reap God's favor:

Do not be deceived: God is not mocked, for whatever one sows, that will he also reap. For the one who sows to his own flesh will from the flesh reap corruption, but the one who sows to the Spirit will from the Spirit reap eternal life. And let us not grow weary of doing good, for in due season we will reap, if we do not give up. So then, as we have opportunity, let us do good to everyone, and especially to those who are of the household of faith.[110]

In short, forgiveness is a form of love that shows compassion, kindness, humility, patience, and tolerance; forgiveness also restores harmony in a Christlike way.[111] With a Christlike heart, we teach others, by example, what the grace and mercy of God looks like. When done in the name of God, our forgiveness is not a burden but an opportunity for joyfulness and thankfulness as described by Paul:

Put on then, as God's chosen ones, holy and beloved, compassion, kindness, humility, meekness, and patience, bearing with one another and, if one has a complaint against another, forgiving each other. As the Lord has forgiven you, so you also must forgive. And above all these put on love, which binds everything together in perfect harmony. And let the peace of Christ rule in your hearts, to which indeed you were called in one body. And be thankful. Let the word of Christ dwell in you richly, teaching and admonishing one another in all wisdom, singing psalms and hymns and spiritual songs, with thankfulness in your hearts to God. And whatever you do, in word or deed, do everything in the name of the Lord Jesus, giving thanks to God the Father through him.[112]

Third, as discussed in chapter 2, healing the pain of a transgression means accepting that pain is comprised of emotional, mental, physical, and spiritual pain, all of which are systemically interrelated. The first task of spiritual formation is to give us a means to provide a gift to the transgressor: the intangible gift of goodness toward the individual, which is Christ's expectation for His followers. Paul told the Christians in Rome, "If your enemy is hungry, feed him; if he is thirsty, give him something to drink. … Do not be overcome by evil, but overcome evil with good." It takes humility to offer food or drink or another gift to a transgressor, and frankly, humility is the first step toward forgiving an offense. As the apostle Peter said,

Humble yourselves, therefore, under the mighty hand of God so that at the proper time he may exalt you, casting all your anxieties on him, because he cares for you. Be sober-minded; be watchful. Your adversary the devil prowls around like a roaring lion, seeking someone to devour. Resist him, firm in your faith, knowing that the same kinds of suffering are being experienced by your brotherhood throughout the world. And after you have suffered a little while, the God of all grace, who has called you to his eternal glory in Christ, will himself restore, confirm, strengthen, and establish you.[113]

As discussed in this chapter, spiritual formation sets the stage for forgiveness[114] by renewing our minds and encouraging Christlikeness.[115] Spiritual formation is a proactive coping response that may begin long before a transgression occurs, or it may be a response after a transgression occurs. Christ's brother James tells us to consider trials of various kinds (for example, transgressions) as joyful opportunities to bolster the steadfastness of our faith.[116] The remainder of this chapter will present a process to encourage you to form a stronger spiritual maturity that includes the following:

- Learning how to pray for yourself and your transgressor
- Developing a method for applying the Bible to your situation
- Meditating on the Word of God and making it come alive in your heart and mind
- Seeking out and fellowshipping with like-minded believers

In the previous two journal exercises you assessed aspects of your spiritual maturity. On day 25, you looked at the state of your heart as the foundation upon which spiritual maturity is formed. On day 26, you assessed how you were then internalizing the disciplines of spiritual maturity. The next journal exercise is intended to help you identify the current state of these disciplines in your life.

Journal Exercise 23a: Current State of Your Spiritual Disciplines

For each of the spiritual disciplines listed below, put a circle around the rating that most describes you (YES) or doesn't describe you.

SPIRITUAL DISCIPLINES	RATING
Prayer Assessment	
1. I focus prayer on discovering how I fit into God's will more than how He fits into mine.	1. Yes No
2. I trust God to answer when I pray, and I wait patiently on His timing.	2. Yes No
3. My prayers include thanksgiving, praise, confession, and requests.	3. Yes No
4. I expect to grow in my prayer life, and I intentionally seek help to improve.	4. Yes No
5. I spend as much time listening to God as I spend talking to Him.	5. Yes No
6. I pray because I am aware of my complete dependence on God for everything in my life.	6. Yes No
7. I maintain an attitude of prayer throughout each day.	7. Yes No
8. I believe my prayers impact my life and the lives of others.	8. Yes No
9. I engage in a daily prayer time.	9. Yes No
Meditation Assessment	
1. I listen to God's Word as it speaks to my heart, and it influences the way I live my life.	1. Yes No
2. I reflect on the works of God's hands in this world.	2. Yes No
3. I rehearse how God's deeds in the world can flow through me.	3. Yes No
4. I reflect on God's law and how it filters into my heart and influences how I live my life.	4. Yes No
5. I reflect on how my behavior has changed or is changing because of my walk with God.	5. Yes No
6. I reflect on the shortcomings and weaknesses that I rely on God for strength to overcome.	6. Yes No
7. I see offenses I have made against God and others, and I seek strength through repentance.	7. Yes No
8. I open my heart as an inner sanctuary for the Holy Spirit to fill me with gratitude, strength, love, and discernment.	8. Yes No

Living in the Word Assessment

1. I regularly read and study my Bible.	1. Yes	No
2. I believe the Bible is God's Word and provides His guidance for life.	2. Yes	No
3. I can answer questions about life and faith from a biblical perspective.	3. Yes	No
4. I replace impure or inappropriate thoughts with God's truth.	4. Yes	No
5. I demonstrate honesty in my actions and conversation.	5. Yes	No
6. I apply the Word of God when it exposes areas of my life that need change.	6. Yes	No
7. Generally, my public self and private self are the same.	7. Yes	No
8. I use the Bible as the guide for the way I think and act.	8. Yes	No
9. I study the Bible for the purpose of discovering truth for daily living.	9. Yes	No

Fellowship with Believers Assessment

1. I forgive others when their actions harm me.	1. Yes	No
2. I admit my errors in relationships and humbly seek forgiveness from the ones I have hurt.	2. Yes	No
3. I allow other Christians to hold me accountable for spiritual growth.	3. Yes	No
4. I seek to live in harmony with other members of my family and my community of believers.	4. Yes	No
5. I place the interests of others above my self-interest.	5. Yes	No
6. I am gentle and kind in my interactions with others.	6. Yes	No
7. I encourage feedback from others to help me discover areas for relationship growth.	7. Yes	No
8. I show patience in my relationships with family and friends.	8. Yes	No
9. I encourage others by pointing out their strengths rather than criticizing their weaknesses.	9. Yes	No
10. My time commitments demonstrate that I value relationships over work/career/hobbies.	10. Yes	No

Interpreting your results

Go back and look at the items you didn't circle. Are these disciplines actions you would like to put more emphasis on in your life? Put an "X" on the of the top three disciplines you would like to work on starting today.

Interpretation

The purpose of this survey is primarily to help you think about some of the behaviors that contribute to spiritual maturity. By rating them "yes" or "no," you have to reflect on the extent to which you are focusing on each of the behaviors. It's this reflection that is important.

As you reflect, you may notice on the list something that requires action on your part. As you reflect on the behaviors on the list, take notice of three types of behaviors:

- behaviors that focus on your own actions
- behaviors that focus on your relationship with God
- behaviors that focus on your relationship with others.

As you go back through the list and reread each behavior, reflect on which of the three types of behaviors you feel it falls under. Overall, which area of behaviors do you feel is your strength (relationship with self, God, others), and which behaviors do you feel need more focus? Use the next exercise to ask God for guidance and strength as you work on these areas of your life.

Journal Exercise 23b: Committing to Improve

Thank You, Lord, for the peace You offer my life. I ask that You give me the desire to continually improve the spiritual disciplines that will draw me closer to You and will help me be a vessel through which You may work to bring love and peace to the world that I touch, particularly as I learn to be more forgiving.

Help me, Lord, to improve these areas of my prayer life:	What I can do with Your help to improve my prayers to You:
Help me, Lord, to improve these areas of my meditation:	What I can do with Your help to improve my meditation:
Help me, Lord, to improve these areas of my study of the Word:	What I can do with Your help to improve my study of the Word:
Help me, Lord, to improve these areas of my fellowship with other Christians:	What I can do with Your help to improve my fellowship:

Father, I release all these requests into Your loving hands of grace. I ask that You give me insight to know how I can love You more, wisdom to fill my heart with Your light, and the strength and courage to live in Your mighty power. In the name of Your Son Jesus, my brother and Savior, amen.

DAY 24

Internalizing Forgiveness through Scripture Study

The reminder of this chapter will provide an introduction to four spiritual disciplines, along with a general set of guidelines for how the disciplines help with the forgiving of one's transgressor. Our discussion will begin with the study of God's Word.

Reading the Word of God is not the same as *studying* the Word of God. We read to inform; we study to understand. The purpose of studying God's Word is to fill our hearts with an understanding of God's will for us. Even Jesus acknowledged His need to know the Word since the desire of His heart was to fulfill His Father's will for His life. Jesus was so successful in achieving this goal that He could say that He was in the Father and the Father was in Him.[117] Similarly, studying God's Word is the means for us to understand God's will; it is our means to being in the will of the Father and allowing Him to direct our steps.

While we may have an established pattern of studying God's Word before we experience a transgression, the Word is also a source of strength after being challenged by a transgression. If our hearts are full of the Word and we choose to act in ways that are consistent with it, we can emulate the mind of Christ, which is to love and forgive. Although our minds are comprised of memories, perceptions, beliefs, information, images, and ideas, when we devote the power of our thinking to understanding the Word of God, we focus our thoughts on Christ. This is the process of renewing our minds and entering into a state of spiritual worship.[118]

We know that we choose between what is good and what is sin based on our thoughts. When we memorize the Word of God, our thoughts are filled with information, images, and ideas that are consistent with God's will: we worship God through a heart that is transformed.[119] This transformation opens the door for the Holy Spirit to lead us to be conformed to the will of God. As the interplay of our thoughts, feelings, and will becomes more Christlike, the Holy Spirit can operate to strengthen us to deal with temptation and tribulation.

When you take His Word into your innermost being, memorize it, and relate it to your own life, you become the person that Christ has called you to be. This indwelling of the Word then spreads to how you relate to others and to yourself.

When Christ is at the center of our will, we reflect Christlikeness and understand our circumstances from His point of view. With the help of the Holy Spirit, we reflect the mind of Christ.[120] The result of our spiritual formation is our transformation, being filled with love, joy, peace, long-suffering, gentleness, goodness, kindness, faithfulness, and self-control: the fruit of the Spirit. In short, the purpose of studying the Word is to learn, understand, and believe God's divine plan for our lives. Following are ideas to aid you as you seek to incorporate the Word into your heart and transform your mind.

Memorization

Memorizing scripture helps us to recall the truths of the Word at critical times in life. As stated earlier, our behavior is influenced by our thoughts. When our thoughts incorporate the Word of God, the result is Christlike behavior. Without memorization of the Word, our thoughts have no ready access to the principles and truths needed to prompt Christlike behavior. Alone in the wilderness after His baptism, Jesus modeled dependence on a thorough knowledge of scripture when Satan tempted Him to spurn God's will and use His power for personal gain. Jesus successfully resisted each of Satan's evil suggestions by quoting scripture.[121]

In an upcoming journal exercise, you will memorize scripture passages concerning forgiveness. But first, the following information will help you determine your preferred means of memorizing the Word. Since people memorize differently based on their learning styles, the following are various approaches to try. First, some people's memorization is enhanced by making their own flash cards and handwriting the verse on one side and the scripture reference on the other. In addition to the standard 3 × 5 index cards, a smaller size of flash cards can be created with a box of blank business cards, available at most printshops. Second, for those who like technology, websites and applications are available that offer a version of Bible flash cards. Finally, some people prefer listening to verses from a recording. Although professional recordings of scripture are available, another effective method is to make your own.

Since deciding what verses to memorize can be difficult, having a systematic approach for selecting scriptures is recommended and will likely produce better results. One approach is to find as many verses as possible on a single topic, which in our case is forgiveness. However, as seen in *Forty Days to Forgiveness*, other topics relate to different aspects of forgiveness, such as the mind of Christ, humility, love, or mercy. The next journal exercise will ask you to go through previous chapters of *Forty Days to Forgiveness* and find verses relating to topics that you want to learn more about. Obviously, this approach can also be used as you read your Bible. Another way to generate topics and related scriptures is to consult a Bible study aid, such as a topical Bible, a Bible concordance, or a Bible dictionary. Once you find your favorite verses for each topic, create a memory aid to help you learn them (recordings or handwritten or electronically generated flash cards), and work on them several times each day.

Bible Reading

Reading the Bible is the doorway to understanding; it is the first step toward Bible study. How can we read in such a way that we remember what we read? I have benefited from highlighting my favorite scriptures, so the following are tips based on my own experiences.

Tip 1: Mark your Bible with a color-coded system. Some people create elaborate color-coding schemes to identify key topics in scripture: purple for verses about God, Jesus, the Holy Spirit; pink for passages about family, marriage, parenting, and other relationships; red for verses dealing with love, kindness, mercy, and grace; etc. Typically, I find all those different colors annoying when I am trying to read, so I simply use a yellow highlighter. However, I purchased a new Bible and developed a color scheme to highlight verses related to forgiveness; I am creating my own "forgiveness Bible," using this color code:

- Red—verses that describe how we deal with "trials and suffering"
- Blue—verses that reference "one another"
- Green—verses that explicitly talk about forgiveness
- Yellow—favorite verses accompanied by notes written in the margins

When I highlight, I do not cover the text; instead, I draw a line under the text. I usually use a ruler because my hands are not very steady, but you may find it easier to draw the line freehand. Finding a highlighter that does not bleed through the thin pages of most Bibles is important to preserve readability. Zebrite Bible markers and dry Bible highlighters do not bleed through. Some people suggest colored pencils, but I have found that over time the wax and pigments rub off on adjacent pages. I use a set of fine-line colored pens[122] that do not bleed through and that create a clean look. You will need to try various pens to see what works best for you.

Tip 2: Memorizing verses. Memorizing the Bible is a great way to begin to study the Word. As you underline your chosen passages on forgiveness (or other topics), make a list of the reference so that you can come back later and make flash cards.

Tip 3: Outlining. Outlining what you read is often helpful because connecting your observations about the text with the cognitive processes required to create an outline engages the mind at a deeper level. First, read the text all the way through. Second, go to the end of the text and scan up to find the beginning of the final thought or idea that is being written about. Third, ask yourself what supports this idea or what questions are answered by this idea. When you have finished this process, find the beginning of the next idea and repeat the process. Continue this way until you get back to the beginning of the text. Finally, read the entire passage again from the beginning, but this time create an outline as you read. An outline summarizes what you are reading and shows how the ideas are related to each other. I usually create a logos outline, which uses numerical labels to help indicate the relationship between major and supporting ideas.

Open your Bible to a verse I used earlier in this chapter, Colossians 3:12–17, and do the following:

1. Read the text from beginning to end.
   a. Go to the end of the text and scan up until you find the beginning of the final idea being written about.
   b. "Do everything in the name of the Lord and give thanks." (This is the last idea in the text. What is the purpose of this command?)
   c. It reinforces "the Word of God living in me richly," which supports living in harmony (a summary of the next idea). And why is that important?
   d. Because being loving sustains the harmony that reflects the peace that we were called to have. (So what? Why is peace important?)
   e. Because we are commanded to forgive, and forgiveness is a natural part of living in harmony. And love, which reinforces harmony, is the central theme of forgiveness.

2. Outline the text.
   a. God's beloved and holy ones are to put on the following:
      i. Compassion
      ii. Kindness
      iii. Meekness
      iv. Patience
      v. Love
      vi. Thankfulness
   b. Putting on these attributes, especially love, ensures harmony among believers.
   c. Harmony is a heart filled with the peace of Christ.
      i. Forgiveness is evidence of harmony.
      ii. We model how Christ forgave us.

    d. The Word of Christ dwells in us and empowers us to:
        i. Teach and admonish one another with wisdom.
        ii. Acknowledge God's role in our fellowship.

Approaches to Bible Study

Another important part of Bible study is to select a focus for study. The study will mean more to you if it is relevant to something going on in your life. The following are some common approaches to identifying how to structure your study, the final one being perhaps the most common, namely, inductive Bible study. We will use that approach in the next journal exercise to focus on a part of forgiveness that will be helpful in your journey.

Approach 1: Follow Bible lessons. A first approach is to work with published Bible lessons, but so many are available that I could not begin to make a recommendation. Rather, I suggest that you read reviews of Bible studies that match your faith tradition. For example, for my Protestant faith tradition, I have found Zondervan to be a reliable publisher. One good study they publish is *Pursuing Spiritual Transformation*, which gets high marks in the reviews. Other publishers represent other faith traditions: Roman Catholic, Pentecostal, Latter-day Saints, Jehovah's Witnesses, and so on.

Approach 2: Listen to instructional presentations. A second approach is to find sermons (podcasts, online sources, or videos) of pastors in your faith tradition on topics of interest to you. Many pastors reference Bible verses as they preach or teach, so consider having a notepad on hand to write down the scripture references. Later, look up these references and make a memory device for them. A website I use that aligns with my faith tradition is One Place. As the name implies, it is one place to find Bible lessons on practically any topic. An example of an instructional video is the series *That We May Know* by Ray Vander Laan, which provides historical and geographical contexts to biblical passages. If you choose to watch a dramatized video, be sure read the biblical texts portrayed to ensure their accuracy.

Approach 3: Choose a topic. This approach was illustrated with my earlier suggestion to choose a topic to study that relates to the most difficult part of your forgiveness journey. Regardless of the focus of study, the first step is to identify where the biblical texts are that relate to your area of interest. As mentioned earlier, books on the topic and reference works (Bible concordance, topical Bibles, etc.) will be helpful. Examples of aspects of forgiveness to study are the following:

- Fruit of the Spirit
- Managing your anger

- Teachings about "one another"
- Pure thoughts
- Living a Christian life in a fallen world
- Fellowship
- Prayer
- Meditation

One way to start a topical study is with the reference material often located at the back of Bibles, typically organized according to topic. For more extensive study, a popular, helpful, and reasonably priced reference work is *Nave's Topical Bible*. A Bible dictionary that I use is *The Interpreter's Dictionary of the Bible*. Like any dictionary, it organizes the topics alphabetically. Bible dictionaries are distinct from topical Bibles in that they provide an explanation of the topic along with scripture references.

Approach 4: Choose a Bible character to study. Another approach is to study a particular biblical figure whose situation is similar to yours. Many stories in the Bible illustrate the challenging situations that God's people have dealt with. To find a person whose situation is similar to yours, you can conduct a Web search using the keywords "Bible characters" and a description of your situation. Bible dictionaries also provide a brief synopsis of people in the Bible, along with references to the biblical passages about them. An obvious but overlooked method of finding a relevant person is to ask your pastor or fellow believers. Finally, simply going to a bookseller website and entering the name of a biblical figure is an effective way to find relevant books and resources.

Approach 5: Choose a book or section of the Bible. Another effective approach is to study a particular book or section of the Bible where the predominant theme reflects your situation. Books of the Bible typically have a theme determined by the original audience. Once again, a Web search with the keywords "books of the Bible" will suggest sites where you can quickly identify which books have themes that relate to your situation. Charles Swindoll has compiled an excellent overview of each book of the Bible called "Insight for Living," which is available online.[123]

Approach 6: Read the text and cross-references. Another approach to Bible study is to read not just the text of interest but also the cross-references for the text. Cross-references are the small footnotes found throughout reference Bibles that direct readers to related passages. Pursuing these cross-references will deepen your understanding and further immerse you in the Word.

Approach 7: Participate in a group Bible study. Joining a Bible study group at your church, another church, online, at a Christian college, or at the home of a friend can be extremely beneficial. You can probably find Bible studies in your area by doing a Web search with keywords "Bible study [your city]."

Approach 8: Follow an inductive Bible study approach. Inductive Bible study means using information in the passage itself to reach a conclusion about what the passage is saying. In an inductive study, the reader tries hard to understand the text from evidence within the Bible itself rather than with the aid of outside information or opinions. A common, but contrasting, approach is deductive Bible study, wherein the reader draws conclusions about a text based on his or her general knowledge of the whole. To help illustrate this concept, think of a certain brand of clothing that you consider high quality and fashionable. If you purchase an item of this brand without looking at it closely, believing it to be well-made based on your general knowledge of the brand, you have employed deductive reasoning. Similarly, drawing conclusions about biblical texts based on your general knowledge is not always as reliable as using the inductive approach. The best way to learn the inductive method of study is to just do it, so I designed a journal exercise (as follows) that directs an inductive Bible study of an aspect of forgiveness.

Journal Exercise 24a: Inductive Bible Study of Forgiveness

The following instructions coordinate with the Bible Study Worksheet, below. Read the instructions and use the worksheet provided to do an inductive study based on the topic of forgiveness.

1. **Choose a passage on forgiveness that you want to study.**
   - Go back through *Forty Days to Forgiveness* and find a section that struck home for you.
   - Go to that section and select a verse that resonates in your mind.
   - Ask the Lord to guide you to gain a good grasp of that scripture and to deepen your love for and knowledge of Him[124] (Ephesians 1:17–19).
   - Write the verse in the space provided in the worksheet, below.

2. **Understand the background of the scripture passage.**
   - What is the general background of the book that contains your verse; who wrote it; and to whom was it written? Read the entire chapter and mentally summarize what it is about and how your verse fits into the message of the chapter.
   - If you are using a study Bible, resist the temptation to read the notes; doing so would be a "deductive" Bible study because the printed notes will likely contain conclusions that you want to discover for yourself.

3. **Make a copy of the verse.**
   - Print the verse from an online Bible application, leaving room in between lines to make notes.[125]
   - Make a flash card for the verse you chose and memorize it.

4. **Select a portion of the verse to study, and mark up what you see.**
   - Narrow down a section for closer study.
   - Use a set of colored pencils/pens/highlighters to look for keywords (the words you think are the most important). Circle these keywords in one color.
   - Circle each of the ideas, themes, and messages in another color. Are they commandments, principles, admonishments, prayers, or instruction? Use a different color for each.
   - Mark repeated or similar words and ideas to look for repetition; they are the parts of the verse that the writer emphasized.
   - Put brackets around words that connect units of thought, such as [now], [therefore], [so that], and [but]. Connecting words between sections of thought indicate how the author is building on what he or she has already said, whether continuing his or her argument, making a conclusion, or introducing a new thought.

5. **Ask questions of the text.**
   - Sometimes the questions you can ask to better understand the verse are obvious; other times they are not. One way to get at the questions is to read the passage from the end to the beginning.
   - Think of questions that naturally arise from what has been said: "What does this say? What does His Word mean? How does this section relate to the rest of the chapter? What would the people who received this message think?"
   - Write as many questions as you can in the space provided on the worksheet.

6. **Answer questions from the text yourself before looking for what others have said.**
   - Often our questions can be answered within the verse or in the chapter where the verse appears. Reading the verse in other Bible translations—*New International Version* (*NIV*), *New Living Translation* (*NLT*), *English Standard Version* (*ESV*), Revised Standard Version (*RSV*), King James Version (*KJV*), THE MESSAGE, *Amplified Bible*—can be helpful. Various websites show different translations of the verse side by side, making comparison easier.
   - Look up any words that are not clear to you in a Bible dictionary.
   - Use cross-references to see where these words or ideas are found elsewhere in the Bible. Many Bibles provide a list of cross-references either in the middle, toward the side, or at the bottom of the page. An alternative is to look up the theme or idea/word in a topical Bible, such as *Nave's Topical Bible* or the *Zondervan Topical Bible*.

7. **Make an elevator speech of your conclusions.**
   - An elevator going up seven floors would take about two minutes. In that time, how would you explain the message of your verse?
   - Try out your speech on others who are believers, such as family or members of your local church, or compare your ideas with the study notes in your Bible.

1. **Verse the study is based on:**

2. **Write out the verse:**

3. **Make a memorization flash card:**
   - Use a 3 × 5 card.
   - Write out the verse on one side.
   - Write the passage reference on the opposite side.

4. **Mark up the verse:**
   - Circle the most important words.
   - Underline repeating words or ideas.
   - Bracket connecting words.

5. **List questions the verse raises:**

Q1. _____

Q2. _____

Q3. _____

6. **Answers to the questions the verse raises:**

Answer Q1. _____

Answer Q2. _____

Answer Q3. _____

7. **Write out an elevator speech:**

Journal Exercise 24b: Assessing Your Bible Study

Assess how you are currently doing with your study of God's Word by completing the assessment below. Scoring: 1 = Almost never; 5 = Regularly

SIGNS OF SPIRITUAL MATURITY	HOW OFTEN I DO THIS (COLUMN 1)	HOW WELL I DO THIS (COLUMN 2)	WHY I DO NOT DO THESE BEHAVIORS WELL
1. I read God's Word regularly.	[1] [2] [3] [4] [5]	[1] [2] [3] [4] [5]	❏ I do not know how.
2. I study God's Word regularly.	[1] [2] [3] [4] [5]	[1] [2] [3] [4] [5]	❏ It is uncomfortable.
3. I can explain my faith to others when asked.	[1] [2] [3] [4] [5]	[1] [2] [3] [4] [5]	❏ I have a better way.
			❏ I do not want to.
4. God's Word drives how I think and act.	[1] [2] [3] [4] [5]	[1] [2] [3] [4] [5]	❏ I try but keep failing.
			❏ I get distracted.
5. God's Word is the standard for my lifestyle.	[1] [2] [3] [4] [5]	[1] [2] [3] [4] [5]	❏ Other reasons
Totals (add the numbers you marked) Put the total in the box below each column.	Total _____	Total _____	Column 1 + 2 = _____ Out of 50 possible

Making Meaning out of Your Results

Studying God's Word is often a challenge for most of us, and few of us study as often or as well as we would like. We often do not know where to start or how to go about it, so we postpone it. It does not get on our schedule and we do not improve. Where are your sore spots? Here are a few ways to look at your results, along with some tips for improving:

1. **The total for column 2 is greater than the total for column 1**
   Meaning: You will benefit from establishing a Bible study on your radar screen of daily activities.

   Tips:

   - Schedule a time for Bible study in your daily activities.
   - Spread your reading throughout the day; it does not have to be done all at once.
   - Listen to Bible reading in audio or video format; try a dramatized version.
   - Listen to Bible teachings on YouTube, through podcasts, by way of popular pastor sermons, etc.
   - Create flash cards of Bible verses and keep them handy to review, or put them on your electronic device.

2. **The total for column 1 is greater than the total for column 2**
   Meaning: You will benefit from establishing a Bible study pattern or routine.

   Tips:

   - Use a Bible study marking system with either a paper Bible or an electronic Bible (for example, the application available from Olive Tree Publishing Company).
   - Try a daily devotional book that includes Bible readings.
   - Follow a plan to read the Bible through in one year.
   - Use a Bible study workbook.
   - Join a Bible study group either at church or online, or create one.

3. **The total for column 1 is the same as or close to the total of column 2**
   Meaning: You have a fairly balanced perspective on your spiritual discipline.

   Tips:

   - Break your pattern and try something new from these tips.
   - No matter how good or poor your score, there is always room to improve.
   - Keep a record/log of the quality and quantity of your Bible study.
   - Start a gratitude journal about your Bible study, including not just quantity and quality but also new learning.

4. **The reasons for low scores can inform your plans to improve**

Tips:

- Consider why those reasons exist, and find ways to resolve the obstacles.
- Ask God for insight on ways you can improve.

Study of the Word	Quotient: _____ out of 50
Ways I can improve	

DAY 25

Internalizing Forgiveness through Meditation

Like scripture study, meditation is a discipline that some Christians practice regularly, contributing to their ability to respond to a transgressor in a Christlike manner. Meditation can also be helpful after a transgression to overcome the vicious cycle of rumination and unforgiveness. Meditation is a thought process that helps us hear God's Word better and visualize how we will obey His Word in our lives. Although reading and memorizing scripture is a key part of spiritual formation, it does not shape us until we meditate on the scripture and let it paint a picture of how it works in our lives. In short, meditation is reflecting on how God's Word influences and directs every situation we encounter in life.

Scripture is the central reference point from which we bring our spiritual and physical lives into balance.[126] When meditating, we contemplate what God's Word means to us. We may also meditate on other aspects of God's work in creating within us a steadfast faith and spirit through creation,[127] our interactions with others, and prayer. As we meditate, we become more connected to the will of God for our lives.[128]

The words for "meditation" and descriptions of it are found fifty-eight times in the Bible (depending on the version of the bible, you may find slightly more or less) and convey the concepts of listening to God's Word,[129] reflecting on God's works, rehearsing God's deeds, and ruminating on God's law, among others. In its simplest form, Christian mediation is the ability to hear God's voice,[130] draw near to Him, and obey His Word. The God of the universe, the Creator of all things, desires our fellowship.[131] Over and over again throughout the biblical narrative, we see God's people in fellowship with Him, living on the basis of hearing His voice and obeying His Word.

Meditation is sometimes referred to as devotional time, and many good devotional books are available or can be found on-line.[132] However, meditation goes beyond devotional reading and contemplative prayer. One difference is that meditation is practiced in a state of solitude, whereas devotional time might be shared with others.[133] Yet meditation is also more than solitude and detachment from the world around us. While the goal of some forms of Eastern meditation is to empty the mind, in Christian mediation we open ourselves to be filled with the mind of God and His presence in the world. The essence of meditation is seeking attachment to God. We let go of preoccupations so we can focus our minds on God and become present to Him. Our minds are naturally designed to make associations and follow tangents; meditation, however, trains the mind to stay focused in order to explore appropriate associations between ourselves, God, and His Word.

Christian meditation leads us to the inner wholeness necessary to give ourselves freely to God. Meditation redirects our lives so we can successfully deal with transgressions and the trials of human life. In meditation we create the emotional and spiritual space that allows Christ to construct an inner sanctuary in our hearts. Inner fellowship of this kind transforms the inner person. The following are some characteristics of meditation:

- Confessing our shortcomings to God and asking for His guidance and strength.
- Reflecting on God's majesty and works in the world around us.
- Reflecting with gratitude on what God has done for us and for others.
- Opening our minds and hearts for Christ to enter into a deeper relationship with us.
- Clearing our minds of all distractions to nurture our fellowship with Christ.
- Challenging our faith to grow by reflecting on how God is working in our lives.
- Reflecting on how we fit into God's greater plan rather than how God fits into our lives.

Regardless of the approach used in meditation, a helpful practice is to write down what you learn from reflecting on God and His Word. Journaling provides a vehicle to organize your thoughts and better understand the impact of meditation on your life. Some choose to journal as part of their meditative practice because it provides a record of their journey to refer back to in difficult times. Writing about a transgression, according to research done by behavioral scientists, helps to cultivate a spirit of forgiveness. For those seeking to overcome a transgression, meditative journaling also provides a way to write about how God's Word and majesty are revealed in the transgression they have experienced.

Personally, I find journaling difficult. Either I write too much or I cannot think of anything to write at all. Too often, I pressure myself by thinking I have to write something profound or fill up a page, but an empty page is not like a plate that we must fill: it is simply a place to record whatever is on our minds. Journaling can take a number of forms:

- **Letter format.** The letter can be to God, yourself, your offender, or people who know of the offense. It is not a letter that you will ever send, but writing it will help you process what you learned during meditation.
- **Story format.** Think of your journal entry as a story that starts with why you chose the Bible verses you did, what happened in the reading of the verses, what they mean to you, and how they will influence your life. Alternatively, you may narrate how what you learned during your meditation time fits into your life story.

- **Artistic format.** You may choose to create a picture or write a poem or song to describe what your meditation has revealed to you or what it means to you. Similarly, you may cut pictures from magazines and paste them into your journal to give an impression of your meditation insights. Even though you may never share any of these creations, they will influence how your time of meditation soaks into your heart.

- **Summarize lessons learned.** I personally like to write bullet points that encapsulate what I have learned during my meditation. I think of them as lessons from God or ways God has spoken to my heart through scripture or devotional readings. Making a list is the easiest way for me to see how meditation influences my heart and my life.

Journal Exercise 25: Assessing Your Meditation Practices

Take a moment to think about your spiritual maturity by responding to the questions below. Follow the directions for summarizing your spiritual quotient. A score of 1 = not at all satisfied with your practice of that discipline, and a score of 5 = completely satisfied.

TABLE 1 Meditation

SIGNS OF SPIRITUAL MATURITY	HOW OFTEN I DO THIS (COLUMN 1)	HOW WELL I DO THIS (COLUMN 2)	WHY I DO NOT DO THESE BEHAVIORS WELL
1. I practice regular quiet time with the Lord.	[1] [2] [3] [4] [5]	[1] [2] [3] [4] [5]	❏ I do not know how. ❏ It is uncomfortable.
2. I see God's hand in many things daily.	[1] [2] [3] [4] [5]	[1] [2] [3] [4] [5]	❏ I have a better way. ❏ I do not want to.
3. I seek Christ's guidance in important decisions.	[1] [2] [3] [4] [5]	[1] [2] [3] [4] [5]	❏ I try but keep failing. ❏ I get distracted.
4. I thank God often for blessings and suffering.	[1] [2] [3] [4] [5]	[1] [2] [3] [4] [5]	❏ Other reasons
5. I replace impure thoughts with Christlike ones.	[1] [2] [3] [4] [5]	[1] [2] [3] [4] [5]	
Add together the numbers that you marked. Put the total in the box below each column.	Total _____	Total _____	Total of column 1 + column 2: _____ out of 50 possible

Making Meaning Out of Your Results

The term *meditation* is often misunderstood, and the practice of meditation is often a challenge for all of us. Meditation is the blending of something *outside* of you with what is *inside* you. For a Christian, meditation may entail reflecting on a verse of scripture and how it impacts his or her life. Here are a few ways to look at your results, along with some tips for improving:

1. **The total for column 2 is greater than the total for column 1**
   Meaning: Meditation is not a regular activity.

   Tips:

   • Put a repeating event on your calendar for meditation; choose a time of day when you are most likely to need an infusion of God's love and power.

- Set the timer on your electronic device for at least ten minutes of meditation.
- Choose a regular place to mediate, or envision a type of spot that is conducive to your silent time with God.

2. **The total for column 1 is greater than the total for column 2**

   Meaning: You would benefit to establish an approach to meditation that you are comfortable with.

   Tips:

   - Use a meditation app on your electronic device.
   - Incorporate meditation into your daily Bible reading or devotional time.
   - Keep a journal of scriptures you meditated on, new insights into God's direction for you, and/or your gratitude for how God has blessed you.
   - Talk to other believers to learn from their meditation practices. Discuss common practices, create new ideas, and demonstrate examples to each other.

3. **The total for column 1 is the same as or close to the total of column 2**

   Meaning: You have a fairly balanced perspective on your spiritual discipline.

   Tips:

   - Break your pattern; try something new from these tips.
   - No matter how good or poor your score, there is always room to improve.
   - Keep a record/log of the quality of your meditation activities.

4. **The reasons for low scores are informative for making improvements**

   Meaning: You are open to learning and improving your Bible study.

   Tips:

   - Look for common themes, and list reasons why those themes exist.
   - Add the items you checked to your gratitude journal, and thank God for insights on ways you can improve.

Category: Meditation	**Quotient: _____ out of 50**
Ways I can improve:	

DAY 26

Internalizing Forgiveness through Prayer

Research in the behavioral sciences has shown that praying and studying the Word of God reduce unforgiveness and promote forgiveness.[134] In a study conducted by Poloma and Gallup, 83 percent of the victims of transgressions reported that God's help was needed to truly forgive someone.[135] If you are a follower of Christ, you already know what prayer is, and you have a method, a rhythm, for how you pray. In this section we will talk about how to take prayer to another level in order to rely on it as a weapon for spiritual warfare. Prayer helps derail unforgiveness in four ways:

1. It guides you to put on the whole armor of God.
2. It causes you to program yourself to replace the growth of negative schema with prayer.
3. It leads you to respond to your transgressor with goodness.
4. It helps you control your thoughts and your tongue.

The Armor of God

Unforgiveness creates a state of unhappiness, imbalance, and negative well-being.[136] Prayer is a key line of both offense and defense to derail the unforgiveness life cycle. As we escalate from emotions, to negative feelings, to a sense of unenforceable rules, and then to negative intentions, we are walking in the flesh, a state triggered by our negative emotions. Paul tells us that our weapons are rooted in Jesus Christ and that our weapons have the power to break down Satan's strongholds.[137]

Why is prayer important? Because it is the most powerful tool we have to combat Satan's efforts or schemes to turn us away from God. Peter tells us to "be sober, be vigilant; because your adversary the devil walks about like a roaring lion, seeking whom he may devour."[138] Satan is searching furiously to gain complete control over this earth, and he attacks wherever he can to bring his plan to fruition. But for all those with a heart for God, resisting Satan is possible.

Satan is the prince of the air and has a prominent role in influencing what happens on the earth.[139] Satan received dominion over this world when he was ejected from heaven for attempting to overthrow God. Since he could not overtake God's heavenly kingdom, his purpose is to act as if he is the god of this earth. If he had his way, he would return to heaven and seek to set himself above God. Since that scheme is impossible, Satan tries to control as much of God's dominion as he can. The world and all things in heaven are under the direct control of God, but Satan, who received practically a free hand to do as he pleases on earth, uses the power he has to gather as many subjects for his kingdom as he can. Jesus calls Satan "the ruler of this world."[140] The apostle Paul calls him "the god of this age."[141]

God did not create us to be robots that are programmed to worship Him. Instead, we have free will to choose to follow God or Satan. God's plan is to provide every opportunity possible to reveal the deceitful schemes the devil employs to turn us to a life of sin. Although Satan's way leads to death and destruction, most of the world is not aware of the fact that they are constantly "under the sway of the wicked one."[142] The devil uses our inherent pride to occupy us with ourselves and our supposed greatness, a distraction that has affected every aspect of humanity.

Satan wants humankind to be so sure of our human abilities that our certainty precludes all need for God. If I were to sum up the devil's desire for us in a nutshell, it would be this: Do as you will. That mentality got Satan ejected from heaven, and when that thought sits at the crossroads of our choice to do what God wills or what we will, it has the same effect on the unsaved: they will be denied entrance to heaven. Satan is not interested in making the world evil but in bringing everyone under his sway; he is interested in gaining followers to prove himself equal to or greater than God. Satan would prefer to show that humankind is only interested in serving God when it suits their purposes or brings them pleasure. If Satan can show that people would rather follow him than God, then he can set himself up to be greater than God in dominion over the world.[143] I do not believe that disciples of Christ can lose their entrance to heaven once they have chosen Christ as their Savior. This is a controversial point, however, because some believe that if we return to a life of sin, doing as we will without regard for God's rule in our lives, then we can lose our salvation. Paul speaks to this question several times:

> *Well then, shall we keep on sinning so that God can keep on showing us more and more kindness and forgiveness? Of course not! Should we keep on sinning when we do not have to? For sin's power over us was broken when we became Christians and were baptized to become a part of Jesus Christ; through his death the power of your sinful nature was shattered.[144]*

Later in the same chapter, he goes on to say,

> *Does this mean that now we can go ahead and sin and not worry about it? (For our salvation does not depend on keeping the law but on receiving God's grace!) Of course not! Do not you*

realize that you can choose your own master? You can choose sin (with death) or else obedience (with acquittal). The one to whom you offer yourself—he will take you and be your master, and you will be his slave.[145]

Even though we are saved under the grace of God, Satan still whispers his lies into every ear, sowing pride and doubt. But we have been given weapons to combat his schemes. The weapons by which we combat the negative feelings and intentions that Satan wants us to ruminate on are, in essence, the armor of God as described in Ephesians 6:14–18:

Stand therefore, having fastened on the belt of truth, and having put on the breastplate of righteousness, and, as shoes for your feet, having put on the readiness given by the gospel of peace. In all circumstances take up the shield of faith, with which you can extinguish all the flaming darts of the evil one; and take the helmet of salvation, and the sword of the Spirit, which is the Word of God.

Paul emphasizes that after we have put on the armor of God (which is putting on Christ), we are to stand strong in prayer. He says, "At all times, pray."[146] Notice that all the elements of the armor are defensive except one: the sword of truth, the Word of God, which we talked about earlier. Here is the point: the Word of God and prayer go together.

Replacing Negative Schemas

A schema is a persistent pattern of thinking that affects what we believe about a situation and how we behave in it. Paul's choice of words in Ephesians 6 is interesting; he says that the whole armor of God enables us to stand against the schemes of the devil. Similarly, in the field of cognitive behavioral sciences, we see negative behaviors triggered by schema, patterns of thought that become programmed within our minds, affecting both our feelings and our responses.

Chapter 3 examines how rumination leads us to create a story about the transgression we experienced. When these negative stories become automatic, they form ruts in the neural pathways that are very difficult to change. These ruts become schemas—maps in our minds that cause us to react to external forces in a predetermined way. The schema may be thought of as schemes of the devil to trip us up; certainly, they are similar to what Paul refers to as "strongholds" of the devil. Strongholds were fortifications built around important areas such as towns or food stores to keep out predators and the enemy. Satan, our enemy, relies on the repetitive nature of rumination to create a stronghold that fortifies our negative thinking and prevents positive thoughts and the light of Christ from entering. Since they fortify our negative intentions as well as our negative thoughts, strongholds make it difficult to respond with love and kindness. When the vicious cycle of unforgiveness forms a stronghold, we become shackled inside, unable to break free on our own.

When we change the schema, that is, our negative stories, we pull down the strongholds of our negative thoughts and behaviors. But how do we change our schema? Prayer is one way to alter our stories: strongholds have no defense against prayer and the Word of God. Prayer releases us from the chains that hold us within Satan's stronghold and opens the door for nurturing positive intentions and forgiveness.

Doing Good

In his letter to the church at Thessalonica, Paul recognizes that continual prayer contributes to our desire to seek "to do good to one another and to everyone,"[147] instead of repaying evil with evil. One approach to changing our schema is to choose to direct some act of goodness or kindness toward the offender. This may be done outwardly or by inwardly rehearsing how we would like to return kindness in our hearts. These thoughts of returning good for evil replace the negative story, or schema, to create a new story or an addendum to the old story. This new narrative replaces the negative intentions and sets the tone for forgiveness.

But why do we have negative thoughts in the first place? Because we cannot help it. God gave us emotions and feelings as warning signals that something is amiss. Only when our emotions and feelings are allowed to rule do we give Satan a means to devour us by filling us with negative thoughts. Such thoughts, in turn, destroy the joy that God has promised.[148] For Christians, emotions and negative feelings are triggers for prayer. As Paul admonished the church in Philippi, Christians today present our needs to God through prayer and supplication with thanksgiving.[149] In the case of unforgiveness, our requests to God move us to a state of spiritual formation, which disrupts the strongholds of negative intentions. Rather than dwelling on cherished ideas of how things "should" be or on the injustice perpetrated against us, Paul instructs us to think on things that are true, honorable, pure, lovely, commendable, and just in the sight of God.[150]

Control Your Thoughts; Control Your Tongue

Most offenses are related to the tongue, and when we respond to a transgression without adequately assessing our words, our tongues can also get us, the victims, into trouble. Indeed, our tongues often move us toward unforgiveness, whether we speak aloud or reply internally. James, the brother of Jesus, tells us that if we can control the tongue, we can control the whole body.[151]

The apostle James provided some insight when he said, "Be slow to speak, and slow to anger."[152]

Slowing down what we say gives the conscious brain time to catch up with the emotional brain. Slowing down our responses and comments gives us time to interpret our emotional experience and emotional expressions from a Christlike perspective. In the case of mental or social threats to our well-being, slowing down what we say gives the mind sufficient time to assess the threat and consider positive responses, such as courage, love, and diplomacy. But sometimes when we tell ourselves to slow down our talking, we do not do so. Paul sums up this principle well in his letter to the church in Rome:

> I do not understand my own actions. For I do not do what I want, but I do the very thing I hate. Now if I do what I do not want, I agree with the law, that it is good. So now it is no longer I who do it, but sin that dwells within me. For I know that nothing good dwells in me, that is, in my flesh. For I have the desire to do what is right, but not the ability to carry it out. For I do not do the good I want, but the evil I do not want is what I keep on doing. Now if I do what I do not want, it is no longer I who do it, but sin that dwells within me.

> So I find it to be a law that when I want to do right, evil lies close at hand. For I delight in the law of God, in my inner being, but I see in my members another law waging war against the law of my mind and making me captive to the law of sin that dwells in my members. Wretched man that I am! Who will deliver me from this body of death? Thanks be to God through Jesus Christ our Lord! So then, I myself serve the law of God with my mind, but with my flesh I serve the law of sin.[153]

So how do we do what we want to do? We can take a lesson from our Lord: He engaged in prayer often in order to be in sync with the will of the Father. Jesus would slow down and withdraw to a private place to commune with God through prayer. If Jesus engaged in prayer in order to stay true to the course set before Him, how much more do we need to pray? Prayer connects us to God in light of whatever circumstance has triggered our negative emotions and feelings, and God answers our prayers by responding to what we ask for.[154]

Prayer serves other purposes besides slowing us down and controlling our thoughts and tongue. Prayer also helps us to persevere in difficult times. Jesus told His disciples to "pray and not give up."[155] Paul said Christians should "devote yourselves to prayer."[156] Paul told the church at Ephesus to pray in the spirit, on all occasions and with all kinds of prayers and requests. He goes on to say that we should be alert against the devil's attempts to lead us into sin by continually praying for ourselves and our fellow Christians.[157]

Like journaling, praying does not come easily to some people—and that's okay. God accepts us where we are and does not expect our prayers to be elegant. In fact, Paul tells us that the Holy Spirit intercedes on our behalf, recounting our prayers with a depth of purpose we could never equal.[158] There are several ways to get better at praying, discussed below, but the most important is simply to pray.

Set Aside Time to Pray

Setting aside time does not mean that you have to schedule prayer into your day. While it is helpful to, as Jesus did, to focus exclusively on prayer, we are also told to pray continually, without ceasing.[159] This teaching means that whenever any need arises, we can immediately take time to pray. Therefore, when a transgression occurs, pray. Ask for guidance; cry out (silently if you must) about your pain; ask for blessings for your offender. It is not necessary always to pray out loud, but it is necessary to pray if you are to overcome the transgression you have experienced.

Follow a Pattern

Jesus taught His disciples to pray in His Sermon on the Mount. He gave us a pattern, not just words to recite. This is often referred to as "the Lord's Prayer," but in actuality it is the disciples' prayer since it was given as instruction to His disciples on how to pray. If we take a close look, we can see a pattern that can serve as a format for us:

- Pray in secret, in your closet or within your thoughts. Your transgressor does not need to hear your prayer; God does.[160]
- Do not use repetitious phrases, but let each word carry its own weight.[161]
- Acknowledge your relationship with God as your Father.[162]
- Give respect and praise to God for His power and might.[163]
- Acknowledge that you accept God's rule over all His kingdom, especially in your heart.[164]
- Acknowledge that your will and requests are subordinate to His; He has a plan for you.[165]
- Acknowledge that He provides all that is good for you, even the basic necessities of life. You can ask for what you need.[166]
- Acknowledge that you have sinned, and ask for His forgiveness and guidance as you go forward.[167]
- Acknowledge your forgiveness of others just as He has forgiven you through His love for us and His sacrifice on the cross.[168]
- Acknowledge your need for God's guidance against sin in a fallen world. Ask for the strength to withstand temptation.[169]
- Claim victory over Satan through the power of Christ.[170]
- Acknowledge the everlasting presence of God.[171] You are under His loving protection forever.

Try to incorporate each thought in the prayer Jesus taught the disciples, but expand on the ideas, applying the ideas to your own life and your own situation. By using this prayer as a pattern, you can present yourself to God in a manner that is pleasing in His sight. This example prayer, short as it is, includes praise to God, words to get your heart right with God, and suggestions for requesting what you need from God.

We often think of prayer as simply talking to God. But there is more to it than that. When we study the great prayers of the Bible, we see many different ways in which God's people have approached Him. Different types of prayers served different purposes. A total of 481 prayers are recorded in the Old and New Testaments; of these, Dave Earley has suggested that 21 of them are "most effective"[172] because the person praying received answers. For our purpose of spiritual formation in the face of a transgression, we can break prayer into seven types:

- **Intercessory prayer**
  This is prayer on behalf of another person. To pray for another, we must first identify with him or her. In the case of forgiveness, when we understand the transgression from the other's point of view and acknowledge that we, too, have transgressed against others, then we can pray more effectively for the one who hurt us.

- **Praise, adoration, and worship**[173]
  As Jesus taught in the disciples' prayer, acknowledging God as Supreme Creator and King of the heavens and earth is a worthy prayer. The Old and New Testaments identify more than a hundred different names for God. Lifting up His names is an appropriate way to praise Him. Our prayer then becomes a form of adoration.[174] When praising God is difficult for you because He has allowed a transgression in your life, consider the next form of prayer.

- **Thankfulness and gratitude**[175]
  All that we have is of God.[176] How often do we overlook this simple truth? Gratitude has been shown to be a powerful agent in the cultivation of happiness and well-being.

- **Forgiveness and confession**[177]
  Forgiveness comes in two varieties, and both are a focus for prayer. Divine forgiveness is when we confess our sins to God and seek His forgiveness. The second type is forgiveness of another person. It is perfectly appropriate to ask God for strength to forgive another. At the same time, confessing the times we have needed forgiveness from others is also a topic for prayer.

- **Contemplative prayer**[178]

  Contemplative prayer is typically done in conjunction with meditation. Reflecting on scripture and the works of God's hand stimulates contemplative prayer that focuses on the insights received from meditation.

- **Watchman prayer**[179]

  Old Testament stories mention watchmen who were positioned as sentinels to protect crops and cities. In the same way, we are to be sentinels against attacks of Satan and his demons, which often come in the form of mistreatment by others. We are told by Christ, Paul, and Peter to "be on alert," praying that we have strength to escape Satan's attempts to devour us like a roaring lion while also being certain that all we do is done in love. Unforgiveness, in essence, is an attack on our ability to respond to another person in a loving way. We must be sentinels of our own hearts, praying that God will strengthen us against the temptation to fall prey to unforgiveness. We are also sentinels for the hearts of our offenders, praying that they will not be overcome by evil but will come to a saving knowledge of Christ.

- **Supplication and petition**[180]

  This type of prayer is surprisingly challenging. James tells us that we ask but do not receive because we ask wrongly.[181] At the same time, Jesus tells us to ask and it will be given to us,[182] while Jeremiah the Old Testament prophet tells us that God knows His plans for us, to prosper us, not to harm us.[183] James goes on to explain that asking wrongly is to make requests based on our passions. God gives us the desires of our hearts when we delight ourselves in Him. God will eventually bring your offender to justice. He looks to us to be patient and to focus on drawing closer to Him. King David, called a man after God's own heart, describes well what God will do for us and what God expects us to do.

What God will do for you:

- Delight yourself in the Lord, and He will give you the desires of your heart.
- Commit your way to the Lord; trust in Him, and He will act. He will bring forth your righteousness as the light and your justice as the noonday.
- In just a little while, the wicked will be no more; though you look carefully at His place, He will not be there.
- For the evildoers shall be cut off, but those who wait for the Lord shall inherit the land.
- But the righteous shall inherit the land and delight themselves in abundant peace.
- For the arms of the wicked shall be broken, but the Lord upholds the righteous.
- The wicked plots against the righteous and gnashes his teeth at him, but the Lord laughs at the wicked, for He sees that His day is coming.

What God desires us to do:

- Be still before the Lord and wait patiently for Him.
- Fret not yourself over the one who prospers in his way, over the man or woman who carries out evil devices!
- Refrain from anger and forsake wrath!
- Fret not yourself; it tends only to evil.
- Know that better is the little that the righteous has than the abundance of many wicked.[184]

In this passage (Psalms 37:1-40) has set up the dynamics between wrongdoers and those who are meek and wait for Him to act. God wants us to have justice, but when we fret over the wrongdoers (i.e., ruminate), we rob God of the space in our minds to work His will. It is common and often natural for us to want to pray that God will rain down vengeance on our offenders. But what He prefers is that we ask with compassion that He deal with our transgressors in His way, in His time, and for His glory. More importantly, however, we should will that God forgive their sins.

While hanging on the cross, Jesus did not ask God to avenge the wrong done by His transgressors; rather, He asked the Father not to hold their sins against them.[185] His words are often misinterpreted as Jesus's "forgiving" His transgressors, but He did not forgiven them. He asked His Father not to hold their sins against them. We are told that Jesus was a man and that he felt the things we experience. I cannot help but believe, therefore, that He struggled with forgiving His tormentors, but He knew that the Father could help Him through His emotions. Jesus also clearly acknowledged that God is the one who deals with transgressors. Jesus was poignantly aware of how His Father could deal with them, but He asked God to "let it go." Like Elijah's confrontation with the priests of Baal, He could have called for God to rain down fire and consume them, or He could have summoned a legion of angels to avenge Him, but He did not.

In a similar way, when Stephen was being stoned, he asked the Lord not to hold this sin against his attackers. Although Stephen could have called upon the Father to deal harshly with his persecutors, he did not. Instead, he asked God to spare them. If Jesus and Stephen knew what God's wrath can do yet did not call upon Him to strike down their tormentors, well, you do the math.[186]

Are you skeptical about whether God answers prayers about forgiveness today? Here's a true story: A friend came to me asking for advice because she was being blocked for a promotion to receive the title and pay for a job she had already been doing for a year. While she wanted to pray that God would give her the promotion, I advised her instead to pray with compassion for the soul of the manager and ask God to soften his heart. Two days later on her way to work, she received a call telling her that the manager had suffered a heart attack and was in a coma. Stunned, she pulled off the road and prayed, "God, I asked you to soften his heart, not to stop it." Think about this situation. How would you feel if God did rain down His wrath on your offender?

Our mission is to honor the Lord's desire that none should perish but that all should be saved.[187] The manager survived the heart attack and after three weeks returned to work. The cashier in the employee cafeteria, a disciple of Christ, talked to him upon his return, asking him how he was doing. He said he felt much better: he felt that his heart had been softened. This statement, the events that prompted it, and the manager's change of heart are not coincidences. God worked His power in that man's life. The key was that my friend prayed for her enemy, asking God to bring what was best for her adversary into his life. God did: He softened his heart. When the executive leadership was reorganized, my friend was offered the title and pay that came with the work she had already been doing. When a new CEO was appointed, he gave her the promotion.

The disciple's prayer is a good example of making supplications with the right intentions: asking for our daily bread, forgiveness, not to be led into temptation, and to be delivered from evil. James tells us that asking rightly means making petitions with humility and asking for closeness with God and the Holy Spirit who dwells in us.[188] By asking for material blessings, in contrast, we run the risk of focusing on the things of this world as opposed to storing up treasures in heaven. In the case of our transgressors, God blesses us when we humbly ask for a spirit of forgiveness to dwell in us so we can do good to them in hopes that they will be saved.

What kind of prayer can you provide for your transgressor? Are you a watchman, keeping a protective eye on your transgressor, looking for ways that you can call upon God to intervene in his or her life? Does your transgressor need a prayer of supplication wherein you ask God to bring peace or healing to his or her troubled mind? Here is a challenging thought: Do you need to thank God for the transgression because God used it to get your attention? In other words, can you find gratitude for the experience you have had?

As a chaplain in a hospital, I see a lot of pain and grief. Many people are there for serious life-threatening illnesses or injuries. Should I ask a person with pancreatic cancer to give thanks to God or a person who fell twenty feet off a ladder to praise God? No, these would not be the questions to ask. Instead, the questions I put to patients are, "How is God using this illness/injury to get your attention? What is He trying to tell you?"

Once I was working the midnight shift at a large hospital, one that had both a palliative care and hospice care section. At 2:00 a.m. I received a page to call the nurses' station in the hospice wing. The nurse explained that a family was gathered around the bed of a parent who had just expired. They wanted a chaplain to come and offer a prayer. When I arrived, three siblings, all adults in their late forties, were in the room. One was standing by the bed holding her mother's hand, and the other two were sitting off to the side, silent, contemplative. I asked who they were, and we introduced ourselves. At that point, I could have prayed. Instead, I asked myself, *How can God use this moment for the benefit of these adult children?*

I sensed tension in the room among the siblings. I also sensed emotional distance between them. In a moment like this, the emotions in the room would eclipse any questions about their relationships with each other; therefore, I asked God to grant me wisdom to know how to help mend any woundedness in the room. A thought then came to me, and I asked the siblings what memories about their mother they would cherish as they went forward.

They started to share, and as they did, I could see that their mother had been a wonderful influence in their lives and in the lives of their children. At one point they expanded on how Christmas would not be the same since their mother went all out decorating, finding special gifts, baking, and cooking. I began to see them soften. I then asked how they would keep that memory alive. They began to negotiate and collaborate on who would do what, where they would do it, when the best time would be for everyone, and how they would coordinate the event. As they began to open up to each other, I saw God soften the strongholds in their hearts that they had brought into the room. I invited them each to thank God for one thing their mother did to influence their lives. As they shared, I incorporated their thoughts into a prayer. When they finished, I asked God to continue blessing this family as the warmth and love of their mother flowed through them. When I left, they were hugging each other. They also hugged me, and I could feel the presence of God embracing them with the presence of the Holy Spirit.

Journal Exercise 26: Assessing Your Prayer Practices

Take a moment to think about your own spiritual maturity by responding to the questions below. Follow the directions for summarizing your spiritual quotient. A score of 1 = not at all satisfied with your practice of that discipline, and a score of 5 = completely satisfied.

TABLE 2 Prayer

SIGNS OF SPIRITUAL MATURITY	HOW OFTEN I DO THIS (COLUMN 1)	HOW WELL I DO THIS (COLUMN 2)	WHY I DO NOT DO THESE BEHAVIORS WELL
1. I pray for God's will more than I pray for what I need.	[1] [2] [3] [4] [5]	[1] [2] [3] [4] [5]	❏ I do not know how. ❏ It is uncomfortable.
2. I am patient for God's response to prayer.	[1] [2] [3] [4] [5]	[1] [2] [3] [4] [5]	❏ I have a better way. ❏ I do not want to.
3. I listen to God as much as I talk to Him.	[1] [2] [3] [4] [5]	[1] [2] [3] [4] [5]	❏ I try but keep failing. ❏ I get distracted.
4. I believe my prayers impact my life as well as others' lives.	[1] [2] [3] [4] [5]	[1] [2] [3] [4] [5]	❏ Other reasons
5. I pray constantly throughout the day.	[1] [2] [3] [4] [5]	[1] [2] [3] [4] [5]	
6. My prayers include praise, confession, and requests.	[1] [2] [3] [4] [5]	[1] [2] [3] [4] [5]	
Add together the numbers you marked. Put the total in the box below each column.	Total _____	Total _____	Column 1 + 2 _____ out of 60 possible

Making Meaning Out of Your Results

Prayer is for you and every person in your sphere of contact. None of us pray as often or as well as we would like. Knowing how, when, for whom, and for what to pray is always a challenge. Below are a few ways to look at your results and some tips for improving:

1. **The total for column 2 is greater than the total for column 1**
   Meaning: Prayer as part of your daily activities seem to be a challenge.

   Tips:

   • Schedule a time for prayer in your daily activities.
   • Do not wait for a specific time to pray; learn to take a break and pray as needed, on the spot, quietly or with others.

2. **The total for column 1 is greater than the total for column 2**
   Meaning: Try establishing a prayer pattern or routine.

   Tips:

   • Read prayers in the Bible to learn new ways of putting your thoughts in front of God.[189]
   • Keep a journal of things you are grateful for and why. Share these in prayer with God.
   • Make a list of people who need God's grace and mercy. Simply state their names for God to know you care.

3. **The total for column 1 is the same as or close to the total of column 2**
   Meaning: You have a fairly balanced perspective on your spiritual discipline.

   Tips:

   • Break your pattern by trying something new from these tips.
   • No matter how good or poor your score, you can improve. Focus on improving.
   • Keep a record/log of the quality and quantity of your prayer.
   • Start a gratitude journal about your prayer life, including quantity, quality, and new learning about prayer.

4. **The reasons for low scores are informative for making improvements**

   Tips:

   • Look for common themes, and list reasons why those reasons exist.
   • Add the items you checked to your gratitude journal, and thank God for the insight on ways you can improve.

Category: Prayer	Quotient: _____ out of 50
Ways I can improve:	

DAY 27

Internalizing Forgiveness through Fellowship

Like prayer, meditation, and study of the Word of God, fellowship is a coping response. As explained in chapter 4, seeking support in the face of transgressions is an active response to achieve positive emotional regulation. God designed us to live in relationship with others. When we are not living in fellowship with Jesus or other believers, we respond to challenging situations in ways that compete negatively with our desire to live a Christlike life. In John's first letter, he makes clear that fellowship is not an optional matter for believers: "If we walk in the light [in fellowship with God] ... this causes us to have fellowship with one another." The outcome of this fellowship is that "the blood of Jesus, His Son, cleanses us from all sin."[190]

This section provides a broader view of fellowship than the common conception that fellowship is a potluck meal after the worship service or some other social gathering with fellow believers. Fellowship is much more than social gatherings. True fellowship relates to our vertical relationship with Jesus Christ, God, and the Holy Spirit, as well as to our horizontal relationship with fellow believers. As we have seen, our vertical relationship is established through the three disciplines of scripture study, prayer, and meditation, but it is also enhanced by fellowship as seen in Jesus's words in the Gospel of John:[191]

> *I am the vine; you are the branches. If you remain in me and I in you, you will bear much fruit; apart from me you can do nothing. If you do not remain in me, you are like a branch that is thrown away and withers; such branches are picked up, thrown into the fire and burned. If you remain in me and my words remain in you, ask whatever you wish, and it will be done for you. This is to my Father's glory, that you bear much fruit, showing yourselves to be my disciples.*[192]

This analogy describes true fellowship. The image of the vine and its branches illustrates our relationship with the Lord. The Vine, Christ, is firmly rooted in the soil, providing stability and nutrients for the branches to thrive, grow, and bear fruit. The branches, if removed from the Vine, quickly wither and die, but when connected to the Vine, they are part of a beautiful and healthy organism that provides sustenance and belonging for every branch. Our horizontal relationship with like-minded believers is also illustrated in this analogy; each Christian needs connection with other disciples to encourage spiritual growth.[193]

A scripture that describes the horizontal element of fellowship is in Acts: "And they [the believers] devoted themselves to the apostles' teaching and fellowship, to the breaking of bread and the prayers."[194] In this passage, the context of the word *fellowship* also includes the concept of edification. In his letter to the Romans, Paul uses *edification* (KJV) to mean building up others and encouraging others to do good. Paul, as well as other New Testament writers, uses the word *edify* to mean "building up" the body of Christ (that is, the church).[195]

The church has evolved since the first century, but if we focus on the context of the passage in Acts, we see that the first-century idea of fellowship was what today is known as the worship service wherein Christians lift holy hands in prayer, sing hymns and spiritual songs, and listen to the teaching of God's Word. It is in the corporate fellowship that we draw strength from one another and edify one another. This is also where the Holy Spirit breathes a spirit of love that encourages us to draw strength from other believers. An inscription over the door of some churches says, "Enter to worship; leave to serve." I would suggest, however, that we worship and serve no matter where we are. As Paul told the Roman Christians, we are to present our bodies as a living sacrifice "for this is your spiritual worship."[196] Presenting our bodies as a living sacrifice means not conforming to the ways of the world and renewing our minds through meditation, prayer, study of the Word, and fellowship.

Our participation in fellowship with other believers is a crucial component of spiritual formation. The commonly accepted idea is that we go to church to worship God, and that "worship" is the purpose of what we do "in church." I found, however, that "worship" is only a partial description of what the Christian assembly does on the first day of the week. Instead, edification, building one another up, is expressly identified by Paul[197] as the purpose and goal of everything we do in the community of believers, also known as the church. If we followed the first-century church's design, our gatherings would be about building up one another rather than trying to perform rituals or obligatory liturgical activities that we have decided are pleasing to God.

The popular mantra today seems to be that our gatherings on Sunday mornings are all about God. The biblical concept of assembling ourselves together, however, is both about our edifying one another and about our corporate praise to God. It is through our edification of one another; singing songs, hymns, and spiritual songs; and teaching from the Word of God that we strengthen the body of Christ and, subsequently, strengthen our relationship with God. Jesus established fellowship with, and among, His disciples for their benefit, not God's. Consequently, it is necessary for us in our fellowship to be constantly working on our own spiritual maturity and on our relationships with one another, both of which are achieved through mutual edification. Certainly, God loves the songs of praise and thankfulness; He loves the reading of the Word; He loves for us to raise our hearts and hands to Him in prayer like a pleasing aroma. But our devotion to Him is manifested each day in everything we do to please Him, not just in the time we spend in church.

Our participation in the fellowship of other believers is a critical component of spiritual formation. There are four types of fellowship:

- Fellowship with the triune God (God the Father, God the Son, and God the Holy Spirit), which happens in both large corporate gatherings and small group gatherings.
- Person-to-person fellowship with another like-minded believer.
- Fellowship with a small community of believers who know each other well and encourage each other to love and to do good works or, as popular vernacular puts it, to "do life together."
- The larger community fellowship, sometimes referred to as "worship."

God is certainly involved in every aspect of fellowship and edification, but thinking that we go to our temples (church buildings) to offer service to a needy God is not biblical. As Paul said to the Athenians, "The God who made the world and everything in it, being Lord of heaven and earth, does not live in temples made by man, nor is he served by human hands, as though he needed anything, since he himself gives to all mankind life and breath and everything."[198]

Over the centuries, the church has certainly evolved to meet our ongoing needs for fellowship, but we need to keep edification at the center of our gatherings. We might say that corporate singing is edifying because the sharing of the words and music builds us up as a community, inspiring us to good works and to praise. We could also say that we are built up in a greater knowledge and understanding of the Lord through the preaching of the Word and that as we pray, we raise up praise, devotion, and requests for the needs of the community, building a strong case for God to hear us since, as Jesus said, He is among His disciples when even two or three are gathered together.[199]

Another meaning of the word *fellowship* in the early church was in reference to things shared in common. While the New Testament church literally shared all things—property, food, wealth, belongings—God's intent is not that we live in communes. Instead, we share a spiritual birthright and heritage within the Christian community: we have the same God, [200] a common salvation,[201] a common faith,[202] and a common place to turn in times of need. We also share spiritual edification through music, preaching, prayer, and reading of the Word.[203]

In the context of forgiveness, our participation in the fellowship of other believers is a critical component of spiritual formation. A shift from negative to positive intentions and the peaceful experience of emotional forgiveness occurs when we are connected to the Vine, which is our interaction with Christ and with other believers. We share our spiritual edification in common, and that edification is a critical part of our ability to overcome unforgiveness. In fact, fellowship with Jesus and like-minded believers is central and critical to our ability to forgive, which, I believe, is one reason Jesus wants us to come together as His body, a community that edifies and supports one another in our efforts to live for Him. Jesus intended for us to love one another because that is how others know we are His disciples.[204] To our Lord and to the New Testament writers, fellowship was a process, not an event. Fellowship is not so much what we "do" as it is who and how we are as followers of Christ.

How, then, does fellowship help us to reach biblical forgiveness? Following are some ways that fellowship helps us overcome our unforgiveness and grow in our relationship with God:

- Fellowship lightens the weight of our unforgiveness for our transgressor when it becomes too heavy to bear alone. When the transgression weighs us down, we can be emotionally and mentally built up by the love and encouragement of our community of believers. In fellowship, we

  ✓ encourage and show honor to one another,[205]
  ✓ comfort each other in our suffering and share in one another's joy, including the joy of forgiving a transgression,[206]
  ✓ find strength because the Lord is in our midst.[207]

- Fellowship is a community of disciples bound together in love to help each other grow in spiritual maturity. Our fellowship with other believers creates a state of mind in which we do not feel alone; instead, we have a place of love and support. We feel comfort and belonging with like-minded believers as we

  ✓ teach and admonish one another,[208]
  ✓ confess our sins to one another,[209]
  ✓ bring one another back to the truth if any have strayed,[210]
  ✓ receive encouragement from having harmony with others, including people different from us, a key element of well-being,[211]
  ✓ feel mutual acceptance,[212]
  ✓ experience joy, unity, and peace,[213]
  ✓ remember Christ's death on the cross as we partake in a worthy manner[214] of the wine ("the fruit of the vine") and the bread that represent His blood and body, sacrificed for us.[215]

- In fellowship, we learn to let our lights shine in the world and to present ourselves to others in a Christlike way. We share our challenges and gain insights into overcoming distractions that block our witness, bolstering our ability to

- ✓ demonstrate a sincere love for Jesus in how we treat others,[216]
- ✓ use our freedom in Christ to serve others,[217]
- ✓ receive God-given opportunities to develop patience,[218]
- ✓ become aware of God-given opportunities to grow in kindness and forgiveness,[219]
- ✓ put ourselves on God's pathway for cultivating spiritual growth.[220]

- • When we share scripture, prayer, and songs of worship and admonition, we

  - ✓ receive mutual encouragement and growth that comes from corporate worship of God,[221]
  - ✓ publicly demonstrate reverence for Christ,[222]
  - ✓ see God's answers to prayers in our lives and in the lives of others,[223]
  - ✓ receive insight from others to be less vulnerable to the deceitfulness of sin,[224]
  - ✓ stir up one another to love and to do good works.[225]

- • Being in fellowship with like-minded believers provides a place where we can explore possibilities for addressing our challenging situations. We can find perspective from others who are not emotionally invested to help us reframe, emotionally regulate, and problem-solve our challenges. The inspiration to approach life's challenges in new ways can help us to

  - ✓ put to death our judgmental spirits,[226]
  - ✓ learn to confess our challenges to a brother or sister and benefit from another's prayers,[227]
  - ✓ grow in humility,[228]
  - ✓ find new ways to make the gospel more visible to a dark world.[229]

I could go on, giving more examples of how fellowship with other believers strengthens us to live as Christ's followers and remain committed to walking with Him. A community of believers reflects how God designed us in His likeness:[230] as He is in fellowship with Jesus, the Holy Spirit, and us,[231] He created us to be in fellowship with Him, Christ, and like-minded people. Christians are blessed with different spiritual gifts, and we all have different experiences and challenges that others can learn from; thus, fellowship provides comfort, encouragement, love, and strength to help us address the hurt of transgressions.

In the next journal assignment, you will look at how strong you feel your fellowship is. This assignment might be even more helpful to you if you ask some others who are close to you to complete this exercise also, and then compare responses with them.

Journal Exercise 27: Assessing Your Fellowship Practices

TABLE 3 Fellowship

SIGNS OF SPIRITUAL MATURITY	HOW OFTEN I DO THIS (COLUMN 1)	HOW WELL I DO THIS (COLUMN 2)	WHY I DO NOT DO THESE BEHAVIORS WELL
1. I meet regularly with a community of believers.	[1] [2] [3] [4] [5]	[1] [2] [3] [4] [5]	❏ I do not know how. ❏ It is uncomfortable.
2. I ask forgiveness when I hurt others.	[1] [2] [3] [4] [5]	[1] [2] [3] [4] [5]	❏ I have a better way. ❏ I do not want to.
3. I accept feedback on my spiritual walk.	[1] [2] [3] [4] [5]	[1] [2] [3] [4] [5]	❏ I try but keep failing. ❏ I get distracted.
4. I am gentle with others.	[1] [2] [3] [4] [5]	[1] [2] [3] [4] [5]	❏ Other reasons
5. I show love toward all people.	[1] [2] [3] [4] [5]	[1] [2] [3] [4] [5]	
6. I express joy in my life.	[1] [2] [3] [4] [5]	[1] [2] [3] [4] [5]	
7. I am patient with others.	[1] [2] [3] [4] [5]	[1] [2] [3] [4] [5]	
8. I endeavor to show goodness to others.	[1] [2] [3] [4] [5]	[1] [2] [3] [4] [5]	
9. I have an unshakable faith.	[1] [2] [3] [4] [5]	[1] [2] [3] [4] [5]	
Add together the numbers you marked. Put the total in the box below each column.	Total _____	Total _____	**Fellowship Quotient** Total of columns 1 + 2 _____out of 90 possible

Making Meaning Out of Your Results

Fellowship is the fourth foundation upon which spiritual maturity is built. Fellowship is necessary because of the way God wired us: we need a safe and secure bond with like-minded believers. In a community, we find strength to engage in spiritual warfare.

1. **The total for column 2 is greater than the total for column 1**
   Meaning: Trying to minimize the distractions from spending the time needed to engage in fellowship would be helpful.

   Tips:

   - *Slow down!* When you are constantly focused on the next thing, you have a hard time being in the moment. Many of the attributes of forgiveness happen as we go through the day and encounter other people.

- Use scripture during the day to keep you close in spirit to the Lord and to your fellowship community.

2. **The total for column 1 is greater than the total for column 2**
   Meaning: You may be engaging in fellowship, but you do not fully feel that the quality of your engagement is what you would like it to be.

   Tips:

   - Read prayers in the Bible to learn new ways of putting your thoughts in front of God.[232]
   - Ask others in your fellowship to assess the quality of your engagement and to share their thoughts about enriching the fellowship experience for you and others.

3. **The total for column 1 is the same as or close to the total of column 2**
   Meaning: You have a fairly balanced perspective on your engagement of fellowship. However, there is always opportunity to improve the quality and frequency of your fellowship behaviors and to show love and compassion in helping others improve as well. Helping each other grow in the Spirit of the Lord is a critical part of fellowship.

   Tips:

   - Begin to see every interpersonal encounter with other believers as an opportunity to encourage and engage.
   - Have a sharing time with other believers wherein you each talk about the quality and frequency of your fellowship and share ideas for improving your relationship with each other and with Christ.

4. **The reasons for low scores are informative for making improvements**
   Meaning: You are open to learning and to improving your fellowship opportunities.

   Tips:

   - Interview a person in your community of believers and share with this individual the challenges you want to address. Hear how he or she would address those things from his or her perspective.
   - Go back through the benefits of fellowship and see how they can help you address the reasons you are challenged in your fellowship engagement.

Category: Fellowship	**Quotient:** _____ **out of 90**
Ways I can improve:	

Summary of Chapter 5

- In the ACTION model, *I* stands for internalization, the thought process of trying to dissect and intellectualize the transgression in order to understand what happened to you.

- In internalizing the transgression, you begin to develop either a worldly or Christlike response; the choice is yours.

- The condition of your heart influences your ability to forgive. Creating a spiritually mature heart pleases God and brings you peace.

- When you internalize with spiritual maturity, you replace your initial negative thoughts about your transgressor with positive thoughts. You replace negative schema with positive schema by controlling your tongue and doing good.

- In the process of viewing the experience through a godly lens, you develop Christlike behaviors, thoughts, and feelings, and others see Christ in you.

- The key to internalizing forgiveness is to practice the disciplines that lead to your ongoing spiritual maturity.

- The four spiritual disciplines you need in your life are prayer, meditation, a stronger knowledge of God's Word, and fellowship with like-minded disciples of Christ in whom you can confide your forgiveness journey.

- The Lord's Prayer is actually the disciples' prayer; it models the many kinds of prayers available to you: intercessory, praise and adoration, gratitude, confession and forgiveness, contemplative, supplication, etc.

- Fellowship, commonly thought of as interaction among believers, is also to be nurtured between you and God: it is vertical as well as horizontal.

Scripture for Strength

I am the vine; you are the branches. If you remain in me and I in you, you will bear much fruit; apart from me you can do nothing. If you do not remain in me, you are like a branch that is thrown away and withers; such branches are picked up, thrown into the fire and burned. If you remain in me and my words remain in you, ask whatever you wish, and it will be done for you. This is to my Father's glory, that you bear much fruit, showing yourselves to be my disciples. (John 15:1–8)

Devotional Prayer

Dear Lord,

Please help me to internalize the image of Your Son as the _____, the Source of my stability and nourishment, and myself as a _____ who is dependent on Him. Also, Father God, please help me to see myself as part of a living, thriving organism, the body of Christ, the _____, where I am able to find encouragement, belonging, guidance, and strength, all benefits of the spiritual discipline of _____.

In addition to this corporate means of growing in spiritual maturity, I also humbly ask for Your strength and blessing as I focus on the spiritual disciplines of _____, _____ and knowledge of Your _____. Lord God, I want those who see me to see Christ in me. As a branch connected to Christ, I want to bear the fruit of bringing others to You, even _____, my transgressor. My goal in this life is to show myself to be Christ's disciple.

In the powerful name of Christ, amen.

Chapter 5 Endnotes

1   Ezekiel 26:36.
2   1 Corinthians 10:13.
3   James 1:2–4.
4   2 Corinthians 11:3.
5   1 Peter 5:8–10.
6   James 1:2–4.
7   1 Peter 5:8–10.
8   2 Corinthians 12:9.
9   2 Corinthians 12:9.
10   Psalms 119:10–11.
11   Luke 23:34; Acts 7:60.
12   Colossians 3:15–16.
13   Galatians 5:22–23.
14   Jeremiah 29:12–14.
15   Matthew 7:7; Luke 11:9.
16   1 Thessalonians 5:16–17.
17   Matthew 11:28–30.
18   Ephesians 4:32; Romans 5:8–10.
19   Matthew 18:23–34.
20   Luke 15:11–32.
21   Luke 17:4; Matthew 18:21.
22   Luke 6:28.
23   Luke 6:23–34.
24   Matthew 7:12.
25   Ephesians 4:32.
26   Acts 11:23.
27   John 16:22.
28   Hebrews 10:22; 1 John 3:20; Romans 12:2.
29   Matthew 6:21.
30   Proverbs 3:5.
31   Proverbs 4:23.
32   Psalms 73:26.
33   John 14:27.
34   Ibid.
35   Psalms 37:4.
36   Matthew 5:8
37   Psalms 19:14.
38   Mark 6:52.
39   Psalms 51:10; Ezekiel 36:26.
40   Jeremiah 17:9.
41   Proverbs 4:23.

42 Luke 6:45; Matthew 12:24.

43 Luke 6:45.

44 2 Corinthians 3:3; Proverbs 6:21.

45 *The Holy Bible: English Standard Version* (Wheaton, IL: Standard Bible Society, 2016).

46 Psalms 51:13.

47 Matthew 6:21; Luke 12:24.

48 Romans 8:1–11.

49 Romans 8:6–7.

50 Revelation 3:16.

51 Matthew 12:35.

52 Luke 6:45.

53 Philippians 4:8.

54 Romans 12:2–3.

55 Jeremiah 17:9.

56 Genesis 8:21.

57 Proverbs 6:14; Mark 7:2.

58 Romans 1:29–30.

59 Matthew 12:24.

60 Romans 1:29–31.

61 1 Corinthians 6:9–10.

62 Galatians 5:19–21.

63 Ephesians 4:31.

64 Colossians 3:8.

65 1 Timothy 6:4–5.

66 James 2:4.

67 Mark 7:20–21; James 3:9–10.

68 Matthew 15:16–20.

69 James 3:6–10.

70 Ephesians 3:17.

71 Colossians 3:15.

72 Romans 8:6; Isaiah 26:3.

73 Hebrews 10:25.

74 2 Timothy 4:7–8.

75 Matthew 5:13–14; 1 Peter 3:15–17.

76 Matthew 5:6.

77 Isaiah 26:3; Philippians 4:7.

78 Isaiah 26:3–4.

79 John 14:15, 15:10.

80 Matthew 22:37–39.

81 Ephesians 6:11–13.

82 1 John 1:7.

83 The role of empathy as a mediator in interpersonal forgiveness has been replicated in too many studies to reference here. Two prominent studies are found in these sources: M. E. McCullough, E. Worthington

Jr., and K. C. Rachal, "Interpersonal Forgiving in Close Relationships," *Journal of Personality and Social Psychology* 73 (1997): 321–36; W. Malcom, S. Warwar, and L. Greenberg, "Facilitating Forgiveness in Individual Therapy as an Approach to Resolving Interpersonal Injuries," in *Handbook of Forgiveness*, ed. E. Worthington Jr. (New York: Routledge, 2005), pp. 384–85.

84 Philippians 2:13.

85 1 John 5:2–4.

86 2 Corinthians 2:5.

87 Romans 12:1–4.

88 Colossians 3:1–4.

89 Luke 6:25–37.

90 Luke 6:45–46.

91 D. E. Davis, J. N. Hook, D. R. Van Tongeren, and E. L. Worthington Jr., "Sanctification of Forgiveness," *Psychology of Religion and Spirituality* 4, no. 1 (2012): 38.

92 1 Peter 1:13.

93 Matthew 13:18–23.

94 Psalms 51:13.

95 John 14:26.

96 Joshua 1:8.

97 1 Timothy 4:4–8; Matthew 5:44–45; 1 Thessalonians 5:17.

98 Deuteronomy 11:19–21; 2 Timothy 2:15.

99 Ecclesiastes 4:12; 1 John 1:7; Hebrews 10:24–25; John 13:34–35.

100 D. Willard, *The Spirit of the Disciplines: Understanding How God Changes Lives* (New York: Harper Collins, 1998), p. 158.

101 Richard Foster, *Celebration of Discipline: The Path to Spiritual Growth* (New York: Harper One, 1978).

102 Romans 6:13.

103 Galatians 5:22–23.

104 1 Peter 5:6–10.

105 1 Peter 3:14–17.

106 Colossians 3:9.

107 Titus 3:3.

108 Matthew 6:15.

109 1 Peter 2:1–3; Hebrews 5:12–14, 6:1; Colossians 1:10.

110 Galatians 6.

111 1 Corinthians 13:4.

112 Colossians 3:12–17.

113 1 Peter 5:6–7.

114 Matthew 5:23; John 15:1–2; Galatians 5:22; Mark 7:21; John 4:23.

115 Romans 12:1–2; Luke 6:47; Ephesians 4:31.

116 James 1:2–4.

117 John 14:10.

118 Romans 12:2.

119 Ibid.

120 Romans 8:28; 1 Corinthians 2:11–16.

121 Matthew 4:1–11.

122 My favorite marking pen is the Pilot Juice gel ink ballpoint pen, 0.38 mm, twelve-color set, Amazon no. LJU-120UF-12C. I use a bookmark as a straight edge for underlining.

123 Charles Swindoll, "Insights on the Bible," Insight.org, accessed August 25, 2020, https://www.insight.org/resources/bible.

124 Ephesians 1:17–19.

125 Several applications for handheld devices provide easy access to the Bible text. My favorite is Olive Tree. One of my favorite websites is Bible Study Tools. Other sites are also good, but many of them have too much advertising for my taste.

126 Foster, *Celebration of Discipline*.

127 Psalms 19:1, 119:27, 143:5–8.

128 Romans 8:26–27.

129 Psalms 119:97, 101–102.

130 John 10:27; Luke 6:47–49; Revelation 3:20.

131 Exodus 33:11.

132 Visit ODB.org.

133 For example, Jesus withdrew to meditate and pray. Matthew 4:1–11, 14:13, 17:1–9, 26:36; Luke 5:16, 6:12; Mark 1:35, 6:31.

134 S. L. Vasiliauskas and M. R. McMinn, "The Effects of a Prayer Intervention on the Process of Forgiveness," *Psychology of Religion and Spirituality* 5, no. 1 (2013): 28–29.

135 M. M. Poloma and G. H. Gallup, "Unless You Forgive Others: Prayer and Forgiveness," in *Varieties of Prayer* (Philadelphia: Trinity, 1991), pp. 85–106.

136 I. Yalçin and A. Malkoç, "The Relationship between Meaning in Life and Subjective Well-Being: Forgiveness and Hope as Mediators," *Journal of Happiness Studies* 6, no. 4 (2015): 915–29.

137 2 Corinthians 10:3–6.

138 1 Peter 5:8.

139 Ephesians 2:2.

140 John 12:31.

141 2 Corinthians 4:4.

142 1 John 5:19.

143 1 Peter 5:8.

144 Romans 12:1.

145 Romans 12:15.

146 Ephesians 6:18.

147 1 Thessalonians 5:15–17.

148 1 Peter 5:8.

149 Philippians 4:6.

150 Philippians 4:8.

151 James 3:1–10.

152 James 1:19–21.

153 Romans 5:15–25.

154 Matthew 7:7.

155 Luke 18:1.

156 Colossians 4:2.

157 Ephesians 6:18.

158 Romans 8:26–27.

159 1 Thessalonians 5:17.

160 Matthew 6:6.

161 James 5:12.

162 John 1:12–13.

163 Colossians 1:11; 1 Chronicles 29:12–13.

164 1 Timothy 1:17.

165 Jeremiah 29:11–12.

166 Matthew 7:7–11; Romans 8:28; James 4:3.

167 Romans 3:23.

168 John 15:12–13; 1 John 3:16–24.

169 James 1:13.

170 Romans 7:24–25; 2 Corinthians 2:14.

171 1 Timothy 6:12, 15–16.

172 D. Earley, *The 21 Most Effective Prayers of the Bible* (Uhrichsville, OH: Barbour, 2005).

173 Psalms 7:17, 57:9; Hebrews 13:15; Revelation 4:9.

174 Psalms 91:14–15.

175 1 Chronicles 16:8–41; Psalms 107:1; 2 Corinthians 1:11.

176 James 1:17; Matthew 7:11; Luke 11:13.

177 Psalms 32:5; Romans 14:11–12; 1 John 1:9.

178 Psalms 19:14, 104:32, 119:11, 15, 18; Ecclesiastes 5:2.

179 Matthew 26:41; 2 Corinthians 13:7; Colossians 1:9; 1 John 5:16.

180 Luke 22:46.

181 James 4:3.

182 Matthew 7:7.

183 Jeremiah 29:11–12.

184 Psalms 37:1-40.

185 Luke 23:34.

186 Acts 7:60.

187 2 Peter 3:9.

188 James 4:5–10.

189 A book you may find helpful: H. Lockyer, *All the Prayers of the Bible* (Grand Rapids, MI: Zondervan, 1990).

190 1 John 1:7.

191 John 15:5; 1 John 1:3–4.

192 John 15:5.

193 There are many ways we can manage our fellowship with God, each of us in our own way. I mention these four ways because they are the four disciplines that we are focusing on in the forgiveness process.

194 Acts 2:42.

195 2 Corinthians 10:8, 13:10; Acts 10:35; 1 Corinthians 8:1, 10:23, 14:17; 1 Thessalonians 5:11.

196 Romans 12:1.

197 1 Corinthians 14:26.

198 Acts 17:24–25.

199 Matthew 18:20.

200 Ephesians 4:6.

201 Jude 3.

202 Titus 1:4.

203 Acts 2:44.

204 John 13:35.

205 Romans 12:10; 1 Thessalonians 5:11.

206 1 Corinthians 12:25–26; 2 Corinthians 13:11; Romans 12:15.

207 Matthew 18:20.

208 Romans 15:14; Colossians 3:15–17.

209 James 5:13–18.

210 James 5:19–20.

211 Romans 15:5.

212 Romans 15:7.

213 2 Corinthians 13:11; 1 Thessalonians 4:18, 5:11.

214 1 Corinthians 11:27.

215 Matthew 26:26–29; Mark 14:22–25.

216 1 John 4:19–20.

217 Galatians 5:31.

218 Ephesians 4:1–2.

219 Ephesians 4:32; Colossians 3:13.

220 Colossians 3:7–10.

221 Colossians 3:16.

222 Ephesians 5:21.

223 2 Thessalonians 1:3; 1 Thessalonians 3:11–12.

224 Hebrews 3:13.

225 Hebrews 10:24–25.

226 James 4:11–5:9.

227 James 5:16.

228 1 Peter 5:5.

229 John 1.

230 Genesis 1:27.

231 1 John 1:2–10.

CHAPTER 6

Opening Your Heart to Forgiveness

Blessed are the merciful, for they shall receive mercy.
Blessed are the peacemakers, for they
shall be called sons of God.
Blessed are those who are persecuted for righteousness'
sake, for theirs is the kingdom of heaven.
Blessed are you when others revile you and persecute you
and utter all kinds of evil against you falsely on my account.
Rejoice and be glad, for your reward is great in heaven,
for so they persecuted the prophets who were before you.

—MATTHEW 5:2–12

Above all else, guard your heart, for it is the wellspring of life.

—PROVERBS 4:23

DAY 28

Opening Your Heart to Forgiveness—Introduction

In chapter 3, I asked you to consider making a commitment to try to forgive your transgressor. Since then, we have talked about how forgiveness is not a feeling; it is an *action*. In the previous chapter we talked about the heart: what it is, how it functions, and its importance in the forgiveness process. We also talked about how Satan can trick us into using our thoughts to build a stronghold around our hearts that keeps our Christ-centered spirit locked inside. In this chapter we will talk about how forgiveness requires that we open up our hearts to the possibility of how our Lord Jesus Christ would respond to our transgressor; to let the Lord flow through us into the life of the transgressor; and to allow others to witness our love for and devotion to our Lord and how we have overcome unforgiveness.

As we become more spiritually mature, each of us begins to develop the mind of Christ within our hearts. Each chapter has presented more and more steps for you to consider as you transition from an unforgiving to a forgiving spirit. Until now, all the exercises have been targeted at how you *think* about forgiving your transgressor. In this chapter, we will move beyond thinking and actions. We will now work on being open to let everything you have learned about forgiveness to take command of your heart. Opening one's heart is the key to forgiveness and is a prerequisite to building a forgiving nature.

Opening Your Heart

Whereas there are actions you can take to forgive an interpersonal transgression, forgiveness comes from your heart. When your heart has an openness to forgive, you will be able to do the following:

- Begin to feel love toward the transgressor and a desire for his or her salvation.
- Feel gratitude for the challenge God has brought into your life.

- Hold on to the faithfulness of the Word of God.
- Be a vessel through which God's shining light may enter the world.

Forgiveness Step 5: Opening Your Heart

Things that inhibit opening your heart. Rank the following inhibitors (1–8) from the thing that is most like you to the thing that is least like you:

_____	I do not feel sympathy toward my transgressor.
_____	I resent what he or she did to me.
_____	I do not feel love toward him or her.
_____	I would find it difficult to act warmly toward him or her.
_____	I am too hurt and bitter to consider opening my heart to him or her.

When we are in a state of unforgiveness, our human nature closes our minds and hearts to prevent us from considering other ways of thinking about the transgression. In this chapter we will explore how to open our hearts to the outcomes of forgiveness: having empathy for the offender that reflects love; being faithful to the Word of God; being a shining light to the offender and the world; acting as a conduit of God's grace; and nurturing gratitude as we seek the heart of God for our peace of mind and the salvation of the offender.[1] Here are the sections of this chapter:

Day 28: Opening Your Heart to Forgiveness—Introduction
Day 29: Opening Strongholds with Gratitude
Day 30: Opening Up to Meet Your Needs
Day 31: Openness to Empathy—the Gift of Forgiveness
Day 32: Opening Up to a New Story
Day 33: Opening the Door to Reconciliation

In some ways this chapter is a summary of lessons in previous chapters, but here they are presented from the perspective of a state of attitude rather than one of a state of mind. Being open to new ideas and change can be very difficult. I think of the pioneers who extended the boundaries of our country. They were walking into unknown regions with very little or no idea of what they would encounter. They were challenged with thinking about everything they would need for their journey and for making a new home when they arrived. While forgiveness is an unknown territory for many people, it has been explored extensively, and *Forty Days to Forgiveness* has provided details about what you need to bring with you on this journey.

But your journey is not over yet. You can set a course and load your wagon, but until you decide to hook up the horses and get on board, your exploration does not commence. In this chapter I invite you to consider climbing onboard the forgiveness wagon and heading out on your journey. With an openness of heart, you will be able to overcome the difficulties you encounter. Just know, all along, that the Lord is on your side, and He *will* provide peace of mind. Now join me for the sixth step of a seven-step journey: opening your heart to forgiveness.

Opening the Door of Strongholds

In the previous chapter I talked about how the heart is the place where our ability to forgive is stored. Luke records Jesus as saying, "The good person out of the good treasure of his heart produces good, and the evil person out of his evil treasure produces evil, for out of the abundance of the heart his mouth speaks."[2] The psalmist also gives us a hint as to what the treasure of the heart is: "I have stored up your word in my heart that I might not sin against you. Blessed are you, O Lord; teach me your statutes!"[3] In the previous chapter we talked extensively about the role the heart plays in the forgiveness process (and its role in our behavior overall). The heart sits at the center of our ability to forgive a transgressor. We also talked about how spiritual maturity comes from a study of the Word of God, prayer, meditation, and fellowship with like-minded believers. But all of this is useless if you cannot protect your heart from corruption or if you cannot access what is in your heart. When Satan lures you into building strongholds around your heart, your ability to express God's love for others is inhibited.

Strongholds are the emotional walls erected around our thoughts, our heart, and our Christlike spirit. Strongholds keep valued possessions locked inside so that no harm befalls them. Satan would like for us to protect our hearts from being known because his ambition is to prevent Christ from being shown to the world through us. The more we fear opening our hearts to others, to the transgressor, and to ourselves, the harder it is for the Christlike spirit of our hearts to be revealed. When the heart is hidden and protected behind a stronghold, the less likely it is that we will be able to forgive, and the less likely it is that the person with the hidden and protected heart will gain and sustain the mind of Christ. It is also less likely that such a person will reap the rewards of the fruit of the Spirit that have been promised to a righteous heart.

At the same time, a stronghold prevents us from freely expressing the Spirit of Christ stored in our hearts. When we cannot express our desire to be Christlike, there's a risk of amplifying a spirit of opposition to our expression of empathy and forgiveness. In his letter to the church in Galatia, Paul put it like this: "But I say, walk by the Spirit, and you will not gratify the desires of the flesh. For the desires of the flesh are against the Spirit, and the desires of the Spirit are against the flesh, for these are opposed to each other, to keep you from doing the things you want to do."[4]

Walking by the Spirit means releasing the Spirit of Jesus Christ that is partially or fully bound up within a stronghold in our hearts. When a stronghold surrounds the Spirit of Christ within our hearts, we are left to behave according to our own judgment or according to the programming of our worldly (fleshly) desires from previous similar experiences. Our worldly programming overlooks the value of forgiveness and seeks less desirable ways to reduce our unforgiveness. After all, forgiveness is countercultural. We fear that forgiving our transgressor may unleash judgment from others. So our instinct to protect our hearts and ourselves becomes triggered. We protect our heart from what people will think about us if we reveal our heart of forgiveness to them. And what are these "fleshly desires"?

Now the works of the flesh are evident: sexual immorality, impurity, sensuality, idolatry, sorcery, enmity, strife, jealousy, fits of anger, rivalries, dissensions, divisions, envy, drunkenness, orgies, and things like these. I warn you, as I warned you before, that those who do such things will not inherit the kingdom of God.

But the fruit of the Spirit is love, joy, peace, patience, kindness, goodness, faithfulness, gentleness, self-control; against such things there is no law. And those who belong to Christ Jesus have crucified the flesh with its passions and desires.[5]

When we implore Christ to help us break down the walls that surround the Christlike spirit in our hearts, we experience the benefits of the spiritual fruit Christ blesses us with. For those of us struggling with forgiveness, the stronghold that keeps us from enjoying the fruit of the Spirit is made up of our having negative intentions and ruminating about our transgressors. However, when our actions match the Christlike spirit in our hearts, we live a life of peace. As Paul says, "If we live by the Spirit, let us also keep in step with the Spirit."

This next passage, arguably more than any other, expresses the heart of how we forgive. God wants us to see people as children of God who are as worthy of His love as we are. We deceive ourselves if we think otherwise.

Brothers, if anyone is caught in any transgression, you who are spiritual should restore him in a spirit of gentleness. Keep watch on yourself, lest you too be tempted. Bear one another's burdens and so fulfill the law of Christ. For if anyone thinks he is something when he is nothing, he deceives himself. But let each one test his own work, and then his reason to boast will be in himself alone and not in his neighbor. For each will have to bear his own load.[6]

What, really, is the harm we are trying to prevent with the stronghold around our hearts? What needs do we have whose fulfillment will be threatened if we do not protect our hearts? Every human being has four fundamental needs; when any of these are not met, we feel that we are in jeopardy of harm, fearing that we have lost the following abilities:

- To be loved by others
- To love ourselves
- To feel worthwhile to others
- To feel worthwhile to ourselves

We all carry around a story about how each of these needs is being fulfilled in our lives. Those stories, in turn, influence the development of our view of ourselves. Some call this "self-esteem." In some Christian circles, however, self-esteem is considered a form of thinking of ourselves as being more important than others: the higher our self-esteem, the less we think we need God and the more we think we are better than others. Certainly, one state of self-esteem embraces seeing oneself as better than others and performing better than others without regard for the role of God in one's life. To prevent this view, some say, we are not to love ourselves or hold ourselves in high esteem, but this is a narrow view of the meaning of self-esteem; in fact, we Christians should evaluate our worth to God, to others, and to ourselves. The study of self-esteem in the behavioral sciences is long and wide, and the theology of self-esteem is likewise extensive. My goal, therefore, is not to give a full explanation of self-esteem[7] but to describe some general principles about how one's self-esteem and self-image affect one's ability to forgive.

Behavioral and theological research offers numerous theories about self-esteem; for our purposes, we will focus on how self-esteem and forgiveness affect each other. Self-esteem reflects an individual's overall subjective emotional evaluation of his or her own worth. It is the decision made by an individual that represents his or her attitude toward the self. Two behavioral scientists[8] offered a definition for self-esteem by distinguishing it from self concept: self concept is how we identify and describe our self: self-esteem is the positive or negative evaluations of the self, as in how we feel about it." Self-esteem, then, is the rating we give ourselves when we compare our image of ourselves against a standard set of measures. Those measures can be based on the social group we associate with, society at large, our academic experiences, and our understanding of God's expectations for us. This is another example of the importance of fellowship with like-minded believers. When we affiliate with others who seek to live by the same standards we do, we can find strength in observing and learning from each other, encouraging each other to good works, and participating in spiritual disciplines that help us to continually align our self-concept with our self-esteem.

Even if we would like to think that God's Word is the only standard we need, the reality is that our self-concept is affected by every environment and experience we encounter. When our self-concept is affected, so is our self-esteem, and self-esteem influences how we behave. Such behaviors as academic achievement, seeking happiness and a sense of well-being, and finding satisfaction in marriage and relationships, amid a multitude of other behaviors, are affected by how we view ourselves against whatever standards exist for the situation we are in. Self-esteem can apply specifically to a particular dimension of ourselves, for example, "I believe I am a good writer, and

I feel happy about that," or to a global dimension, such as, "I believe I am a bad person, and I feel bad about myself in general." Just like the two types of forgiveness, state and trait, we can see our worth differently in a particular situation (state esteem) overall feeling of our worth that influences how we see ourselves in general (trait esteem). Each of the four basic needs outlined above describes a different form of esteem. In other words, we all have:

- The need to feel worthwhile to others is affected by the need for respect from others in the form of recognition, success, and admiration.
- The need to feel worthwhile to oneself may be reflected in the need for self-respect in the form of self-love, self-confidence, skill, or aptitude.

When either one of these two needs is not met, we are driven to seek ways to fulfill it because self-esteem serves a protective function by reducing our anxiety about harm coming upon us. Self-esteem is important because it shows us how we view ourselves and how we value ourselves. Thus, it affects the way we are, the way act in the world, and the way we relate to everyone else.

The other two needs, which also have an influence on our ability and willingness to forgive, are affected by whether or not we are able to forgive.

- The need to be loved by others is reflected in our need to see others respond to our patience, kindness, and civility. When a transgressor treats us in an impatient, unkind, disrespectful way, we translate that negative response as "I am not lovable or likable."
- When we are unable to forgive or when our forgiveness is rebuffed, we may be left feeling that we are not capable of loving others. That feeling affects our self-concept and our self-esteem because of our belief that we should be able to love others. Therefore, because we don't have this ability, we feel worthless.

Another behavioral scientist theorized that the origin of many people's mental health problems is that they despise themselves and consider themselves worthless and incapable of being loved. When people have a low regard for themselves, that is, see themselves as unlovable they have a lower regard for the world around them, and the people in that world. In other words, how you feel about yourself in light of the transgression you experienced influences your ability to forgive the transgressor. This can be true for several reasons:

1. If you believe others will think less of you if you forgive your transgressor, you may feel that forgiveness is a sign of weakness, a trait you do not want to project to other people. If other people think you are unable to stand your ground in light of a transgression, they may not project behaviors toward you that make you feel worthwhile.[10]

2. When forgiveness interacts with beliefs about good and evil, right and wrong, and justice and injustice, we may believe that the transgression represents a violation of reasonable expectations for how we are to be treated. For a transgression to be damaging, we must first have a sense of the self that we feel has been hurt. In other words, our sense of ourselves affects whether we interpret a transgression as hurtful and whether the hurt should activate some response on our part. When we experience a behavior from someone that we see as a threat, our brains go into action to try to eliminate the threat.[11] Research has shown, however, that people with high self-esteem are no more forgiving than those with low self-esteem because a person with a high level of stable self-esteem is more likely to have a high level of confidence in his or her ability to resolve the hurt without resorting to forgiveness.[12]

3. How we respond to a transgression may distort our self-concept and ultimately our self-esteem. The transgression may remind us of a similar transgression we committed in the past. This memory may make us feel a sense of self-condemnation. In this way, our unforgiveness is a way to deny our own faults. By being unforgiving of someone else, we transfer our guilt to them by telling ourselves, *He [or she] is just as bad as I am, so I am not as bad as I thought.* The problem, however, is that when we are protecting our self-esteem, we find it difficult to offer empathy to the transgressor.[13]

Let's get back to how the openness of your heart fits into self-esteem. Depending on the situation, each of us demonstrates some type of emotions, feelings, and behaviors more than others. In other words, we all carry an emotional imprint that influences how we respond in any situation. Our emotional imprint affects how we interpret obstacles in our path and influences how we respond.[14] The apostle Paul, as mentioned earlier, said that he did not understand his own actions. He described the flesh as an unconscious influence on his actions that caused him to do what he did not want to do. Although he had the right motive within, his sinful nature eclipsed it.[15] In current parlance, we could say that our sinful nature is expressed through our emotional brain and our emotional temperament.

In chapter 2, we talked about negative intentions that give rise to stories about the hurt that becomes the state of rumination we carry around. These stories that we tell ourselves and others become our internal "truth" about what happened and its impact on us; the stories take on a life of their own and often continue even after some resolution (such as reducing unforgiveness or forgiveness) occurs. The Bible talks about carrying around negative thoughts and suggests that we *do not* try to stop thinking about them. Given human nature, when we try to stop something, we become more fixated and less likely to be able to stop. Instead, Paul gave us another formula in his letter to the church at Philippi:[16] "Finally, brothers, whatever is true, whatever is honorable, whatever is just, whatever is pure, whatever is lovely, whatever is commendable, if there is any excellence, if there is anything worthy of praise, think about these things."[17]

This seems easier said than done; however, we have instruction on *how* to think on these things. Paul tells us in the previous and following verses that the peace of God will guard our hearts and minds if we do the following:

- Rejoice in the Lord always.
- Let our reasonableness be known to everyone.
- Replace anxiety with prayer, supplication, and thanksgiving, letting our requests be made known to God.
- Practice the things we have learned from the Word.

The truth is, what is in our hearts influences what we think about, what we believe, and what we need to protect. We can store up both Christlike and un-Christlike preferences in our heart, but as the writer of Proverbs says, "Above all else, guard your heart, for it is the wellspring of life."[18] When we think unforgiving thoughts or consider negative actions toward an offender, we become unforgiving because the vicious cycle of rumination and unforgiveness creates a stronghold or prison that overpowers our ability to think forgiving and loving thoughts. Forgiveness is the path that releases us.

As noted in chapter 5, strongholds in ancient times were fortifications built around important areas such as towns and the enlightenment that is sparked food storage structures to keep out predators and enemies while locking inside whatever was valued. Unforgiveness is a stronghold in our minds created by Satan; Satan's strongholds in our mind are like the fortresses that prevented intruders. Problem is, what fortresses keep inside are also prevented from being shared outside the fortress walls. In our case, fortresses that keep the kinds of things Paul told us to think about inside. In other words, Satan's strongholds inhibit our ability to show our Christlike thoughts with others. It's as if Satan has built the stronghold to prevent us from accessing our Christlike thoughts from being shared. Negative intentions, bitter thoughts, anger, resentment, revenge are the brick and mortar of strongholds. When the vicious cycle of unforgiveness forms a stronghold, our knowledge of God becomes shackled inside. The stories that we ruminate on about the transgression fortify the walls that keep our positive intentions and Christlike behavior from surfacing. Paul says this about battling strongholds: "For though we walk in the flesh, we are not waging war according to the flesh. For the weapons of our warfare are not of the flesh but have divine power to destroy strongholds."[19]

In his letter to the Ephesians, Paul talks about the warfare we wage in the heat of unforgiveness and how we are battling unseen forces of evil. He tells us that prayer is a critical weapon in this battle. Prayer breaks the strongholds of negative intentions to help us stand firm against Satan's devices.[20] When we pray, we begin to change our negative stories. With God's help, through prayer, we break down our stories about the transgression and allow Christlike thoughts to escape from the strongholds that imprison us in a state of unforgiveness. Prayer is one way to alter our stories: strongholds have no defense against prayer and the Word of God. Prayer is within our control; it is a proactive way to take back our thoughts from the prison of strongholds.

Forgiveness is the ultimate means to breaking down strongholds. Forgiveness releases us from the bondage of rumination and unforgiveness in four ways:

1. Forgiveness releases us from the negative effects of anger, anxiety, and depression. When we are anxious about how we are being treated and we become imprisoned in the vicious cycle of unforgiveness, we rob ourselves of the peace that God has planned for us.

2. Forgiveness passes on the love Christ has shown for us to our transgressor, breaking the bonds of unforgiveness and giving us access to Christlike thoughts and intentions. Jesus told us to pass along the love He has for us, and we show our love by keeping His commandments and following His example. His example is having love for others.[21]

3. Forgiveness sows seeds for salvation for our transgressor. Our Christlike patience for others may influence them to see Christ in us, causing them to have an interest in their own salvation.[22]

4. Forgiveness keeps us in a right relationship with God. Jesus tells us that we show our love for Him and others when we lay down our lives for them.[23] Forgiveness is a form of subordinating our sense of hurt and alienation by putting to death our focus on ourselves.

Journal Exercise 28a: The Stronghold of Unforgiveness

This exercise is intended to help you identify your positive and negative intentions. In the picture below, write all the negative things you are thinking about your transgressor on the outside walls of the fortress; these thoughts are the brick and mortar of your stronghold. Next, write the Christlike traits you would like to allow to show to the transgressor and others inside the fortress walls.

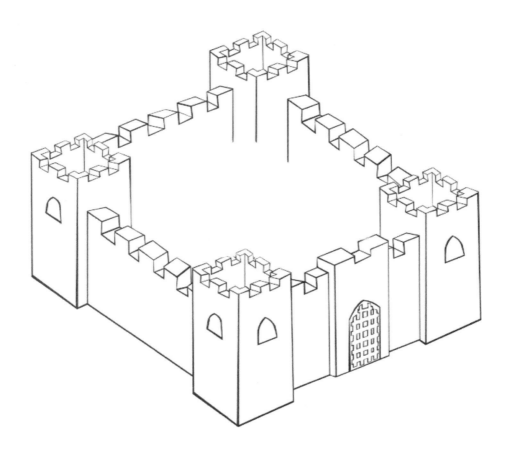

Journal Exercise 28b: Prayer for Release from Strongholds

In the following exercise you will begin your prayer journey for breaking down the strongholds of unforgiveness. Fill in the blanks in the outline below before you turn to God in prayer to ask for the release of these strongholds that prevent positive, Christlike thoughts.

Our Father, we know that Your will is for us to rely on You for strength in our time of trials. I pray, Lord, that You would help me with my unforgiveness for

_____.

The following negative thoughts are holding me captive:

List the items you wrote on the stronghold walls:

Release me from these negative thoughts so that I will feel these positive thoughts toward my transgressor instead:

List the items you wrote on the stronghold walls:

Be with me. Guide and strengthen me as Your Holy Spirit works in my mind to release me from the bondage of unforgiveness that I am trying to overcome.

In Your Son's name, amen.

DAY 29

Opening Strongholds with Gratitude

Another way to open the prison of unforgiveness and destroy the strongholds around our hearts is to have a disposition of gratitude. Paul tells us that as the grace received through the sacrifice of our Lord "extends to more and more people, it may increase thanksgiving, to the glory of God."[24] When we walk with the Lord, we abound in thanksgiving for every good thing.[25] In his letter to the church at Philippi, Paul plainly states the importance of gratitude: "Do not be anxious about anything, but in everything by prayer and supplication with thanksgiving let your requests be made known to God. And the peace of God, which surpasses all understanding, will guard your hearts and your minds in Christ Jesus."[26]

Gratitude is critical for forgiveness. Gratitude pokes holes in the stronghold walls of negative rumination and allows our Christlike spirit to be seen from our heart. Throughout *Forty Days to Forgiveness*, many references have been made to gratitude, but so far we have not dealt directly with its role. Gratitude is not just a key feature of the forgiveness process; it is also a critical element of a life of wholeness and well-being. Following are some suggestions to cultivate gratitude:

- Incorporate a gratitude journal into your Bible study practice to acknowledge the positive role of gratitude in your life.
- Use a gratitude journal to reflect on what God has done for you and others around you. Gratitude has been shown to be a powerful agent in the cultivation of happiness and well-being.
- Keep a prayer journal as you offer gratitude and thanksgiving in your prayers.[27] All that we have is of God.[28] How often do we overlook this simple truth?
- Learn God's Word from like-minded believers, singing to the Lord and edifying one another with songs to create a spirit of gratitude that lubricates the transition from your natural instinct to a spirit of grace to love.
- Open your heart as an inner sanctuary for the Holy Spirit to fill you with gratitude, strength, love, and discernment.

Forgiveness helps us to experience gratitude to God as we remember that we are passing to another the love God has shown to us by forgiving us of our transgressions.[29]

Research has shown that gratitude is a doorway to forgiveness[30] and that forgiveness leads to happiness and well-being.[31] Research from the behavioral sciences also shows that "gratitude predicts more prosocial behavior, lower depression, fewer post-traumatic stress disorder symptoms, stronger social bonds, and higher levels of commitment to religion."[32] All of these conditions have been shown to affect happiness and well-being.

Gratitude may be defined as the "positive emotional reaction to receiving a benefit that is perceived to have resulted from the good intentions of another."[33] A grateful disposition leads to such positive behaviors as empathy and compassion, as well as to psychological, physical, and spiritual well-being.[34] One of the most effective ways to capitalize on the happiness that comes from gratitude is by engaging in prayer and journaling.[35] Research has shown that keeping a gratitude journal is a way to focus on experiences that make us happy, giving us an increased awareness of and appreciation for their value and meaning and how they provide for our needs in some way. People who keep a gratitude journal tend to exhibit more positive effects on their physical, emotional, and mental health and well-being.[36] Gratitude, in addition, has a positive effect on empathy, forgiveness, and one's disposition to help others. One key activity that can also affect one's gratitude and willingness to forgive is to pray on a regular basis.[37]

Journal Exercise 29: Overcoming Strongholds with Gratitude

Find a journal to keep your gratitude notes in. Following are thirty-one thought starters for writing in your gratitude journal, one for each day of the month:

1. List five small ways that you can share your gratitude today.
2. Write about a person in your life for whom you are especially grateful and why.
3. What skills or abilities are you thankful to have?
4. What aspect of a challenge you are currently experiencing can you be thankful for?
5. How is your life different from a year ago? What changes are you thankful for?
6. What activities and hobbies would you miss if you were unable to do them?
7. List five body parts that you are grateful for and why.
8. What aspects of where you live are you grateful for?
9. What are you taking for granted today that you can be thankful for?
10. List five people in your life who are hard to get along with, and record at least one quality for each that you are grateful for.
11. What material items are you most grateful for?
12. What music are you thankful to be able to hear and why?
13. Who has done something this week to help you out (or make your life easier)? How can you thank this person?
14. What foods or meals are you most thankful for?
15. What elements of nature are you grateful for and why?
16. What part of your morning routine are you most thankful for?
17. Write a letter to someone who has positively influenced your life, however big or small.
18. What is something you are grateful to have learned this week?
19. When was the last time you laughed uncontrollably? Relive the memory in your journal.
20. What aspects of your work environment are you thankful for?
21. What about your surroundings (home, neighborhood, city, etc.) are you thankful for?
22. What experiences have you had that you are grateful for?
23. What happened today/yesterday/this week/this month/this year that you are grateful for?
24. What opportunities do you have that you are thankful for?
25. What have others in your life done that you are thankful for?
26. What have others done to benefit your life—even strangers?
27. What relationships are you thankful for?

28. What are you taking for granted that, if you stop to think about, you are grateful for?

29. What aspects of the challenges/difficulties you have experienced (or are currently experiencing) can you be thankful for? (What have you learned? How have you grown?)

30. What are you able to offer others that you are grateful for?

31. What opportunities to help others are you thankful for?

DAY 30

Opening Up to Meet Your Needs

The fundamental reason we react as we do to transgressions is that our needs are not being met or our expectations regarding our proper treatment are being challenged. As stated earlier, all people need to love and be loved and to feel worthwhile to themselves and others. Transgressions challenge these basic needs. For example, when we experience betrayal, we feel unlovable; otherwise, why would we be betrayed? When we do not receive what we feel is due to us, we do not feel worthwhile to others; otherwise, why would someone withhold what we need? When something is taken away from us, we do not feel worthwhile to ourselves; otherwise, we would have received what was denied. It is human nature to rely on others to help us feel okay, happy, satisfied, and in a state of positive well-being.

God, knowing what we need,[38] provides for our needs, whether physical, emotional, spiritual, or mental, when we call out to Him for help.

> *"For I know the plans I have for you, declares the Lord, plans for wholeness and not for evil, to give you a future and a hope. Then you will call upon me and come and pray to me, and I will hear you. You will seek me and find me when you seek me with all your heart."*[39]

This verse makes clear that God expects us to seek Him, yet many of us do the opposite and hold God responsible for making sure our needs are met. As a chaplain, I see patients daily who believe that God has let them down or who believe that God will provide a miracle to return them to better health. When we do this sort of thing, we are looking for God to fit Himself into our plans rather than looking for how we can fit into His plans. In an earlier part of my career, I traveled extensively, often to unfamiliar airports with poor signage. Many times I have stood waiting for a shuttle bus to take me to the car rental center, only to see the bus stop elsewhere. I found it almost comical that if I was not standing exactly where the bus stopped, I would not be getting on the bus. In reality, though, how reasonable would I be if I expected the bus driver to stop in an undesignated area? Similarly, we are being unreasonable if we expect God to intervene in our needs every time we ask. To have such an expectation is a trap because thinking that God is going to arrive and respond to our every felt need is like waiting for a bus when we are not standing in the right spot. God wants us to come to Him. As Jesus said, "Come to me all you who are heavy laden, and I will give you rest." Jesus also said that no one comes to the Father except through Him. Sometimes our expectations of God do not line up with His plans for us.

The key is to seek Him. Jesus tells us that we are to ask for what we need through prayer. When we seek what we need through His love and fatherhood, He provides.[40] We often ask, however, with a time frame in mind that may not match God's timing. How often have we asked God to work Himself into our plans for our lives rather than asking Him to work us into His plans? When we worry excessively about the denial of some need, our sense of peace that comes from reliance on God is eclipsed.[41] Here is a formula, also presented earlier, to help us understand about how God's timing for our requests works:

- If the request is wrong, God says "no."
- If the timing is wrong, God says "slow."
- If you are wrong, God says "grow."
- If the request is right, you are right, and the timing is right, God says "go."

Several theories have been formulated to explain what needs must be met in order to live a life of positive well-being. One theory that is virtually universal and has withstood the test of time was put forth in the 1950s by the behavioral scientist Abraham Maslow. He theorized that we are motivated to meet certain needs that are common to all people. At the most fundamental level is our basic physiological needs such as food, air, water, clothing, shelter, warmth, and rest. God designed us in a body that is vulnerable to absent basic resources. In the garden of Eden, God formed clothes for Adam and Eve when they realized they were naked, meeting their need for warmth and protection. God also met the physical needs of the Israelites when they were in the desert by providing food and water. Jesus tells us in His Sermon on the Mount that God provides for the lilies of the field and the birds of the air, and we are more important than they are. After this sermon, Jesus met the crowd's basic need for nourishment by providing food for them.

The next level in Maslow's hierarchy is the need for safety and security, which includes physical safety, job security, health, and well-being. When we feel threatened by harm, we are wired to react with protective behaviors: to fight or flee. Earlier we discussed how God provided a way of escape when the safety and security of His people was threatened. Today we often do not understand when harm comes to us, but scripture assures us that God knows the plans He has for us—plans to prosper us, not harm us. We also know that there is good in all that we experience when we follow the Lord and are called to His purpose.[42]

Maslow's next category is our need for love and belonging, which includes loving others and feeling loved. The most basic level of love, however, is the love Christ has shown for us through His sacrifice and suffering to redeem us. God has also provided the fellowship of believers as a space where we can love and be loved and find a sense of belonging to a community. More importantly, Christ came to give us an example of how to demonstrate love for others, which Paul describes in 1 Corinthians 13.

Maslow describes the fourth level as esteem needs, that is, to feel worthwhile to ourselves and to others. The second greatest commandment, to love others and treat them as we would like be treated, suggests that we care enough about ourselves to have a firm foundation for how we treat others. At the same time, Paul tells us not to think more highly of ourselves than we should, which suggests that some level of positive self-regard is needed, but it must be kept in check so that we do not subordinate others to elevate our own feelings of value and importance.

The next needs theorized by Maslow are our cognitive needs, which center around our desire to know things—to understand the world around us, how it works, and our place in it. Paul told Timothy to build his cognitive understanding of God by studying God's Word to show himself approved by God.[43] God designed us with a natural curiosity about the world, and He charged us to use our understanding to be good stewards of His creation.

Aesthetic needs, Maslow's sixth level, motivate us to desire the experience of beauty, order, and balance and to appreciate creativity. We experience the glory and majesty of God through the magnificent works of His hands, and we also experience beauty through the creative talents He has bestowed on us and others.

Finally, Maslow stated that we all have a need to know that we are improving our own lives and the lives of others. We need to know that we are striving toward a goal outside ourselves, such as altruism and a pursuit of Christlikeness. Forgiveness has been described by one behavioral scientist as "an altruistic gift,"[44] meaning that forgiveness enables us to rise above our circumstances. For Christians, we rise above when we break down the strongholds that imprison our Christlike spirit and invite the Holy Spirit into our hearts. Paul instructs Christians to move on toward the higher calling of a life in Christ, and he challenges us to run the race that is set before us.[45] When we follow the teachings of Christ, seek His face, and live in a way that glorifies Him, the satisfaction and fulfillment we experience indicates that our highest needs are being met.

The following diagram illustrates these needs and how they relate to each other:

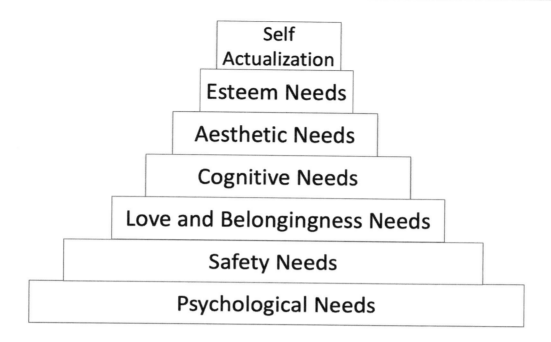

Maslowshierarchy

These needs are building blocks: each one builds upon the success of others. When our needs at the lower levels are not met, focusing sufficiently on our needs at a higher level is difficult. If we are struggling to survive physically, for example, focusing on our sense of belonging and social well-being is impossible. Although every person desires to move up the hierarchy toward self-actualization, progress is often disrupted by failure to meet a lower-level need. Some life experiences such as divorce and job loss can cause a person to fluctuate between the levels of the hierarchy. Therefore, not everyone moves through the hierarchy in a unidirectional manner. Similarly, when a transgression threatens any of these needs, our progress may be arrested as we fixate on the transgression. From a Christian perspective, however, Jesus said to avoid being anxious about our needs being met. We are to know that as His children, He cares for our needs. In His Sermon on the Mount, He taught the following: "Do not be anxious, saying, 'What shall we eat?' or 'What shall we drink?' or 'What shall we wear?' For the Gentiles seek after all these things, and your heavenly Father knows that you need them all. But seek first the kingdom of God and his righteousness, and all these things will be added to you."[46]

When we forget Jesus's admonition, transgressions that deprive us of any basic need become serious roadblocks to our sense of well-being. Our reaction should be to trust God through whom all good things come,[47] even our basic needs. God does not attend to just some of our needs; He is over all of life and all our needs. When we forget that He is in control and is working for what is best for us, we become obsessed with trying to meet our own needs without regard for the role He plays. He wills, however, that we rely on Him through prayer when our needs are not being met.[48]

Paul told the church at Corinth that his desire was not to meet his own needs but to meet the needs of others so that they would be saved.[49] Unfortunately, when we experience a transgression, we tend to focus on how our own needs are not being met, and we lose sight of the needs of our transgressors. We can change that pattern, however, and focus instead on the salvation of the transgressor by considering his or her needs. While it is not for us to satisfy the needs that prompt the transgressor to treat us poorly, we can focus on the person without accepting his or her behavior. When we do this, we can more easily offer the gifts of empathy and compassion, meeting our own need for becoming Christlike, which in turn increases our joy and well-being.

Spiritual warfare is going on all around us, conducted by Satan and his angels (demons) against Jesus and His angels. Satan's intent, in part, is to wreak havoc on the earth by convincing humanity that we all may do as we will: we do not have to listen to God. Satan's message has become a theme in our society, confirming Jesus's prophecy that in the end times people will become lovers of themselves. What illustrates this fact better than the epidemic of addiction to mobile devices and social media?

Another aspect of spiritual warfare is that answers to our prayers are sometimes hindered from reaching us. The Bible relates how God's faithful servant Daniel fasted and prayed for the Lord to thwart the king of Persia from hindering the completion of the temple. Satan was trying to influence the king's thinking, and Daniel was praying for the Lord to intercede and not allow Satan to gain a foothold, but the answer to Daniel's prayer was delayed. Gabriel the archangel appeared to Daniel to explain: "Since the first day that you set your mind to gain understanding and to humble yourself before your God, your words were heard, and I have come in response to them. But the prince of the Persian kingdom [Satan and his forces] resisted me twenty-one days. Then Michael [another archangel] came to help me because I was detained."[50] Although Daniel had to wait, the Lord did intervene.[51]

Satan is indeed the "ruler of this world; the prince of the power of the air; the god of this age" who deceives the whole world.[52] His territory is this fallen world; he and his demons are active in national affairs, business affairs, and the affairs of individuals such as you. To put it simply, Satan does not want you to forgive anyone. He does not want you to forgive your transgressor, yourself, God, or anyone else because forgiveness would align you with God and His purposes, and that is the battle Satan is fighting. We see this spiritual battle in the biblical account of Job. Satan wanted to prove that if Job, a wealthy man, lost everything he had, he would curse God and turn away from Him. But that did not happen. Instead, Job exercised his free will to turn his heart toward God, not away from Him. Satan's objective is to influence all of us to shake our fists at God when life does not go the way we want. When someone commits a transgression against us and we refuse to forgive, Satan's battle plan is working. Forgiveness is contrary to everything he stands for. The animosity in your heart and the vicious cycle of rumination about the transgression are devices Satan uses to battle God's ability to work through you to shed His light in the world.

Journal Exercise 30a: Meeting Your Needs

Use this scale to assess what needs in your life are being hindered by the transgression you experienced. If the transgression is having little or no effect, put an X on the 1. If it is having a major effect, put an X on 5.

NEEDS	
Basic life sustainment: food, air, water, clothing, warmth, shelter, rest	[1] [2] [3] [4] [5]
Safety and security: job security; health; well-being; safety from physical, emotional, or social harm; protection from the elements; security; order; law; stability; freedom from fear	[1] [2] [3] [4] [5]
Love and belonging: feeling loved by others and capable of loving others; having intimate relationships and friends; having trust and acceptance; affiliating and being part of a group (family, friends, coworkers)	[1] [2] [3] [4] [5]
Self-worth: feeling worthwhile to self and others; having a sense of improving life through your own accomplishments or through association with others; having a feeling of importance, achievement, mastery, independence, status, dominance, prestige, self-respect, respect from others	[1] [2] [3] [4] [5]
Cognitive needs: knowledge and understanding; curiosity; exploration; having a sense of meaning and predictability	[1] [2] [3] [4] [5]
Aesthetic needs: appreciation for and attainment of order, beauty, balance, form; engaging in creative activities	[1] [2] [3] [4] [5]
Self-actualization: having a sense of reaching toward a higher goal outside yourself, such as altruism and a pursuit of Christlikeness; realizing personal potential; achieving self-fulfillment; seeking personal growth and peak experiences	[1] [2] [3] [4] [5]

Journal Exercise 30b: A Letter to the Transgressor

You have written letters to the person who hurt you other times during this journey. This one is a little different. In this letter, focus on how the transgression has affected your needs, and explain how you are relying on God to intervene in His timing. I'm providing space here but no template like in previous letters I've suggested you write. Your situation is unique, unlike anyone else's, and your letter will also be unique. One possibility is to think of this as a letter of encouragement to yourself and a letter of gratitude and praise to God. Take your time, meditate, and discover what your heart tells you needs to be said. As before, this is not a letter I'm asking you to send; it is for your eyes only.

Dear _____,
(continue to write your true thoughts at this point on your journey)

DAY 31

Openness to Empathy—the Gift of Forgiveness

Earlier we discussed how forgiveness benefits the forgiver (you) as much as it benefits the transgressor. For both individuals, forgiveness is a gift. We often think of a gift as something we give to another on special occasions, such as a birthday or holiday, or upon accomplishment of a worthy goal. In this sense, *Webster's Dictionary* defines *gift* as "a thing given willingly to someone without payment; a present: the act, right, or power of giving."

There is, however, another way to view a gift: as a special favor we possess given freely by God. In this sense, a gift is a special trait that we have been endowed with by our Maker.

As mentioned in earlier chapters, our natural or instinctual response to a transgression is to protect ourselves. We may protect ourselves by hiding from the transgressor, making the best of the situation, pretending the event did not happen, or striking back verbally or physically in vindictive or vengeful ways in order to feel that we have achieved justice. These responses may help us think we have resolved our pain, but in reality these responses to a transgressor are artificial forms of justice; they are instinctual, driven by our emotional motivations to reduce our feelings of unforgiveness, but these protective responses do not bring emotional freedom from the pain of being harmed. In many cases, these instinctive responses may actually exacerbate the situation and lead to further acts of transgression.

God endowed us with a variety of traits that are modeled after Him since He made us in His image. One particular character trait comes from the heart, not from the primitive part of the brain that is programmed to protect. God has given each of us the ability and desire to forgive. Forgiveness is part of God's fundamental nature. It is so fundamental that the entire Bible, God's covenant with us as children of the Creator, is centered on how He forgives us of the instinctual and earthly programming that separates us from Him. He sent His Son to earth to live a life that teaches us how to live in God's will and the proper godly way to live, yet He also sent Jesus to sacrifice His life for us, "us" being the sum total of all humankind. God wills for all to be saved. Jesus said, "But I tell you, love your enemies and pray for those who persecute you, that you may be sons of your Father in heaven. He causes His sun to rise on the evil and the good, and sends rain on the righteous and the unrighteous."[53] When we love the Lord and are offering forgiveness to others, all the outcomes will be for good, and we are to count those outcomes with joy.[54] God uses the trials in our lives, such as transgressions against us, to build our spiritual maturity and bring us to greater completion as his agents on this earth.

God loves all people equally, even the person who murdered your family, even the person who manipulated the promotion that should have been yours, even the person your spouse had an affair with, even the person who cut in line in front of you while waiting for a cappuccino. It was through His death that Jesus was able to descend into the abyss of hell and take spiritual death away from Satan. When He was resurrected from the grave, He was resurrected with power over Satan's ability to kill our eternal souls.

This scenario was enacted to forgive us of the sinfulness that separates us from the righteousness of God. Jesus's death fulfilled the need for blood sacrifices to atone for the shortcomings and misdeeds (sins) committed by God's people. At the very core of our being, at the core of our devotion to God, at the core of our pursuit of sanctification, is the ability to demonstrate forgiveness. This act is one of the most primary behaviors that we can perform that aligns us with the righteous nature of God. Without forgiveness for our transgressors, we are separated from God by His unforgiveness of us.[55] As I have emphasized throughout *Forty Days to Forgiveness*, forgiveness is an act that allows the love of God for all people to flow through us into the transgressor and into any who witnessed the transgression or heard stories about it. Therefore, when we offer forgiveness to someone who has harmed us, we are drawing upon another gift that God bestowed into our hearts: the capability to love.

For the injured person, forgiveness is a gift that helps to resolve the emotional and psychological pain incurred by the transgressive experience. By being gifted with God's nature of forgiveness, our forgiving actions help resolve the tension that exists between our instinctual nature to protect ourselves and our godly nature to reflect the light of Christ. When we tap into the gift of forgiveness that dwells in our hearts, we also prepare the way for our compassion to flow toward the offender and other involved persons, whether flowing in direct action or through our supplication to God on their behalf. When you offer forgiveness to a transgressor through your loving behavior toward him or her, God's gift is flowing through you. When forgiveness is offered as a gift to your transgressor, it can set the stage for the Lord to further His work of grace, love, and salvation in that person's life.

Jesus talks of treating others with a compassion that meets their needs. To have compassion is to identify with the pain and suffering of others and to act to ease their discomfort by meeting their needs in some way. Not all compassion, however, is demonstrated overtly. This is particularly true in the case of dangerous enemies and transgressors who are no longer accessible to us. Paul says that the best way to deal with our enemies is to meet their needs overtly in some way, to give them a gift that they do not deserve: "Beloved, never avenge yourselves, but leave it to the wrath of God, for it is written, 'Vengeance is mine, I will repay, says the Lord.' To the contrary, 'If your enemy is hungry, feed him; if he is thirsty, give him something to drink; for by so doing you will heap burning coals on his head.' Do not be overcome by evil but overcome evil with good."[56]

Jesus carries the idea of meeting the needs of others farther to include those less fortunate than we are. He tells us that when we show compassion and meet the needs of others, we are serving Him.[57] While the foregoing passage describes serving a physical need, not all who are less fortunate are in need of physical comfort. Quite the contrary: most people are in spiritual need.[58] While God does care about our physical condition, He is more concerned about our spiritual needs. We are to forgive other people, whether they are marginalized physically and/or spiritually. Compassion is a form of love because we are doing good for others without conditions and without expecting the good to be returned. In fact, treating others as we would treat ourselves is part of the greatest commandment: "Love the Lord your God with all your heart and with all your soul and with all your mind, and love your neighbors as yourself, treating them as you wish to be treated." [59]

Jesus freely accepted being tortured to death and was then resurrected to life so that we might have eternal life in the kingdom He has prepared for us.[60] He passed to us the love the Father had for Him without our doing anything to deserve it. When He ascended into heaven, He instructed his followers to continue His legacy by passing that love along to others. Just as He gave us a gift, He wants us to pass that gift to others as we see a need. When people commit transgressions against others, they are expressing a need: a need to elevate themselves by subordinating us, a need to harm us for their own gain, a need to control a situation to their own advantage, or a need to commit evil to satisfy the wiles of the devil. An important saying in counseling is, "All behavior makes sense in context." We may not agree with transgressors' behavior or understand how their unique needs developed, but when we understand the context of their lives that gave rise to their behaviors, we may begin to understand their challenges and realize that our Lord can use us to help them.

If you are like me, you are probably thinking, *I understand there are reasons why my transgressor thought it was okay to harm me. And I understand that he [or she] has had hardship in life. But so have I! What about me? When do I get justice? Should I be able to hurt other people, too, because I've encountered potholes in the road I have traveled?* Earlier chapters have described forgiveness as a close cousin to, but a separate process from, justice. Earlier chapters also emphasized that forgiveness does not let the transgressor off the hook of accountability. The questions we are still trying to answer are, Can the transgressor do anything to evoke forgiveness from you? Will seeing justice done release you from the emotional bond that connects you to the transgressor through the vicious cycle of unforgiveness? The answer is to both is *no*, at least not completely.

The transgressor may prompt you to forgive by asking for your pardon, by apologizing, by paying restitution for the damage he or she caused, or by being incarcerated. In the final analysis, however, only you can prompt yourself to take the actions necessary to experience the emotional freedom that comes with forgiveness. The steps you take to experience emotional forgiveness are required of *you*, internally, from your heart. You have been gifted in your heart by your Maker to forgive; forgiveness is, in fact, a divine act. Expecting the transgressor to do something to right the wrong before you forgive is not a pathway to full emotional freedom. Waiting for the transgressor to seek your forgiveness or receive punishment is to put yourself in a harmful untenable position. As stated earlier, it is like you drinking poison and hoping the transgressor will die.

Regardless of the wrongdoer's needs and reasons for committing the transgression, the role of a follower of Christ is to act out of patience and kindness, not arrogance or rudeness. As Christians, we do not insist on our own way, show irritability, or engage in resentful behaviors. Our role is clearly delineated in scriptures: We do not repay a wrongdoing with another wrongdoing. Instead, we rejoice in the truth that God loves our enemies as much as He loves us.[61] Furthermore, our role is to acknowledge that what others intend for evil, God uses for good. When Joseph's brothers asked for his forgiveness, Joseph responded, "Do not be afraid. Am I in the place of God? You intended to harm me, but God intended it for good to accomplish what is now being done, the saving of many lives."[62]

When our actions express concern for the needs of another, and when we can see a situation from another's perspective, we are giving the gift of empathy. Empathy is a "skill that helps us feel and understand the emotions, circumstances, intentions, thoughts, and needs of others [so] that we can offer sensitive, perceptive, and appropriate communication and support."[63] To have empathy for a transgressor is an act of grace that we offer to ourselves on behalf of someone who has not earned it; moreover, we offer empathy because we walk in the light of Christ's love. While empathy for the offender may help heal his or her woundedness that led to your injury, empathy is not exclusively for your offender. Empathy is part of the process that you engage in to break the strongholds that lock in your Christlike loving disposition.

You likely recall my earlier statement that the Bible has no examples of interpersonal forgiveness. Why not? I think God wants us to emulate how He has forgiven us.[64] His love for us is the ultimate form of empathy: it is perfect and unchanging.[65] He knows us inside and out and knows our needs even before we do. In essence, God's entire covenant with humankind is a story of forgiveness and reconciliation, as expressed by Paul in his letter to the church in Colossae:

> *Put on then, as God's chosen ones, holy and beloved, compassionate hearts, kindness, humility, meekness, and patience, bearing with one another and, if one has a complaint against another, forgiving each other. As the Lord has forgiven you, so you also must forgive. And above all these, put on love, which binds everything together in perfect harmony. And let the peace of Christ rule in your hearts, to which indeed you were called in one body. And be thankful.*[66]

Besides its compelling message, something else is interesting about this letter: Paul wrote it while imprisoned in Rome. If I were in prison, I cannot imagine that I would be thinking this way.

I believe that Paul is modeling for us the spirit of love that echoes Christ's love for us. It is a love with which we *can*, with the Lord's help, approach our transgressors.

Jesus commanded us to forgive others, yet He also assured us that we can carry His yoke, the symbol of living under His control. He said, "Come to me, all who labor and are heavy laden, and I will give you rest. Take my yoke upon you, and learn from me, for I am gentle and lowly in heart, and you will find rest for your souls. For my yoke is easy, and my burden is light."[67] By Christ's own words, biblical forgiveness should not feel like a burden; rather, it should be an outgrowth of our decision to follow the Lord's example. Unfortunately, it is not natural; forgiveness is hard. It is mentally and emotionally challenging. Exchanging negative ruminations for positive Christ-centered thoughts goes against our programming to protect ourselves.

When I think of protecting myself, images of Jason Bourne, James Bond, and other heroes come to mind. When I watch them in movies, their ability to protect themselves seems so natural that I almost believe that the actors who play these characters can actually fight as they appear to on-screen. But such is not the case. These actors spend hours and hours learning the moves that appear so natural on-screen. If I were to walk up to Matt Damon on the street and take a swing at him, I doubt that he would respond like Jason Bourne does in a movie. I think this situation is similar to protecting ourselves from transgressions. Treating someone who has harmed us with love and compassion is not natural. Doing so takes practice, study of the Word, prayer, and meditation, the workout equipment of the spiritual gymnasium. Does simply knowing God's desire to work through us to bless others make us better able to forgive? Probably not without practice and persistence. Just as actors have to be committed to perfect their skills, we have to be committed to opening our hearts to the thoughts and behaviors that reflect love, compassion, and—at the core of forgiveness—empathy.

Can you imagine what it must be like for people who do not have Christ to show forgiveness? Christians can call upon the Lord for help to face the challenges of being hurt. Because we have received the comfort that comes from being forgiven, with practice we can pass that comfort to our transgressors, as Paul describes in Colossians:

> *Blessed be the God and Father of our Lord Jesus Christ, the Father of mercies and God of all comfort, who comforts us in all our afflictions, so that we may be able to comfort those who are in any affliction, with the comfort with which we ourselves are comforted by God. For as we share abundantly in Christ's sufferings, so through Christ we share abundantly in comfort, too. If we are afflicted, it is for your comfort and salvation; and if we are comforted, it is for your comfort, which you experience when you patiently endure the same sufferings that we suffer. Our hope for you is unshaken, for we know that as you share in our sufferings, you will also share in our comfort.*[68]

Although the subject of empathy was discussed earlier in *Forty Days to Forgiveness*, it must be examined more thoroughly in order to complete step five of ACTION, opening up to forgiveness.

As defined a bit earlier, empathy is a form of meaning-focused coping: "It is a means to cope with transgression by changing one's interpretation of the offense by looking at the transgression from the transgressor's perspective in order to feel compassion and concern for him or her."[69] Karla McLaren, a researcher and philosopher who specializes in the art of empathy, says that each of our emotions has a specific form of genius that we can tap into to inform our ability to forgive. She is the source of this previously quoted definition: "Empathy is a social and emotional skill that helps us feel and understand the emotions, circumstances, intentions, thoughts, and needs of others, such that we can offer sensitive, perceptive, and appropriate communication and support."[70]

Empathy has been found to be the pivotal behavior that stands between negative and positive intentions.[71] There are a variety of definitions for empathy, but all include these components: seeing things from another person's perspective; understanding the other's point of view of a situation; and using that understanding to guide one's behavior toward the other person. Empathy is also characterized by asking the transgressor questions to clarify his or her perspective on the transgression, but empathy does not mean having to accept this explanation as accurate or sufficient. Rather, to have empathy is to gain insight in order to separate the person from his or her behavior.

Empathy, McLaren says, is a process, not a result. She describes six essential elements of empathy. One component has to do with cognitive understanding of the other person, while another relates to the visceral, feeling experience that empathy opens in us. The following are her six elements of empathy from the perspective of forgiveness:[72]

1. **Emotional contagion**, which is the capacity to both feel and share emotions in common with transgressors. Some call this mirroring and have suggested that a physiological component of the brain stimulates mirroring behaviors. Mirroring is a standard item of equipment that we are born with. A good example of it is a child responding in like manner to his or her mother's smiling and cooing.

2. **Empathic accuracy**, which is knowing and being able to recognize and name emotional states, thoughts, and intentions in yourself and your transgressor. This was the focus of Chapter 2: Acknowledging the Transgression.

3. **Emotional regulation**, which is having self-awareness of the emotional states you are experiencing, being able to detect what is prompting them and how they are affecting you, and being aware of your thinking about them. This has come to be known as the emotional intelligence quotient or EQ. Your EQ is your ability to recognize your own emotions and those of others, to discern between different feelings associated with those emotions, to label them appropriately, to use emotional information to guide your thinking and behavior, and to manage and/or adjust your emotions to adapt to the experience you are having with your transgressor.[73]

4. **Perspective taking**, which is another coping strategy. It requires you to use your imagination to sense what the transgressor might be thinking or feeling in order to help you see the transgression through his or her lens.

5. **Concern for others**, which results when you are able to feel the emotions of your transgressor, identify and name them, recall your own experiences with similar emotions, and find a synchronicity between your emotions and those of the transgressor. Your sensitivity to the transgressor's needs increases, and your ability to access your Christlike responses blossoms.

6. **Perceptive engagement**, which is your ability to discern actions toward and responses to your transgressor (whether imagined or actually expressed to your transgressor) that are helpful to meeting his or her needs. In some cases, you may only be able to help by lifting these needs to God in prayer. In other cases, you may be able to offer a gift of empathy and compassion as Paul discusses in his letter to the Romans.[74]

Most of these elements of empathy have already been addressed over the course of *Forty Days to Forgiveness*. The next step in the upcoming journal exercise is for you to engage in a process to bring these elements together to build a greater level of empathy for your transgressor. Empathy, like forgiveness, is not a feeling that you wait to pour over you like a waterfall; it requires actions coupled with thinking and feelings. In other words, empathy is a coping strategy that we choose to employ that eventually can become a natural and automatic response to a transgression. Empathy is not a coping skill unique to a particular group of people; rather, it is a skill that can be learned by men and women, children and the aged, rich and poor. As shown in an earlier chart of coping skills, empathy is an active meaning-making strategy: it compares our ideas of how the world should be to another person's views of the world, regardless of our relationship to him or her. Another author defines *empathy* as "a constant awareness of the fact that your concerns are not everyone's concerns and that your needs are not everyone's needs, and that some compromise has to be achieved moment by moment."[75] This writer goes on to say that empathy is not self-sacrifice but an ongoing, ever-evolving way of living. Empathy pushes us into new worlds of understanding what others deem important, which may differ from what we feel is important. Like forgiveness, empathy requires repeated effort to remove the barriers created by our unenforceable rules. Researchers have found that a portion of the human brain is dedicated to empathy.[76] We can nurture and develop that part of our brain to reclaim a skill that was once common among humankind.

Being empathic means accepting that all emotions are good when expressed appropriately. Unfortunately, many of us learn in early childhood to distrust our emotions, to categorize them as positive or negative, and to be suspicious of them. For some, emotions have been portrayed as unwelcome, irrational, and even dangerous. Emotions, however, always truly reflect the internal experiences of the person experiencing them, even though the person may not be expressing them appropriately. If we can decipher emotions, intentions, nuances, social space, and nonverbal language, we can see deeply into people's lives. We can see the issues they think they are hiding, we can understand how they approach life and relationships, and we can become skilled at getting to the essence of who they are. Skilled empathy is the bridge to understanding the perspectives of others and imagining what life feels like for them: how they approach a situation, what their intentions are, how they will respond to others. The point is not to ask yourself what you would do in their place, but to understand what they would do.

Three actions can help us harness the power of empathy to reframe or reinterpret the transgression. This new point of view then gives us a broader perspective on the transgression. First, we can acknowledge that *we are equally capable of inflicting a transgression on another person.* While the transgression committed against us may seem far worse than anything we have ever done, we have all, nonetheless, hurt others and needed forgiveness. When we consider that we have inflicted harm on others, we can be grateful for the gift of forgiveness that has been granted to us. Our thankfulness and gratitude for our own forgiveness is a reason to consider forgiveness for our transgressor. As Paul says, "For all have sinned and fall short of the glory of God and are justified by his grace as a gift, through the redemption that is in Christ Jesus, whom God put forward as a propitiation by his blood, to be received by faith."[77]

Second, we can *assess the situation that led the transgressor to inflict harm on us.* Everyone has a past, and our current behaviors are influenced by the responses we have used in the past to protect ourselves from harm. When we look at the transgressor through the lens of past events in his or her life, we shed light on why the offense was committed. In some cases, we may learn that the transgression is out of character and can be recognized as a slip-up, oversight, or mistake. Remember, however, that understanding the history of a transgressor does not mean we accept his or her behavior; it simply helps us see the transgressor from a different, compassionate, and empathic perspective.

Third, we can *look at the situation from the perspective of what the transgressor might have been thinking, feeling, or concluding about the transgression.* Considering what the person was feeling that led to the transgression or what he or she may be feeling since having inflicted harm is empathy. When we understand the other person's feelings, we can identify with them and engage those feelings in ourselves. In sharing these interrelated feelings, we can distinguish between what we would do in the same conditions and the better question of what would be logical for the other person to do. Sharing the same feelings leads us to show empathy and compassion for the pain that led the transgressor to commit the offense or for the pain the transgressor may be experiencing, but not showing, since the offense.

Before we get to the journal exercise, two key points made in earlier chapters should be reiterated. First, forgiveness does not require the other person to be involved. In other words, our empathy is not necessarily *expressed* to the transgressor. It could be if you want to pursue reconciliation or restoration of your relationship, but at this stage in your forgiveness journey, empathy for the transgressor is actually intended to help you find a different perspective on the transgression in order to help you cope positively.

Empathy helps us to find meaning in the transgression, not to justify it, but to help us better understand the circumstances and the person who committed the hurt against us. Our empathy provides a perspective to help us do three things:

1. Understand the transgressor well enough to be able to offer a prayer of supplication that God will work His will in his or her life.
2. Exchange negative intentions with positive ones. When we understand the transgressor better, we can see how pursuing our negative intentions would drive him or her farther from God, not toward Him.
3. Separate the offender from the offense. Behind every transgression is a child of God, and God wills that all should come to Him for salvation. We can be either an open or closed door for Christ's love. Although we may not be the one who leads our transgressors to Christ, we can sow seeds that God in His timing can grow into a follower of Christ.

Despite our efforts, the actions of some transgressors cannot be explained or understood, and some transgressions are irrational, evil, and dangerous. Some hurts are so heinous that repeated attempts at empathy will not be sufficient to understand the transgressors, and some transgressors' circumstances are too complex to be understood. Still, God understands all transgressors and their circumstances; therefore, we can ask God to help us find compassion, and we can still offer a prayer of supplication for our transgressors. Each of us is part of a greater good that the Lord Jesus Christ brought to earth; without us, God would need a change of plans to reap the harvest of souls that He seeks. The following two exercises will help you nourish your empathy for the person who offended you. In a previous chapter you did the "empty chair" activity. In my doctoral research, participants in a forgiveness workshop found this to be the most impactful activity. I've included it again here, and I encourage you to dive deeper this time into your emotions and what you believe would be the emotions of your transgressor if you were him or her.

Journal Exercise 31a: Openness to Build Empathy

I'm going to ask you to repeat the activity that you did in an earlier chapter. Now that you have come along on your forgiveness journey, think carefully about how you and the transgressor might interact if you had the chance to do so.

1. For this activity, you will need three chairs and a close friend, prayer partner, or sympathetic family member. Set three chairs as shown in this diagram.

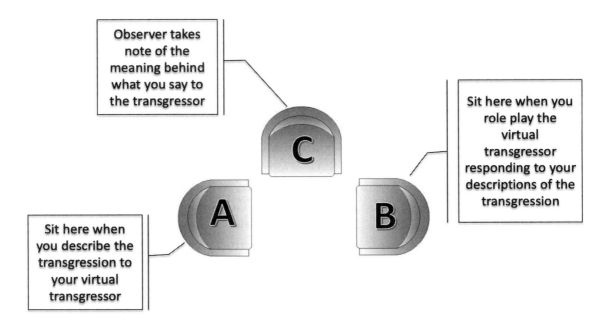

Empathy Exercise

2. To begin, your partner sits in chair C as you sit in chair A and pretend that your transgressor is in chair B. Describe the transgression as if the person is actually in the chair.
3. Next, sit in chair B and face the chair you were just in, chair A. Verbalize aloud what you think the transgressor would say in answer to your description of the transgression and its effect on you. Here are some questions you can consider from the perspective of the transgressor:

   a. What wounds did he or she suffer from others that could have made him or her more likely to hurt you?

b. What extra pressures or stresses were in this person's life at the time he or she offended you?

c. What is he or she like when not embroiled in a situation where he or she **commits an offense against someone?**

d. What is this person like from a spiritual perspective. Does he or she need God's grace and salvation?

Note: These questions are not meant to excuse or condone; rather, they are intended to help you better understand the other person's areas of pain, those areas that make him or her vulnerable and human.

4. Now go back to chair A and continue your conversation with the transgressor, responding to the reaction that you just created for him or her.

5. Return to chair B and respond to what you just said from the point of view of the transgressor.

6. Repeat this process until you have a better understanding of the transgression from your transgressor's point of view.

7. Ask your partner (who has been observing this process from chair C) to give his or her reaction. This person might ask what you meant by something you said or may help clarify the transgressor's responses to your descriptions of what happened.

8. When the observer is through, take a few moments to pray before going on the next step.

9. In this final step, you will need paper and a pencil/pen. Write a letter from the transgressor to you, describing what happened (or is happening) from his or her point of view. Read the letter to your partner and ask him or her to reflect on whether you have accurately and completely described what happened from the transgressor's perspective.

Journal Exercise 31b: Prayer for Empathic Release

In the following exercise you will continue your prayer journey for breaking down the strongholds of unforgiveness by expressing your empathic insights into your transgressor. Fill in the prayer outline that follows before you turn to God in prayer to ask Him to release the strongholds that prevent Christlike thoughts and empathy.

Gracious Father, I pray for Your wisdom that I might gain insights into my transgressor in order to see from his or her point of view. As I try to do this, may I rely on You to help me imagine, or express, compassion and love.

List the feelings that you imagine the transgressor might have that you do not relate to or understand:	*List the feelings that you are experiencing as you grow in empathy toward your transgressor:*

Release me from negative thoughts so that I might feel these positive thoughts toward my transgressor.

List the negative thoughts you were ruminating on when you were first transgressed:	List the positive thoughts that are replacing negative ones as you grow in empathy toward your transgressor:

Please be with me, guiding me and strengthening me as Your Holy Spirit works in my mind and heart to release me from the bondage of unforgiveness that I am trying to overcome.

In Your Son's name, amen.

DAY 32

Opening Up to a New Story

When we encounter a transgression, what we're doing is experiencing an actual violation or an infraction of some cherished rule governing how we should be treated. These rules are often unenforceable and leave us feeling hurt and offended. How we cope with the stress of the violated rules affects the stories we tell ourselves about the transgression. As stories about the unenforceable rules continue, they give way to negative intentions: thoughts of actions that we would like to take to correct the transgression in order to see justice done. We often visualize and anticipate how we would repay the offender for the transgression.

Negative intentions add fuel to stories about the hurt that we think about over and over. Rumination is the ongoing fixation on the feelings associated with the transgression that we cannot get out of our conscious minds. The stories often become the problem more so than the actual transgression. Everett Worthington Jr., a prominent researcher of forgiveness, puts it like this: "Rumination triggers the emotion. The content of the rumination strongly affects the negative emotion. As people ruminate about sad aspects of a situation, they may become depressed. If they ruminate about injustice and frustrated goals, they may become fearful and anxious. If they have unforgiving ruminations, they may experience unforgiveness."[78]

In short, the thought cycle of rumination fuels the intensity of our stories about the transgression, making us unhappy as we think about how we want to react to our transgressor in harmful ways. To forgive, we must intentionally open up space in ourselves to allow positive thoughts to form, and we must reframe how we look at the transgression. Reframing the transgression, as explained earlier, means looking at it from perspectives other than our own and formulating a new story about it.[79] There are three types of stories that we tell ourselves about the transgression: stories about the transgressor, stories about the act of the transgression, and stories about how we have been affected by the offense.

Stories about the transgressor. The story we tell ourselves about our transgressors is often about their flaws and shortcomings. We tend to conceptualize them as demons or agents of evil.

A wider perspective, however, often changes our stories about them. Thinking about what their lives have been like may shed some light on their motivations for the transgression. When we think about them from the spiritual perspective, we come to realize that they are loved by God just as we are.[80] When we see them from the perspective of a soul to be salvaged,[81] we can begin to formulate a different story that leads us to a new perspective. This, however, is difficult work. As we learn about others' situations, we may begin to judge whether their situations warrant the treatment we have received from them. It is important to remember that their situation does not justify their actions. The purpose of having an understanding of their lives and backgrounds is to help us relate to them, not their behavior, with empathy and compassion.

Stories about the act of the transgression itself are from our perspective and are influenced by how we have experienced similar transgressions in the past. Transgressions have a cumulative effect even if they are not committed by the same person. The more we experience a particular type of transgression, the worse it feels when it happens again. In addition, we see the transgression as being worse than the transgressor sees it.[82] The stories we tell ourselves often center on whether we think the transgression was accidental, deliberate, or retaliatory. When we look past how the transgression has affected us to how we can cope with it, we begin to alter our perception of the transgression. We begin to write a new story based on how we can solve the problem, how we can control our emotional response to the transgression, or how we can look at the transgression with fresh insight from a new perspective.

Stories about how we have been affected by the offense come about when we think about the way(s) in which our lives have been altered in the wake of the transgression. Our needs may not get met as a result of the transgression; the role we play in a situation may have been altered from what we had envisioned; and our goals for what we want to accomplish may have been disrupted. When we look at the transgression from the perspective of how good can come from it, however, we begin to alter our story about the transgression. We know that all things work together for good for those who love God and are called to His purposes.[83] Our purpose is to let the light of Christ shine through us[84] to influence the transgressor and the witnesses of the transgression to know the Lord. Through prayer and meditation, and by doing good to our transgressor,[85] we can overcome what seemed overwhelming at the time.

Journal Exercise 32: Rewriting Your Story

This journal exercise is designed to help you piece together a new story about your transgression. In order to do this exercise, you will need to go back and review some of the journal exercises you have done earlier. This reflection time will help you to open your heart to telling a new story about your circumstances.

Take your time. Pray and meditate as you work on each part. If it helps, revisit the scriptures referenced in the endnotes.

This is an important part of your journey. This is where you begin to tell a story of how God has redeemed you from the vicious cycle of unforgiveness that has haunted you. This journal exercise is made up of five parts, each of which might take several days to complete. I encourage you to take your time and reflect on each one to evaluate what you have learned. Here is an overview of the parts:

Part 1. **A**cknowledging the Hurt's Effect in Your Story
Part 2. **C**ommitting to Use Your Strengths to Write a New Story
Part 3. **T**ransitioning to a Godly Perspective
Part 4. **I**nternalizing Spiritual Maturity
Part 5. **O**pening Your Heart to Forgiveness

As you work through this exercise, my prayer is that God will put a new story on your heart, a story that includes God, that comes through reflection and contemplation, and that begins to release you from the vicious cycle of unforgiveness.

New Story Part 1: Acknowledging the Hurt's Effect in Your Story

Go to chapter 2, day 5, and transfer your scores to the following list:

_____	I am mad about what happened.	_____	I want to restart my relationship with the person who hurt me, acting as if nothing happened.
_____	I am bitter about what the transgressor did to me.	_____	I have accepted an excuse or explanation for what he or she did, and I have tried to move on.
_____	I try to avoid him or her.		
_____	I want to withdraw from him or her.	_____	I tolerate what my transgressor has done to me, and I accept him or her despite his or her flaws.
_____	I ought to just forget what happened and move on; what happened was not really that bad.		

Describe in the space below a story about how these are affecting you *now*:

New Story Part 2: Committing to Use Your Strengths to Write a New Story

At this point in your journey, you can see that you have strengths that can help you to overcome the difficulties you identified in the previous exercise. Go back to chapter 4, journal exercise 17b, and identify the top three strengths that would be most helpful to you in overcoming your unforgiveness.

Coping strength 1:

Have you used this strength in response to your transgressor? [Yes] [No]

What result has the use or nonuse of this strength produced?

Describe how and when this strength could be used to have a positive effect on your ability to forgive:

Coping strength 2:

Have you used this strength in response to your transgressor? [Yes] [No]

What result has the use or nonuse of this strength produced?

Coping strength 3
Have you used this strength in response to your transgressor? [Yes] [No]
What result has the use or nonuse of this strength produced?
Describe how and when this strength could be used to have a positive effect on your ability to forgive:

New Story Part 3: Transitioning to a Godly Perspective in Your Story

Using your forgiveness strengths, go back to chapter 4, journal exercise 16, and review your answers to the journal activity. Reflect on what you wrote at that time to identify what will help you most to overcome the negative intentions you have toward your transgressor. Each section that follows asks for you to write a description of your visualization of how each strength will influence your well-being. Choose only three of the strengths that you would like to work on now.

Forgiveness strength 1:

What actions can you take to apply this strength to your commitment to forgive?

What positive thoughts do you think this strength will cultivate to replace negative intentions (refer to day 32)?

Forgiveness strength 2:

What actions can you take to apply this strength to your commitment to forgive?

What positive thoughts do you think this strength will cultivate to replace negative intentions (refer to day 32)?

Forgiveness strength 3:

What actions can you take to apply this strength to your commitment to forgive?

What positive thoughts do you think this strength will cultivate to replace negative intentions (refer to day 32)?

New Story Part 3 (cont.): Benefits of Forgiveness to Your Well-Being

Go back to journal exercise 20 and review your answers to the activity to assess your well-being. Write any statements below that you rated with a 3 or below. In this section you will begin to build the part of your story that describes how forgiveness will affect areas of your well-being that you rated as not being very strong. Describe which positive thoughts from journal exercise 31b will reinforce each aspect of your well-being.

Career well-being

How will your positive thoughts about your transgressor improve your career well-being?

Social well-being

How will transitioning to positive thoughts about your transgressor improve your social well-being?

Financial well-being

How will transitioning to the positive thoughts about your transgressor that you listed earlier improve your financial well-being?

Physical well-being

How will transitioning to the positive thoughts about your transgressor that you listed earlier improve your physical well-being?

Community well-being

How will transitioning to the positive thoughts about your transgressor that you listed earlier improve your community well-being?

New Story Part 4: Internalizing Spiritual Maturity

Spiritual Disciplines to Support Your Journey

Go back to chapter 5 and review your answers to the activity to assess the spiritual thoughts that cultivate forgiveness. In the left column below, write the top three signs of spiritual maturity (rated at 4 or above in satisfaction) that you feel will help you to forgive.[86] In the right-hand column, describe one action that you would like to take to move the needle forward on these signs of spiritual maturity.

Action plan to "team up" with God to develop these signs of spiritual maturity	
Signs of spiritual maturity	
People who can help you with these action steps	1. 2. 3.

New Story Part 5: Opening Your Heart to a New Story of Forgiveness

ROUGH DRAFT OF THE NEW STORY, STEP 1

New Story Part 5 has three steps. This one, the first step, requires reviewing your recent work in New Story Parts 1–4.

Integrating Your Thoughts

Go back through the exercises you just completed in New Story Parts 1–4 and read silently all the information that you wrote into your journal.

Consolidating Your Learning

As you read what you wrote, you are learning a new way of thinking about the transgression. Repeat step 1, except this time sit in a comfortable chair in front of a mirror. Sit sideways to the mirror so that looking in the mirror will reflect either your right or left side.

Next, now that you have thought about a new narrative for the story you have been ruminating on, what can you say to God to release you from your negative thoughts and feelings in order to accept and integrate the new, positive thoughts into your narrative?

STEP 2: CREATING A PRAYER OUT OF YOUR STORY

This is a continuation of the foregoing step. In step 1, you were working silently and privately. In this step, you reach out in fellowship, first with God and at the end with fellow believers.

Creating Your Story as a Prayer

Create a prayer with your new story by reflecting on what you read in step 1. The template that follows is a guideline, but you may want to add more to the prayer. However, try not to shortcut any of the directions outlined for you.

Prayer Template

Thank You, Lord, for leading me on this journey of discovery toward peace and harmony with You and with my transgressor. I ask that You give me the desire to continually improve the spiritual disciplines that draw me closer to You and that help me be a vessel through which You bring love and peace to the world that I touch, particularly as I learn to be more forgiving by showing …

DAY 32: OPENING UP TO A NEW STORY

Please give me wisdom, Lord, to understand the ways this transgression has hurt me, and help me to give those hurts to You so that I might overcome them.

Summarize what you wrote in Part 1: Acknowledging the Hurt's Effect (above).

Help me, Lord, to continue to use my strengths to build my ability to cope with this transgression as You desire in order to glorify You.

Summarize what you wrote in Part 2: Committing to Use Your Strengths to Write a New Story.

Help me, Lord, to continue to build my strength to cope with this transgression and to strengthen my spiritual disciplines.

Summarize what you wrote in Part 3: Transitioning to a Godly Perspective.

Next, read the prayer you created in step 3 out loud in front of the mirror. I would kneel as I read it, facing a mirror.[87]

Finally, in this last step, read your prayer aloud with a prayer partner or with a small Bible study group whose members you are close with.[88] *List who you can invite to share in this prayer with you:*
1.
2.
3.
4.
5.

FORTY DAYS TO FORGIVENESS   329

DAY 33

Opening the Door to Reconciliation[89]

The purpose of this section is not to examine the mechanics of how to reconcile, but to understand the types of reconciliation and the role that forgiveness plays in setting the stage for reconciliation. One question commonly asked about forgiveness is whether forgiving others requires us to continue our relationship with them. This question, of course, regards people with whom we already have a relationship; however, not all transgressions are committed by such people. While the primary goal of forgiveness is to replace negative intentions toward a transgressor with positive ones, unforgiveness closes the door to reconciliation through ill will toward another or actively seeking another's harm. Paul makes clear that we are not to act out our unforgiveness but to leave justice to the Lord.[90] The opposite of vengeance is reconciliation. Forgiveness can open the door for reconciliation with the following kinds of transgressors:

- a fellow disciple of Christ
- a person with whom we have an ongoing relationship (family member, boss, business acquaintance, friend)
- a person who physically violated us in some way
- a neighbor or enemy
- someone who is no longer available.

The first two in the list are people with whom we are bound in an ongoing relationship; with the last three, this is not necessarily the case. Chapter 3 explained that forgiveness and reconciliation are required of Christians for fellow believers and family and, additionally, that forgiveness is a stepping-stone to living peacefully with enemies and people not of the body of Christ. Forgiveness is also required for a deeper relationship with God. Jesus tells us that if we have anything against *anyone*, we are to forgive those people as we pray; otherwise, we distance ourselves from the Father. Still, not all reconciliation is necessary or possible.

Reconciliation is a process of reuniting with someone after a relationship has been broken. In our context, *reconciliation* is the restoration of a relationship that has been broken by the unfair or unjust treatment of one person toward another. In contrast, *forgiveness* is replacing feelings of retaliation and dislike toward the transgressor with empathy and grace, which may or may not include restoring a relationship. Reconciliation is based on a hope that we can proceed in a relationship without pain, hurt, or suffering. People decide whether, how, and when to reconcile based on mutual cooperation between the offended and the transgressor. Reconciliation is based on the idea that there is some benefit to restoring and continuing the relationship even though the relationship will be changed forever as a result of the transgression and cannot be restored to what it was before. The relationship may not be as trusting and close, or in some cases it may be strengthened, but it will never be the same.

In chapter 3 we talked about whether we need to stay in an abusive relationship. The answer is no. We can forgive the abuser without tolerating the abuse. Forgiveness is based on separating the offender from the offense, meaning that the transgressor is to be forgiven, but God does not expect us to remain in a relationship where we are being threatened or harmed. Rather, scripture gives multiple examples of God making provisions for His people to escape the threat of abuse. We are told to pray for our enemies and do good to those who persecute us, but we can follow these directives without continuing in a harmful relationship. Indeed, we can follow them better once we have removed ourselves from the prospect of further harm.

In the Gospel of Matthew,[91] Jesus describes what we are to do when a fellow disciple transgresses against us. As explained earlier, we are first to go to the transgressor and explain the fault. If we are heard and the transgressor repents, then we can reconcile. However, if the person does not listen to us, then we are to take a few other believers with us and, ultimately, present the situation to the church. Once the church has gotten involved and the transgressor still does not repent, then we are to treat the person as an outsider if he or she continues sinning against us. Jesus makes clear that we do not have to continue subjecting ourselves to the sinful behaviors of another, but we do have a responsibility to seek resolution with the person before we break ties. This process, however, does not absolve us from the requirement to forgive, no matter the transgressor's response; it is, rather, a path toward deciding whether or not to reconcile.

In some cases, reconciliation or restitution may come before forgiveness. In the case of an ongoing relationship, we may enter into discussions about the transgression, seeking explanations and reacting to those explanations with more clarity about the transgression. Discussions may also open the door for the transgressor to become more aware of the extent to which he or she has injured us and offer an apology or restitution.

The apostle Paul's directives to forgive are always in one of three contexts: creating unity in the body of Christ; doing good to those who transgress against us; or receiving divine forgiveness of our sin and deepening our relationship with God. Paul also places an emphasis on being reconciled to brothers or sisters who have transgressed against us after we have forgiven them and they have repented. There are no references, however, to being reconciled with a transgressor who is not of the body of Christ. We are, however, admonished[92] to possess a loving spirit toward our neighbor and those who commit evil against us, persecute us, and despitefully use us. Love and forgiveness go hand in hand. Forgiveness opens the door to the possibility of reconciliation in four ways.

1. **Forgiveness helps us question the wrongdoing.**
   Part of the forgiveness process is to look at the transgression from differing points of view. We have a tendency to justify our own behaviors quickly without considering all the perspectives involved. Forgiveness prompts us to seek clarification about the transgression, which opens the door to dialogue and better mutual understanding of the transgression for both the transgressor and the transgressed.

2. **Forgiveness helps us clarify the wrong that was done.**
   One step in the forgiveness process is to acknowledge the wrong that has been done (chapter 2). During this process, we may find the transgression to be less harmful than we initially thought. Once we objectively identify the effect the transgression is having on us, we may open the door to better communication with the transgressor.

3. **Forgiveness takes the offender into account.**
   When we forgive, we consider the offender's background, redeeming attributes, and motives for the transgression. While a better understanding of what motivated the transgression does not justify the offending act, it does help us consider empathy and the gift of forgiveness for the offender, which is a stepping-stone to reconciliation.

4. **Forgiveness opens the door to salvation.**
   As we work on our spiritual formation, our views of the transgressor and the transgression evolve. Looking at the transgressor from a Christlike perspective makes us question how we can reflect Christ's love to him or her. This demonstration of love sets the stage for the transgressor to experience Christ and salvation.

While these four benefits of forgiveness can open the door to your consideration of reconciliation, they also may not. By virtue of the forgiveness process itself, you may uncover truths about the transgression or the transgressor that dissuade you from seeking reconciliation. You may find that reconciliation would return you to a harmful situation or that the transgressor has no interest in a dialogue that assures you of no repeat offense. If either of these is the case, then your forgiveness rests in lifting up the offender's name to God in prayer and letting God address your needs.[93] You may also offer acts of kindness and consideration, if the opportunity presents itself, as long as these are not intended to produce a particular result or change the transgressor's lack of interest in reconciliation.[94]

Reconciliation is an emotional decision. Before making it, you need to ask yourself whether the costs and benefits of reconciling make moving toward it worthwhile. We are not required to reconcile in all circumstances, but "if possible, so far as it depends on you, live peaceably with all." Use the following exercise to assess the advantages and disadvantages for reconciling:

Journal Exercise 33a: Opening Your Heart to Reconciliation

Use the following chart to list the advantages and disadvantages of reconciling with your transgressor:

ADVANTAGES OF RECONCILING FOR YOU	DISADVANTAGES OF RECONCILING FOR YOU

Journal Exercise 33b: Checklist for Considering Reconciliation

Put a check mark in front of any statement that applies to your forgiveness journey.

Has your forgiveness process helped you question the wrongdoing?

☐ I have considered all the points of view involved.

☐ I have sought greater clarification about the transgression.

☐ My transgressor and I have a mutual understanding of the transgression.

Has forgiveness helped you clarify the wrong that was done?

☐ I have acknowledged the wrong that was done to me (chapter 2).

☐ I have come to better understand the transgression and have considered whether it was less harmful than I initially thought.

☐ I have objectively identified the effect of the transgression on me.

☐ I have described how the offender's behavior has hurt me and how I would prefer to be treated in the future.

Has your forgiveness taken the offender into account?

☐ I have considered the offender's background, redeeming attributes, and motives that may have prompted the transgression.

☐ I have separated the offender from the offense and have acknowledged that the reasons behind the offense do not justify the offending act.

☐ I have considered empathy and the gift of forgiveness for the offender.

☐ My heart has been softened toward the offender.

Has your forgiveness opened the door for the salvation of the offender or witnesses?

☐ My work on spiritual formation has altered my view of the transgressor.

☐ I am looking at the transgressor from a Christlike perspective.

☐ I have considered ways to reflect Christ's love to the offender.

☐ I have opened the door for the transgressor to come to a better understanding of his or her need for a Savior.

Interpreting Your Responses

Review the checked items (above) and consider the progress you have made on your forgiveness journey. Pray that the Lord will continue to strengthen you and guide you as you strive to achieve full emotional peace.

Chapter 6 Summary

1. The key concept of this chapter is opening your heart to forgiveness, which is based on considering how our Lord Jesus would respond to your transgressor and being open for others to witness your love for and devotion to Jesus so that the light of Christ shines through you.

2. Opening your heart in order to open the door to your strongholds is necessary if you seek to forgive. When the heart is hidden and protected by a stronghold, you are less able to forgive and less likely to gain and sustain the mind of Christ.

3. Gratitude is a doorway to forgiveness, and forgiveness leads to happiness and well-being.

4. When transgressions threaten the fulfilment of our basic needs, we must open our hearts to God's promise that He will meet all our needs.

5. God's gift of forgiveness to us is the heart of the Bible. In addition, God gave us another gift: the ability and desire to forgive others, which brings peace to the forgiver and the forgiven.

6. Developing empathy (which has six essential elements) for your transgressor allows the Lord's goodness to flow through you into the life of the transgressor.

7. Opening your heart to forgiveness includes writing a new story of the transgression. This is an important part of your journey because you begin to tell the story of how God has redeemed you from the vicious cycle of unforgiveness that has haunted you.

8. The chapter ends by examining the various types of reconciliation and asking you to consider whether taking this additional step would be helpful to you.

Devotional

Dear Father in Heaven,

Your Word instructs and encourages me as I move closer to forgiving my transgressor, _____. The gospel writer Luke quotes Jesus as saying, "The good person out of the good treasure of his heart produces good, and the evil person out of his evil treasure produces evil, for out of the abundance of the heart his mouth speaks" (Luke 6:44-45). These verses show me that the condition of my _____ must be pleasing to You. Lord, I ask that You cleanse my heart and help me to open it so that I may embrace Your ways and that I may exhibit forgiveness, just as You have forgiven me.

Lord, Your Word also gives me detailed instructions on what You expect from me:

Put on then, as God's chosen ones, holy and beloved, compassionate hearts, kindness, humility, meekness, and patience, bearing with one another and, if one has a complaint against another, forgiving each other. As the Lord has forgiven you, so you also must forgive. And above all these, put on love, which binds everything together in perfect harmony. And let the peace of Christ rule in your hearts, to which indeed you were called in one body. And be thankful.

Dear God, of these listed qualities, I need Your help to develop _____ , _____, and _____. If these qualities are visible in my life, then I can be a conduit for the light of Christ to shine through me to my transgressor, as well as to all who observe my obedience and devotion to You.

Finally, Father, I ask that You hear my pleas to open my heart to embrace gratitude and empathy. I trust that You will meet my needs. Help me to continue to write a new story of my transgression, one that focuses on how You redeemed me from bitterness and brought me to peace.

I pray all this in the holy and powerful name of Christ Jesus, Your Son.

Amen.

Chapter 6 Endnotes

1   Mark 16:15; John 15:9–10, 12; 1 Peter 3:9.

2   Luke 6:44–45.

3   Psalms 119:11–12.

4   Galatians 5:16.

5   I presented a more detailed explanation of this scripture in an earlier chapter.

6   Galatians 5:16–6:5.

7   A website that gives a practical explanation of the types of esteem and what we can do to improve our esteem is found at https://positivepsychologyprogram.com/self-esteem/.

8   E.R. Smith and D.M. Mackie (2007). *Social Psychology*, 3rd ed. (London: Psychology Press, 2007).

9   State vs. trait forgiveness, presented in chapter 1.

10 J. J. Exline and R. F. Baumeister, "Expressing Forgiveness and Repentance," in *Forgiveness: Theory, Research, and Practice*, ed. M. E. McCullough, K. I. Pargament, and C. E. Thorensen (New York: Guilford Press, 2000), pp. 149–50.

11 See the section in an earlier chapter about coping with transgressions.

12 A. B. Newberg, E. G. d'Aquili, S. K. Newberg, and V. deMarici, "The Neurological Correlates of Forgiveness," in *Forgiveness: Theory, Research, and Practice,* pp. 102–3.

13 E. L. Worthington Jr., *Forgiveness and Reconciliation: Theory and Application* (New York: Routledge, 2006), pp. 189–90.

14 Newberg, d'Aquili, Newberg, and deMarici, V, "The Neurological Correlates of Forgiveness," pp. 103–7.

15 Romans 7:15–20.

16 Philippians 4:4–9a.

17 Philippians 4:8.

18 Proverbs 4:23.

19 2 Corinthians 10:4.

20 Ephesians 6:12, 18.

21 John 15:9–12.

22 1 Peter 3:9.

23 John 15:12–15.

24 2 Corinthians 4:15.

25 Colossians 2:7.

26 Philippians 4:6–7.

27 1 Chronicles 16:8–41; Psalms 107:1; 2 Corinthians 1:11.

28 James 1:17; Matthew 7:11; Luke 11:13.

29 Ephesians 4:32; Colossians 3:13.

30 R. D. Carlisle and J. Tsang, "The Virtues: Gratitude and Forgiveness," in *APA Handbook of Psychology, Religion, and Spirituality*, vol. 1, *Context, Theory, and Research*, ed. K. I. Pargament (Washington, DC: American Psychological Association, 2013), pp. 423–37.

31 J. C. Karremans, P. A. M. Van Lange, J. W. Ouwerkerk, and E. S. Kluwer, "When Forgiving Enhances Psychological Well-Being: The Role of Interpersonal Commitment," *Journal of Personality and Social Psychology* 84, no. 5 (2003): 1011–26.

32 K. J. Bao and S. Lyubomirsky, "The Rewards of Happiness," in *The Oxford Handbook of Happiness*, ed. S. A. David, I. Boniwell, and A. C. Ayers (Oxford: Oxford University Press, 2014).

33 J. Tsang, "Gratitude and Prosocial Behavior: An Experimental Test of Gratitude," *Cognition and Emotion* 20: 138–40.

34 Carlisle and Tsang, "The Virtues"; D. F. Landry, K. C. Rachal, W. S. Rachal, and G. T. Rosenthal, "Expressive Disclosure Following an Interpersonal Conflict: Can Merely Writing about an Interpersonal Offense Motivate Forgiveness?" *Counseling and Clinical Psychology Journal* 2, no. 1 (2005) full article.

35 Ibid

36 Worthington, *Forgiveness and Reconciliation*, pp. 78–79.

37 Carlisle and Tsang, "The Virtues."

38 Matthew 6:8, 32.

39 Jeremiah 29:11–13a.

40 Matthew 7:7–11.

41 Luke 12:27–34.

42 Romans 8:28.

43 2 Timothy 2:15.

44 Worthington, *Forgiveness and Reconciliation*, pp. 25–27.

45 Colossians 3:2; Philippians 3:14; Hebrews 12:1–2; 2 Timothy 4:7–8.

46 Matthew 6:31–33.

47 James 1:16.

48 Proverbs 3:5–6.

49 1 Corinthians 10:33.

50 Daniel 10:12–14.

51 Genesis 20.

52 John 12:31; Ephesians 2:2; 2 Corinthians 4:4; Revelation 12:9.

53 Matthew 5:44–45; also 2 Peter 3:9; John 3:16; Romans 5:8.

54 Romans 8:28.

55 Luke 11:12, 14.

56 Romans 12:19–21

57 Matthew 25:45.

58 Romans 3:23.

59 Matthew 7:12, 22:37–40.

60 John 14:1–4.

61 Matthew 5:45–47; 1 Corinthians 13:4–7.

62 Genesis 50:15.

63 Luke 7:47; Colossians 3:13.

64 Colossians 3:13.

65 Matthew 6:8; Luke 12:7; Hebrews 13:21.

66 Colossians 3:12–16.

67 Matthew 11:28–30.

68 Colossians 1:3–7.

69 Worthington, *Forgiveness and Reconciliation*, pp. 50–53.

70 K. McLaren, *The Art of Empathy: A Complete Guide to Life's Most Essential Skill* (Boulder: Sounds True, 2013), p. 1.

71 Three significant texts about empathy are M. E. McCullough, E. L. Worthington, and K. C. Rachal, "Interpersonal Forgiving in Close Relationships," in *Dimensions of Forgiveness: Psychological Research and Theological Perspectives*, ed. E. Worthington (1979), pp. 259–61; R. Enright and R. Fitzgibbons, *Forgiveness Therapy: An Empirical Guide for Resolving Anger and Restoring Hope* (Washington, DC: APA Press, 2015); and N. Wade and E. Worthington, " In Search of a Common Core: A Content Analysis of Interventions to Promote Forgiveness," *Psychotherapy: Theory, Research, Practice, Training* 42, no. 2 (2005): 167.

72 I encourage you to study McLaren's book and find the resources on her website that will help you to develop a clearer vocabulary of emotional states and the skills needed to use your understanding of those states to deal with your transgressor. Her website is https://karlamclaren.com.

73 D. Goleman, *Emotional Intelligence* (New York: Bantam, 1995); N. Lowrey, "Examining the Relationship between Emotional Intelligence and Interpersonal Forgiveness among Internet Users," PhD diss., Walden University, 2016), https://scholarworks.waldenu.edu/cgi/viewcontent.cgi?article=3843&context=dissertations.

74 Romans 12:19–21.

75 R. Krznaric, *Empathy: Why It Matters and How to Get It* (New York: Perigee, 2014), p. xxi.

76 Ibid.

77 Romans 3:23; also Romans 14:10–12.

78 Worthington, *Forgiveness and Reconciliation*, p. 46.

79 Ibid, p. 84.

80 Matthew 5:45.

81 1 Timothy 2:4.

82 Worthington, *Forgiveness and Reconciliation*, p. 38.

83 Romans 8:28.

84 Ephesians 5:8; 1 Peter 2:9.

85 Doing good toward a transgressor may not be possible or advisable in some situations, except in our positive intentions to do good should the opportunity present itself.

86 Working on the spiritual strengths that you are most satisfied with may seem counterintuitive. In a deficit-based model for change, that would be true. However, as you rewrite your story, we are taking a strengths-based approach. In chapter 5 you did an activity to decide what you can do to improve the areas of spiritual maturity that you feel need work (pp. 61, 69, 90, 103). At this point, in order to rewrite your story in a way that is motivating and encouraging, leveraging your strengths is important.

87 I have found from my experience as a chaplain that kneeling beside a patient when I pray with him or her creates a feeling that we are in a sacred space, kneeling before our Lord in humility and love. One knee, two knees—it doesn't matter. If you cannot physically kneel, consider raising your arms to God as you read your prayer.

88 According to the research I conducted for my doctoral dissertation regarding how people learn to forgive, this is the most critical step. Participants in a workshop (one that included many of the exercises in this book) said that sharing their stories aloud with others made the greatest impact on their willingness and ability to forgive their transgressors. Please do not shortcut this step. It takes courage to be this vulnerable with others, but with God's help, you can do it.

89 Matthew 5:24; Romans 12:14–21, 14:10–12.
90 Romans 12:19.
91 Matthew 18:15–17.
92 The most well-known passage is 1 Corinthians 13. See also Romans 12:21; Luke 6:27–31.
93 Romans 12:19.
94 Romans 12:20.

CHAPTER 7

Next Steps to Sustain Emotional Freedom

You keep him in perfect peace whose mind is stayed on you, because he trusts in you.

—ISAIAH 26:3

DAY 34

Next Steps for Emotional Healing—Introduction

The steps you have been working through in the ACTION process got you started on the forgiveness journey. As time goes on, however, you may be triggered by something that reminds you of the transgression you have overcome. When this happens, it is easy to fall back into the trap of unforgiveness. As stated earlier, unforgiveness is one of the most powerful and lethal darts Satan can shoot us with. This chapter suggests a series of steps that will help you avoid falling back into the vicious cycle of unforgiveness.

Forgiveness is not an event that happens and then everything goes back to how it was before. Forgiveness is an ongoing process. As you complete the work in *Forty Days to Forgiveness*, you will begin to discover how the forgiveness process changes you spiritually and emotionally. In this section we will explore the next steps—the *N* in ACTION—you can take to embrace the changes you are experiencing and reduce the tendency to return to negative thoughts or behaviors. You will be challenged to continue the forgiveness journey; you may find that revisiting some of the exercises in *Forty Days to Forgiveness* is helpful to sustain your state of forgiveness.

Forgiveness Step 6: Next Steps to Sustain Emotional Freedom

You can build strength to resist any temptation to return to negative thoughts or behaviors by doing the following:

- Practicing the disciplines that lead to ongoing spiritual maturity.
- Developing the feelings, thoughts, and actions that reveal Christ in you.
- Nurturing a preference for prayer and meditation in all things.
- Building a stronger knowledge of God's Word.

- Nurturing fellowship with like-minded disciples of Christ in whom you can confide your forgiveness journey.

Things that inhibit taking the next steps to sustain forgiveness. In contrast to the foregoing list, the following are characteristics and habits that interfere with sustaining forgiveness. Rank the following inhibitors from what is most like you (1) to what is least like you (8).

_____   I treat those who treat me badly the same as they treat me.

_____   I cannot usually forgive and forget an insult.

_____   I continue to feel upset when I think of the transgression and the transgressor.

_____   I don't care about the one who transgressed against me.

_____   I feel bitter about many of my relationships.

_____   I recall hurts that fuel my resentment even after I have forgiven someone.

_____   I do not always forgive those who have hurt me.

_____   I am not a forgiving person.

This section will by no means complete the forgiveness process, but it will set the stage for the ongoing journey toward emotional freedom. In this chapter, we will review the following nine steps:

Day 34: Next Steps for Emotional Healing—Introduction
Day 35: Love, Grace, and Gratitude
Day 36: Character Strengths
Day 37: A Dynamic Narrative
Day 38: Nurturing Positive Intentions
Day 39: Reconciliation
Day 40: Reflecting on Your Progress

Prayer for God's Guidance

My Gracious God,

Hold me in Your hands of grace as I continue my forgiveness journey.

I know that peace will come in Your timing, not mine. Please empower me to overcome a view of myself as someone who … [name the top three inhibitors to forgiveness, above].

I trust You to see me through to the end of this journey. May the progress I make daily reflect You, Your love and goodness, and Your Son's great mercy.

In Jesus's name, amen.

Finding Peace in Forgiveness

Temperament and Forgiveness

It is your thirty-fourth day of working on forgiving the transgressor you chose in chapter 2. As we come to the end of our time together, it is important to remember that having an unforgiveness relapse is possible. This section discusses why forgiveness is so hard for us and how to anticipate and prepare for the potential relapse. The emotional freedom that we seek through forgiving a transgressor can be elusive, like the ebb and flow of ocean tides. In previous sections we talked about how our brains are hardwired to protect ourselves from harm. That is *what* we do; however, *how* we protect ourselves is not hardwired. Each of us has an emotional temperament that forms over time. As we encounter threats to our well-being, we find ways of responding that supply our need for protection. A temperament, the way we tend to respond to the world around us, is part of the personality. An emotional temperament is a disposition that prewires us to respond in predictable ways emotionally to situations we experience. Dr. Judith Orloff[1] has categorized five emotional types. Since our focus is forgiveness, I will describe each emotional temperament from the perspective of how it affects one's response to transgressions.

    The intellectual responds to threats by analyzing the situation and using logic and reason to determine how the threat may affect him or her. This type most likely goes into a problem-solving mode and ignores the emotions that the transgression has sparked. The intellectual may rationalize away a transgression, ignore it, or trivialize it in ways that keep him or her in a vicious cycle of emotional unforgiveness.

The Empath uses intuition to assess the emotional state of the one presenting a threat and responds with feeling, sensitivity, and concern for his or her well-being. As you have learned, the empath is the type most likely to overcome the emotional effects of a transgression. However, if taken to an extreme, the empath may overlook the accountability of the transgressor, which may impede transgressors from accepting responsibility for and the consequences of their actions.

The Rock is emotionally strong. This emotional type sizes up a situation and demonstrates strength and leadership to resolve the threat in decisive, practical ways. This type may deny, dismiss, or diminish the importance of a transgression and may never really resolve the deep emotional feelings that hold him or her captive to the vicious cycle of unforgiveness.

The Gusher is a person whose feelings are worn on his or her sleeve; this emotional type is quick to express emotions in the face of even the slightest threat, creating attention and drama. This person can stir up others and manipulate them into feeling sympathy for his or her misfortune.

The Emotional Vampire is the person who can turn almost any threat around and make it a problem for everyone else but himself or herself. Another drawback of this emotional type is that the "vampire" is a complainer and a stick-in-the-mud at a party; he or she alienates others by sucking them into a situation and then emotionally draining them.

Do you see yourself in any of these emotional styles? I encourage you to go back to the exercise on day 9 and see if any of those descriptions still apply to how you are reacting to your transgressor and the transgression. While we all have a tendency to respond to threats according to a particular emotional type, in reality we possess features of all the various types, and depending on the situation, we may demonstrate any of them to a greater or lesser degree. Our emotional type affects our usual interpretation of obstacles in our paths and influences how we typically respond, but our emotional type does not limit our range of possible responses to various situations.

As mentioned before, the apostle Paul said that he did not understand his own actions; he described the flesh (the worldly, non-Christ-centered nature) as an unconscious influence on his actions that caused him to do what he did not want to do. He emphasized that he had the right motive within, but his worldly nature eclipsed his acting on the right motive.[2] Similarly, we could say that our sinful nature finds expression through our emotional temperament, and we do not always respond as we wish.

Attachment and Forgiveness

Secondly, we often find forgiveness difficult because transgression creates the perception of an unsafe attachment to others. In an earlier section we talked about how important it is for each of us to feel lovable and loved by others and to feel worthwhile to ourselves and to others. This desire for love, validation, acknowledgment, care, compassion, and protection begins early in life. The way the primary caregiver attends to a child's needs forms a pattern of expectations for how the child's future needs will or will not be met. Although I agree with the old adage that we cannot go on blaming our parents for our behavior in our later years, like it or not, behavioral science research shows that the way parents or primary caregivers do or do not attend to the needs of babies and young children shapes the neural pathways that endure throughout life.[3] These ways of experiencing care gradually result in four types of attachment styles: secure, dismissive, preoccupied, and fearful-avoidant.

The **secure attachment style** is created when the child receives reliable care when it is needed. This causes the child to develop a sense of security that his or her needs will continue to be met. The result is an underlying strong sense of self. Such children generally become secure and independent adults.

The **fearful-avoidant style** is caused by disorganized and unreliable care that creates feelings that the child's needs may or may not be met, which leads the child to become detached from his or her feelings of non-care or, in extreme cases, a feeling of abandonment that motivates the child to seek other means of care (a flight response) or to act out inappropriately in order to get the attention of his or her caregiver (a fight response). The result is an overemphasis on a desire for safe relationships in which all needs are met. Without realizing it, such a person perceives a failure in his or her needs being met as a reason to flee or fight in order to gain the attention of others.

The **dismissive attachment style** is often a derivative of the avoidant style, just described. These children become conditioned to writing off their caregivers as being unreliable, and therefore the children become aggressive or passive-aggressive toward their caregivers out of sense of disappointment or anger. The result is that these children grow up to be highly cerebral, overthinking problems or seeing problems where they do not actually exist. Often they respond to stressful situations by avoiding their source.

Finally, the **preoccupied attachment style** is caused by capricious care that is adequate sometimes and not adequate at other times. The result is that the child becomes self-critical and lacks confidence that he or she will receive the type of positive relationships he or she seeks from a caretaker. The child may overemphasize seeking approval and validation from others and become worried and untrusting when they feel rejected. Generally, they are clingy and overly dependent on others instead of being dependent on themselves.

In short, our response to a transgressor may be colored by our prewired attachment style. Although these attachment styles preprogram how we cope with relational challenges throughout our lives, they can be reprogrammed to some extent: we *can* learn new ways of coping, as described in earlier sections. However, the underlying attachment style exists like a shadow and is likely to reemerge in times of threat and stress. More about this will be said later.

The Bible and Personality

While I have not used the term *personality* previously, I am using it now to refer to those aspects of our behavior that are imprinted on how we think and behave, particularly on instinct, attachment style, and temperament. While much more is involved in making up our personalities, for the purposes of *Forty Days to Forgiveness*, we will focus only on these three things.

While instinct, temperament, and attachment style may influence our reactions to a transgression, they do not define how we choose to react. Each of us has the choice to make changes in our mindsets as we have talked about in earlier sections of *Forty Days to Forgiveness*. Instinct, temperament, and attachment all play a role in our predisposed ways of behaving. However, the heart can trump the automatic programmed response we give when we react to others. If we had no control over ourselves, then why would the Bible give us instruction? The instruction we receive on forgiveness, human interaction, relationships with others, etc., is intended to help us reprogram how we think about and respond to the world around us.

The Bible encourages God's people to carry positive thoughts in place of negative ones. What we know from behavioral science is that changing habitual ways of thinking (i.e., rumination) is somewhat like changing habits. Habits can be changed more effectively when the undesirable behavior is replaced by a more preferred behavior. Habits are formed from repetition of a behavior over time with repeating satisfactory results. Once habits are formed, neural pathways are created in the mind, and these are relatively durable. These neural pathways form something called "schema" or schematics for how to achieve the same satisfactory results over and over again. These schemas are difficult to reprogram by trying to simply change our thoughts in order to change them directly. Therefore, we should *not* try to stop the negative thoughts, because when we try to stop something, human nature leads us to become even more fixated and less likely to stop. Instead, we have the formula Paul gives in his letter to the church at Philippi: "Finally, brothers, whatever is true, whatever is honorable, whatever is just, whatever is pure, whatever is lovely, whatever is commendable, if there is any excellence, if there is anything worthy of praise, think about these things."[4]

Paul does not tell us to stop thinking badly. Instead, he tells us what to think about. Additionally, Paul gives instruction on *how* to think on these things. He tells us in the previous and following verses that the peace of God will guard our hearts and minds if we do the following:

- Rejoice in the Lord always.
- Let our reasonableness be known to everyone.
- Replace anxiety with prayer and supplication, doing this with thanksgiving.
- Let our requests be made known to God.
- Practice what we have learned in the Word.

Wow! Can the Bible be any more prescriptive than that? The ACTION process you have been learning describes the steps to thinking as Paul instructs. After progressing through these ACTION stages of forgiveness during this forty-day journey, you may feel that you have forgiven your transgressor. You may have your rumination under control, and you may have formed new ways of thinking positively (i.e., new schema). There is a risk, however, that unforgiveness may resurface. Following are a few reasons why; you can possibly think of more:

- You continue to interact with the transgressor, and you see that his or her behavior has not changed.
- The transgressor has died, leaving negative energy directed toward you.
- The transgressor is no longer present, but the effects of the transgression linger on.
- You continue to want to see the transgressor pay the price for his or her hurtful behavior.
- Your need to establish justice eclipses your desire to minister to your transgressor.
- People other than your transgressor have directed the same offense toward you.

In short, without the person bringing any further harm to you, you may find yourself once again thinking or acting angrily or fearfully toward, or feeling angry or fearful about, him or her. Your transgressor may repeat the exact same transgression (or one similar) that will remind you of the hurt, which can retrigger the same neuropathway, launching you back into the vicious cycle of unforgiveness. You may also experience "microtransgressions," bits and pieces of the behaviors similar to the original transgression that remind you of the intense hurt. These microbehaviors can be just as triggering of your emotions and negative ruminations as experiencing the full transgression. These are called "flashbacks."

This is what we see with people experiencing posttraumatic stress disorder (PTSD). While all transgressions are not traumatic, they can still trigger subtle versions of what a person with PTSD experiences. Here is what I mean: When a recurrence of the transgression or microbehaviors occurs, the mind can relapse into reexperiencing the full original event that programmed the PTSD. This happens because the amygdala does not make a distinction between past and current threats to our well-being. Flashbacks can release powerful stress hormones, as well as a nervous system response, to protect us from harm: sweating, increased heart rate, elevated blood pressure, trembling. The flashbacks send us back into a coping mode, discussed in previous chapters. In other words, the amygdala is like a smoke detector. It does not tell us where the smoke is, how much smoke there is, or why there is smoke; it just tells us that there is smoke.

As with smoke detectors, we learn that some perceived threats are false alarms; other times there may be a "microsmoke" condition that is not an actual fire. It is sometimes difficult to know the difference between harmless smoke and smoke from an actual fire. The reason we cannot just think our way into controlling our response is because the part of the brain that controls our interpretation of the transgression (the amygdala) is inhibited from maintaining control in the face of stress,[5] either partially or completely, depending on the seriousness of our fear regarding another transgression. What happens (to a greater or lesser extent) is that we lose track of time and become trapped in the experience of the retriggered behavior. In other words, having become trapped in the moment the transgression occurred, we lose the ability to distinguish between past, present, and future. The way to control this response is to keep the mind grounded in the present.[6] We can do this by practicing the spiritual disciplines (chapter 5).

Even without a retriggering experience, you might doubt the resilience of your forgiveness or question whether you have truly forgiven. You may be partially correct in this, or you may still be at the stage of decisional forgiveness only. Regardless of such concerns, you have worked hard and have experienced either complete or partial emotional forgiveness as compared to the beginning of your journey.

Yet the risk remains that memories of the transgression and the concomitant unforgiving feelings will resurface. Even the mental energy expended simply to avoid encounters with your offender can trigger memories of pain and unforgiveness. Instead, think of the transgression as your being burned by a hot stove: the experience introduces a new respect for the painful encounter, and you act accordingly. When you see the person who hurt you and feel the negative feelings arise once again, you can respond in two ways: recall the transgression and entertain in your thoughts the pain, anger, and fear you felt the first time you were transgressed, or recall what you have learned from the offense. The first approach will lead you back into the vicious cycle of unforgiveness, while the second can help you overcome unforgiveness.

Mastering unforgiveness in this manner comes from your willingness to commit to forgive and from God's guiding presence throughout your spiritual formation. Our spiritual formation conditions our brains to respond differently to the offender and to cope with our fear, anger, and pain in new ways. We have talked extensively about what actions help us forgive and, conversely, what actions merely reduce unforgiveness.[7] Later in this chapter you will review how the various lessons in *Forty Days to Forgiveness* can be reemployed to help you overcome future encounters with your transgressor.

What if you were to see the person again? What feelings might you feel? If you do feel anger, what will you do? Can you pray for the offender as a means to help you hold onto your forgiveness? Doing so may be difficult, so below is a prayer to guide and strengthen you:

> Lord, make me an instrument of Your peace.
> Where there is hatred, let me sow love;
> where there is injury, pardon;
> where there is doubt, faith;
> where there is despair, hope;
> where there is darkness, light;

and where there is sadness, joy.
O Divine Master,
grant that I may not so much seek
to be consoled as to console;
to be understood as to understand;
to be loved as to love;
for it is in giving that we receive;
it is in pardoning that we are pardoned;
and it is in dying that we are born to eternal life.
Lord, make me an instrument of Your peace.[8]

Journal Exercise 34: Forgiveness Readiness Survey Revisited

Compare how you feel about forgiving your transgressor now to the rating you gave earlier. Rate how you currently feel about each of the three types of forgiveness listed below in relationship to the transgression you selected.

Type 1: Decisional forgiveness. Have you made a decision to work toward forgiveness in your chosen situation even though you may still find it difficult to forgive? On the scale, 1 represents "have not committed" and 10 represents "fully committed" to forgive.

[1] [2] [3] [4] [5] [6] [7] [8] [9] [10]

What would it take for you to move to the next number?

Type 2: Granting forgiveness. How ready are you not to seek retaliation, vengeance, or apology; not to talk negatively about the offender; and (as much as is in your power) to seek to live peacefully with him or her?

Not ready [1] [2] [3] [4] [5] [6] [7] [8] [9] [10] Ready

What would it take for you to move to the next number?

Type 3: Emotional forgiveness. To what degree are you experiencing less and less negative emotion about the offense and feeling at peace about granting forgiveness?

Less [1] [2] [3] [4] [5] [6] [7] [8] [9] [10] More

What would it take for you to move to the next number?

Interpreting Your Results

Add together your scores for each of the three questions. Divide this result by 30, which represents the highest possible score for all the categories. This is your forgiveness quotient. This score reflects how sustainable you feel your forgiveness is. It is also a barometer of how you have progressed in your forgiveness journey.

My totals for all three questions: _____

Divide this total by 30.

My current forgiveness quotient: _____

My forgiveness quotient in journal exercise 3b: _____

You may not be seeing measurable progress. That's okay. If you feel you have not improved your forgiveness quotient as much as you would like, be gentle with yourself. The journey takes time and may require you to revisit some of the action steps.

DAY 35

Love, Grace, and Gratitude

This day has a short reading in order to encourage you to spend more time on the exercise. My prayer for you is that the exercises you have completed up to this point have been helping and are still helping you to progress toward the peace that blossoms from emotional forgiveness. If you are still feeling the negative emotions that are triggered by remnants of resentment and bitterness toward your transgressor, do not be hard on yourself. Emotional forgiveness requires an intentional process over a period of time. In this section we will focus on exercises to help you sustain your journey toward positive emotions.

The key goal of the forgiveness process is to replace negative thoughts and emotions toward a transgressor with positive ones. The behavioral sciences provide some guidance on cultivating positive emotions through the following practices: (1) loving-kindness meditation, which involves directing warm and tender feelings toward others; (2) expressing gratitude for the good things that have happened because of others; (3) knowing your positive character traits and acknowledging how they support your quest for positive emotions; and (4) writing a meaningful narrative about an event. We will start by working on a loving-kindness meditation.

Loving-Kindness

Depending on your progress toward emotional peace, you may still be experiencing negative emotions toward your transgressor. If you still feel negative and resentful, this is nothing to be ashamed of; such feelings are a sign that your journey continues. Take any lingering pain to God in prayer, asking Him to strengthen you on your journey. Supplement this with meditation and fellowship with other believers.

Jesus, who was tempted in every way we are,[9] emerged from His suffering and sorrows through love and compassion for all those He encountered. He was strengthened through prayer and living within the Father's will for Him. When we try to follow His example on our own strength alone, we may inadvertently amplify our pain and suffering by ruminating on the transgression. When we are not walking with the Lord through our spiritual formation, we may be tempted to continue to carry the weight of unforgiveness, but when we approach the throne of grace in prayer, we receive comfort as our Lord intercedes to strengthen us to break the strongholds that have prevented our positive thoughts from emerging.

Gratitude

Thinking about what is going wrong in our lives is natural. We think about experiences from the past that have had negative effects on us, and we fear upcoming events that might be similarly harmful. We contemplate such future events in the hope that we will be able to respond in ways that will help us avoid the difficulties of a negative experience. However, there is a fine line between healthy and unhealthy troubleshooting. Dwelling on what is or may be going wrong in our lives sets us up for anxiety and depression.[10] When we are in an anxious or depressed state, we are not functioning at our best. One result of this is that we tend to make bad decisions and damage our relationships with others. In anxious and depressed states, we also run the risk of ruminating on what may go wrong, which begins to form into a story of worst-case scenarios. Once we carry around a story about negative experiences, we are lured into following the path of the story. Breaking free and operating as our best selves becomes difficult.

An antidote to thinking about what is or may be going wrong in our lives is to think about what did or may go well. We all have experiences every day that we can be thankful for. Paul tells the church at Ephesus to give thanks always and for everything to God the Father in the name of our Lord Jesus Christ.[11] Similarly, the psalmist often illustrates thanks to the Lord for His goodness and great deeds.[12] The Psalms also tell us that giving thanks blesses God and gives praise to Him for His favor and loving-kindness.[13]

This point in your forgiveness journey is a good time to strengthen your emotional resilience, and expressing gratitude is one way to do this. In a previous chapter we talked about how gratitude is acknowledging the good things that have happened to us because of others, and you were encouraged to record what you are grateful for in a journal. Some of the benefits of keeping a gratitude journal include the following:

- Lowering stress levels
- Feeling calm at night and sleeping better
- Gaining new perspective on what is important and what you truly appreciate in your life

- Gaining clarity on what you want more of in your life and what you can cut from your life
- Learning more about yourself and becoming more self-aware

Your gratitude journal is an important part of the next steps you take for sustaining emotional freedom from unforgiveness. Your journal is a safe zone for your eyes only, so you can write anything you feel without judgment. On days when you feel blue, read back through your gratitude journal to readjust your attitude and remember that you have great people and many other blessings in your life.

You may have started to keep a journal when we talked about it earlier. Starting a journal and maintaining one can be difficult because it is something else to remember to do, but the results will be worth the effort required. Keep adding to your journal until it becomes a habit; many people find that keeping a gratitude journal does not feel like a chore because it is a peaceful time to sit and contemplate on what they are thankful for. The words will flow from you; fifteen minutes just might turn into thirty. Gratitude works its magic by serving as an antidote to negative emotions. Gratitude is like white blood cells for the soul, protecting us from cynicism, entitlement, anger, and resignation.

If you did not start your gratitude journal before or started and then did not maintain it, the next exercise is intended to encourage an ongoing practice of gratitude journaling. If you have not done so, get a journal to write in. It does not have to be fancy; drugstores sell composition books for a couple of dollars. Once a week, write down three things that went well. Describe why they went well, and give praise to God for how He showed up in the blessing you experienced. Blessings can be big or small. After writing your blessings, find a friend or family member to read them aloud to. Below are some suggestions to consider as you begin:

- **Do not just go through the motions.** Journaling is more effective if you first make the conscious decision to become happier and more grateful. Motivation to become happier plays a role in the efficacy of journaling.
- **Go for depth over breadth.** Elaborating in detail about something you are grateful for carries more benefits than a making a superficial list of many things.
- **Get personal.** Focusing on *people* for whom you are grateful makes more of an impact than focusing on *things* for which you are grateful.
- **Try subtraction, not just addition.** One effective way to stimulate gratitude is to reflect on what your life would be like *without* certain blessings.
- **Savor surprises.** Try to record events that were unexpected or surprising as these tend to elicit stronger levels of gratitude.
- **Do not overdo it.** Writing occasionally (once or twice per week) is more beneficial than daily journaling. People who wrote just three to five statements of gratitude in their journals once a week for six weeks reported distinct boosts in happiness.

Journal Exercise 35a: Love and Grace Meditation

Chapter 5 discusses the difference between prayer and meditation: Prayer is intentional communication between you and God, and meditation is contemplating how God is showing up in your spiritual experiences. A meditation session may begin or end with prayer and may include scriptures that influence your perspective on how God is showing up in the world around you and inside you. Here is one approach to help you meditate on the nature and role of loving-kindness in and around you.

Prep work: The cornerstone of this meditation is love. The Bible is filled with advice about loving God and others, and the two greatest commandments are to love God and to love our neighbors as ourselves. As with any meditation, you should get comfortable physically and emotionally. Turn off any alarms or phones that may distract you.

1. Get into a relaxed state by noticing your breathing. Breathe in deeply through you nose. Feel your chest rise. Hold your breath for a bit, then exhale slowly through your nose. Do this a few times until you feel relaxed.
2. Let your breathing return to its natural rhythm. Pay attention to the natural rhythm of your breath. Pay attention as it flows in and out of your chest.
3. Begin your meditation by envisioning Jesus. Jesus encourages us to abide in Him, like the branch of a vine. Visualize God's life like a river of white light flowing from Jesus into you. Think of yourself as a branch on a tree with Jesus's love flowing up through the trunk and into your heart.
4. Let your mind float as you wander back to a loving state toward God with everything you have. See God's love as being an open watering well, available for all. See yourself walking around the well, loving all people as God does.
5. Repeat the breathing that you did in step 1 as you slowly come back from the well, noticing where you are, seeing the room around you as a sacred place where God has touched you. Take a deep breath. Begin moving your hands and feet. Gently start moving your head. Then very slowly start to open your eyes.

Journal Exercise 35b: Gratitude Journal

You may have already started a gratitude journal and have developed your own style and rhythm. That's great. If you have not, here is a refresher for what a typical journal looks like:

Sample Gratitude Journal

Day 1 Blessings

1. Today God blessed me with the opportunity to enjoy His sunshine.
   I took a walk today to enjoy the feeling of the sun on my face and the warmth of the air.

2. I am thankful for the blessing of having friends.
   Today I received a call from Jerry, and we are getting together for coffee. It will be a blessing to talk with him about the progress I am making on my forgiveness journey.

3. A conflict I've been having at work was resolved today.
   Today I met with a coworker to discuss progress on a project we are working on together. We reached agreement on the next steps and a timetable, something we were in disagreement about.

DAY 36

Character Strengths

In this exercise, you will focus on knowing your positive character strengths and acknowledging how they support your quest for positive emotions. Character strengths are the positive parts of you that affect how you think, feel, and behave; they are the keys to being your best self. When we apply our character strengths effectively, we benefit others and ourselves. Character strengths are different from your other strengths, such as your unique skills, talents, interests, and resources, because character strengths reflect the *real* you—who you are in your heart. We will take a look at what the behavioral sciences say about character traits, and then we'll see what the Bible says.

We could create a book about the work that has been done in the behavioral sciences on character traits. However, one simple model applies well to our journey. According to Martin Seligman, a prominent behavioral scientist, character strengths fall into six categories:[14]

Wisdom

Wisdom is more than intelligence or knowledge; it is the ability to use intelligence and knowledge to think, choose, and act in new ways that are beneficial and productive. Wisdom comes from what we learn through experiences; it helps us know whether to try a particular thing or to choose an alternative action. Solomon, the wisest man on earth (until Christ came), said, "The fear of the Lord is the beginning of wisdom, and the knowledge of the Holy One is insight."[15] Wisdom begins with reverence and awe for God and His Word. Wisdom includes our curiosity and interest in the world; our ongoing love of learning; our judgment, critical thinking, and open-mindedness; our ingenuity, originality, practical intelligence, and street smarts; social, personal, and emotional intelligence; and a healthy perspective of the world.

Courage

Courage is mental or moral strength in the face of adversity to venture, persevere, and withstand danger, fear, or difficulty while taking action that leads to worthy results. Courage is bolstered by our reliance on the Lord for strength and deliverance.[16] Courage is not being fearless. It is, instead, the ability to do the right thing in the face of fear. Doing the right thing comes from being grounded in the Word of God. With His Word indwelling us, we are equipped to stand in the face of adversity with courage. Our courage in the Lord comes from spiritual formation: knowledge of His truth through the Word, faith in His unfailing love, confidence in our salvation, an indwelling of the Spirit, and standing fast through prayer.[17] Courage includes valor and bravery in the face of adversity; perseverance, industriousness, and diligence to achieve attainable goals; and integrity, genuineness, and honesty to live our lives in authentic ways.

Humanity and Love

Humanity is a character strength that causes one to reach outside oneself to create and maintain positive social interactions with friends, family, acquaintances, and strangers. As followers of Christ, our role is to reflect His glory and be a light in dark places.[18] Our strength of humanity includes kindness and generosity that acknowledges the worth of others, loving others, and allowing ourselves to be loved.

Justice

In this context, justice as a character strength is demonstrated in how we go beyond one-on-one relationships to relate to larger groups such as our family, our community, the nation, and the world. Justice is not to be confused with judgment, which is the process of determining whether someone has violated a standard. Justice has to do with how we work with others. It is the absence of fighting and quarreling.[19] Justice is behaving in ways that bring joy to others.[20] Justice as a character strength includes excelling as a member of a group; having a sense of duty, teamwork, and loyalty; having a standard of fairness and equity that transcends one's own personal feelings and biases; and showing leadership to get things done in an orderly and effective way in collaboration with others.

Temperance

Temperance is self-restraint and the demonstration of moderate appetites and desires. The temperate person does not suppress motives but waits for opportunities to satisfy them so that no harm is done to self or others. Temperance is the ability to exercise self-control and steadfastness and to let obedience to God drive one's decisions.[21] Temperance is acting upon what you value rather than what you desire; the prudence, discretion, and caution to say and do what you will not later regret; and the humility and modesty to reflect the love of Christ.

Transcendence

Transcendence is the emotional strength to reach outside ourselves to connect to the future and to God. We often forget that when we put on Christ as our Savior and Lord, we become immortal beings, living with one foot on this earth and the other in heaven (the kingdom of God). Transcendence is our willingness and ability to renew our minds constantly to know Christ and focus on things above.[22] Transcendence includes an appreciation for beauty and excellence; gratitude for blessings that we never take for granted; hope, optimism, and future-mindedness; a sense of purpose, faith, and focus on a life in God; forgiveness and mercy; playfulness and humor to see the silver lining in every storm cloud; and a zest, passion, and enthusiasm to look forward to what the day has in store for us.

When developing our character strengths, simply *using* them is not enough. Instead, each of us must discover how to draw upon them in the right amount and in the right situations to create the outcomes we want as well as the outcomes that glorify God. Character strengths aid our efforts to cope with transgressions and support our journey to replace negative thoughts about offenders with positive thoughts about them. To find your character strengths, take the VIA (Values in Action) survey on this website: www.authentichappiness.com.[23] When you finish, print your report and use it in the exercise to follow.

Just as the behavioral sciences provide numerous descriptions of character, so does God's Word. One prominent list of character strengths is found in Jesus's Sermon on the Mount, which has come to be known as the beatitudes. When we look at character strengths that influence our ability to be forgiving, many come into play, such as the fourteen listed in chapter 4, day 16. Two journal exercises followed to help you think about how to put these strengths into practice. Specifically, in journal exercise 16a, you rated how well you demonstrate each of the fourteen traits, and in journal exercise 16b, you developed a plan for how you can benefit from those strengths on your forgiveness journey. These strengths are not like a grocery list where you put each one in your basket; these traits are more like a perennial garden. You plant perennial flowers once, and ideally they bloom every year, provided they are attended to. Keeping out weeds, watering, fertilizing, and providing ample sunlight are all necessary in order to enjoy the full bloom of your garden.

The best way to think about your character strengths is to know that they operate along a continuum: at one end you underplay your strengths, and at the other end you overplay your strengths. In the middle you find the golden mean where you apply your strengths effectively in different situations to create your desired results. In this way, your character strengths form a foundation upon which your ability to cope with offenses rests. When we suffer from a deep level of blindness about areas in which we have character strength, we tend to underuse our strengths. Perhaps you can think of a time when your strong character strengths would have been helpful but you did not draw from them. At other times, however, when we are passionate and excited about using them, we are prone to overplay our personality strengths. The emphasis of this section is how to tend to the garden of your forgiveness strengths.

If we overplay a character strength such as hope in a work situation where we see many opportunities to make great things happen, we might overextend and overcommit ourselves. In the middle is the sweet spot where we draw on our character strengths to be our best selves in a situation. Think of the times when you were engaged and energized, enjoying what you were doing. These are probably times when you leaned on a character strength, and the empowering experience then reinforced that strength.

Journal Exercise 36: Assessing Character Strengths

In the following exercise, list the top five strengths that you found from the VIA survey, and then answer the two questions for each strength. If you are not able to take the VIA survey, you can refer back to the descriptions of the character strengths found earlier in this section.

Character strength 1:
Describe one example of how this strength has been helpful in the past:
Describe a way this strength can help you show forgiveness for your transgressor:

Character strength 2:
Describe one way this strength has been helpful in the past:
Describe a way this strength can help you show forgiveness for your transgressor:

Character strength 3:

Describe one way this strength has been helpful in the past:

Describe a way this strength can help you show forgiveness for your transgressor:

Character strength 4:

Describe one way this strength has been helpful in the past:

Describe a way this strength can help you show forgiveness for your transgressor:

Character strength 5:

Describe one way this strength has been helpful in the past:

Describe a way this strength can help you show forgiveness for your transgressor:

DAY 37

A Dynamic Narrative

As discussed in chapter 2, when we are not able to cope with a transgression, fear and anger can overtake us and send us into a vicious cycle of rumination. As we ruminate, we begin to fabricate a story, or narrative, about what happened to us, how we have been a victim of someone's careless or malicious behavior, and how we think we should respond. As we mull over the story in our minds, our fear or anger is amplified, as are our negative intentions toward the transgressor. Although fear can be a healthy response because it alerts us to take action to avoid hurt, fear can capture us in a vicious cycle if we ruminate on it. The result can then be a return to unforgiving feelings.

Anger is an instinctive response to a threat and to the frustration of our goals, our desires, and our belief that our rules about how we should be treated have been violated. When we have not coped with the transgression fully, anger is a common result. Anger is a negative emotional state that may grow into hostility and aggression and a desire to harm or injure the individual who hurt us. The story that we form about our transgression affects how we see and interpret the world around us and how we see ourselves in that world. This narrative gets in the way of the positive emotions that help us forgive others. When we judge the world around us based on our internal rules for how we should be treated, our internal expectations drive how we treat others.

A good metaphor to help us think about how we see the world, according to Everett Worthington, is to consider a pencil.[24]

A pencil has a short life, yet it can make a significant mark that can communicate volumes, just like you can. The tiniest things you do and say can make a profound mark on others and, ultimately, on you.

A pencil is not a pen. Its mistakes can be corrected with effort, but correcting the mistakes often means standing the pencil on its head. In order for you to ignore the actions that your expectations advocate, you may have to turn your "head" upside down to show love and seek forgiveness instead of revenge.

What is inside the pencil is what counts. As is the case with you, what is inside the pencil is responsible for the mark it makes. When you hold positive thoughts toward others captive by having a stronghold of negative emotions and feelings, you may treat others in angry and unforgiving ways. What is hidden within the strongholds, Christ and His power, is what needs to shine through you.

Pencils need to be ground down and sharpened regularly, so do not despise the sharpening that you must undergo from God. Often the hurts and wounds you feel as painful are God's sharpening you so you can be His instrument to write the love of Christ on the hearts of those who hurt you and on the hearts of others who see how you react to your injuries.

God uses suffering from our transgressions to build us up and remove our weaknesses,[25] resulting in praise, glory, and honor to God as Christ is revealed through us.[26] One way suffering sharpens us is by challenging us to think about what we are here for. What is the purpose of our existence, and what is the meaning of our existence? When people find meaning in suffering, they come to a new understanding about what has happened in the past. They begin to create a new narrative that puts suffering in a new perspective, knowing that they have learned something valuable from the experience. Finding purpose changes our attitude toward the future and provides motivation for how we want to show up going forward. As disciples of Christ, our purpose is to glorify God, to serve Him above all else. As Peter says, "Though now for a little while, if necessary, you have been grieved by various trials, so that the tested genuineness of your faith—more precious than gold that perishes though it is tested by fire—may be found to result in praise and glory and honor at the revelation of Jesus Christ."[27]

Our innermost needs and emotions come to the surface in adversity and suffering. Adversity is like a fire that brings the impurities in our lives to the surface to be skimmed off like the impurities that are skimmed off melted gold. Like fire working on gold, suffering can destroy impurities within us to cleanse and strengthen us. Heartaches and problems that seem beyond our ability to endure may be the very things that God permits to cause us to realize the importance of trusting Him. Adversity and suffering are, in a sense, gifts that draw us into a closer relationship with Him.

An openness to learning and growing from the suffering you have endured will help you find your way to forgiveness and healing. Ask yourself, "What have I learned from this experience?" Did your experiences make you a stronger person, a more empathic and compassionate person, a person who is more spiritually mature? As with the sharpening of a pencil, how has your suffering sharpened your commitment to walk the path to which Christ has called you?

Through His own suffering, Christ set the pattern for how we are to walk in obedience to the will of the Father.[28] Furthermore, Christ is able to help us in our suffering from temptations and adversity.[29] Our suffering is also a means through which we grow in our Christlikeness[30] because our suffering presents us the opportunity to do good to others. Christ has assured us that He will provide a way to escape adversity, and in our suffering from adversity, we build endurance to withstand future challenges. Our resilience to withstand adversity strengthens the Christlikeness in our hearts.[31] Every transgression is unique and requires each of us to find our own path through it, but all of us have Christ's example and help as we travel through adversity.

Journal Exercise 37a: Creating a Dynamic Narrative

Complete each sentence that follows to help you think about the story you have created about your transgression experience and the story you would like to create as your forgiveness journey continues. First, acknowledge the feelings this transgression has elicited by returning to the exercises that are part of journal exercise 7.

As a result of this transgression, I have felt …

Think about the coping strategies you have tried to help you respond positively to the transgression. Can you think about *new ways* to solve the problems the transgression represents, new ways to regulate your emotions, or new ways to look at the transgression from new perspectives? It may be helpful to return to day 9 to revisit the section on coping.

I have tried to cope with this transgression by ...

A way of coping I have not tried that may be more helpful is ...

Have you thought about what background story might shed light on your offender's transgression? Creating a separation in your mind between the backstory and the here and now helps to distinguish the offender from the transgression and is a stepping-stone to showing empathy and compassion.

What I have learned about my offender that helps me to understand his or her transgression against me is ...

Forgiveness is the process of letting go of the negative intentions we have toward our transgressors and replacing them with positive thoughts.

The negative thoughts I have harbored toward my transgressor include ...

The positive thoughts I have decided to cultivate toward my transgressor include ...

Journal Exercise 37b: A Dynamic Narrative

When we walk with the Lord, harmful events in our lives can lead to opportunities for God to strengthen us. No matter what the transgression is, God can use it to bless and strengthen us.

Prompt: Out of the experience of this transgression, I can see that God has blessed me by strengthening me in the areas of (check all that apply):

Wisdom
☐ curiosity and interest in the world and an ongoing love of learning
☐ my judgment, critical thinking, and open-mindedness
☐ ingenuity, originality, practical intelligence, and street smarts
☐ social, personal, and emotional intelligence

Courage
☐ valor and bravery in the face of adversity
☐ perseverance and industriousness
☐ diligence to achieve attainable goals
☐ integrity, genuineness, and honesty to live my life in an authentic way

Humanity and love
☐ kindness and generosity that acknowledges the worth of others
☐ loving others and allowing myself to be loved

Justice
☐ excelling as a member of a group, maintaining a sense of duty, teamwork, and loyalty
☐ being committed to a fairness and equity that transcends my personal feelings and biases
☐ showing leadership to get things done in an orderly and effective way in collaboration with others

Temperance
☐ self-control to act upon what I value and not what I desire
☐ prudence, discretion, and caution to act in ways that I will not regret later and to say things I will not regret later
☐ the humility and modesty to reflect the love of Christ

Transcendence
☐ appreciation for beauty and excellence
☐ gratitude for my blessings, never taking them for granted
☐ hope, optimism, and future-mindedness
☐ a sense of purpose, faith, and focus on a life in God
☐ forgiveness and mercy
☐ playfulness and humor to see the silver lining in every storm cloud
☐ a zest, passion, and enthusiasm to look forward to what the day has in store for me

Journal Exercise 37c: A Letter to the Transgressor

Earlier you wrote a letter to the transgressor whom you are working on forgiving. You have also done the "empty chair" exercise twice to help you imagine what a conversation between you and the offender might be like. In this exercise I'm offering some prompts to help you think about what you might say to the transgressor in a different way. Write a letter that you will not send to your transgressor describing how you currently feel about the transgression. Keep the following thoughts in mind as you write:

- ❏ Recall when the transgression occurred and how long you have been angry about it.
- ❏ Is your anger rising from this one event, from multiple events, or from a reminder of something that happened to you before?
- ❏ On a scale of 1 to 10, how angry are you now (1 is "not angry" and 10 is "seething with anger")?
- ❏ What struggles has the transgression caused you to endure?
- ❏ What have you learned about the transgressor? In what ways are you feeling empathy for him or her?
- ❏ What have you learned about yourself? Can you see how God is using this transgression to bring about some good for you or for the transgressor?

A Letter to the Transgressor

Dear _____,

On _____ [date] I experienced some hurtful [behavior/words/actions] from you. As a result, I have experienced [describe what pain or suffering you have endured] …

```



```

Since then, I have learned that you may have committed this transgression because of [describe what you have learned about the transgressor] …

```



```

Even though the transgression has been hurtful, I have learned [describe what you have learned about yourself through this process of forgiveness] …

```



```

I have made a decision to try to be forgiving. I am / am not feeling forgiveness at this time. In order to be forgiving, I will [describe what will help you forgive or continue forgiving your transgressor] …

```



```

Sincerely,

_____

DAY 38

Nurturing Positive Intentions

Forty Days to Forgiveness has included many exercises to help you overcome the vicious cycle of unforgiveness. When you reencounter situations, you may find it helpful to revisit the same exercises. This section involves a troubleshooting chart to help you identify which exercises would be most beneficial for you. Also included are examples from the Bible to help you reprogram your narratives for dealing with your transgressors; remember, however, that positive intentions do not necessarily have to be played out in real life. Some ways you can nurture positive intentions include the following actions:

- ❏ Incorporating positive intentions into prayer
- ❏ Writing about your positive intentions, particularly in a gratitude journal
- ❏ Writing letters that you may or may not send
- ❏ Rehearsing your positive intentions in an empty-chair activity
- ❏ Associating your positive intentions with your own character strengths

These are just a few ideas. There are many more ways that positive intentions can be a game changer for you. In the final stroke of empathy and love, you are seeking to have your positive intentions inform and fuel a new narrative about your experiences with your transgressor.

Journal Exercise 38: Reflecting on Growth

For this exercise, reflect on the growth you have made in your forgiveness journey. Go back in *Forty Days to Forgiveness* and select one journal exercise that you found particularly helpful in reprogramming negative intentions, turning them into positive intentions toward your transgressor. Repeat that activity and then share the results with a prayer partner. Here is a sample prayer that may help to reinforce your engagement in the activity you choose:

Gracious Lord,

You are the God of all. You make the rain fall on the righteous and the unrighteous, the just and the unjust.

I pray, Father, that You help me renew my mind with positive Christlike thoughts toward _____ [the one who transgressed / hurt you].

Be with _____ [the one who transgressed / hurt you] and help him [or her] to find the path to Your grace and love so that he [or she] may reflect You.

Nourish in me a thirst for Your Word and a hunger to learn Your ways as I develop my mind to be more like Yours.

Search my heart and find the impurities that keep me wrapped up in my own pain and hurt. Help me purge those thoughts and replace them with Your love and truth.

Thank You for Your Son, who died for us that we might have eternal life with You. I pray that Your love for us and Christ's death may be a source of nourishment for the one who hurt me as You soften his [or her] heart toward You and toward others.

In Your Son's name, amen.

DAY 39

Reconciliation

As explained earlier, forgiveness and reconciliation are different. Forgiveness is the emotional release of negative intentions toward the transgressor, replaced by positive Christlike thoughts and behavior, which can be done without the participation of the transgressor. Looking to the transgressor to participate in your forgiveness process is counterproductive: it is like you drinking poison and hoping that the transgressor dies.

Reconciliation is not forgiveness. The Bible includes examples of reconciliation without any mention of forgiveness. Instead, reconciliation is the set of steps taken to restore relationship with offenders in order to continue in fellowship/friendship/partnership with them. Like forgiveness, reconciliation requires a decision on the part of the wounded person to try to reconcile; unlike forgiveness, reconciliation requires the cooperation of the offender. Interestingly, the Bible does not paint a clear picture of the process to forgive, but in a number of places it provides clear examples of the steps to reconcile:

- ❏ Joseph reconciled with his brothers by giving them a dependable food supply, providing space for them to settle, and allaying their fears of reprisal.
- ❏ Jacob met his brother Esau in the desert with gifts to show his love, his repentance, and his desire to have a relationship again.
- ❏ God continued to reconcile Moses to Himself after Moses's failure to follow His instruction.
- ❏ God's whole plan of salvation is to reconcile humankind to Himself following humankind's fall in the garden of Eden.

There are a number of reasons why we might want or need to reconcile with someone who has committed an offense against us.[32] Following are some common reasons, but you may think of others that apply to your situation more specifically:

- ❏ We place a value on the other person and find comfort or satisfaction in our time with him or her.
- ❏ We think reconciliation will bring about forgiveness or be a less painful way to move forward without the hard work of forgiveness.
- ❏ We realize that not reconciling may leave the transgressor lonely, friendless, or missing the benefits of the relationship.
- ❏ We feel that our integrity and character are apparent in our desire for a relationship to succeed.
- ❏ Reconciliation helps to reduce the injustice of the transgression, especially when there is restitution, repentance, and apology on the part of the transgressor.
- ❏ The transgressor has asked to reconcile and may have stated some of these very reasons for reconciling.
- ❏ The offender is a person with whom you are in Christian fellowship and you will continue to encounter him or her.

So where does that leave us? We have talked in several sections about what the New Testament says about reconciliation: it clearly tells us to be reconciled to those with whom we are in fellowship in the body of Christ, as well as our families and others with whom we are in close relationship. In the case of others, we are told to let our light shine so that all may see our good works. We are also instructed to turn the other cheek when we are wronged and to do our part to build bridges between others and the kingdom of God. But this is all easier said than done. Following are the recommended steps for reconciling with a transgressor:

First, have a goal in mind. The purpose of reconciliation is *not* to restore a relationship to what it was before the transgression. Once a transgression is committed, it cannot be undone, and the relationship will never be the same. It may be better. It may be worse. It may be terminated. In my days as an organizational change consultant, I emphasized that change is inevitable, pointing out that my clients could not control whether or not change occurred in their organizations. All they could do was to anticipate change and influence it toward the desired results. Knowing the desired result is an important first step. Without a clear image of the desired result, your attempts to reconcile will likely result in frustration or disappointment. You may even worsen your situation.

Second, discuss your differences and work out a solution. Jesus gave specific instructions regarding reconciliation. He told His followers that if they have a complaint against a brother to go directly to him and reconcile. Otherwise, the situation may deteriorate to the point of becoming a legal matter.[33] Jesus spelled out three steps in this process; it is important to note that these steps are for a person in the same church fellowship as you:

1. Upon awareness of the transgression, the offended person is to go to the offender alone and voice his or her complaint. The implications are that we are not to talk about the offense to others and that we and the transgressor are to work out the issue between ourselves.

2. If the offender does not listen or refuses to work out a solution, the injured person is to take one or two others (a limited number) with him or her and approach the transgressor again.

3. If the transgressor still refuses to work out the issue, tell the church and discuss discipline, up to and including withdrawing fellowship.

Third, absorb the infraction with grace and love. Jesus said that we are blessed when people persecute us or make hateful statements about us. Here are some thoughts on reconciling with an unbeliever or someone we are not in fellowship with:

1. Go the extra mile to accommodate even unreasonable requests. In the case of a boss, subject yourself to his or her direction unless doing so would compromise your moral standards. On the other hand, the first step of reconciling with a brother or sister in Christ can also apply. You may choose to approach the offender in a spirit of reasonableness and work out a solution that is a win-win.

2. Turn the other cheek. This is an interesting and often misunderstood direction from Christ. We might think it to mean we are not to hold the infraction against the offender. However, as discussed earlier, if we are in a harmful, dangerous situation, God does not expect us to remain in harm's way. We have numerous examples of taking action to protect ourselves, beginning with Joseph and Mary taking Jesus to Egypt to thwart Herod's plan to kill Him.

   Here's another way to look at this directive: Given that Jesus specified the right cheek, which is the one that is hit when someone backhands you, you are to offer up the other cheek, the left, so the person may slap you in a forehanded way. A backhanded slap is a sign of disrespect from a person believing himself or herself to be in a superior position to you. A forehanded slap is a strike delivered to the face of a person on equal footing. In any event, the directive to turn the other cheek seems distinctly not to mean that you shouldn't hold something against someone who offends you. It isn't about your thoughts or feelings. It is about offering the other person the opportunity to hit you properly, not as a disobedient slave or a misbehaving child, but as an adult of equal standing. In this way, being on equal footing, we have a choice as to whether to continue to be transgressed or to remove ourselves from the situation, such as Peter suggests in the next point.

3. Flee the presence of evil, injustice, and danger. Peter tells us to shun evil and do good, and to seek and pursue peace.[34]

4. Overcome evil with good. Jesus told us that when we do good to others, meeting their needs, it is as if we are doing good to Him. Working out differences with others can be

a form of bringing peace to a situation. We serve a God of peace. In fact, peace is one of the blessings that God gives to those who love Him and keep His commandments. God actually taught His people to use the word *peace* (*shalom*) to greet others and part from others.[35]

What would reconciliation mean for you? Would it restore trust? Would it repair a broken relationship and make it stronger? Would it restore the benefits of being in relationship with the person who transgressed against you? On the other hand, would it keep you in a dangerous or harmful situation? Would it compromise your Christian integrity? Would it simply make you feel like you did your part to show piety without actually restoring the relationship and resolving negative intentions? In the next exercise, you will consider what to do about reconciling with the person you have been working to forgive.

Journal Exercise 39: To Reconcile or Not to Reconcile

Benefits/Drawbacks

On the left side of this chart, list all the specific benefits that reconciliation would bring to you and possibly to your transgressor. On the right side, list all the drawbacks of reconciliation.

Benefits of reconciling	Drawbacks of reconciling

Scoring

If the benefits outweigh the drawbacks, put a 5 here; if not, put a 0: _____

Physical Safety

On a scale of 1 to 10, rate how physically safe you would feel if you were to continue in a relationship with your transgressor.

Score: _____

TOTALLY UNSAFE									TOTALLY SAFE
1	2	3	4	5	6	7	8	9	10

Emotional Safety

Using the same chart, rate how emotionally safe you would feel if you were to continue in a relationship with your transgressor.

Score: _____

Goals: List what you and others will see/experience if you reconcile.   •   •   •
Do you realistically feel these goals can be achieved?   **Score:** Yes (5 points) or no (0 points) _____
The Transgression   Put a check next to any of the following *emotions* that the idea of reconciliation brings up for you. Subtract 1 point from 12 for each check mark.

❐ Fear	❐ Surprise	❐ Jealousy	❐ Guilt
❐ Sadness	❐ Disgust	❐ Envy	❐ Indifference
❐ Anger	❐ Disappointment	❐ Shame	❐ Other

Score (subtract 1 point from the number 12 for each check mark): _____
Unenforceable Rules   What rules governing how you feel you should be treated will be resolved by reconciling?

Do you feel that your **expectations** for how you should be treated in the future will be met if you reconcile?

Score: Yes (5 points) or no (0 points) _____

Coping
What coping methods have helped you through your forgiveness process?

Will your way of coping with your transgressor improve?
Score: Yes (5 points) or no (0 points) _____

Grievances
What grievances will reconciliation resolve? (Look at journal exercise 6a.)

❏ **Hurt feelings** (which may arise from being criticized or teased in a hurtful way)
❏ **Betrayal** (which made you feel rejected. This usually happens between close friends, work associates, or romantic partners)
❏ **Active dissociation** (an act that explicitly rejected you)
❏ **Passive dissociation** (subtle, unclear attempts to make you feel unwanted)
❏ **Being unappreciated** (experiencing a heightened sense of rejection and dismissiveness)
❏ **Unfair treatment** (receiving different treatment than others)
❏ **Unjust treatment** (receiving treatment that violates some law or common rule)
❏ **Abuse** (being intimidated, manipulated, or controlled for the personal gain of the transgressor)
❏ Other

Score (1 point subtracted from the number 9 for each check mark): _____

Unforgiveness

Put a check in front of any of the following actions that you believe will help reduce your unforgiveness:

❏ Apology   ❏ Revenge   ❏ Retaliation   ❏ Criticism

❏ Restitution   ❏ Reciprocation   ❏ Grudge   ❏ Stonewalling

❏ Defensiveness   ❏ Contempt   ❏ Avoidance   ❏ Verbal aggression

Score (subtract 1 point from 12 for each check mark): _____

Justice/Accountability

List any actions that you think might be needed to correct the transgression:

What is the transgressor accountable for?

What are you accountable for?

Score: Do you feel both of you can be accountable for your parts in reconciling?

Yes (5 points) or no (0 points) _____

Action Plan

Explain your plan to involve your transgressor in working toward reconciliation. Make two lists: things you have control over and things your transgressor has control over.

Actions I have control over:

Actions the transgressor has control over:

Score: Do you feel you can both be accountable for your actions toward reconciling? Yes (5 points) or no (0 points) _____

Interpreting Your Results

In the previous assessment activity, you were challenged to think about reconciling with the person who transgressed against you. In this section you will interpret your answers in order to rate the importance and potential of reconciling.

POTENTIAL FOR SUCCESSFUL RECONCILIATION		
SURVEY CATEGORY	TOTAL POSSIBLE	YOUR SCORE
❑ Benefits/drawbacks	5	
❑ Physical safety	10	
❑ Emotional safety	10	
❑ Goals	5	
❑ Transgression	12	
❑ Unenforceable rules	5	
❑ Coping	5	
❑ Grievances	9	
❑ Unforgiveness	12	
❑ Justice/accountability	5	
❑ Action plan	5	
Total score	83	

DAY 40

Reflecting on Your Progress

Forty Days to Forgiveness has included many exercises to help you overcome the vicious cycle of unforgiveness. As you move forward, you may find it helpful to revisit these same exercises. The following troubleshooting chart will help you identify which exercises might be of benefit again:

Journal Exercise 40a: Reflecting on Your Forgiveness Journey

Rate each of the ACTION forgiveness steps on a scale of 1 to 5 with 1 being very difficult/helpful and 5 being not difficult / not helpful.

ACTION FORGIVENESS PROCESS STEPS	DIFFICULTY	HELPFULNESS
Chapter 2: Acknowledging that a wrong has been done and gaining insight into the painful effects the injustice has had on you	[1] [2] [3] [4] [5]	[1] [2] [3] [4] [5]
Chapter 3: Committing to trying to forgive the offending person and working on replacing unforgiving thoughts and actions with positive ones	[1] [2] [3] [4] [5]	[1] [2] [3] [4] [5]
Chapter 4: Transitioning from the vicious cycle of negative feelings and unenforceable rules to a state of Christian forgiveness	[1] [2] [3] [4] [5]	[1] [2] [3] [4] [5]
Chapter 5: Internalizing the process of forgiveness through spiritual formation	[1] [2] [3] [4] [5]	[1] [2] [3] [4] [5]
Chapter 6: Opening your heart to the outcomes of forgiveness	[1] [2] [3] [4] [5]	[1] [2] [3] [4] [5]

Examine your scores. Are there any steps that you rated as not very helpful that you also rated as very difficult? If so, your forgiveness journey may benefit from your going back and revisiting those chapters. Some of these processes may have been painful to address, causing you to hurry through the exercises or do them superficially. Look at the journal exercises again to see if you would respond to them differently now that you have completed all of them. The forgiveness process sometimes requires a second pass through the exercises because the first try is often too challenging to move us forward toward emotional forgiveness.

Journal Exercise 40b: Forgiveness Tune-Up

This worksheet may look intimidating. However, it is not a worksheet to be completed; it is a troubleshooting guide. Any items in the previous exercise with low ratings are areas you may want to revisit. This worksheet will help you pinpoint the journal exercises that correspond to areas that are still a struggle for you. You may need to revisit the exercises now and in the future if you feel the vicious cycle of rumination threatening the forgiveness you have worked so hard to achieve.

Forgiveness Step 1: Acknowledging the Hurt		
Behaviors that promote forgiveness	Unlike me Like me	Actions to review to improve
1. Focusing on who you are working on forgiving and why	[1] [2] [3] [4] [5]	Journal Exercise 1b: Selecting the Transgressor Journal Exercise 3b: Forgiveness Readiness Survey
2. Making a commitment to try to replace unforgiving thoughts with positive ones	[1] [2] [3] [4] [5]	Journal Exercise 4a: What Do You Need? Journal Exercise 4b: Getting a New Perspective
3. Making a commitment to try to see the transgression from God's perspective	[1] [2] [3] [4] [5]	Journal Exercise 5: Your Forgiveness GPS Journal Exercise 6a: Acknowledging How You Are Affected Journal Exercise 6b: Acknowledging Degrees of Transgression
4. Resolving transgressions by actively coping through positive, assertive means	[1] [2] [3] [4] [5]	Journal Exercise 7: Acknowledging Emotions and Feelings Journal Exercise 8: Unenforceable Rules Journal Exercise 9: Coping with Offenders Journal Exercise 10a: Acknowledging Your Negative Intentions Journal Entry 10b: Acknowledging Your Rumination Journal Entry 10c: Reducing Unforgiveness

Behaviors that inhibit forgiveness	Write in actions to boost behaviors that promote forgiveness:
5. I do not like the transgressor.	
6. I cannot forgive a friend for just anything.	
7. I'll keep as much distance between us as possible.	
Behaviors that inhibit forgiveness	Write in actions to boost behaviors that promote forgiveness:
8. I do not try to act toward him or her in the same way I did before he or she hurt me.	
9. I do not try to forgive others even when they feel guilty for what they did.	
10. I'll live as if he or she does not exist or is not around.	
11. Some things I could never forgive anyone, even a loved one.	
12. I rehearse schemes of revenge in my mind.	
13. I try to excuse the transgressor's behavior and let him or her off the hook.	
14. I tell numerous people about the rotten character of the offender.	

Forgiveness Step 2: Committing to Try to Forgive

Behaviors that promote forgiveness	Unlike me Like me	Actions to review to improve
1. Making a commitment to try to replace unforgiving thoughts with positive ones	[1] [2] [3] [4] [5]	Journal Exercise 11: Readiness to Forgive Journal Exercise 12: Motivations for Unforgiveness Journal Exercise 13a: Justice, Fairness, Safety
2. Making a commitment to try to see the transgression from God's perspective	[1] [2] [3] [4] [5]	Journal Exercise 13b: Knowing When You Have Forgiven Journal Exercise 14: What Forgiveness Looks Like
3. Resolving transgressions by actively coping through positive, assertive means	[1] [2] [3] [4] [5]	Journal Exercise 15a: Deciding to Commit to Trying to Forgive Journal Exercise 15b: Committing to Trying to Forgive

Behaviors that inhibit forgiveness	Write in actions to boost behaviors that promote forgiveness:
4. I do not like the transgressor.	
5. I cannot forgive a friend for just anything.	
6. I'll keep as much distance between us as possible.	
7. I do not try to act toward him or her in the same way I did before he or she hurt me.	
8. I do not try to forgive others even when they feel guilty for what they did.	
9. I'll live as if he or she does not exist or is not around.	
10. Some things I could never forgive anyone, even a loved one.	
11. I rehearse schemes of revenge in my mind.	
12. I try to excuse the transgressor's behavior and let him or her off the hook.	
13. I tell numerous people about the rotten character of the offender.	

Forgiveness Step 3: Transitioning to a Godly Perspective

Behaviors that promote forgiveness	Unlike me Like me	Actions to review to improve
1. Transferring the negative thoughts that are going around in your head about the transgression into positive thoughts	[1] [2] [3] [4] [5]	Journal Exercise 16: Finding Your Forgiveness Strengths Journal Exercise 17a: Coping Style Journal Exercise 17b: Coping Action Planner
2. Looking at the ways the transgression has created disappointments from a different point of view	[1] [2] [3] [4] [5]	Journal Exercise 18: Your Anger Style Journal Exercise 19a: Negative to Positive Intentions Journal Exercise 19b: Visualization Activity
3. Transitioning from intending for bad things to happen to your transgressor to showing love, empathy, and compassion toward him or her	[1] [2] [3] [4] [5]	Journal Exercise 20: Activity to Assess Well-Being Journal Exercise 21a: Activity to Build Empathy Journal Exercise 21b: Mindful Empathy
4. Transitioning from seeing the transgressor as a villain to a child of God	[1] [2] [3] [4] [5]	

Behaviors that inhibit forgiveness	Write in actions to boost behaviors that promote forgiveness:
5. I seek revenge and ways to make him or her pay.	
6. I contemplate ways to hurt him or her in the same way he or she hurt me.	
7. I want to see him or her miserable, and I wish that something bad would happen to him or her.	
8. I would find it difficult to act warmly toward him or her.	
9. I resent what he or she did to me.	
10. I keep thinking about the offense to avoid working on the hurt productively.	

Forgiveness Step 4: Internalizing Spiritual Maturity

Behaviors that promote forgiveness	Unlike me Like me	Actions to review to improve
1. Beginning to practice the disciplines that lead to ongoing spiritual maturity	[1] [2] [3] [4] [5]	Journal Exercise 22a: Setting Your Mind on Things Above Journal Exercise 22b: Inhibitors to Spiritual Maturity
2. Developing feelings, thoughts, and actions so that others will see Christ in you	[1] [2] [3] [4] [5]	Journal Exercise 23a: Current State of Your Spiritual Disciplines Journal Exercise 23b: Committing to Improve
3. Nurturing a preference for prayer and meditation in all things	[1] [2] [3] [4] [5]	Journal Exercise 24a: Inductive Bible Study of Forgiveness Journal Exercise 24b: Assessing Your Bible Study
4. Building a stronger knowledge of God's Word	[1] [2] [3] [4] [5]	Journal Exercise 25: Assessing Your Meditation Practices Journal Exercise 26: Assessing Your Prayer Practices
5. Nurturing fellowship with like-minded disciples of Christ in whom you can confide your forgiveness journey	[1] [2] [3] [4] [5]	Journal Exercise 27: Assessing Your Fellowship Practices

Behaviors that inhibit forgiveness	Write in actions to boost behaviors that promote forgiveness:
6. People close to me probably think I hold a grudge too long.	
7. I will not help my transgressor if he or she needs something.	
8. I want him or her to get what he or she deserves.	
9. If I see him or her, I will not act friendly.	
10. I am going to get even.	
11. I will try to get back at him or her.	
12. I want to cut off the relationship with him or her.	
13. I want to demand an apology and receive justice and atonement.	

Forgiveness Step 5: Opening Your Heart to Forgiveness

Behaviors that promote forgiveness	Unlike me Like me	Actions to review to improve
1. Beginning to feel love toward the transgressor and a desire for his or her salvation	[1] [2] [3] [4] [5]	Journal Exercise 28a: The Strongholds of Unforgiveness Journal Exercise 28b: Prayer for Release from Strongholds Journal Exercise 29: Overcoming Strongholds with Gratitude
2. Feeling gratitude for the challenge God has brought into your life	[1] [2] [3] [4] [5]	Journal Exercise 30a: Meeting Your Needs Journal Exercise 30b: A Letter to the Transgressor
3. Holding on to the faithfulness of the Word of God	[1] [2] [3] [4] [5]	Journal Exercise 31a: Openness to Build Empathy
4. Being a vessel through which God's shining light may enter the world	[1] [2] [3] [4] [5]	Journal Exercise 31b: Prayer for Empathic Release Journal Exercise 32: Rewriting Your Story Journal Exercise 33a: Opening Your Heart to Reconciliation Journal Exercise 33b: Checklist for Considering Reconciliation

Behaviors that inhibit forgiveness	Write in actions to boost behaviors that promote forgiveness:
5. I do not feel sympathy toward the transgressor.	
6. I resent what he or she did to me.	
7. I do not feel love toward him or her.	
8. I would find it difficult to act warmly toward him or her.	
9. I am too hurt and bitter to consider opening my heart to my transgressor.	

Forgiveness Step 6: Next Steps to Sustain Emotional Freedom

Behaviors that promote forgiveness	Unlike me Like me	Actions to review to improve
1. Practicing the disciplines that lead to ongoing spiritual maturity	[1] [2] [3] [4] [5]	Journal Exercise 34: Forgiveness Readiness Survey Revisited Journal Exercise 35a: Love and Grace Meditation
2. Developing the feelings, thoughts, and actions that reveal Christ	[1] [2] [3] [4] [5]	Journal Exercise 35b: Gratitude Journal Journal Exercise 36: Assessing Character Strengths
3. Nurturing a preference for prayer and meditation in all things	[1] [2] [3] [4] [5]	Journal Exercise 37a: Creating a Dynamic Narrative Journal Exercise 37b: A Dynamic Narrative
4. Building a stronger knowledge of God's Word	[1] [2] [3] [4] [5]	Journal Exercise 37c: A Letter to the Transgressor Journal Exercise 38: Reflecting on Growth
5. Nurturing fellowship with like-minded disciples of Christ in whom you can confide your forgiveness journey	[1] [2] [3] [4] [5]	Journal Exercise 39: To Reconcile or Not to Reconcile Journal Exercise 40a: Reflecting on Your Forgiveness Journey Journal Exercise 40b: Forgiveness Tune-Up

Behaviors that inhibit forgiveness	Write in actions to boost behaviors that promote forgiveness:
1. I treat those who treat me badly the same as they treat me.	
2. I cannot usually forgive and forget an insult.	
3. I continue to feel upset when I think of the transgression and the transgressor.	
4. I do not care about the one who transgressed against me.	
5. I feel bitter about many of my relationships.	
6. I recall hurts that fuel my resentment, even after I have forgiven someone.	
7. I do not always forgive those who have hurt me.	
8. I am not a forgiving person.	

Concluding Remarks

You've been through a long journey as you've read this book and completed the journal exercises. I pray you will be blessed as you continue to seek God in your unforgiveness challenges.

I would like to encourage you to consider encouraging others with your journey. Go to my website "forgivenessinaction.com" and share in the community forum there. Here are some things to consider sharing.

- Reflect on the parts of this book that resonated with you and share them.
- Share things you've found helpful that may not be part of any of the exercises or readings in this field guide.
- Note any part of the book that you may not have agreed with and why.

I don't intend for this book to be the final word on learning to forgive, but the beginning of an ongoing dialogue. As each person shares their experiences, thoughts, reflections, and insights we will grow our understanding of how to forgive and how to sustain the progress we've made on our journeys.

Notice I use the word *our* in the previous sentence. I'm part of this equation too. I will benefit from what you share and will share in return with my own insights on my journey. May the Lord bless you on your road to emotional peace, and your journey toward a closer relationship with Him.

Chapter 7 Summary

1. Despite hard work and progress toward forgiveness, many people who have suffered a transgression eventually experience a resurgence of negative feelings, particularly fear and anger. This final chapter reviews pertinent information and provides next steps for returning to a state of peace and positive emotions.

2. Understanding one's temperament—the Intellectual, the Empath, the Gusher, or the Emotional Vampire—improves one's ability to forgive effectively.

3. One's attachment style—secure, fearful-avoidant, dismissive, or preoccupied—is prewired to some extent and also affects how a person forgives.

4. The key to forgiveness is to replace negative thoughts and emotions toward transgressors with positive ones, a process aided by loving-kindness meditation (journal exercise 35a) and expressing gratitude, especially by keeping a gratitude journal (day 35b).

5. Character strengths, such as wisdom, courage, humanity and love, justice, temperance, and transcendence, also support one's quest for positive emotions. See journal exercise 36.

6. If fear and anger arise and threaten to return you to the vicious cycle of rumination, an important next step is to create a dynamic narrative that embraces the possibility of learning and growing from suffering and adversity. See journal exercises 37a, 37b, and 37c.

7. Reasons to reconcile are discussed on day 39, followed by an outline of biblical instructions for approaching reconciliation. Deciding whether to try to reconcile is the focus of journal exercise 39.

8. The chapter ends with a troubleshooting list (reference guide to the contents of *Forty Days to Forgiveness* and accompanying journal exercises) to revisit in order to continue one's forgiveness journey effectively.

Devotional

Dear Father in Heaven,

I have learned on this forgiveness journey that my emotional peace is dependent on my mind's being filled with positive thoughts and intentions, especially toward my transgressor. Trying to stop negative thoughts, though, is usually futile; rather, I must proactively fill my mind as the apostle Paul instructed with whatever is true, honorable, just, pure, lovely, commendable, and excellent.

Lord God, I truly want to be a person who is filled with Your qualities. I humbly ask You to guide me as I submit to you in obedience and develop the godly characteristics of _____.
I know that these qualities in my life will reflect You to everyone around me and perhaps even guide some to You.

Lord, I also ask that You give me wisdom as I determine whether or not to attempt to reconcile with my transgressor. In the words of the prayer of Saint Francis of Assisi, I ask that You "make me an instrument of your peace. Where there is hatred, let me sow _____;
where there is injury, _____; where there is doubt, _____; where there is despair, _____;
where there is darkness, _____; and where there is sadness, _____."

Thank You, Father, for Your presence on this forgiveness journey. May my life bring You glory and honor.

In the name of Your holy Son, amen.

Chapter 7 Endnotes

1   J. Orloff, *Emotional Freedom: Liberate Yourself from Negative Emotions and Transform Your Life* (New York: Harmony, 2009), pp. 99–142. I highly recommend this book for anyone whose emotions seem to run away with them upon perception of any threat or even when there is no threat at all.

2   Romans 7:15–20.

3   Arguably the most comprehensive research synthesis on the topic of attachment is *Becoming Attached: First Relationships and How They Shape Our Capacity to Love* (1998) by Robert Karen. See in particular pp. 394–408.

4   Philippians 4:4–9a.

5   The dorsolateral prefrontal cortex and thalamus.

6   This is a simplified description of a reaction to complete or partial reexperiencing of the transgression. For a more complete description, see Bessel Van Der Kolk, *The Body Keeps the Score: Brain, Mind, and Body in the Healing of Trauma* (New York: Penguin, 2015), pp. 66–73.

7   E. L. Worthington and S. J. Sandage, "How Attachment Affects Spirituality and Why Spirituality Transformation May Be Needed to Forgive," in *Forgiveness and Spirituality in Psychotherapy: A Relational Approach* (Washington, DC: American Psychological Association, 2016), 70–76, 79.

8   Often attributed to the thirteenth-century Saint Francis of Assisi and referred to as "the prayer of Saint Francis of Assisi." In its modern form, this prayer was first seen in 1912 as "a beautiful prayer to say during Mass" in the December 1912 issue of the small devotional French publication *The League of the Holy Mass*. It was popularized in 1915 by Marquis Stanislas de La Rochethulon, president of the Anglo-French association Souvenir Normand. At that time this prayer was referred to as "a work of peace and justice, inspired by the testament of William the Conqueror, who is considered to be the ancestor of all the royal families of Europe." La Rochethulon sent this prayer to Pope Benedict XV in the midst of World War I.

9   Hebrews 4:15–16.

10 Matthew 6:34.

11 Ephesians 5:20.

12 Psalms 106:1, 107:1, 118:19.

13 Psalms 97:12, 105:1, 109:30, 136:3.

14 M. E. P. Seligman, *Flourish: A Visionary New Understanding of Happiness and Well-Being* (New York: Atria, 2011), pp. 243–65.

15 Proverbs 9:10.

16 Psalms 56:3–4; Joshua 1:9–11; Isaiah 41:10–14.

17 Ephesians 6:13–18.

18 Matthew 5:16; Luke 11:34.

19 James 4:1–2.

20 Proverbs 21:15.

21 Galatians 5:23; Titus 2:12; 2 Peter 1:6; Romans 13:14.

22 Romans 12:1–2; Colossians 3:1–4.

23 If do not have access to a computer, use the survey at the end of this chapter to identify the character features of your best self by giving the survey to at least three people who know you well and asking them to honestly answer the questions. Then use their answers to fill in the following exercise.

24 E. L. Worthington, "The Path to Forgiveness: Six Practical Sections for Becoming a More Forgiving Person," http://www.evworthington-forgiveness.com/diy-workbooks.

25 Hebrews 12:1–17; Romans 8:18–30; 2 Corinthians 1:3–12, 4:7–5:5, 11:24–12:10.

26 1 Peter 1:7.

27 1 Peter 1:6–7.

28 Hebrews 5:8.

29 Hebrews 2:18, 4:15.

30 Romans 8:17; 2 Corinthians 4:16–17.

31 Romans 5:3–5.

32 A good description of some steps to take in reconciliation can be found in *Forgiveness and Reconciliation: Theory and Practice* by Everett L. Worthington Jr. (2006), pp. 197–221.

33 Matthew 18:15–17.

34 1 Peter 3:11.

35 An excellent primer on making peace from a biblical perspective is Ken Sand's book *The Peace Maker: A Biblical Guide to Resolving Personal Conflict* (Grand Rapids, MI: Baker Books, 2004).

Index

A

Abuse 20, 35, 38, 48, 65, 67, 70, 71, 80, 85, 113, 125, 131, 132, 133, 137, 145, 165, 168, 207, 331, 384

Accountability 8, 77, 136, 137, 175, 305, 348, 385, 387

Acknowledging 10, 27, 51, 53, 54, 55, 56, 60, 63, 64, 69, 71, 72, 73, 74, 78, 79, 84, 93, 94, 97, 98, 101, 104, 114, 153, 255, 308, 318, 319, 329, 356, 357, 361, 389, 390

Action 9, 10, 11, 13, 15, 16, 18, 23, 24, 26, 27, 28, 38, 54, 56, 57, 59, 60, 61, 62, 64, 65, 66, 67, 68, 72, 74, 75, 76, 77, 79, 80, 81, 82, 83, 85, 86, 87, 90, 91, 93, 94, 95, 96, 97, 101, 102, 107, 108, 113, 117, 118, 120, 123, 124, 127, 128, 129, 130, 134, 135, 136, 137, 139, 149, 151, 155, 156, 158, 159, 165, 166, 171, 177, 180, 182, 184, 191, 196, 203, 206, 208, 209, 220, 227, 228, 253, 270, 281, 284, 287, 288, 304, 305, 306, 307, 309, 310, 311, 316, 317, 322, 323, 324, 326, 345, 348, 351, 352, 355, 361, 362, 363, 367, 375, 376, 380, 385, 386, 387, 389, 390, 391, 392, 393, 394, 395, 396, 397, 398, 399, 400, 401

    Taking action 86, 101, 117, 118, 362, 380

Aggressive 77, 80, 101, 119, 175, 177, 196, 349

Altruism 156, 221, 298, 301

Amygdala 72, 351, 352

Anger xv, xviii, 7, 16, 33, 34, 35, 36, 37, 38, 42, 45, 46, 54, 59, 61, 64, 66, 70, 72, 73, 74, 75, 76, 77, 78, 80, 81, 84, 88, 90, 93, 97, 101, 103, 104, 112, 113, 119, 120, 121, 122, 124, 131, 132, 133, 138, 139, 143, 145, 153, 159, 166, 167, 168, 174, 175, 176, 177, 178, 179, 180, 181, 184, 190, 196, 197, 198, 199, 206, 211, 221, 223, 224, 234, 252, 257, 284, 288, 289, 341, 349, 352, 358, 367, 374, 383, 394, 403

Assertive 77, 80, 101, 108, 175, 177, 196, 390, 392

Attitudes 26, 37, 54, 75, 79, 80, 211, 212, 223, 226, 282, 285, 358, 368

B

Beatitudes 103, 363

Beneficence 7, 108, 109, 114, 130, 179, 181, 189, 217

Bitterness xviii, 7, 20, 27, 38, 42, 59, 76, 93, 97, 114, 119, 124, 131, 138, 139, 158, 179, 181, 211, 338, 356

Boundaries 15, 24, 35, 45, 48, 49, 77, 85, 125, 127, 130, 134, 142, 168, 175, 282

Brother 12, 16, 17, 19, 20, 24, 33, 37, 91, 101, 105, 114, 131, 132, 138, 150, 154, 182, 204, 211, 219, 225, 229, 252, 266, 284, 287, 306, 332, 350, 378, 379, 380

C

Christ ii, xviii, xix, xx, 3, 5, 7, 8, 9, 11, 19, 20, 21, 23, 24, 25, 35, 36, 37, 38, 44, 53, 66, 74, 76, 77, 109, 111, 112, 114, 131, 132, 133, 142, 143, 149, 150, 153, 154, 155, 157, 158, 159, 160, 164, 166, 174, 176, 179, 180, 181, 183, 184, 195, 196, 197, 201, 203, 204, 205, 206, 207, 208, 210, 211, 212, 213, 214, 215, 216, 217, 220, 221, 223, 224, 225, 230, 231, 233, 234, 244, 246, 249, 250, 251, 253, 254, 256, 258, 262, 263, 264, 265, 266, 268, 270, 271, 281, 283, 284, 289, 292, 298, 304, 306, 307,

310, 311, 317, 330, 331, 332, 335, 337, 338, 345, 346, 348, 357, 361, 362, 363, 368, 373, 377, 379, 380, 396, 400

Atoning blood of 158

Christlike 10, 87, 112, 151, 153, 154, 158, 174, 175, 203, 211, 212, 214, 217, 221, 223, 224, 230, 231, 243, 246, 253, 262, 265, 270, 283, 284, 288, 289, 290, 291, 292, 298, 300, 306, 309, 314, 332, 335, 377, 378

Commandments iii, 4, 17, 21, 32, 111, 158, 205, 206, 207, 214, 215, 237, 289, 298, 305, 359, 381

Grace 7, 16, 23, 24, 25, 40, 42, 43, 60, 101, 111, 112, 115, 147, 156, 158, 160, 164, 179, 182, 183, 193, 195, 205, 219, 220, 221, 224, 225, 229, 232, 250, 251, 261, 282, 292, 304, 306, 310, 313, 331, 346, 347, 356, 357, 359, 377, 380, 400

Greatest commandment 111, 298, 305, 359

Heart like 207, 214

Intimate relationship with 111

Light of 26, 77, 111, 124, 157, 176, 179, 196, 201, 203, 207, 221, 251, 253, 286, 304, 306, 317, 337, 338

Lord xiii, xx, 1, 4, 5, 12, 17, 19, 25, 27, 33, 36, 37, 38, 42, 47, 51, 102, 105, 109, 111, 112, 130, 131, 143, 150, 154, 155, 156, 157, 164, 178, 195, 196, 197, 204, 205, 212, 213, 214, 218, 219, 220, 223, 224, 225, 229, 233, 237, 246, 253, 254, 256, 257, 258, 262, 264, 265, 268, 270, 271, 281, 283, 288, 291, 292, 296, 297, 300, 304, 305, 306, 307, 311, 317, 328, 329, 330, 336, 337, 338, 341, 350, 352, 353, 357, 361, 362, 363, 373, 377, 402, 404

Mercy iii, 7, 12, 20, 23, 24, 25, 43, 53, 75, 101, 102, 111, 112, 115, 131, 134, 138, 147, 164, 180, 189, 217, 220, 221, 223, 224, 231, 232, 261, 279, 307, 347, 363, 373

Peace of xv, 29, 38, 57, 93, 108, 110, 112, 123, 135, 142, 153, 155, 195, 196, 197, 209, 212, 224, 233, 282, 283, 288, 292, 306, 338, 350

Relationship with ii, 3, 8, 15, 17, 19, 20, 21, 23, 29, 31, 33, 35, 38, 43, 54, 55, 56, 64, 65, 66, 67, 71, 89, 90, 108, 110, 111, 130, 131, 132, 157, 158, 195, 204, 214, 215, 220, 224, 228, 244, 254, 262, 263, 265, 268, 289, 319, 330, 331, 368, 378, 381, 382, 383, 397, 402

Cognitive processing 208

Committing 10, 18, 107, 114, 117, 120, 135, 141, 151, 153, 155, 166, 174, 195, 229, 306, 318, 320, 329, 389, 392, 396

Compassion ii, xv, 7, 9, 10, 19, 23, 27, 38, 87, 92, 94, 102, 109, 112, 113, 114, 138, 149, 157, 163, 179, 180, 181, 189, 196, 197, 203, 206, 214, 217, 220, 221, 224, 233, 257, 268, 293, 300, 304, 305, 307, 308, 309, 310, 311, 314, 317, 349, 356, 371, 394

Coping 35, 36, 56, 59, 61, 64, 80, 84, 85, 86, 87, 88, 89, 90, 91, 92, 93, 95, 101, 104, 108, 109, 114, 117, 130, 142, 144, 150, 153, 159, 163, 164, 165, 166, 167, 168, 169, 170, 171, 172, 173, 189, 196, 197, 199, 225, 262, 308, 309, 320, 321, 339, 349, 351, 370, 384, 387, 390, 392, 394

Emotional regulation 85, 91, 92, 262, 308

Positive iii, 7, 10, 27, 32, 35, 55, 56, 60, 64, 77, 80, 81, 84, 85, 86, 87, 90, 91, 92, 94, 95, 96, 107, 108, 109, 110, 117, 120, 123, 125, 129, 130, 131, 134, 142, 143, 149, 150, 154, 157, 158, 159, 163, 164, 165, 166, 169, 170, 171, 172, 173, 174, 175, 179, 180, 181, 182, 183, 184, 189, 190, 191, 196, 197, 203, 221, 222, 223, 251, 252, 253, 262, 264, 270, 285, 288, 290, 291, 292, 293, 296, 297, 298, 307, 308, 309, 311, 315, 316, 320, 321, 322, 323, 324, 325, 327, 330, 341, 346, 349, 350, 356, 357, 361, 362, 363, 367, 368, 372, 376, 377, 378, 389, 390, 392, 394, 403, 404

Processes 16, 110, 123, 139, 157, 163, 164, 222, 233, 389

Reframing 34, 82, 156, 166, 316

Stress 5, 8, 12, 32, 48, 59, 60, 61, 74, 80, 84, 85, 86, 87, 90, 92, 97, 104, 108, 113, 117, 138, 145, 150, 163, 164, 165, 167, 170, 183, 184, 189, 192, 196, 197, 199, 213, 293, 313, 316, 349, 351, 352, 357

D

Deciding 24, 79, 112, 119, 140, 153, 208, 231, 331, 392, 403

Decision xix, 28, 30, 89, 92, 95, 109, 114, 128, 130, 135, 136, 137, 151, 153, 166, 191, 209, 210, 212, 222, 246, 285, 307, 333, 354, 357, 358, 363, 375, 378

Decisional forgiveness 30, 92, 129, 153, 352, 354

To try to forgive 10, 12, 28, 63, 107, 109, 114, 115, 128, 135, 136, 141, 142, 151, 153, 174, 180, 281, 392

Demonizing 60, 120

Depression xviii, 33, 64, 73, 74, 84, 88, 120, 289, 293, 357

Devotional 11, 44, 102, 143, 197, 241, 243, 245, 247, 271, 338, 404, 405

Distributive 123

E

Emotion-focused 85, 86, 87, 101, 165, 166, 169, 196

Emotions xv, xviii, 3, 5, 26, 31, 32, 48, 56, 57, 59, 60, 61, 64, 65, 66, 72, 73, 74, 75, 76, 77, 78, 79, 80, 81, 85, 86, 87, 88, 94, 97, 101, 103, 108, 113, 115, 118, 124, 129, 145, 153, 159, 163, 165, 166, 168, 169, 175, 178, 179, 181, 189, 190, 191, 196, 197, 203, 208, 212, 222, 223, 249, 252, 253, 257, 259, 287, 306, 308, 309, 311, 316, 340, 347, 348, 351, 355, 356, 358, 361, 367, 368, 370, 383, 390, 403, 405

Emotional freedom xviii, xx, 5, 7, 11, 56, 103, 109, 120, 153, 174, 197, 215, 303, 305, 306, 343, 345, 346, 347, 358, 400, 405

Emotional healing 10, 345, 346

Emotional peace 6, 12, 15, 26, 28, 29, 36, 57, 108, 110, 111, 117, 118, 124, 125, 126, 213, 214, 220, 336, 356, 402, 404

Emotional release 378

Fear 35, 36, 38, 59, 61, 64, 66, 72, 73, 74, 77, 78, 80, 81, 84, 88, 103, 113, 115, 120, 121, 126, 153, 159, 165, 166, 174, 175, 177, 179, 180, 181, 190, 208, 223, 283, 284, 301, 352, 357, 361, 362, 367, 378, 383, 403

Triggers 36, 59, 73, 74, 84, 94, 113, 119, 124, 163, 164, 165, 208, 252, 316, 351, 352

Empathy xv, 7, 8, 9, 16, 27, 60, 92, 94, 102, 108, 109, 113, 114, 120, 130, 149, 150, 156, 157, 166, 179, 180, 181, 189, 190, 191, 192, 194, 196, 200, 203, 206, 212, 215, 221, 273, 282, 283, 287, 293, 300, 303, 306, 307, 308, 309, 310, 311, 312, 314, 315, 317, 331, 332, 335, 337, 338, 341, 371, 374, 376, 394, 398

Enemies 3, 19, 20, 23, 26, 28, 33, 110, 126, 131, 175, 199, 215, 216, 288, 303, 304, 306, 330, 331

Love of xiii, 24, 109, 125, 131, 197, 204, 206, 220, 221, 259, 304, 361, 363, 368, 373

Pray for 3, 18, 20, 42, 49, 53, 131, 182, 206, 207, 225, 255, 260, 303, 314, 331, 352

Envy 42, 59, 61, 73, 93, 97, 112, 119, 153, 211, 224, 284, 383

F

Fear 35, 36, 38, 59, 61, 64, 66, 72, 73, 74, 77, 78, 80, 81, 84, 88, 103, 113, 115, 120, 121, 126, 153, 159, 165, 166, 174, 175, 177, 179, 180, 181, 190, 208, 223, 283, 284, 301, 352, 357, 361, 362, 367, 378, 383, 403

Feeling iii, 5, 7, 10, 16, 18, 26, 27, 29, 31, 32, 35, 36, 39, 40, 53, 56, 57, 59, 60, 65, 66, 69, 72, 73, 74, 78, 80, 81, 86, 87, 90, 91, 93, 94, 95, 96, 97, 100, 101, 108, 109, 110, 113, 114, 116, 118, 119, 120, 124, 125, 129, 136, 149, 153, 158, 159, 163, 166, 168, 174, 175, 177, 180, 181, 184, 187, 190, 191, 194, 197, 199, 203,

208, 209, 210, 211, 212, 217, 220, 221, 222, 223, 230, 249, 251, 252, 253, 270, 281, 286, 287, 298, 301, 303, 308, 309, 310, 314, 316, 327, 331, 341, 345, 348, 349, 351, 352, 355, 356, 357, 360, 362, 367, 368, 369, 373, 374, 375, 380, 384, 389, 390, 396, 398, 400, 403

Feelings iii, 5, 7, 10, 16, 18, 26, 27, 29, 31, 32, 35, 36, 39, 40, 53, 56, 57, 59, 60, 65, 66, 69, 72, 73, 74, 78, 80, 81, 86, 87, 90, 91, 93, 94, 95, 96, 97, 100, 101, 108, 109, 110, 113, 114, 116, 118, 119, 120, 124, 125, 129, 136, 149, 153, 158, 159, 163, 166, 168, 174, 175, 177, 180, 181, 184, 187, 190, 191, 194, 197, 199, 203, 208, 209, 210, 211, 212, 217, 220, 221, 222, 223, 230, 249, 251, 252, 253, 270, 281, 286, 287, 298, 301, 303, 308, 309, 310, 314, 316, 327, 331, 341, 345, 348, 349, 351, 352, 355, 356, 357, 360, 362, 367, 368, 369, 373, 374, 375, 380, 384, 389, 390, 396, 398, 400, 403

Anger xv, xviii, 7, 16, 33, 34, 35, 36, 37, 38, 42, 45, 46, 54, 59, 61, 64, 66, 70, 72, 73, 74, 75, 76, 77, 78, 80, 81, 84, 88, 90, 93, 97, 101, 103, 104, 112, 113, 119, 120, 121, 122, 124, 131, 132, 133, 138, 139, 143, 145, 153, 159, 166, 167, 168, 174, 175, 176, 177, 178, 179, 180, 181, 184, 190, 196, 197, 198, 199, 206, 211, 221, 223, 224, 234, 252, 257, 284, 288, 289, 341, 349, 352, 358, 367, 374, 383, 394, 403

Negative xv, xviii, 7, 8, 10, 28, 31, 33, 36, 39, 40, 42, 43, 59, 60, 61, 64, 65, 71, 73, 74, 75, 77, 80, 81, 84, 85, 86, 87, 88, 89, 90, 91, 92, 93, 94, 95, 96, 97, 101, 103, 108, 109, 110, 113, 117, 118, 119, 120, 121, 122, 123, 124, 129, 130, 131, 134, 136, 139, 142, 143, 149, 153, 154, 157, 158, 159, 163, 164, 165, 169, 170, 174, 175, 179, 180, 181, 182, 189, 190, 195, 196, 197, 203, 204, 206, 211, 212, 221, 223, 224, 249, 251, 252, 253, 264, 270, 284, 285, 286, 287, 288, 289, 290, 291, 292, 307, 308, 309, 311, 315, 316, 322, 323, 324, 327, 330, 345, 350, 351, 352, 355, 356, 357, 358, 363, 367, 368, 372, 377, 378, 381, 389, 390, 394, 403, 404, 405

Positive iii, 7, 10, 27, 32, 35, 55, 56, 60, 64, 77, 80, 81, 84, 85, 86, 87, 90, 91, 92, 94, 95, 96, 107, 108, 109, 110, 117, 120, 123, 125, 129, 130, 131, 134, 142, 143, 149, 150, 154, 157, 158, 159, 163, 164, 165, 166, 169, 170, 171, 172, 173, 174, 175, 179, 180, 181, 182, 183, 184, 189, 190, 191, 196, 197, 203, 221, 222, 223, 251, 252, 253, 262, 264, 270, 285, 288, 290, 291, 292, 293, 296, 297, 298, 307, 308, 309, 311, 315, 316, 320, 321, 322, 323, 324, 325, 327, 330, 341, 346, 349, 350, 356, 357, 361, 362, 363, 367, 368, 372, 376, 377, 378, 389, 390, 392, 394, 403, 404

Triggers for 252

Fellowship xix, 10, 11, 19, 20, 21, 112, 132, 154, 174, 203, 204, 213, 215, 220, 221, 222, 223, 224, 227, 229, 234, 235, 243, 244, 262, 263, 264, 265, 266, 267, 268, 269, 270, 276, 283, 285, 298, 328, 346, 356, 378, 379, 380, 396, 400

Works of the flesh
Unenforceable rules 56, 59, 61, 79, 83, 93, 101, 150, 163, 164, 190, 249, 309, 316, 383, 387, 389, 390

Forgive i, iii, xv, xviii, xix, xx, 1, 3, 4, 5, 6, 7, 9, 10, 12, 13, 14, 15, 16, 18, 19, 20, 21, 23, 24, 25, 26, 28, 29, 32, 33, 35, 36, 37, 38, 39, 40, 43, 44, 45, 46, 55, 57, 63, 87, 90, 92, 102, 103, 105, 107, 108, 109, 110, 111, 112, 113, 114, 115, 116, 117, 125, 128, 129, 130, 131, 132, 135, 136, 137, 138, 139, 140, 141, 142, 144, 145, 151, 153, 154, 155, 157, 158, 161, 163, 166, 171, 172, 173, 174, 179, 180, 184, 187, 188, 196, 197, 198, 200, 204, 205, 206, 207, 209, 213, 222, 224, 227, 230, 233, 249, 255, 257, 264, 270, 275, 281, 283, 284, 285, 286, 293, 300, 303, 304, 305, 306, 307, 308, 316, 320, 321, 322, 323, 324, 326, 330, 331, 332, 337, 338, 341, 346, 352, 354, 367, 375, 378, 381, 389, 391, 392, 393, 401, 402, 403, 405

GPS 61, 101, 390

Trying to 10, 34, 55, 60, 73, 77, 87, 88, 90, 101, 107, 108, 109, 110, 111, 113, 116, 117, 120, 125, 129, 135, 138, 140, 141, 166, 175, 184, 222, 232, 258, 263, 267, 270, 284, 291, 300, 305, 315, 350, 389, 392, 404

Forgiveness i, ii, iii, v, xiii, xv, xvi, xvii, xviii, xix, xx, 3, 4, 5, 6, 7, 8, 9, 10, 11, 12, 13, 14, 15, 16, 17, 18, 19, 20, 21, 22, 23, 24, 25, 26, 27, 28, 29, 30, 31, 32, 33, 34, 35, 36, 37, 38, 39, 43, 44, 45, 46, 47, 48, 49, 54, 55, 56, 57, 60, 61, 63, 65, 76, 85, 88, 89, 90, 91, 92, 93, 94, 96, 102, 103, 104, 107, 108, 109, 110, 111, 112, 113, 114, 115, 116, 117, 118, 123, 124, 125, 126, 128, 129, 130, 131, 132, 133, 134, 135, 136, 137, 138, 139, 141, 142, 143, 144, 145, 149, 150, 151, 153, 155, 156, 157, 158, 159, 160, 161, 163, 164, 170, 175, 178, 179, 180, 181, 183, 184, 189, 190, 191, 196, 197, 198, 199, 200, 201, 203, 204, 205, 207, 209, 210, 211, 214, 215, 220, 221, 222, 223, 224, 227, 230, 231, 232, 233, 234, 236, 237, 243, 244, 249, 250, 252, 254, 255, 257, 258, 262, 264, 265, 266, 267, 270, 273, 274, 275, 276, 279, 281, 282, 283, 284, 285, 286, 287, 288, 289, 292, 293, 298, 300, 303, 304, 305, 306, 307, 308, 309, 310, 311, 312, 316, 318, 322, 323, 324, 325, 326, 327, 330, 331, 332, 335, 336, 337, 338, 339, 340, 341, 345, 346, 347, 348, 350, 351, 352, 354, 355, 356, 357, 360, 363, 364, 365, 366, 367, 368, 369, 372, 373, 375, 376, 377, 378, 379, 384, 388, 389, 390, 391, 392, 393, 394, 395, 396, 397, 398, 399, 400, 401, 403, 404, 405, 406

Dispositional 9

Situational 65

Trait iii, 9, 112, 179, 286, 290, 303, 339, 356, 361, 363

Fruit of the spirit 64, 112, 153, 154, 157, 184, 223, 231, 234, 283, 284

G

God ii, xiii, xv, xviii, xix, xx, 3, 4, 5, 6, 7, 8, 9, 10, 11, 12, 13, 16, 17, 18, 19, 20, 21, 22, 23, 24, 25, 26, 27, 28, 32, 33, 35, 36, 37, 38, 40, 43, 44, 48, 53, 54, 55, 56, 64, 65, 74, 75, 76, 77, 92, 101, 102, 108, 110, 111, 112, 113, 114, 115, 120, 125, 126, 131, 132, 133, 136, 141, 142, 143, 147, 149, 150, 151, 154, 155, 156, 157, 158, 159, 160, 164, 166, 169, 174, 175, 176, 179, 180, 183, 193, 194, 195, 196, 197, 201, 203, 204, 205, 206, 207, 208, 209, 210, 211, 212, 213, 214, 215, 216, 217, 218, 220, 221, 222, 223, 224, 225, 226, 227, 228, 230, 231, 232, 233, 234, 235, 240, 242, 243, 244, 245, 246, 247, 249, 250, 251, 252, 253, 254, 255, 256, 257, 258, 259, 260, 261, 262, 263, 264, 265, 266, 267, 268, 270, 271, 274, 276, 279, 281, 282, 283, 284, 285, 288, 289, 291, 292, 293, 296, 297, 298, 299, 300, 302, 303, 304, 305, 306, 307, 309, 310, 311, 313, 314, 317, 318, 326, 327, 328, 330, 331, 332, 337, 338, 341, 345, 347, 350, 352, 356, 357, 358, 359, 360, 361, 362, 363, 368, 373, 374, 377, 378, 379, 380, 381, 390, 392, 394, 396, 398, 400, 402, 404

Accountability 8, 77, 136, 137, 175, 305, 348, 385, 387

Godly perspective 10, 61, 101, 107, 147, 149, 153, 154, 155, 158, 210, 318, 322, 329, 394

God's works 141, 243

His Word xiii, xix, 28, 154, 159, 205, 214, 221, 230, 238, 243, 244, 257, 361, 362

Plan of salvation 115, 378

Punishment 26, 108, 118, 120, 123, 126, 138, 306

Gratitude xv, 156, 179, 180, 184, 194, 200, 226, 241, 244, 247, 255, 258, 261, 270, 281, 282, 292, 293, 294, 302, 310, 337, 338, 339, 340, 346, 356, 357, 358, 360, 363, 373, 376, 398, 400, 403

Journal xvii, xx, 9, 10, 11, 12, 13, 14, 21, 22, 28,
29, 30, 40, 41, 43, 48, 61, 68, 69, 71, 73,
78, 83, 89, 97, 98, 99, 100, 101, 103, 104,
110, 115, 116, 121, 127, 128, 134, 140,
141, 142, 145, 160, 168, 169, 171, 176,
177, 180, 181, 182, 185, 192, 194, 196,
199, 200, 217, 218, 225, 226, 229, 231,
234, 236, 237, 240, 241, 244, 245, 246,
247, 260, 261, 266, 267, 274, 275, 290,
291, 292, 293, 294, 301, 302, 309, 310,
312, 314, 318, 320, 322, 325, 327, 334,
335, 339, 340, 354, 355, 357, 358, 359,
360, 363, 365, 369, 373, 374, 376, 377,
382, 384, 389, 390, 392, 394, 396, 398,
400, 402, 403
  Practicing 166, 200, 214, 220, 221, 345,
352, 400
Grudges xviii, 7, 17, 34, 36, 42, 48, 60, 62, 76, 93,
97, 119, 136, 138, 139, 145, 180, 204, 224,
385, 397

H

Happiness 8, 64, 80, 102, 104, 129, 157, 174, 183,
184, 194, 199, 200, 210, 255, 275, 285, 292,
293, 337, 340, 358, 405
Hatred 37, 42, 76, 93, 97, 119, 179, 181, 195, 210,
211, 352, 404
Heart ii, xiii, xv, xvii, xviii, xx, 4, 9, 10, 11, 12, 17,
20, 21, 26, 28, 32, 36, 37, 38, 42, 44, 64, 72,
74, 75, 76, 84, 108, 109, 111, 112, 114, 126,
131, 141, 150, 151, 154, 155, 157, 158, 175,
180, 196, 197, 201, 203, 204, 205, 206, 207,
208, 209, 210, 211, 212, 213, 214, 215, 216,
217, 218, 219, 220, 221, 222, 223, 224, 225,
226, 229, 230, 231, 233, 244, 245, 249, 252,
254, 255, 256, 257, 258, 259, 264, 270, 279,
281, 282, 283, 284, 287, 288, 292, 296, 298,
300, 302, 303, 304, 305, 306, 307, 315, 318,
327, 334, 335, 337, 338, 350, 351, 359, 361,
368, 377, 389, 398, 399
  Spiritual heart 208, 212
Hostility 18, 34, 42, 59, 84, 92, 93, 97, 119, 124,
165, 166, 168, 179, 180, 181, 367

I

Intentions 36, 48, 59, 60, 61, 67, 77, 81, 85, 86, 88,
91, 92, 93, 94, 95, 97, 101, 102, 108, 109, 117,
118, 119, 120, 122, 124, 125, 130, 134, 136,
139, 142, 143, 149, 150, 153, 154, 157, 158,
159, 163, 164, 165, 174, 179, 180, 181, 182,
189, 190, 191, 196, 197, 204, 206, 211, 212,
221, 222, 223, 224, 249, 251, 252, 258, 264,
284, 287, 288, 289, 290, 293, 306, 308, 309,
310, 311, 316, 322, 323, 324, 330, 341, 346,
367, 372, 376, 377, 378, 381, 390, 394, 404
  Negative xv, xviii, 7, 8, 10, 28, 31, 33, 36, 39,
40, 42, 43, 59, 60, 61, 64, 65, 71, 73, 74,
75, 77, 80, 81, 84, 85, 86, 87, 88, 89, 90,
91, 92, 93, 94, 95, 96, 97, 101, 103, 108,
109, 110, 113, 117, 118, 119, 120, 121,
122, 123, 124, 129, 130, 131, 134, 136,
139, 142, 143, 149, 153, 154, 157, 158,
159, 163, 164, 165, 169, 170, 174, 175,
179, 180, 181, 182, 189, 190, 195, 196,
197, 203, 204, 206, 211, 212, 221, 223,
224, 249, 251, 252, 253, 264, 270, 284,
285, 286, 287, 288, 289, 290, 291, 292,
307, 308, 309, 311, 315, 316, 322, 323,
324, 327, 330, 345, 350, 351, 352, 355,
356, 357, 358, 363, 367, 368, 372, 377,
378, 381, 389, 390, 394, 403, 404, 405
  Positive iii, 7, 10, 27, 32, 35, 55, 56, 60, 64,
77, 80, 81, 84, 85, 86, 87, 90, 91, 92,
94, 95, 96, 107, 108, 109, 110, 117, 120,
123, 125, 129, 130, 131, 134, 142, 143,
149, 150, 154, 157, 158, 159, 163, 164,
165, 166, 169, 170, 171, 172, 173, 174,
175, 179, 180, 181, 182, 183, 184, 189,
190, 191, 196, 197, 203, 221, 222, 223,
251, 252, 253, 262, 264, 270, 285, 288,
290, 291, 292, 293, 296, 297, 298, 307,
308, 309, 311, 315, 316, 320, 321, 322,
323, 324, 325, 327, 330, 341, 346, 349,
350, 356, 357, 361, 362, 363, 367, 368,
372, 376, 377, 378, 389, 390, 392, 394,
403, 404

Internalization 198, 270

Internalize 154, 203, 204, 206, 221, 270, 271

Internalizing 10, 154, 200, 201, 203, 204, 220,
221, 225, 230, 243, 249, 262, 270, 318, 326,
389, 396

J

Justice 6, 26, 36, 37, 42, 56, 68, 75, 93, 96, 97, 99,
108, 109, 117, 120, 123, 124, 125, 126, 127,
136, 137, 142, 144, 189, 204, 256, 257, 287,
303, 305, 316, 330, 351, 362, 373, 385, 387,
392, 397, 403, 405
Civil 123, 127
criminal 25, 115, 123, 127
Fairness, 108, 109, 120, 123, 125, 126, 127,
136, 137, 142, 189, 362, 373, 392
Gap iii, 36, 65, 66, 124
Safety 38, 66, 109, 120, 121, 122, 123, 125,
127, 131, 132, 136, 137, 142, 297, 301,
382, 383, 387, 392

L

Ladder of inference 95

Love ii, xiii, xviii, 3, 4, 5, 7, 8, 17, 19, 20, 21, 23,
24, 25, 27, 33, 37, 38, 42, 43, 60, 64, 66, 69,
76, 94, 102, 103, 109, 110, 111, 112, 114, 115,
125, 130, 131, 133, 137, 149, 153, 155, 156,
157, 158, 160, 174, 175, 179, 180, 181, 183,
194, 195, 196, 197, 199, 204, 206, 212, 214,
215, 217, 219, 220, 221, 223, 224, 226, 229,
230, 231, 232, 233, 237, 246, 252, 253, 254,
256, 259, 263, 264, 265, 266, 267, 268, 281,
282, 283, 284, 285, 286, 289, 292, 293, 296,
297, 298, 301, 303, 304, 305, 306, 307, 311,
314, 317, 328, 332, 335, 337, 338, 341, 346,
347, 349, 352, 353, 356, 359, 361, 362, 363,
367, 368, 373, 376, 377, 378, 380, 381, 394,
398, 399, 400, 403, 405
Loving kindness
And meditation 203, 221, 262, 307, 317, 345,
359, 396, 400

M

Meaning-focused 85, 87, 90, 91, 101, 165, 166, 169,
196, 308

Meditation i, 112, 165, 174, 194, 195, 203, 204, 209,
215, 220, 221, 222, 224, 226, 229, 235, 243,
244, 245, 246, 247, 248, 256, 262, 263, 270,
283, 307, 317, 345, 356, 359, 396, 400, 403

Motivation 28, 75, 121, 122, 124, 135, 156, 209,
303, 317, 358, 368, 392

Myths 8, 56, 90, 142

N

Narrative 60, 98, 243, 252, 327, 346, 356, 367, 368,
369, 373, 376, 400, 403
Rewriting 34, 318, 398

Neighbor 3, 5, 17, 19, 20, 23, 33, 37, 111, 215, 284,
305, 330, 332, 359

O

Offense xvii, 5, 9, 10, 13, 14, 15, 18, 20, 24, 26, 28,
29, 31, 33, 34, 35, 36, 37, 40, 41, 42, 44, 54,
55, 56, 59, 60, 65, 67, 70, 71, 73, 77, 81, 82,
84, 87, 88, 91, 92, 94, 96, 98, 99, 101, 108,
109, 113, 115, 118, 119, 125, 126, 129, 130,
131, 134, 138, 140, 141, 150, 156, 160, 163,
166, 168, 169, 175, 221, 225, 226, 244, 249,
252, 308, 310, 311, 313, 316, 317, 331, 332,
335, 340, 351, 352, 355, 364, 378, 380, 395
Hating the 115
Repeating 120, 125, 130, 239, 246, 350

Opening ii, 10, 33, 244, 279, 281, 282, 283, 292,
296, 307, 316, 318, 327, 330, 334, 337, 389,
398, 399

P

Passive-aggressive 77, 101, 175, 177, 196, 349

Personality 48, 200, 212, 221, 274, 339, 347,
350, 364

Prayer xv, 12, 22, 24, 25, 33, 37, 42, 44, 48, 53, 75,
76, 102, 109, 112, 136, 141, 143, 150, 165,
166, 174, 182, 184, 192, 195, 197, 203, 204,

206, 207, 214, 215, 218, 220, 221, 222, 224, 226, 229, 235, 237, 243, 249, 251, 252, 253, 254, 255, 256, 257, 258, 259, 260, 261, 262, 263, 264, 266, 268, 270, 271, 275, 276, 283, 288, 289, 291, 292, 293, 297, 300, 307, 309, 311, 312, 314, 317, 318, 328, 329, 332, 341, 345, 347, 350, 352, 356, 357, 359, 362, 376, 377, 396, 398, 400, 404, 405

Procedural 123

R

Reconciliation ii, 5, 8, 9, 15, 16, 19, 20, 35, 38, 56, 91, 96, 102, 103, 104, 108, 109, 113, 115, 131, 137, 198, 199, 282, 306, 310, 330, 331, 332, 333, 334, 335, 337, 339, 340, 341, 346, 378, 379, 381, 382, 383, 384, 386, 387, 398, 403, 406

Relationship ii, xviii, 3, 4, 8, 9, 14, 15, 16, 17, 19, 20, 21, 23, 24, 29, 31, 32, 33, 34, 35, 38, 43, 45, 48, 49, 54, 55, 56, 64, 65, 66, 67, 71, 84, 87, 89, 90, 91, 92, 94, 108, 110, 111, 118, 125, 129, 130, 131, 132, 134, 142, 145, 157, 158, 184, 185, 189, 190, 195, 200, 204, 211, 214, 215, 220, 224, 227, 228, 232, 233, 244, 254, 259, 262, 263, 265, 268, 274, 275, 285, 289, 294, 301, 309, 310, 319, 330, 331, 341, 346, 349, 350, 354, 357, 362, 368, 378, 379, 381, 382, 383, 397, 401, 402, 405

   Broken xvii, xviii, 9, 16, 123, 164, 250, 256, 331, 381

   Intimate 66, 71, 111, 131, 301

   Peaceful 70, 108, 170, 264, 358

   Reconciling 9, 16, 24, 91, 115, 131, 134, 333, 334, 379, 380, 381, 382, 383, 385, 386, 387

   With God xv, xviii, 3, 5, 19, 20, 21, 23, 27, 33, 38, 43, 55, 64, 65, 108, 110, 111, 114, 157, 164, 195, 206, 207, 213, 216, 222, 226, 227, 228, 230, 247, 253, 254, 255, 258, 261, 262, 263, 265, 276, 288, 289, 300, 304, 326, 328, 330, 331, 341

Repression 88, 94

Resentment 7, 35, 42, 59, 86, 90, 93, 94, 97, 119, 120, 121, 122, 124, 179, 181, 206, 221, 288, 346, 356, 401

Restorative 123, 124

Restoring equality 125

Retributive 123

Revenge 6, 26, 27, 36, 42, 60, 62, 86, 89, 91, 92, 93, 94, 96, 97, 99, 108, 117, 118, 124, 137, 144, 150, 167, 179, 181, 288, 367, 385, 391, 393, 395

Rumination 34, 36, 60, 62, 74, 85, 93, 94, 95, 98, 101, 108, 109, 114, 118, 119, 120, 130, 134, 153, 154, 158, 159, 163, 164, 174, 180, 189, 196, 200, 213, 221, 223, 224, 243, 251, 287, 288, 289, 292, 300, 307, 316, 350, 351, 367, 390, 403

   Vicious cycle of 10, 21, 59, 60, 74, 85, 93, 102, 108, 111, 117, 118, 120, 130, 134, 149, 153, 154, 155, 158, 159, 163, 164, 165, 166, 170, 174, 180, 184, 189, 191, 196, 243, 252, 288, 289, 300, 305, 318, 337, 345, 348, 351, 352, 367, 376, 388, 389, 390, 403

S

Scripture study 204, 222, 230, 243, 262

Self-concept 285, 286, 287

Self-esteem 124, 285, 286, 287, 339

Social 15, 48, 59, 65, 70, 104, 108, 124, 131, 137, 165, 169, 184, 185, 188, 189, 190, 196, 199, 200, 253, 262, 274, 285, 293, 299, 300, 301, 308, 309, 325, 339, 361, 362, 373

Spirit xv, 9, 20, 21, 25, 35, 38, 64, 65, 109, 112, 120, 124, 125, 142, 143, 151, 153, 154, 155, 156, 157, 159, 170, 174, 184, 197, 210, 212, 215, 221, 223, 224, 226, 230, 231, 232, 234, 243, 244, 251, 253, 258, 259, 262, 263, 264, 266, 268, 274, 281, 283, 284, 291, 292, 298, 307, 315, 332, 362, 380

   Fruit of the 64, 112, 153, 154, 157, 184, 223, 231, 234, 265, 283, 284

   Holy spirit 9, 21, 25, 35, 65, 112, 120, 125, 151, 153, 154, 157, 159, 184, 197, 215,

221, 223, 224, 226, 230, 231, 232, 253, 258, 259, 262, 263, 264, 266, 291, 292, 298, 315

Indwelling of 125, 153, 157, 215, 231, 362

Spiritual ii, xvi, xix, 9, 10, 11, 21, 33, 38, 59, 65, 68, 70, 76, 87, 101, 108, 112, 115, 129, 144, 147, 153, 154, 155, 158, 163, 180, 184, 191, 193, 198, 200, 201, 203, 204, 207, 208, 210, 212, 215, 216, 217, 218, 219, 220, 221, 222, 223, 224, 225, 226, 227, 228, 229, 230, 231, 234, 240, 241, 243, 244, 246, 247, 249, 252, 255, 260, 261, 263, 264, 265, 266, 267, 270, 271, 274, 283, 284, 285, 293, 296, 300, 304, 305, 307, 313, 317, 318, 326, 328, 329, 332, 335, 341, 345, 352, 357, 359, 362, 389, 396, 400

Formation 87, 153, 154, 158, 180, 184, 191, 198, 200, 204, 220, 221, 222, 225, 231, 243, 252, 255, 263, 264, 332, 335, 352, 357, 362, 389

maturity xv, 9, 10, 11, 112, 144, 153, 154, 201, 203, 204, 214, 215, 216, 217, 218, 219, 221, 222, 224, 225, 228, 240, 246, 260, 263, 265, 267, 270, 271, 283, 304, 318, 326, 341, 345, 396, 400

Spiritual maturity 9, 10, 11, 112, 144, 153, 154, 203, 204, 215, 216, 217, 218, 219, 221, 222, 224, 225, 228, 246, 260, 263, 265, 267, 270, 271, 283, 304, 318, 326, 341, 345, 396, 400

Stress 5, 8, 12, 32, 48, 59, 60, 61, 74, 80, 84, 85, 86, 87, 90, 92, 97, 104, 108, 113, 117, 138, 145, 150, 163, 164, 165, 167, 170, 183, 184, 189, 192, 196, 197, 199, 213, 293, 313, 316, 349, 351, 352, 357

Strongholds xv, 159, 199, 206, 249, 251, 252, 259, 281, 282, 283, 284, 288, 289, 290, 291, 292, 294, 298, 306, 314, 337, 357, 368, 398

Prayer and 22, 25, 203, 221, 252, 275, 289, 292, 293, 317, 332, 345, 350, 356, 359, 396, 400

Release from 291, 398

Styles i, 77, 87, 90, 104, 136, 137, 164, 165, 167, 168, 170, 175, 176, 177, 178, 196, 231, 348, 349, 350, 360, 394, 403

Suffering 6, 8, 24, 27, 111, 118, 123, 125, 157, 158, 160, 194, 205, 223, 225, 231, 232, 246, 265, 298, 304, 307, 331, 356, 357, 368, 375, 403

T

Teachable moment 205

Temptation xvii, 8, 9, 44, 111, 133, 167, 204, 205, 206, 230, 237, 254, 256, 258, 345, 368

Carnal 210, 212

Desires 6, 7, 10, 19, 23, 32, 57, 59, 74, 79, 80, 86, 88, 90, 94, 109, 110, 111, 112, 114, 119, 141, 142, 150, 154, 164, 175, 182, 189, 207, 208, 209, 210, 213, 214, 221, 222, 223, 224, 229, 230, 243, 250, 252, 253, 256, 257, 258, 262, 281, 283, 284, 298, 299, 300, 303, 307, 328, 329, 337, 348, 349, 351, 363, 367, 373, 378, 379, 398

Worldly appetite 210

Thinking xviii, 6, 25, 29, 30, 59, 60, 64, 69, 80, 87, 91, 93, 101, 110, 113, 114, 117, 118, 120, 121, 124, 139, 149, 150, 151, 166, 168, 174, 179, 182, 184, 190, 191, 205, 208, 211, 217, 220, 230, 244, 251, 264, 281, 282, 285, 287, 290, 297, 300, 305, 306, 308, 309, 310, 317, 327, 350, 351, 357, 361, 373, 395

Thoughts iii, xv, xx, 7, 8, 10, 12, 25, 26, 27, 28, 33, 34, 36, 42, 43, 55, 57, 59, 60, 64, 65, 66, 70, 73, 78, 86, 90, 91, 92, 94, 95, 96, 99, 101, 102, 107, 109, 110, 114, 117, 118, 119, 120, 121, 123, 124, 128, 130, 131, 140, 142, 143, 149, 151, 153, 157, 158, 164, 165, 166, 168, 177, 178, 179, 180, 181, 187, 189, 190, 191, 194, 195, 196, 197, 203, 205, 206, 209, 210, 211, 212, 213, 214, 215, 216, 220, 221, 222, 223, 227, 230, 231, 233, 235, 237, 243, 244, 246, 249, 250, 251, 252, 253, 254, 255, 258, 259, 261, 268, 270, 281, 283, 287, 288, 289, 290, 291, 294, 302, 305, 306, 307, 308, 314, 315, 316, 322, 323, 324, 325, 326, 327, 332, 335, 345, 350, 352, 356, 357, 363, 368, 371, 372, 374, 377, 378, 380, 389, 390, 392, 394, 396, 400, 402, 403, 404

Negative xv, xviii, 7, 8, 10, 28, 31, 33, 36, 39, 40, 42, 43, 59, 60, 61, 64, 65, 71, 73, 74, 75, 77, 80, 81, 84, 85, 86, 87, 88, 89, 90, 91, 92, 93, 94, 95, 96, 97, 101, 103, 108, 109, 110, 113, 117, 118, 119, 120, 121, 122, 123, 124, 129, 130, 131, 134, 136, 139, 142, 143, 149, 153, 154, 157, 158, 159, 163, 164, 165, 169, 170, 174, 175, 179, 180, 181, 182, 189, 190, 195, 196, 197, 203, 204, 206, 211, 212, 221, 223, 224, 249, 251, 252, 253, 264, 270, 284, 285, 286, 287, 288, 289, 290, 291, 292, 307, 308, 309, 311, 315, 316, 322, 323, 324, 327, 330, 345, 350, 351, 352, 355, 356, 357, 358, 363, 367, 368, 372, 377, 378, 381, 389, 390, 394, 403, 404, 405

Positive iii, 7, 10, 27, 32, 35, 55, 56, 60, 64, 77, 80, 81, 84, 85, 86, 87, 90, 91, 92, 94, 95, 96, 107, 108, 109, 110, 117, 120, 123, 125, 129, 130, 131, 134, 142, 143, 149, 150, 154, 157, 158, 159, 163, 164, 165, 166, 169, 170, 171, 172, 173, 174, 175, 179, 180, 181, 182, 183, 184, 189, 190, 191, 196, 197, 203, 221, 222, 223, 251, 252, 253, 262, 264, 270, 285, 288, 290, 291, 292, 293, 296, 297, 298, 307, 308, 309, 311, 315, 316, 320, 321, 322, 323, 324, 325, 327, 330, 341, 346, 349, 350, 356, 357, 361, 362, 363, 367, 368, 372, 376, 377, 378, 389, 390, 392, 394, 403, 404

Tongue 166, 174, 212, 249, 252, 253, 270
   is a fire 212

Transgression xviii, 3, 5, 6, 7, 8, 9, 10, 13, 14, 15, 16, 17, 18, 20, 22, 24, 25, 26, 33, 34, 35, 36, 38, 39, 41, 43, 48, 53, 54, 55, 56, 57, 59, 60, 61, 64, 65, 66, 67, 68, 69, 70, 71, 72, 73, 74, 76, 77, 78, 79, 80, 81, 82, 84, 85, 86, 87, 88, 90, 91, 93, 94, 95, 98, 101, 104, 107, 108, 109, 111, 113, 114, 117, 118, 123, 124, 125, 126, 127, 128, 129, 130, 131, 135, 136, 138, 140, 141, 142, 149, 153, 154, 155, 156, 159, 160, 163, 164, 165, 166, 167, 168, 169, 170, 174,

175, 179, 183, 184, 188, 189, 191, 192, 193, 194, 195, 196, 203, 204, 205, 206, 207, 209, 211, 212, 213, 214, 215, 220, 223, 225, 230, 243, 244, 249, 251, 252, 254, 255, 258, 262, 265, 266, 270, 281, 282, 284, 286, 287, 288, 293, 296, 299, 300, 301, 302, 303, 304, 305, 306, 307, 308, 309, 310, 311, 312, 313, 316, 317, 318, 327, 329, 330, 331, 332, 335, 337, 338, 339, 345, 346, 347, 348, 350, 351, 352, 354, 357, 363, 367, 368, 369, 370, 371, 373, 374, 375, 379, 380, 383, 385, 387, 390, 392, 394, 401, 403, 405

Transgressor ii, xv, 7, 8, 9, 10, 12, 13, 14, 15, 16, 17, 18, 19, 20, 21, 24, 25, 26, 27, 28, 34, 35, 38, 39, 40, 43, 55, 56, 57, 59, 60, 64, 66, 68, 70, 71, 73, 77, 79, 80, 81, 83, 84, 85, 86, 87, 88, 89, 90, 91, 92, 94, 96, 97, 98, 99, 100, 101, 102, 107, 108, 109, 111, 113, 114, 115, 117, 118, 119, 120, 123, 124, 125, 126, 127, 128, 129, 130, 131, 134, 135, 136, 138, 139, 140, 142, 149, 150, 151, 153, 154, 155, 156, 157, 159, 160, 161, 162, 163, 164, 165, 166, 167, 171, 172, 173, 174, 175, 178, 179, 180, 182, 183, 189, 191, 192, 193, 195, 196, 203, 204, 206, 209, 210, 211, 212, 213, 214, 215, 217, 220, 221, 223, 224, 225, 230, 243, 249, 254, 257, 258, 265, 270, 271, 281, 282, 283, 284, 286, 287, 289, 290, 291, 300, 302, 303, 304, 305, 306, 307, 308, 309, 310, 311, 312, 313, 314, 315, 316, 317, 319, 320, 321, 322, 325, 328, 330, 331, 332, 333, 334, 335, 337, 338, 341, 346, 347, 348, 349, 351, 352, 354, 356, 365, 366, 367, 372, 374, 375, 376, 377, 378, 379, 380, 382, 383, 384, 385, 386, 390, 391, 393, 394, 397, 398, 399, 400, 401, 403, 404

Transitioning 10, 147, 149, 150, 154, 156, 159, 184, 196, 318, 322, 325, 329, 389, 394

Treasure of 201, 210, 283, 338

troubleshooting 357, 376, 388, 390, 403

U

Unforgiveness ii, xviii, xx, 7, 9, 10, 11, 21, 27, 32, 34, 36, 39, 40, 41, 48, 53, 54, 56, 57, 59, 60,

61, 62, 63, 73, 74, 80, 81, 84, 85, 88, 90, 92,
93, 94, 95, 96, 99, 100, 101, 102, 103, 108,
111, 114, 116, 117, 121, 123, 124, 125, 129,
130, 133, 134, 135, 141, 149, 150, 151, 153,
154, 155, 158, 159, 163, 164, 166, 170, 174,
175, 180, 183, 184, 191, 196, 203, 204, 205,
207, 210, 215, 217, 221, 223, 224, 243, 249,
252, 256, 264, 265, 281, 282, 284, 287, 288,
289, 290, 291, 292, 303, 304, 305, 314, 315,
316, 318, 320, 330, 337, 345, 347, 348, 351,
352, 357, 358, 376, 385, 387, 388, 390, 392,
398, 402
   and rumination 109, 130, 153, 163, 189,
      200, 224
   reducing 34, 48, 57, 60, 94, 96, 99, 117, 123,
      163, 286, 287, 390
Unrighteousness 211, 212, 214

V

Values 66, 77, 124, 126, 175, 208, 209, 210, 211,
    212, 215, 222, 227, 284, 286, 293, 298, 363,
    373, 379
Vengeance 17, 25, 30, 37, 88, 94, 111, 114, 130, 133,
    138, 158, 166, 174, 180, 257, 305, 330, 354
Vicious cycle 10, 21, 56, 59, 60, 74, 85, 93, 95, 102,
    108, 111, 117, 118, 120, 130, 134, 149, 150,
    153, 154, 155, 158, 159, 163, 164, 165, 166,
    170, 174, 179, 180, 184, 189, 191, 196, 243,

252, 288, 289, 300, 305, 318, 337, 345, 348,
351, 352, 367, 376, 388, 389, 390, 403

W

Well-being 6, 7, 8, 15, 23, 32, 33, 35, 36, 48, 56, 57,
    59, 64, 65, 66, 67, 68, 70, 71, 72, 80, 81, 84,
    85, 87, 94, 102, 103, 107, 108, 110, 111, 120,
    126, 132, 135, 142, 143, 144, 153, 157, 163,
    164, 166, 174, 180, 182, 183, 184, 185, 186,
    187, 188, 189, 194, 196, 200, 205, 221, 249,
    253, 255, 265, 275, 285, 292, 293, 296, 297,
    299, 300, 301, 322, 325, 337, 339, 347, 348,
    351, 394, 405
   Emotional xiii, xv, xvii, xviii, xx, 5, 6, 7, 9, 10,
      11, 12, 13, 15, 26, 28, 29, 31, 33, 34, 35,
      36, 38, 43, 54, 55, 56, 57, 65, 68, 72, 73,
      80, 81, 84, 85, 91, 92, 103, 107, 108, 109,
      110, 111, 117, 118, 120, 124, 125, 126,
      128, 129, 133, 153, 164, 165, 166, 168,
      174, 178, 183, 189, 190, 191, 197, 208,
      213, 214, 215, 220, 225, 244, 253, 259,
      262, 264, 283, 285, 287, 293, 296, 301,
      303, 304, 305, 306, 308, 317, 333, 336,
      341, 343, 345, 346, 347, 348, 352, 355,
      356, 357, 358, 361, 363, 367, 373, 378,
      383, 387, 389, 400, 402, 403, 404, 405
   Homeostasis 124
Works of the flesh 111, 112, 284
Worldly programming 284